ISABELLA LUCY BIRD (1831-1904), the daughter of a clergy-man, grew up in Tattenhall, Cheshire. Early in life she suffered from a spinal complaint and in 1854 she was sent by her doctor to America and Canada to improve her health. She published *The Englishwoman in America* in 1856 and *Aspects of Religion in the United States* in 1859. In 1860 her father died, and Isabella, with her mother and sister Henrietta, moved to Edinburgh. From there she made several excursions to the Outer Hebrides, writing ar-ticles on the island crofters and on subjects ranging from the poetry of John Donne to ragged schools. She continued to suffer from back trouble, insomnia and depression until, at the age of forty, she set off for Australia, continuing to Hawaii where her health miraculously improved. She wrote *Six Months in the Sandwich Islands* (1875) and climbed the world's largest volcano, Mauna Loa.

In 1873, Isabella Bird set off for the Rocky Mountains; her 'Letters from the Rocky Mountains' were published in the maga-zine *Leisure Hour* in 1878 and later published as *A Lady's Life in the Rocky Mountains* (1879). After a period at home she set off once more, this time to the northern Japanese island of Hokkaido and to the Native States of Malaya. As a result of these two journeys she published *Unbeaten Tracks in Japan* (1880) and *The Golden Chersonese* (1883).

In 1881 Isabella Bird married Dr John Bishop. He died in 1886, and three years later she set off on her travels to western Tibet and Ladakh, the deserts of Persia and Kurdistan, the Korean peninsular and the remote interior of China. These remarkable expeditions were recorded in *Journeys in Persia and Kurdistan* (1891), *Among the Tibetans* (1894), *Korea and Her Neighbours* (1898) and *The Yangtze Valley and Beyond* (1899).

Isabella Bird returned from the Far East in 1898; making her final journey at the age of seventy, she visited Morocco, touring the country on a black stallion given her by the Sultan. She died in Edinburgh in 1904.

Virago publishes *Jou.........................ne I*.

CHURCH OF MAR SHALITA KOCHANES. *Frontispiece vol. II.*

ISABELLA L. BIRD

JOURNEYS
IN
PERSIA
AND
KURDISTAN

Volume II

WITH A NEW INTRODUCTION BY

SHUSHA GUPPY

Published by VIRAGO PRESS Limited 1989
20-23 Mandela Street, London NW1 0HQ

First published by John Murray 1891
Virago Press edition reproduced from the John Murray edition

Introduction copyright © Shusha Guppy 1989

A CIP catalogue record for this book
is available from the British Library

Printed in Great Britain by Cox & Wyman Ltd.,
Reading, Berkshire

LIST OF ILLUSTRATIONS

IN VOLUME II.

INTRODUCTION

Isabella Bird arrived in Persia in January 1890. She had long harboured a desire to visit the country, but aged nearly sixty and in poor health, had abandoned the idea on account of the journey's difficulties and dangers. Now a chance encounter had enabled her to realise her old plan. Travelling in India the previous October, she had met Major Herbert Sawyer, an Intelligence Officer in the Indian Army bound for Persia on a secret mission, and he had offered to accompany her as far as the capital, Teheran.

Brave, intelligent and extremely handsome, Sawyer was thirty-eight, and 'distracted' by his wife's recent death. His offer seemed 'the acme of good fortune', as many a Memsahib Bovary would have been delighted to be entrusted with the task of consoling him. 'But I cannot spend much sympathy on him because the more distracted men are the sooner they remarry!' confessed Isabella. She had always preferred travelling alone, unimpeded by the needs of others.

They sailed from Karachi aboard the S.S. Assyria and arrived with the New Year at the port of Basra – in present-day Irak – 'one of the least desirable places to which Europeans are exiled by the exigencies of commerce'. There they took the S.S. Mejidieh up the Tigris to Baghdad. Isabella was the only woman among a heterogeneous group of Englishmen, one of whom was George Curzon, then M.P. for Southport and later Viceroy of India. He was collecting material for his magnum opus, *Persia and the*

Persian Question, published soon after Isabella's own book *Journeys in Persia and Kurdistan* in 1893.

Persia was then the subject of intense rivalry between the two Great Powers of the day, Britain and Russia. In a series of wars earlier in the century, Persia had lost all her trans-Caucasian dominions to Russia (They are now the Soviet Republics of Central Asia). From being an empire that had stretched from the Indus to the Nile, she had shrunk to her present size, and was a backward, underpopulated country run by despotic Shahs and feudal chieftains. Russia's ultimate aim was to reach the warm waters of the Persian Gulf, which Curzon believed would threaten India, Britain's greatest possession, without which 'the British Empire could not exist'. The solution, Curzon believed, was 'to strengthen and make Persia *something*'.

But Isabella had little time for power politics. She was moved more by the feminine instincts of curiosity and compassion, and her reactions to situations and people sprang from deeply religious and humanitarian beliefs. Born in October 1931, she was the daughter of a clergyman and brought up in an atmosphere of piety and public benefaction – and she had more affinity with another fellow passenger, Dr Bruce, a missionary going to a Mission in Julfa, the Christian suburb of Isfahan.

Isabella's family had 'breathed causes', and she espoused many throughout her life. As a young girl she had helped create cottage industries producing Harris Tweed in the Highlands, and had encouraged emigration to Canada to relieve poverty in the aftermath of the Potato Famine; she had struggled with the Edinburgh Town Council to spend more money on slums, and had spent the proceeds from her first book, *The English Woman in America* buying fishing boats for the fishermen of Skye and Mull, where her family spent their holidays.

Her first journey to America, which had ignited her wanderlust and released her writing powers had been undertaken on health grounds. As a child she had developed a spinal condition, that culminated in an operation at eighteen for the removal of a tumour on her spine. She could have resigned herself to an invalid's life and 'adorned a sofa all her days', but she was made of a stouter stuff, took up exercises to overcome her weakness, and cultivated her wide-ranging interests in French, history, botany and the Scriptures. Nonetheless she suffered from insomnia, pain, and such *recherché* Victorian ailments as 'nervous prostration', recognising their partly psychosomatic nature her family doctor recommended a sea voyage. As soon as she set sail her pains all but vanished, and later, throughout her life, her health improved in direct ratio to the hardships of her journeys: 'It is rather a sad fact . . . but knocking about, open air life in combination with sufficient interest is the one in which my health and spirit are best,' she wrote to John Murray, her publisher and life-long friend.

On a second journey to America in 1857 she had met Emerson and Thoreau, and on her return wrote *Aspects of Religion in the United States.* Then for over a decade she remained in Scotland, writing on a variety of subjects for scholarly periodicals, and spending her resources on philanthropic causes. She had settled in Scotland with her mother and younger sister Henrietta after her father's death in 1860. But, racked with ill health, her body and soul craved 'the savage freedom her genteel cage and sailed for the Sandwich Islands. Unable to move her head – considered too heavy for her spine – before she left, she became healthy on arrival, galloped through the luxuriant tropical landscape, climbed the 17,000 feet volcano of Maura Loa, 'the Matterhorn of the Pacific', and camped on the edge of the crater. She returned to England via the United States, where she spent some time in a sanatorium, lived with settlers in their cabins, made forays into the snow-bound mountains, and experienced the nearest thing to romance with a certain whisky-swilling, gun-toting, one-eyed Jim Nugent, an Irish trapper, her 'dear desperado'. The result of these journeys was two books she published in 1875 and 1879 respectively: *The Hawaiian Archipelago* and *A Lady's Life in the Rocky Mountains.* With the royalties from these, she financed her next trip – to Japan, Malaya and China – and published *Unbeaten Tracks in Japan* and *The Golden Cherosonese and the Way Thither*, on her return, confirming her reputation as one of the finest travel writers of her time.

In June 1880, Isabella's beloved sister Henrietta died of typhoid, and she was disconsolate – it was for her that she had kept her detailed journals, and written the long letters which formed the basis of her books. A year later she married Dr John Bishop, her long-standing and devoted suitor, and settled down to the 'dutiful life of a doctor's wife'. But within a year her husband contracted erysipelas, a painful and lingering skin disease, which led to his death four years later. Alone and bereft, Isabella returned to Scotland and threw herself into charitable work, 'tending Henrietta's poor', writing for learned journals, and lecturing at the Royal Scottish Geographical Society. But again beset with ill health, she had now conceived the plan for a journey to India, Tibet and Persia.

Before leaving she took a three-month nursing course at St Mary Abbott's Hospital, London, and learnt the dressing of wounds and the rudiments of minor surgery. Then she set sail. 'I have only one formidable rival in Isabella's heart, and that is the high tableland of Central Asia,' Dr Bishop once remarked, and it was in his memory that Isabella founded the John Bishop Memorial Hospital for Women and Children in Islamabad (later she would finance other such establishments in various parts of the East under the aegis of the Church Missionary Society). While the hospital was being built she made expeditions to the Himalayas, Balistan or Little Tibet, and climbed the 18,000 feet Kaila Mountain. *Among the Tibetans* was based on those forays.

★

In Baghdad the S.S. Mejidieh's passengers dispersed towards their various destinations. Isabella hired the services of a facto-tum and four mules, and together with Major Sawyer joined a caravan of merchants and pilgrims returning from the Shrines of Kerbala and Nejef: 'I felt better at once in the pure exhilarating desert air and nervousness about the journey was left behind,' she wrote. Soon they were on the ancient pilgrims' road through the mountains of Kurdistan, famous for its hazards at the best of times. But now was the season of heavy snows, with the piercing, searing *Sooz* blowing down from the mountains and impeding progress, and Isabella describes in grim details the hardships of the journey, the filthy overcrowded carvanserais, sleeping on floors thick with decades of sludgy manure, the poverty-stricken, disease-ridden lives of the inhabitants of these desolate wastes. But she is transported by the beauty of the landscape: 'The uplift silent world of snow and mountain on whose skirts for some miles grew small apple and pear trees, oak, ash, hawthorn, each twig a coral spray.' A journey that would take a day or so by car or train nowadays, lasted forty-six days – during which Isabella lost twenty-two pounds in weight – with pauses in Kermanshah, Isfahan and Qum.

In Teheran she stayed three weeks at the British Delegation and vistied the city: 'A stroll through Teheran bazaars shows the observer the extent and rapidity with which Europe is ruining the artistic taste of Asia,' she observed. She was introduced to Nasseruddin Shah, whose Marble Palace and gardens lived up to the European romantic image of Persia as the land of the Nightingale and the Rose, of sumptuous palaces and golden thrones. Then she left for Isfahan to join Major Sawyer on his 'cartographical' survey through the Zagros mountains, the abode of the fierce nomadic Bakhtiari tribes – despite their differences, the short, plump, kindly widow and the irascible dashing officer had grown to respect each other and become 'good comrades'.

Isabella's first stop was Qum, a town built around the Shrine of Fatimah the Innocent, sister of Imam Reza, the eighth Imam of the Duodecimal Shiites. It is a centre for theological studies and to its many cemeteries are brought bodies from all over Persia to be buried close to the Saint. So Persians describe Qum as 'a town whose imports are corpses and exports mullahs'. She was not to know that ninety years later it would become the birthplace of the revolution which toppled the Shah and brought to power one of its mullahs – Ayatollah Khomeini – but she was shocked by the religious fanaticism that forced her to disguise herself in order to move about, and prevented her from visiting the Shrine.

In Isfahan she stayed with Dr Bruce at his Mission in Julfa, visited the Armenian churches, and got involved in the Mission's work. 'Isfahan is half the world,' a Persian saying goes, for in the seventeenth century the Safavids made it their capital and built it into one of the most beautiful cities in the world, rivalled only by Venice. But again 'the fury of Islam', expressed in open hostility and insults, prevented her from seeing its gorgeous palaces and exquisite mosques. Only once was she taken to an *andaroon* (women's quarters of a seigneurial house) where pallid women idled away their lives in gossip and intrigue.

At the end of April Isabella left Isfahan to begin the most original and interesting part of her Persian adventure – the journey with the Bakhtiaris. From time immemorial these tribes have lived in the folds of the high jagged Zagros range, their way of life unchanged. Alexander failed to subdue them, and even the Arabs left them alone – they only converted to Islam six centuries after the rest of the country. Every spring they migrate with their flocks of sheep and goat from their winter quarters in the plains of Khuzistan (by the Persian Gulf) to summer pastures in the highlands near Isfahan, and return in the autumn. This second volume of *Journeys in Persia and Kurdistan* starts with Isabella living and moving through the mountains with the Bakhtiaris. Every dawn she is roused by Sawyer's cry of 'to boot and saddle', and starts the day's ride along the stony path that winds around the precipitous slopes: 'This is a purely nomadic life . . . we never know in the morning where we shall be at night, if a place is nice and there is water we decide to camp there. I *like* it!' She describes the majesty of the mountains, rising to the 15,000 feet high summit of Zardeh-Kuh (the Yellow Mountain, so called because its snow-

clad heights shine golden in the sun), the velvety green valleys
dotted with wild flowers, the glassy rivers swollen with melted
snow, the cool breeze carrying the smell of jasmine, thyme and
tamarisk, and the flocks of storks fishing by lake Seligun. At every
stop swarms of tribesmen and women come to see the *hakeem*
(doctor) with their gastro-enteritis, trichomas and septic wounds.
Her large medicine chest gets depleted and she is frequently
robbed of her personal possessions and animals. With characteristic charity she blames the tribesmen's savagery and brigandage
upon their extreme poverty and harsh living conditions. She is
appalled by Sawyer's frankly imperialistic attitude, which treats
the 'natives' with utter contempt: 'His behaviour is a frightful
political mistake and a mistake in every way,' she affirms. At one
point she threatens to leave him unless he improves. He does.

This journey with the Bakhtiaris, originally planned for two
months, lasted three and a half. Sawyer's mission completed the
two companions separated in Bojnurd and he returned to India.

In the early 1970s I too travelled with the Bakhtiaris on their
spring migration. I had not then read Isabella Bird's book – it was
before Virago Press rescued such treasures from oblivion – but
now I find her experiences tally with my own. I too took a
medicine chest, was called *hakeem*, and provided the only medical
care on the six-week journey. The tribes had been considerably
subdued by the then strong central government, but their lives
had not changed. The Black Gold that had brought about an
unprecedented economic boom ran beneath their land, and already many of their young men were leaving the millenial way of life
in favour of menial but remunerative work in the oil fields. Today,
by all accounts, the Bakhtiaris' number has been further diminished by revolution and the long war with Irak, with dire consequences in the shortage of the meat that their flocks had provided.

In Bojnurd Isabella acquired a new horse, *Boy*, and continued
her ride through Western Persia and Kurdistan, along a road
hardly ever taken by European travellers. She reached Lake
Urumyeh at harvest time: 'Here the winepress is at work, there

girls are laying clusters of grapes on terraces prepared for the purpose, to dry for raisins, women are gathering cotton and caster-oil seeds, little boys are taking buffaloes to bathe, men are driving and loading buffalo carts, herding mares . . . in the innumerable villages the storehouses are being filled; the women are making large cakes of animal fuel, the cranes are spinning in the sun, and the swaddled infants bound in their cradles are lying in the fields and vineyards while their mothers are at work.'

Crossing the mountains into Turkey Isabella headed for Trebizond on the Black Sea, via Van and Erzerum. She took a boat along the coast, and then the Orient Express back to London, arriving on Boxing Day, 1891.

During her nine months' stay in Persia, Isabella came to understand well the country and its people. She admired Nasseruddin Shah for the skill with which he negotiated the difficult straits between the Charybdis and Scilla of Russia and Britain to gain time and concessions. She saw the need for radical reform, while deploring the inevitable loss of traditions that made the country unique. She lamented the demise of those skills which produced the lustrous faience, the exquisite miniatures, and the magnificent carpets, while expressing indignation at the working conditions of artisans and women weavers. She did not know that such contradictions would one day provide powerful weapons for demagogues, and feed the conflagration of 1979. Read in the light of recent history, Isabella Bird's *Journeys in Persia and Kurdistan* evinces an uncanny topicality, as if the decades that followed her journey, especially those between the two World Wars, during which genuine progress was made in education, the judiciary, communications, women's rights, had been just a lucky parenthesis. Today women have been humiliated back into purdah, justice has again become 'Islamic', and dissent is ruthlessly crushed. The nightingale sings no more, and the rose is red with the blood of 'martyrs'. But then really good books do not age; they just acquire a patina. In them each generation can examine its own reflection, and ponder the future.

Isabella Bird's Persian journey was the most arduous of her life, and she meant it to be her last. Back in Britain she settled down in East Anglia and Kensington, indulged her new passion for photography, wrote, lectured at the Royal Geographical Society, and took up tricycling for exercise. But soon her *furor vagandi* reasserted itself, and she was off to Japan, Korea and China. Her two-volume book, *Korea and her Neighbours*, published in 1898 provided 'the sole information in the West on that country,'* and won her yet more popular and critical acclaim. It was followed by *The Yangtze Valley and Beyond*, equally well received. Then a year after her return to England she was off again, this time to Morocco and the Atlas mountains. But she was too ill thereafter to write the account of this final odyssey. She died in 1904, and was buried in Edinburgh with the remains of her husband.

It would be easy to recognise in Isabella Bird Bishop, with her indomitable spirit, her courage, her intellectual vigour, a feminist *avant la lettre*. But as her perceptive biographer Pat Barr remarks, she could not be: her whole upbringing and religious and moral beliefs resisted such conscious formulation of a feminist philosophy. Indeed she considered her own hunger for adventure and movement 'an unnatural aberration' unsuited to the majority of women. 'She evinced no great sympathy for the majority of women and usually preferred the company of energetic adventurous men.'** Yet the recipient of her deepest affection was a woman – her sister Henrietta – as were some of her most intimate and devoted friends. On the one occasion when she could have championed the cause of women, she demurred: in 1893 she was elected to the Royal Scottish Geographical Society, and later was one of the fifteen 'well qualified ladies' to become a member of the Royal Geographical Society. Some of the more traditionalist members objected – even Curzon who greatly admired Isabella's powers of description and observation sided with the opposition: 'The fellowship as it stands at present is not worth making any trouble,' said Isabella scornfully, yet she confessed to John Murray a 'lurking satisfaction in having vindicated a woman's right to do what she can do well,' and was delighted that reviewers 'made no puerile remarks on the feminine authorship of the book, or awarded praise or blame on that score'. Like many women of her ilk she advanced the cause of women in the best possible way, by setting an example with her own life and work.

*Edward Bosworth, *Journal of the British Institute of Persian Studies*, Volume 27, 1989.
**Pat Barr, *A Curious Life for a Lady*. John Murray, 1970.

LETTER XVI

Two days before we left Chigakhor fierce heat set in, with a blue heat haze. Since then the mercury has reached 98° in the shade. The call to "Boot and Saddle" is at 3.45. Black flies, sand-flies, mosquitos, scorpions, and venomous spiders abound. There is no hope of change or clouds or showers until the autumn. Greenery is fast scorching up. "The heaven above is as brass, and the earth beneath is as iron." The sky is a merciless steely blue. The earth radiates heat far on into the night. "Man goeth forth to his work," not "till the evening," but in the evening. The Ilyats, with their great brown flocks, march all night. The pools are dry, and the lesser streams have disappeared. The wheat on the rain-lands is scorched before the ears are full, and when the stalks are only six inches long. This is a normal Persian summer in Lat. 32° N. The only way of fighting this heat is never to yield to it, to plod on persistently, and never have an idle moment, but I do often long for an Edinburgh east wind, for drifting clouds and rain, and even for a chilly London fog! This same country is said to be buried under seven or eight feet of snow in winter.

On leaving Chigakhor we crossed a low hill into the Seligun valley, so fair and solitary a month ago, now brown and dusty, and swarming with Ilyats and their flocks, and Lake Albolaki has shrunk into something little better than a swamp. A path at a great elevation above a stream and a short rocky ascent brought us to the top of the pass above Naghun, a wall of rock, with an altitude of 7320 feet, and a very stiff zigzag descent upon Isfandyar Khan's garden, where the heat made a long halt necessary. The view from the Naghun Pass of the great Ardal valley is a striking one, though not so striking as one would suppose from the altitude of the mountains, which, however, do not nearly reach the limit of perpetual snow, though the Kuh-i-Kaller, the Kuh-i-Sabz, the great mass of the Kuh-i-Gerra, the range of the Kuh-i-Dinar, and the Kuh-i-Zirreh are all from 11,000 to 13,000 feet in height. Even on the north side the range which we crossed by the Gardan-i-Zirreh exceeds 9000 feet. The Karun, especially where it escapes from the Ardal valley by the great Tang-i-Ardal, is a grand feature of the landscape from the Naghun Pass.

On leaving Naghun we were joined by Aziz Khan, a petty chief, a retainer of Isfandyar Khan, who has been deputed to attend on the Agha, and who may be useful in various ways.

Between Naghun and Ardal, in an elevated ravine, a species of *aristolochia*, which might well be mistaken for a pitcher-plant, was growing abundantly, and on the Ardal plain the " sweet sultan " and the *Ferula glauca* have taken the place of the *Centaurea alata*, which is all cut and stacked.

A hot and tedious march over the Ardal plateau, no longer green, and eaten up by the passage of Ilyat flocks, brought us to the village of Ardal, now deserted and melancholy, the great ibex horns which decorate the roof of the Ilkhani's barrack giving it a spectral look in its loneliness. The night was hot, and the perpetual passing of Ilyats, with much braying and bleating, and a stampede of mules breaking my tent ropes, forbade sleep. It was hot when we started the next morning, still following up the Ardal valley and the Karun to Kaj, a village on bare hummocks of gravel alongside of the Karun, a most unpromising-looking place, but higher up in a lateral valley there was a spring and a walled orchard, full of luxuriant greenery, where we camped under difficulties, for the only entrance was by a little stream, leading to a low hole with a door of stone, such as the Afghans use for security, and through which the baggage could not be carried. The tents had to be thrown over the wall. There was little peace, for numbers of the Kaj men sat in rows steadily staring, and there were crowds of people for medicine, ushered in by the *ketchuda*.

Four miles above Ardal is a most picturesque scene, which, though I had ridden to it before, I appreciated far more on a second visit. This is the magnificent gorge of the Tang-i-Darkash Warkash, a gigantic gash or rift in the great range which bounds the Ardal and Kaj valleys on the north, and through which the river, on whose lawn-like margin the camps were pitched at Shamsabad, find its way to the Karun. A stone bridge of a single arch of wide span is thrown across the stream at its exit from the mountains. Above the bridge are great masses of naked rock, rising into tremendous precipices above the compressed water, with roses and vines hanging out of their clefts.

Below, the river suddenly expands, and there is a small village, now deserted, with orchards and wheat-fields in the depression in which the Darkash Warkash finds its way across the Kaj valley, a region so sheltered from the fierce sweep of the east wind, and so desirable in other respects, that it bears the name of Bihishtabad, the *Mansion of Heaven*.

Geographically this *tang* has a great interest, for the water passing under the bridge is the united volume of the water system to which three out of the four districts known as the Chahar Mahals owe their fertility, and represents the drainage of 2500 square miles. It will be remembered that we entered the Chahar Mahals by the Kahva Rukh Pass, and crossed that portion of them lying between Kahva Rukh and the Zirreh Pass, which is politically, not geographically, a portion of the Bakhtiari country, and is partially Christian.

I started at five the next morning to follow the left bank of the Karun for nearly a whole march, sometimes riding close beside it among barley-fields, then rising to a considerable height above it. It is occasionally much compressed between walls of conglomerate, and boils along furiously, but even where it is stillest and broadest, it is always deep, full, and unfordable, bridged over, however, at a place where there are several mills. An ascent from it leads to the village of Rustam-i, where the people were very courteous and put me on the road to Ali-kuh, a village not far from the river, at the foot of a high range very much gashed by its affluents, one of which is very salt.

Ali-kuh is quite deserted, and every hovel door is open. There is nothing to tempt cupidity. The people, when they migrate to the high pastures, take all their goods with them. There was not a creature left behind who could tell me of a spring, and it was a tiresome search before I came, high upon the hillside, on a stream tumbling down under willows over red rock, in a maze of campanulas and roses. The first essential of a camping-ground is that there should be space to camp, and this is lacking; my servants sleep in the open, and my bed and chair are propped up by stones on the steep slope. Scorpions, " processional " caterpillars, earwigs, and flies abound. It is very pretty, but very uncomfortable. The stream is noisy, and a rude flour mill above has the power, which it has exercised, of turning it into another channel for irrigation purposes. There are some large Ilyat camps above, and from these and from Rustam-i the people have been crowding in.

The wild flowers about Ali-kuh are in great profusion just now, the most showy being hollyhocks—white, pink, and mauve, which affect the cultivated lands. Three parasitic plants are also abundant, one of them being the familiar dodder. Showy varieties of blue and white campanulas, a pink mallow, a large blue geranium, chicory, the blue cornflower, and the scarlet poppy all grow among the crops.

In the course of a day's expedition to the summit of the Ali-kuh Pass large Ilyat camps abounded, and the men were engaged in stacking the leaves and the blossoming stalks of the wild celery for fodder later in the season. These flower-stalks attain a height of over six feet. These, and the dried leaves of the *Centaurea alata*, which are laid in heaps weighted down with stones, are relied upon by the nomads for the food of their flocks on the way down from the summer to the winter pastures, and much of their industry, such as it is, is spent in securing these " crops."

This Ali-kuh Pass, 9500 feet in altitude, is on the most direct route from Isfahan to the Bazuft river, but is scarcely used except by the Ilyats. It is in fact horribly steep on the Ali-kuh side. The great Bakhtiari ranges on its south-west side, and a deep valley below, closed by the great mass of Amin-i-lewa, are a contrast to the utterly shadeless and mostly waterless regions of Persia proper which lie eastwards, blazing and glaring in the summer sunshine. There is a little snow and some ice, and the snow patches are bordered by a small rosy primula,

delicate white tulips, and the violet *penguicula* so common
on our moorlands. Mares with mule foals were grazing
at a height of over 9000 feet.

The Khan of Rustam-i, married to a daughter of the
Ilkhani, " called." He is very intelligent, has some idea
of conversation, and was very pleasant and communicative. He says the " Bakhtiaris love fighting, and if
there's a fight can't help taking sides, and if they have
not guns fight with stones," and that " one Bakhtiari can
beat ten Persians"! I asked him if he thought there
would be fighting at Chigakhor, and he said it was very
likely, and he and his retainers would take the Ilkani's
side. He showed me with great pleasure a bullet wound
in his ankle, and another in his head, where a piece
of the skull had been removed. He wishes that " the
English" would send them a doctor. " We would gladly
receive even a *Kafir*," he said. Mirza politely translated
this word Christian. He says they " suffer so much in
dying from want of knowledge." I explained to him the
virtues of some of their own medicinal herbs, and he at
once sent his servant to gather them, and having identi-
fied them he wrote down their uses and the modes of
preparing them.

With the Khan was his prim little son, already, at
ten years old, a bold rider and a good shot, the pale
auburn-haired boy whom his grandmother, the Ilkhani's
principal wife, offered me as a present if I would cure
him of deafness, debility, and want of appetite! I gave
him a large bottle of a clandestinely-made decoction of
a very bitter wormwood, into which I put with much
ceremony, after the most approved fashion of a charlatan,
some tabloids of *nux vomica* and of permanganate of
potash. When I saw him at the fort of Chigakhor he
was not any better, but since, probably from leading a
healthier life than in Ardal, he has greatly improved, and

being strong is far less deaf, and consequently the virtues of wormwood have forced themselves on the Khan's attention.

The boy had suffered various things. He had been sewn up in raw sheepskins, his ears had been filled with fresh clotted blood, and he had been compelled to drink blood while warm, taken from behind the ear of a mare, and also water which had washed off a verse of the Koran from the inside of a bowl. It transpired that the Khan, who is a devout Moslem and a *mollah*, could not allow his son to take my medicine unless a piece of paper with a verse of the Koran upon it were soaked in the decoction.

I asked him why the Bakhtiaris like the English, and he replied, "Because they are brave and like fighting, and like going shooting on the hills with us, and don't cover their faces." He added after a pause, "and because they conquer all nations, and do them good after they have conquered them." I asked how they did them good, and he said, "They give them one law for rich and poor, and they make just laws about land, and their governors take the taxes, and no more, and if a man gets money he can keep it. Ah," he exclaimed earnestly, "why don't the English come and take this country? If you don't, Russia will, and we would rather have the English. We're tired of our lives. There's no rest or security."

It may well be believed that there are no schools, though some deference is paid to a *mollah*, which among the Bahktiaris means only a man who can write, and who can read the Koran. These rare accomplishments are usually hereditary. The chiefs' sons are taught to read and write by *munshis*. A few of the highest Khans send their sons to Tihran or Isfahan for education, or they attend school while their fathers are detained as hostages in the capital for the good behaviour of their clans. There they learn a few words of French and English, along with pure Persian and Arabic, and the few other branches of the education of a Persian noble. They are fine manly boys, and ride and shoot well from an early age. But the worst of them is that they never are " boys." They are little men, with the stiffness and elaboration of manner which the more important Khans have copied

STONE LION AND GUIDE.

from the Persians, and one can never fancy their abandoning themselves to " miscellaneous impulses."

Killa Bazuft, Bazuft Valley, June 18.—A few days ago we left the last village of the region behind, to enter upon a country not laid down in any maps. It is a wild land of precipitous mountain ranges, rising into summits from 11,000 to 13,000 feet high, enclosing valleys and gorges or cañons of immense depth, some of them only a few feet wide, a goodly land in part, watered by springs and streams, and green with herbage and young wheat, and in part naked, glaring, and horrible.

It is very solitary, although at times we come upon Bakhtiaris in camp, or moving with their flocks, much darker in complexion and more uncivilised in appearance than those of Ardal and its neighbourhood. From these camps Aziz Khan procures guides, milk, and bread. The heat increases daily, and the hour of getting up is now 2.45. There are many forlorn burial-grounds, and their uncouth stone lions, more or less rudely carved, are the only permanent inhabitants of the region. Wheat and barley grow in nearly all the valleys, and clothe the hill-slopes, but where are the sowers and the reapers, and where are the barns ? Cultivation without visible cultivators is singularly weird.

Although the Bakhtiaris expend great labour on irrigation, their methods of cultivation are most simple. They plough with a small plough with the share slightly shod with iron; make long straight furrows, and then cross them diagonally. They do not manure the soil, but prevent exhaustion by long fallows. After they come up to the mountains they weed their crops carefully, and they look remarkably clean. In reaping they leave a stubble five or six inches long. There is a good deal of spade husbandry in places where they have no oxen, or where the arable patches are steep. The spades are much longer than ours, and the upper corners of the sides are turned over for three inches.

A spade is worked by two men, one using his hands and one foot, and the other a rope placed where the handle enters the iron, with which he gives the implement a sharp jerk towards him.

In the higher valleys they grow wheat and barley only, but in the lower rice, cotton, melons, and cucumbers are produced, and opium for exportation. They plough and sow in the autumn, and reap on their return to their "yailaks" the following summer. Their rude water mills, and the hand mills worked by women, grind the wheat into the coarse flour used by them.

It appears from the statements of the *Mollah-i-Murtaza*, Aziz Khan, an intelligent son of Chiragh Ali Khan, and others, that the tenure of arable lands is very simple and well understood. "From long ago" certain of such lands have been occupied by certain tribes, and have been divided among families. Some of the tribes possess documents, supposed to secure these rights, granted by Ali Mardan Khan, the Bakhtiari king of Persia, in the anarchical period which followed the death of Nadīr Shah. Those of them who are without documents possess the lands by right of use. Nearly all the tribes have individual rights of tillage, and have expended much labour on their lands in irrigation and removing stones. A fee for the use of these lands is paid to the Ilkhani every year in money or cattle.

For pasturage there is only the right of "use and wont," and the grazing is free. For camping-grounds each tribe has its special "use and wont," subject to change by the order of the Ilkhani, but it was out of quarrels concerning these and the pasture lands that many of the feuds at present existing arose.

We left Ali-kuh in a westerly direction, followed and crossed the Karun, left it at its junction with the Duab, ascended this short affluent to its source, crossed the Gardan-i-Cherri at an elevation of 9200 feet, and descended 4000 feet into the Bazuft or Rudbar valley, where the camps now are. The road after leaving Ali-kuh, where the slopes were covered with pink and white hollyhocks, keeps along a height above the Karun, and then descends abruptly into a chasm formed of shelves of conglomerate, on the lowest of which there is just room for a loaded mule between the cliffs and the water at the narrowest part. Shadowed by shelf upon shelf of rock, the river shoots

KARUN AT PUL-I-ALI-KUH.　　*To face p.* 10, *vol. II.*

through a narrow passage, as though impatient for its liberation from an unnatural restraint, and there is what I hesitate to call—a bridge. At all events there is a something by which men and beasts can cross the chasm— a rude narrow cradle of heavy branches, filled with stones, quite solid and safe, resting on projections of rock on either side. The Karun, where this Pul-i-Ali-kuh crosses it, is only nine feet six inches in width. I found the zigzag ascent on the right bank a very difficult one, and had sundry falls.

Two hours more brought us to the junction of the Karun and Duab ("two rivers") above which the former is lost to view in a tremendous ravine, the latter coming down a green valley among high and mostly bare mountains, on a gravelly slope of one of which we camped, for the purpose of ascending a spur of a lofty mountain which overhangs the Karun. On such occasions I take my mule, Suleiman, the most surefooted of his surefooted race, who brings me down precipitous declivities which I could not look at on my own feet. After crossing the Duab, a green, rapid willow-fringed river, by a ford so deep as to be half-way up the bodies of the mules, and zigzagging up a steep mountain side to a ridge of a spur of Kaisruh, so narrow that a giant might sit astride upon it, a view opened of singular grandeur.

On the southern side of the ridge, between mountains of barren rock, snow-slashed, and cleft by tremendous rifts, lying in shadows of cool gray, the deep, bright, winding Duab flows down the green valley which it blesses, among stretches of wheat and mounds where only the forgotten dead have their habitation,—a silver thread in the mellow light. On the northern side lies the huge Tang-i-Karun, formed by the magnificent mountain Kaisruh on its right bank, and on the left by mountains equally bold, huge rock-masses rising 3000 feet perpendicularly, and topped by battlements of terra-cotta rock, which took on vermilion colouring in the sunset glow. Through this mighty gorge the Karun finds its way, a green, rapid willow-fringed stream below the ridge, and visible higher up for miles here and there in bottle-green pools, everywhere making sharp turns in its stupendous bed, and disappearing from sight among huge piles of naked rock. Even on this splintered ridge, at a height of 8000 feet, there were tulips, celery in blossom, mullein, roses, legions of the *Fritillaria imperialis*, anemones, blue linum, and a wealth of alpine plants.

There also are found in abundance the great umbelliferous plants—*Ferula glauca*, *Ferula candelabra*, and the *Ferula asafœtida*. The latter I have never seen elsewhere, and was very much rejoiced to procure some of its "tears," though the odour will cling to my gloves till they are worn out. Hadji had heard that it is found in one or two places in the Bakhtiari country, but up to this time I had searched for it in vain. There also for the first time I found the *Astragalus verus*, the gum tragacanth of commerce. The ordinary tragacanth bush, the "goat's thorn," the *Astragalus tragacantha*, which is found everywhere on the arid hillsides, produces a gummy juice but no true gum, and its chief value is for kindling fires.

Following up the Duab, through brush of tamarisk, *Hippophae rhamnoides*, and Indian myrtle, above the cultivated lands, and passing burial mounds with their rude stone lions with their sculptured sides, we camped in a valley at the foot of the Gardan-i-Cherri and Kuh-i-Milli, close to the powerful spring in the hillside which is the source of the stream, where there was abundant level ground for three camps. The next evening Karim, the man who so nearly lost his arm some time ago, was carried past my tent fainting, having been severely kicked in the chest by the same horse that lacerated his arm. "I *am* unlucky," he murmured feebly, when he came to himself in severe pain.

I have crossed the Gardan-i-Cherri twice, and shall cross it a third time. It marks a great change in the scenery, and the first intimation of possible peril from the tribesmen. The ascent from the east, which is extremely rugged and steep, is one of 2000 feet in three and a half miles. Near the top were many Ilyats camping without their tents, a rough-looking set, with immense flocks, and on the summit the Agha, who was without his attendants, met some men who were threatening both in speech and gesture.

From the top there is a wonderful view into an unknown land. The ranges are heavily wooded, and much broken up into spurs and rounded peaks. Between the great range, crossed at a height of 9550 feet by the Cherri Pass, and a wall-like range of mighty mountains of white limestone with snow on them hardly whiter than themselves, lies the Bazuft valley, 4000 feet below, and down upon it come sharp forest-covered spurs, often connected by sharp ridges of forest-covered rocks cleft by dark forest-filled ravines, with glimpses now and then of a winding peacock-green river, flowing at times through green lawns and slopes of grain, at others disappearing into gigantic cañons—great forest-skirted and snow-slashed mountains apparently blocking up the valley at its higher end. At the first crossing all lay glorified in a golden veil, with indigo shadows in the rifts and white lights on the heights.

The first part of the descent is fearfully rough, a succession of ledges of broken rock encumbered here and there with recently dead horses or mules, and the whole downward course of 4000 feet is without a break, the climate getting hotter and hotter as one descends. At 8000 feet the oak forests begin. This oak bears acorns nearly three inches long, which are ground and made into bread. All other vegetation is dried and scorched, and the trees rise out of dust. In this forest we came upon a number of Ilyats, some of whom were lying under a tree, ill of fever, and Aziz Khan insisted that then and there I should give them quinine.

At the bottom of this unalleviated descent there is a shady torrent, working a rude flour mill; a good deal of wheat speckled with hollyhocks, white campanulas, and large snapdragons; some very old tufa cones, and below them level lawns, eaten bare, fringed with oaks, with dry wood for the breaking; and below again the translucent, rapid, peacock-green, beautiful Bazuft. But not even the sound of the rush of its cool waters could make one forget the overpowering heat, 100°, even in the shade of a spreading tree.

I know not which is the more trying, the ascent or the descent of the 4000 feet of ledges and zigzags on the southern face of the Gardan-i-Cherri. The road is completely encumbered with stones, and is being allowed to fall into total disrepair, although it is the shortest route between Isfahan and Shuster. Things are undoubtedly deteriorating. The present Ilkhani is evidently not the man to get and keep a grip on these turbulent tribesmen. I notice a gradual weakening of his authority as the distance from Ardal increases.

When Hussein Kuli Khan, the murdered father of Isfandyar Khan, was Ilkhani, he not only built substantial bridges such as those over the Karun in the Tang-i-Ardal and at Dupulan, but by severe measures compelled every tribe using this road in its spring and autumn migrations to clear off the stones and repair it. As it is, nearly all our animals lost one or more of their shoes on the descent. The ascent and descent took eight hours.

Some of the cliffs on the right bank of the Bazuft are

of gypsiferous rock, topped with pure white gypsum, resting on high, steep elevations of red and fawn coloured earths, with outcrops of gravel conglomerate.

Yesterday was spent in a very severe expedition of twenty-four miles from Mowaz to the lofty plateau of Gorab, mostly through oak forest, crossing great cañons 800 feet deep and more, with almost precipitous sides, descending upon the awful gorge through which the Bazuft passes before it turns round the base of the Kuh-i-Gerra, the monarch of this mass of mountains. The ascents and descents were endless and severe as we crossed the mountain spurs. It was a simple scramble up and down rock ledges, among great boulders, or up or down smooth slippery surfaces. Even my trusty mule slipped and fell several times. Often the animals had to jump up or down ledges nearly as high as their chests, and through rifts so narrow as only just to admit the riders. In some places it was absolutely necessary to walk, and in attempting to get down one bad place on my own feet I fell and hurt my knee badly—a serious misfortune just at present.

After twelve miles of a toilsome march the guide led us up among the boulders of a deep ravine to the treeless plateau of Gorab, an altitude of 8000 feet, where the air was fresh and cool. The scenery is on a gigantic scale, and the highly picturesque Bazuft is seen passing through magnificent cañons of nearly perpendicular rock, and making sharp turns round the bases of lofty spurs, till after a course of singular beauty it joins the Karun at Shalil. It is glorious scenery, full of magnificence and mystery. This beautiful Ab-i-Bazuft, which for a long distance runs parallel with the Karun within fifteen or eighteen miles of it, is utterly unlike it, for the Karun is the most tortuous of streams and the Bazuft keeps a geographically straight course for a hundred miles. Springs bursting

from the mountain sides keep it always full; it passes
nearly ice-cold among lawns and woods, and its colour is
everywhere a pure peacock-green of the most exquisite
tint, contrasting with the deep blue-green of the Karun.
Shuster is only seven marches off, and in the direction
in which it lies scorched barren hills fill up the distance,
sinking down upon yellow barren plains, softened by a
yellow haze, in which the imagination sees those vast
alluvial stretches which descend in an unbroken level to
the Shat-el-Arab and the Persian Gulf. Many a lofty
range is seen, but the eye can rest only on the huge
Gerra mass, with the magnificent snowy peak of Dalo-
nak towering above all, bathed in a heavenly blue.

The shelter-tent was pitched till the noonday heat
moderated. Abbas Ali and Mehemet Ali were inside it,
and I was reading *Ben Hur* aloud. Aziz Khan was
lying half in and half out, with a quizzical look on his
face, wondering at a woman knowing how to read. Not
a creature had been seen, when as if by magic nine or
ten Lurs appeared, established themselves just outside,
and conversed with Aziz. I went on reading, and they
went on talking, the talk growing disagreeably loud, and
Aziz very much in earnest. Half an hour passed thus,
the Agha, who understood their speech, apparently giving
all his attention to *Ben Hur*.

I did not hear till the evening that the topic of the
talk was our robbery, with possible murder, and that
Aziz was spending all his energies on dissuading them,
telling them that we are guests of the Ilkhani and under
the protection of the Shah, and that they and their tribe
would be destroyed if they carried out their intention.
They discovered that his revolvers were not loaded—he
had in fact forgotten his cartridges, and one said to the
others, "Don't give him time to load."

While the tent was being packed, I sat on a stone

watching the Lurs, dark, handsome savages, armed with
loaded clubbed sticks, and the Agha was asking them
about the country, when suddenly there was a *mêlée*, and
the semblance of an attack on him with the clubs. He
seemed to shake his assailants off, lounged towards his
mule, took his revolver from the holster, fired it in the
air, and with an unconcerned, smiling face, advanced
towards the savages, and saying something like calling
attention to the excellences of that sort of firearm, fired
two bullets close over their heads. They dread our arms
greatly, and fell back, and molested us no further. Till
later I did not know that the whole thing was not a
joke on both sides. Aziz says that if it had not been
for the Agha's coolness, all our lives would have been
sacrificed.

In returning, the Agha, walking along a lower track
than we were riding upon, met some Lurs, who, thinking
that he was alone, began to be insolent, and he heard
them say to each other, " Strip him, kill him," when their
intention was frustrated by our appearance just above.
After crossing the Serba torrent with its delicious shade
of fine plane trees, the heat of the atmosphere, with the
radiation from rock and gravel, was overpowering. I
found the mercury at 103° in my shady tent.

Aziz Khan now pays me a visit each evening, to give
me such information as is attainable regarding the people
and locality, and, though he despised me at first, after
Moslem fashion, we are now very good friends. He is a
brave man, and made no attempt to magnify the danger
at Gorab, merely saying that he was devoutly thankful
that we had escaped with our lives. He remonstrated
with me for pitching my tent in such a lonely place,
quite out of sight of the other camps, but it was then
too dark to move it. He said that there was some risk,
for the Lurs had declared they would " rob us yet," but

he should watch all night. I knew he would, for the
sake of his Arab mare!

This morning, soon after leaving Mowaz, the Sahib's
guide galloped up, saying that his master had been
robbed of "everything" the night before, and was
without the means of boiling water. Orders were
given for the camps to close up, for no servants to ride
in advance of or behind the caravan, and that no Ilyats
should hang about the tents.

Although the Bakhtiari Lurs are unified under one
chief, who is responsible to the Shah for the security of
the country, and though there has been a great improvement since Sir A. H. Layard's time, the advance, I
think, is chiefly external. The instincts and traditions
of the tribes remain predatory. Possibly they may no
longer attack large caravans, but undoubtedly they rob,
when and where they can, and they have a horrid habit
of stripping their victims, leaving them with but one
under garment, if they do not kill them. They have a
gesture, often used by Aziz Khan in his descriptions of
raids, which means stripping a man to his shirt. The
word used is skin, but they are not such savages as this
implies. The gesture consists in putting a finger into the
mouth, slowly withdrawing it, and holding it up with a
look of infinite complacency. Aziz admits with some
pride that with twenty men he fell upon a rich caravan
near Shiraz, and robbed it of £600.

To-day's march has been mainly through very
attractive scenery. We crossed the Ab-i-Mowaz, proceeded over slopes covered with wheat and flowers, and
along a rocky path overhanging the exquisitely tinted
Bazuft, forded the Ab-i-Nozi, at a place abounding in
tamarisks bearing delicate, feathery pink blossoms, and
ascended to upland lawns of great beauty, on which
the oaks come down both in clumps and singly,

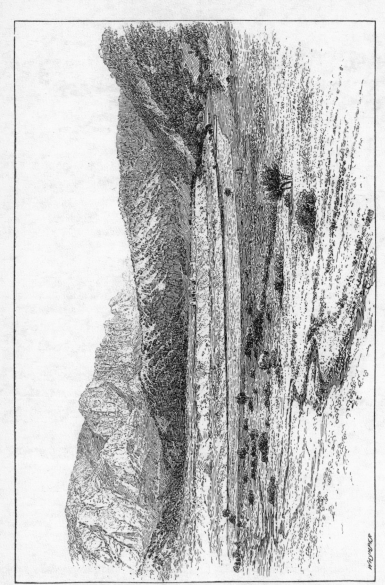

To face p. 19, vol. II.

KILLA BAZUFT.

as if planted. The views from this natural park are glorious. Besides the great ranges with which I have become familiar, the Safid-Kuh, or "white mount," on the right bank of the river, at present deserves its name, its snows descending nearly to the forests which clothe its lower heights. A deep chasm conceals the Tabarak stream up to the point of its foamy junction with the Bazuft, which emerges on the valley by an abrupt turn through a very fine cañon.

We crossed the pure green waters by a broad ford, and camped on the right bank on a gravel plateau above it, on which is Killa Bazuft, a large quadrangular stone fort with round towers at the corners, an arcaded front, a vaulted entrance, and rooms all round the quadrangle. It is now ruinous. Some irrigated land near it produces rice and mosquitos. The Sahib's camp is pitched here. He has been badly robbed, both of clothing and cooking-pots, and was left without the means of cooking any food.

Dima, June 26.—We retraced our steps as far as the source of the Duab, crossed into the Shamisiri valley, and by a low pass into the Karun valley, forded the Karun by a strong deep ford, crossed a low range into the Zarin valley, where are some of the sources of the Zainderud, from thence marched to the Tang-i-Ghezi, through which the Zainderud, there a vigorous river, passes into the Chahar Mahals, went up the Kherson valley, crossed Gargunak, and by a very steep and rugged descent reached this camp, a place of springs, forming the upper waters of the Zainderud. These days have been severe, the heat great, and the incidents few.

The ascent of the Gardan-i-Cherri was difficult. The guide misled us, and took us through a narrow rift in the crest of a ridge on broken ledges of rock. We camped at a height of 9000 feet in the vicinity of snow. The new arrangement, which is necessary for safety, does not increase comfort, for the Arab horses, noisy, quarrelsome fellows, are in camp, and the mules shake their bells and sneeze and bray at intervals all night.

The descent of 2000 feet into the Shamisiri valley, over bare gravel chiefly, was a very hot one. It is a wide, open valley with stony hills of no great height enclosing it, with much green sward along the river banks, above which, running to a great height on the hillsides, are stretches of irrigated wheat. So far as I have yet seen, the wheat is all "bearded." It is a most smiling valley; so cultivated, indeed, and so trim and free from weeds are the crops, that one naturally looks for neat farm-houses and barns. But one looks in vain, for except the ruins of some Armenian villages there are no traces of inhabitants, till night comes, when the glimmer of camp fires here and there high up on the hillsides shows the whereabouts of some migratory families.

I start so early as to get in to the camping-ground about nine now, and the caravan, two hours later, comes in with mules braying, bells ringing, horses squealing for a fight, servants shouting. Then the mules roll, the tent-pegs are hammered down, and in the blazing, furnace-like afternoons the men, who have been up since 2 A.M., take a prolonged siesta, and a solemn hush falls on the camp. After the Gorab affair I loaded my revolver, and now sleep with it under my pillow, carry it in my holster, and never have it out of my reach. I *think* I should only fire it in the air if I were attacked, but the fact of being known to be armed with such a weapon is more likely than anything else to prevent attack. No halt is now made on the march.

The sick people who appeared at Shamisiri, from no one knows where, were difficult and suspicious, and so they have been since. The dialect of Persian has some-

what changed, and Aziz Khan now interprets the strange
accóunts of maladies to Mirza, and he interprets to me.
When they crowd almost into the tent, Aziz, when
appealed to, pelts them with stones and beats them with
a stick, and they take it very merrily.   He thinks that
I have appliances in the " leather box " for the cure of
all ills, and when he brings blind people, and I say that
I cannot do anything for them, he loses his temper.
No matter where we camp, dark, handsome men spring up
as if by magic, and hang about the fires for the rest of the
day.   From among these the guides are usually selected.

Numbers of "patients" appear everywhere, and the
well assemble with the sick round my tent.   At Berigun
the people were very ignorant and obstinate.   After spending a whole hour on two men, and making medicines up
for them, they said they would have the " Feringhi's ointment," but "nothing that goes down the throat."   Another
said (and he had several disciples) that he would not take
the medicine "for fear it should make him a Christian."
One man, who has fever, took away four quinine powders
yesterday for four days, and came back to-day deaf and
giddy, saying that I have killed him.   He had taken
them all at once !

It is very pleasant to see how very fond the men are
of their children, and how tender and loving they are to
their little girls.   The small children are almost always
pretty, but by three years old the grace and innocence of
childhood are completely lost, and as in Persia there are
no child faces; indeed, the charm of childhood scarcely
survives the weaning-day.   If they are sick the fathers
carry them for miles on their backs for medicine, and
handle them very gently, and take infinite pains to understand about the medicine and diet.   Even if both father
and mother come with a child, the man always carries
it, holds it, is the spokesman, and takes the directions.

Several men have offered me mares and cows if I will cure their children. All the "patients" ask finally, "What must I eat, and not eat?"

The Bakhtiaris have often asked me whether it is unwholesome to live so much as they do on cheese and sour milk. They attribute much of their dyspepsia to their diet. They live principally on *mast* or curdled milk, buttermilk, cheese, *roghan* or clarified butter, *nān*, a thin leavened cake, made of wheat or acorn flour, bannocks of barley meal, celery pickled in sour milk, *kabobs* occasionally, and broth flavoured with celery stalks and garlic frequently. They never use fresh milk. They eat all fruits, whether wild or cultivated, while they are quite unripe. Almonds are eaten green.

They hunt the ibex and shoot the francolin and the bustard, and make soup of them. They are always on the hills after game, and spare nothing that they see. I have seen them several times firing at red-legged partridges sitting on their nests. They use eggs considerably, boiling them hard. Alcohol in any form is unknown among them, and few, except the Khans, have learned the delights of tea and coffee. Buttermilk, pure water, and *sharbat*, when they can get lime-juice, are their innocent beverages. The few who drink tea use it chiefly to colour and flavour syrup. They eat twice in the day. Though their out-of-doors life is healthy and their diet simple, they rarely attain old age. A man of sixty is accounted very old indeed. The men are certainly not polite to their wives, and if they get in their way or mine they kick them aside, just as rough men kick dogs.

We have been marching through comparatively lowland scenery, like the Chahar Mahals, from which we are not far. At Shamisiri, except for the fine peak of Dilleh, there are no heights to arrest the eye. The hills

FORDING THE KARUN.

To face p. 23, vol. II.

on the north side are low, gravelly, and stony, with perpendicular outbreaks of rock near their summits.   To
the south they are of a different formation, with stratifica-
tion much contorted.   The next march was over low
stony hills, with scanty herbage and much gum tragacanth, camel thorn, and the *Prosopis stephaniana,* down
a steep descent into the Karun valley, where low green
foot-hills, cultivated levels, and cultivation carried to a
great altitude on the hillsides refresh the tired eyes.   The
Karun, liberated for a space from its imprisonment in
the mountains, divides into several streams, each one a
forcible river; winds sinuously among the grass, gleams
like a mirror, and by its joyous, rapid career gives animation to what even without it would be at this season
a very smiling landscape.   Crossing the first ford in
advance of the guide, we got into very deep water, and
Screw was carried off his feet, but scrambled bravely to
a shingle bank, where we waited for a native, who took
us by long and devious courses to the left bank.   The
current is strong and deep, and the crossing of the caravan
was a very pretty sight.

We halted for Sunday at Berigun, an eminence on
which are a ruinous fort, a graveyard with several lions
rampant, and a grove of very fine white poplars, one of
them eighteen feet in circumference six feet from the
ground.   A sea of wheat in ear, the Karun in a deep
channel in the green plateau, some herbage-covered foot-
hills, and opposite, in the south-west, the great rocky,
precipitous mass of the Zard Kuh range, with its wild
crests and great snow-fields, made up a pleasant landscape.   The heat at this altitude of 8280 feet, and in
the shade, was not excessive.

The next day's march was short and uninteresting,
partly up the Karun valley, and partly over gravelly hills
with very scanty herbage and no camps, from which we

came down abruptly into the elevated plain of Cheshmeh
Zarin (the Golden Fountain) at a height of 8500 feet,
the plain being about five miles by two and a half.
Receding hills with some herbage upon them border the
plateau, and the Zard Kuh, though at some distance,
apparently blocks up the western end. A powerful
spring bursts from under a ridge of rock half-way down
the plain, and becomes at once a clear gentle stream, fifty
feet broad, which passes through the level green sward
in a series of turns which are quite marvellous. Smooth
sward, green barley, many yoke of big oxen ploughing up
rich black soil, dark flocks of thousands of sheep and
goats, asses, mares, mules, cows, all feeding, large villages
of black tents, one of them surrounding the white pavilion
of a Khan, saddle-horses tethered, flocks being led to and
fro, others being watered, laden asses arriving and departing, butter being churned, and carpets being woven,
form a scene of quiet but busy industry which makes
one feel quite " in the world." This stream is one of
the chief sources of the Zainderud.

From this cheerful camping-ground we marched over
low hills, forded the Zainderud several times, and came
upon several Ilyat camps on low, rich pasture lands.
These nomads had no tents, but dwelt in booths without
fronts, the roofs and backs being made of the tough
yellow flowering stalks of the celery. The path follows
the left bank of the river, there a full, broad stream,
flowing through the Tang-i-Ghezi, through rounded hills,
and scenery much like that of the Cheviots. At the
Tang-i-Ghezi we camped, and this morning crossed a low
hill into a heavily-grassed valley watered by the Kherson,
ascended a shoulder of Gargunak, and halted at Aziz
Khan's tents, where the women were very hospitable,
bringing out cows' milk, and allowing themselves to be
photographed.

An unpleasant *contretemps* occurred to me while we
were marching through some very lonely hills.   If Mirza
rides as he should, behind me, his mule always falls out
of sight, and he is useless, so lately I have put him in
front.   To-day I dropped a glove, and after calling and
whistling to him vainly, got off and picked it up, for I
am reduced to one pair, but attempt after attempt to get
on again failed, for each time, as I put my hand on the
saddle, *Screw* nimbly ran backwards, and in spite of my
bad knee I had to lead him for an hour before I was
missed, running a great risk of being robbed by passing
Lurs.   When Mirza did come back he left his mule in a
ravine, exposed to robbers, and Aziz Khan was so infuriated that he threatened to " cut his throat."   Aziz
despises him as a " desk-bred " man for his want of " out-
doorishness," and mimics the dreamy, helpless fashion
in which he sits on his mule, but Mirza can never be
provoked into any display of temper or discourtesy.

From Aziz's camp we had a very steep and rugged
descent to this place, Cheshmeh Dima, where we have
halted for two days.   Three streams, the head-waters
of the Zainderud, have their sources in this neighbourhood, and one of them, the Dima, rises as a powerful
spring under a rock here, collects in a basin, and
then flows away as a full-fledged river.   The basin or
pool has on one side a rocky hill, with the ruins of a fort
upon it, and on the three others low stone walls of very
rude construction.   The Lurs, who soon came about us,
say that the ruined fort was the pleasure palace of a great
king who coined money here.   The sides of the valley
are dotted with camps.   Opposite are the large camp and
white tent of Chiragh Ali Khan, a chief who has the reputation of being specially friendly in his views of England.

The heat yesterday was overpowering, and the crowds
of Bakhtiari visitors and of sick people could hardly be

received with benevolent equanimity. This great heat
at an altitude of 7600 feet is most disappointing. These
head-waters of the Zainderud, rising in and beautifying
the Zarin, Kharba, and Dima valleys, unite before reaching the Tang-i-Ghezi, from which they pass to Isfahan, and
are, as has been stated before, eventually lost in a swamp.
This is the most watery region I have seen in Persia.
Besides the gushing, powerful springs which form vigorous
streams at the moment of their exit from the mountain
sides, there are many moist, spongy places in the three
valleys, regularly boggy, giving out a pleasant *squish* under
a horse's tread, and abounding in plants associated in my
ideas with Highland bogs, such as the *Drosera rotundi-
folia*, which seems to thrive on a small red fly unknown
to me. These waters and swampy places occupy a small
area, just within the Outer range, below the southern
slopes of the Kuh-i-Rang.

From this place I made an expedition of thirty miles
up a very fine valley, much of which is irrigated and
cultivated, by an ascent of 2500 feet to the Gal-i-Bard-i-
Jamal, a pass 10,500 feet in altitude, with a tremendous
descent into an apparent abyss, from whose blue depths
rise the imposing mass of the Kuh-i-Shahan, and among
other heights Faidun, a striking peak of naked rock, super-
imposed on a rocky ridge. At this height the air was
really cool, and it was an escape from the heat of Dima.

This region seems much disturbed. We heard of
bloodshed two days ago, and to-day in the Kharba
valley of fighting among the Kuh-i-Shahan mountains with
the loss of twelve lives, and horsemen passed us armed
with long guns and swords on their way to tribal war.
I fear I shall have to return to Isfahan. Things are
regarded as looking very precarious farther on, and every
movement, retrograde or forward, is beset with difficulties.

                                        I. L. B.

LETTER XVII

From Dima we ascended to high tablelands, having the
snowy Zard Kuh ever in sight, one nameless peak being
at present pure white, and descended into and crossed
the Shorab, a fertile valley, on one side of which is the
famous cleft called Kar Kanun, an artificial gash across
a spur of the Kuh-i-Rang of the same name. After
winding among mountains we descended on the Karun,
whose waters, clear, rapid, and peacock-green, fertilise a
plain of fine flowery turf lying at the base of hills, with
another branch of the Karun between them and the Zard
Kuh.

It is a lovely plain, bright and smiling, contrasting
with the savage magnificence of the Zard Kuh, which
comes down upon it with its peaks, chasms, and
precipices, and glittering fields of unbroken snow.
It was given up to mares and foals, but green platforms
high above, and little hollows in the foot-hills were
spotted with Ilyat tents, and in the four days which
we spent there the camps were never free from Ilyat
visitors. The Sahib came in the first evening with one
man badly hurt, and another apparently in the first stage
of rheumatic fever. A small tent was rigged for this poor
fellow, who was in intense pain and quite helpless, with a
temperature of 104°, and every joint swollen. The usual
remedies had no effect on him. I had had a present of

a small quantity of *salol*, a newish drug, with directions
for its use, and his master Hadji undertook to make
him take it regularly, and hot tea when he fancied it, and
at the end of twenty-two hours he was not only free
from fever but from pain, and was able to mount a
mule.[1]

There are two definite objects of interest close to the
plain of Chaman Kushan, the reputed source of the Karun
and the great artificial cleft of Kar Kanun.   I visited the
first on a misty day, which exaggerated the height of the
mountains, and by filling their chasms with translucent
blue atmosphere gave a rare loveliness to the whole, for
it must be said that the beauties of Persian scenery are
usually staring, hard, and unveiled.   The fords of two or
three rivers, including the Karun, some steep ascents and
descents, a rough ride along a stony slope of the Zard
Kuh, and the crossing of a very solid snow-bridge took us
to the top of a cliff exactly opposite the powerful springs
in which the Karun has its reputed origin.

Over this source towers the mighty range of the Zard
Kuh,—a colossal mountain barrier, a mass of yellow and
gray limestone, with stupendous snow-filled chasms, huge
precipices, and vast snow-fields, treeless and destitute of
herbage except where the tulip-studded grass runs up to
meet the moisture from the snow-fields.   It is the birthplace of innumerable torrents, but one alone finds its way
to the sea.

These springs are in a lateral slit in a lofty limestone precipice below a snow-field, at one end of

[1] For the benefit of other travellers I add that the dose of *salol* was
ten grains every three hours.   I found it equally efficacious afterwards in several cases of acute rheumatism with fever.   I hope that the
general reader will excuse the medical and surgical notes given in these
letters.   I am anxious to show the great desire for European medical aid,
and the wide sphere that is open to a medical missionary, at least for
physical healing.

To face p. 29, vol. II.

SAR·I·CHESHMEH·I·KURANG.

which, as if from a shaft, the most powerful of them wells up, and uniting with the others in a sort of grotto of ferns and mosses pours over a ledge in a sheet of foam, a powerful waterfall, and slides away, a vigorous river of a wonderful blue-green colour, under a snow-bridge, starting full fledged on its course. The surroundings of this spring are wild and magnificent. A few Bakhtiaris crept across the lower part of the face of rock, and perched themselves above it. The roar of the water, now loud, now subdued, made wild music, and the snow-bridges added to the impressiveness of the scene.

Of course the geographical interest of this region is engrossing.[1] This remarkable spring, called by the Bakhtiaris Sar-i-Cheshmeh-i-Kurang ("the head source of the Kurang"), and until this journey held to be the real source, is not, however, the actual birthplace of the Karun or Kurang, which was afterwards traced up to its head-waters in the magnificent Kuh-i-Rang.[2]

A few words on this, the one real river of which Persia can boast, and which seems destined to play an important part in her commercial future, will not be out of place. From its source it is a powerful and important stream, full, deep, and flowing with great velocity for much of its upper course between precipices varying in height from 1000 to 3000 feet. It is a perennial stream, fordable in very few places, and then only in its upper waters. Varying in width usually from fifty to a hundred yards, it is compressed at the Pul-i-Ali-kuh into a breadth of about nine feet.

The steepness and height of its banks make it in

---

[1] A few geographical paragraphs which follow here and on p. 35 are later additions to the letter.

[2] Although the correct name of this river is undoubtedly Kurang, I have throughout adopted the ordinary spelling *Karun*, under which it is commercially and politically known.

general useless for irrigation purposes, but some day it
may be turned to account as a great " water power." Its
windings, dictated by the singular formation of the mountain ranges (for I reject the idea of it having " carved "
its channel), are almost phenomenal. After flowing south-
east for a hundred miles from its source, it makes an
acute bend, flows for fifty miles to the south-west, and
then making another fantastic turn it flows in an exactly
opposite direction to that of its earlier course, proceeding
north-west to Shuster for a hundred miles.

It is calculated that the distance from the Kuh-i-Rang
to Shuster as the crow flies is seventy-five miles, but the
distance travelled by the waters of the Karun is 250
miles, with an aggregate fall of 9000 feet.

Besides being fed on its journey through the Bakhtiari country by many mountain-side fountain springs of
pure fresh water, as well as by salt streams and springs,
it receives various tributaries, among the most important
of which are the Ab-i-Bazuft and a stream which, though
known locally under various names, may be called from
the Chigakhor basin in which it rises the Ab-i-Chig-
akhor, which makes a course of ninety miles to get over
a distance of twenty; the Darkash Warkash flowing in
from the Chahar Mahals near Ardal, the Dinarud rising
in the fair valley of Gorab, and the Ab-i-Cherri or Duab.

This mountain range, the Zard Kuh, in whose steep
side at a height of over 8000 feet the Sar-i-Cheshmeh-
i-Kurang wells up so grandly, is rather a series of rock
summits and precipices than a range of mountains. In
late June its naked shelves and battlements upbore great
snow-fields, and its huge rifts or passes—the Gil-i-Shah,
nearly 11,700 feet in altitude, and the Pambakal, 11,400
—were full of snow. But even in four days it melted
rapidly, and probably by August little remains except a
few patches, in the highest and most sunless of the rifts.

ZARD KUH RANGE.   *To face p. 30, vol. II.*

It is only on the north side that the snow lasts even into July.

The marked features of this range are its narrow wall-like character, its ruggedness on both sides, its absence of any peaks rising very remarkably above the ordinary jagged level of the barrier, its lack of prominent spurs, and its almost complete nakedness. It is grand, but only under rare atmospheric conditions can it be termed beautiful. Its length may be about thirty miles. It runs from north-west to south-east. Some of its highest summits attain an elevation of 13,000 feet. Its name is a corruption of Sard Kuh, "cold mountain."

After fording various snow streams and taking a breakneck goat track, we reached the great snow pass of Gil-i-Shah, by which the Bakhtiaris come up from the Shuster plains on the firm snow in spring, returning when the snow is soft in autumn by a very difficult track on the rocky ledges above. In the mist it looked the most magnificent and stupendous pass I had ever seen, always excepting the entrance to the Lachalang Pass in Lesser Tibet, and an atmospheric illusion raised the mountains which guard it up to the blue sky. I much wished to reach the summit, but in a very narrow chasm was fairly baffled by a wide rift in a sort of elevated snow-bridge which the mule could not cross, and camped there for some hours; but even there nomads crowded round my tent with more audacity in their curiosity than they usually show, and Mirza heard two of them planning an ingenious robbery.

The heat was very great when I returned, 100° in the shade, but rest was impossible, for numbers of mares and horses were tethered near my tent, and their riders, men and women, to the number of forty, seized on me, clamouring for medicines and eye lotions. I often wonder at the quiet gravity of Mirza's face as he interprets their grotesque accounts of their ailments. A son of Chiragh

Ali Khan came to tell me that the "Feringhi ointment" had cured a beautiful young woman of his tribe of an "abscess in her nose"! An instance of real benefit hardly consoles for many failures, and any cure increases the exhausting number of "patients." On one day on that plain there was no rest between eleven and five.

Small events occurred tending to show that the good order which the Ilkhani's government secures is chiefly round the centre of rule. Stories of tribal disputes with violence, and of fights arising out of blood feuds came in daily, and recent sword cuts and bullet wounds were brought to the *Hakīm*. One day there was a disturbance in camp owing to a man attacking Hassan for preventing a woman from entering my tent in my absence. I learned very soon after coming into this country that the Bakhtiaris are dangerously sensitive about their women, although the latter are unveiled and have an amount of latitude unusual in the East. I have more than once cautioned my servants on this point, for any supposed insult to a female relative of a Bakhtiari would have by custom to be wiped out in blood. This extreme sensitiveness has its good side, for even in the midst of the tribal wars and broils which are constantly occurring female honour is always secure, and a woman can travel safely alone through the wildest regions; a woman betraying her husband would, however, almost certainly be put to death. One night the camps were threatened by robbers, upon whom Aziz Khan fired.

Solitary as is now the general aspect of the surrounding country, it must have been crowded with workmen and their food providers within the last two centuries, for in the beginning of the seventeenth century Shah Abbas the Great, the greatest and most patriotic of modern Persian kings, in his anxiety to deliver Isfahan once for all from the risk of famine, formed and partly executed

the design of turning to account the difference in level
(about 300 feet) between the Karun and Zainderud, and by
cleaving an intervening mountain spur to let the waters
of the one pass into the other.   The work of cleaving
was carried on by his successors, but either the workmen
failed to get through the flint which underlies the free-
stone, or the downfall of the Sufari dynasty made an end
of it, and nothing remains of what should have been a
famous engineering enterprise but a huge cleft with tool
marks upon it in the crest of the hill, "in length 300
yards, in breadth fifteen, and fifty feet deep."[1]   Above
it are great heaps of quarried stones and the remains of
houses, possibly of overseers, and below are the remnants
of the dam which was to have diverted the Karun
water into the cleft.

On a cool, beautiful evening I came down from this
somewhat mournful height to a very striking scene, where
the peacock-blue branch from the Sar-i-Cheshmeh unites
with the peacock-green stream from Kuh-i-Rang, the
dark, high sides of their channels shutting out the mountains.   Both rivers rush tumultuously above their union,
but afterwards glide downwards in a smooth, silent
volume of most exquisite colour, so deep as to be unfordable,
and fringed with green strips of grass and innumerable
flowers.   On emerging from the ravine the noble mass of
the Zard Kuh was seen rose-coloured in the sunset, its
crests and spires of snow cleaving the blue sky, and the
bright waters and flower-starred grass of the plain gave
a smiling welcome home.

The next march was a very beautiful one, most of
the way over the spurs and deeply-cleft ravines of the
grand Kuh-i-Rang by sheep and goat tracks, and no
tracks at all, a lonely and magnificent ride, shut in
among mountains of great height, their spurs green with

---

[1] *Six Months in Persia.*—Stack.

tamarisk, salvias, and euphorbias, their ravines noisy
with torrents, bright springs bursting from their sides
with lawn-like grass below, and their slopes patched with
acres of deep snow, on whose margin purple crocuses,
yellow ranunculuses, and white tulips were springing.
But the grand feature of the march is not the mighty Kuh-
i-Rang on the right, but the magnificent Zard Kuh on
the left, uplifting its snow-fields and snow-crests into the
blue of heaven, on the other side of an ever-narrowing
valley. At the pass of Gal-i-Gav, 11,150 (?) feet in
altitude, where we have halted for two days, the Zard
Kuh approaches the Kuh-i-Rang so closely as to leave
only a very deeply cleft ravine between them. From
this pass there is a very grand view, not only of these
ranges, but of a tremendous depression into which the
pass leads, beyond which is the fine definite mountain
Kuh-i-Shahan. This pass is the watershed between the
Karun and Ab-i-Diz, though, be it remembered, the latter
eventually unites with the former at Band-i-Kir. All is
treeless.

The Kuh-i-Rang is the only " real mountain " seen on
the journey hitherto. It is unlike all others, not only
in its huge bulk and gigantic and far-reaching spurs, but
in being *clothed*. Its name means the " variegated mountain." It has much Devonshire red about it, but clad
as it is now with greenery, its soil and rock ribs cannot
be investigated.

It is a mountain rich in waters, both streams and
springs. It is physically and geographically a centre, a
sort of knot nearly uniting what have been happily
termed the "Outer" and "Inner" ranges of the Bakhtiari
mountains, and it manifestly divides the country into
two regions, which, for convenience' sake, have been
felicitously termed the Bakhtiari country and Upper Elam,
the former lying to the south-east and the latter to the

north-west of this most important group of peaks, only just under 13,000 feet, which passes under the general name Kuh-i-Rang.

A prominent geographical feature of this region is that from this point south-eastwards the valleys run parallel with the great ranges, and are tolerably wide and level, carrying the drainage easily and smoothly, with plenty of room for the fairly easy tracks which usually run on both banks of the rivers.

The reader who has followed the geographical part of my narrative will, I hope, have perceived that the openings through the Outer and Inner ranges in the region previously traversed are few and remarkable, the Tang-i-Ghezi and the Tang-i-Darkash Warkash piercing the Outer, and the Tang-i-Dupulan the Inner range.

The Kuh-i-Rang is the definite water-parting and the originating cause of two drainage systems, and it may be seen from the map, as was beautifully obvious from the summit of one of the peaks over 11,000 feet in height, that it marks a singular change in the "lie of the land," inasmuch as the main drainage no longer runs parallel to the main ranges, but cuts them across, breaking up Upper Elam into a wild and confused sea of mountains, riven and gashed, without any attempt at uniformity.

This cutting through the ranges at right angles by rivers which somehow must reach the sea, probably through channels formed by some tremendous operations of nature, presents serious obstacles to the traveller, and must effectually prevent commerce flowing in that direction. The aspect of Upper Elam as seen from the Kuh-i-Rang is of huge walls of naked rock, occasionally opening out so as to give space for such a noble mountain as the Kuh-i-Shahan, with tremendous gorges or cañons among them, with sheer precipices 4000 and 5000 feet high, below which blue-green torrents, crystalline in their purity, rage and boom, thundering on their way to join the Ab-i-Diz. The valleys are short, and elevated from 6000 to 7000 feet, and the tracks dignified by the name of roads pass along them and at great altitudes on the sides of the main ranges, but are compelled continually to make dips and ascents of many thousand feet to reach and emerge from the fords of the rivers which dash through the magnificent rifts and cañons.

To the south-east of the Kuh-i-Rang the formation is orderly and intelligible ; to the north-west all is confusion and disorder, but a sublime confusion. Two great passes to the north and south of this magnificent mountain are the only ways of communication between the region of Upper Elam and the Bakhtiari country. The northern pass was ascended from Dima. The Kharba, one of the head-streams of the Zainderud, rises on it and fertilises a beautiful valley about fourteen miles in length. That pass, the Gal-i-Bard-i-Jamal (the pass of Jamal's stone), the stone being a great detached rock near the summit, and the Gal-i-Gav (the Cattle Pass) on the southern side, are both over 10,000 feet in altitude. They are seldom traversed by the natives, and only in well-armed parties, as both are very dangerous.

The Kuh-i-Rang must now be regarded as the true birthplace of the Zainderud and the Karun, though their sources have hitherto been placed in the Zard Kuh. A tributary of the Ab-i-Diz, and locally considered as its head-water, rises also in the Kuh-i-Rang.

Aziz Khan, who had gone to his tents, has returned with a very nice young servant and another mare, and with him noise and " go." He has such a definite personality, and is so energetic in his movements, that the camps are dull without him. He is a fearful beggar.

He asks me for something every day, and for things he can make no possible use of, simply out of acquisitiveness.   He has got from me among many other things a

AZIZ KHAN.

new embroidered saddle-cloth, a double-bladed knife, an Indian *kamarband*, many yards of silk, a large pair of scissors, bracelets for his wife and daughter, and working materials, and now he has set his heart on a large combination knife, which is invaluable to me.   "What use

is that knife to a woman ? " he asks daily.   Now he says
that. I have given him many things but I have never
given him money, and he must have a purse of money.

"Why can you do so much more than our women?"
he often asks.   His astonishment that I can read, and
yet more that I can write, is most amusing.   "Can
many women in your country write ? " he asked.   "Can
your Queen read and write ?   Can she embroider as you
do ?"   At first he thought that I only pretended to
write, but was convinced when I sent a letter to the
Ilkhani.

He usually appears when a number of sick people
come, interprets their dialect into good Persian for Mirza,
and beats and pelts them with stones when they crowd
too closely, but they do not care.   Sometimes when I say
that nothing that I have can do a sick person any good
he begs "for my sake" that I will try, and when I still
decline he goes away in a tantrum, cursing, and shaking
his wide *shulwars* with an angry strut, but is soon back
again with fresh demands.

He spreads his prayer-carpet and goes through his
devotions thrice a day, but somehow "Aziz Khan pray-
ing" seems to suggest some ludicrous idea, even to his
co-religionists.   "Feringhis don't fear God," he said to
me; "they never worship."   I told him he was wrong,
that many are very devout.   He said, "Does —— pray ?"
mentioning a European.   I said "Most certainly," and
he walked away with the sneering laugh of a fiend.   He
is a complete child of nature.   He says what he thinks,
and acts chiefly as he pleases, but withal there is a
gentlemanliness and a considerable dignity about him.
I think that his ruling religion is loyalty to Isfandyar
Khan, and consequent hatred of the Ilkhani and all his
other enemies.   Going through a pantomimic firing of an
English rifle he said, " I hope I may shoot the Shah with

this one day!" "For what reason?" I asked. "Because he murdered Isfandyar Khan's father, and I hate him." I asked him if he liked shooting, and he replied, "I like shooting men!"

He has done a good deal of fighting, and has been shot through the lung, arm, and leg, besides getting sword cuts, and he takes some pride in showing his wounds. I think he is faithful. Mirza says that he has smoothed many difficulties, and has put many crooked things straight, without taking any credit to himself. His most apparent faults are greed and a sort of selfish cunning.

There are many camps about the Gal-i-Gav, and crowds, needing very careful watching, are always about the tents, wanting to see Feringhi things, most of the people never having seen a Feringhi. It is a novel sight in the evenings when long lines of brown sheep in single file cross the snow-fields, following the shepherds into camp.

This Gal-i-Gav on the Kuh-i-Rang marks a new departure on the journey, as well as the establishment of certain geographical facts. It will be impossible for the future to place the source of the Karun in the Zard Kuh range, for we followed the stream up to the Kuh-i-Rang, or to indulge in the supposition that the mountains which lie to the north-west are "covered with eternal snow," which in this latitude would imply heights from 17,000 to 20,000 feet.

It is indeed a disappointment that, look where one may over the great area filled up by huge rock barriers and vast mountains, from the softer ridges bounding the fiery Persian plains to the last hills in which the Inner range descends upon the great alluvial levels of Khuzistan, not a peak presents itself in the glittering snowy mantle which I have longed to see. Snow in forlorn patches or

nearly hidden in sunless rifts, and the snow-fields of the
Zard Kuh will remain for a time, but eternal snow is—
nowhere, and it does not appear that the highest of the
peaks much exceeds 13,000 feet, either in Upper Elam
or the Bakhtiari country.

Great difficulties are ahead, not only from tracks
which are said to be impassable for laden animals, but
from the disturbed state of the country. From what I
hear from Aziz Khan and from the guides who have
come up here, I gather that the power of the Ilkhani,
shaky enough even nearer Ardal, all but dwindles
away here, and is limited to the collection of the tribute,
the petty Khans fighting among themselves, and doing
mainly what is right in their own eyes.

It is somewhat of a satisfaction to me that it is impossible now to go back, and that a region absolutely
unexplored lies ahead, doubtless full, as the previously
untraversed regions have been, of surprises and interests.

I. L. B.

LETTER XVIII

Camp Gokun, *July 6*.

A descent of 5000 feet brought us into the grand and narrow gorge of the Sahid stream, with willow, walnut, oak, maple, pear, and crab along its banks, knotted together by sprays of pink roses, with oaks higher up, and above them again overhanging mountains of naked rock, scorched, and radiating heat.

Quite suddenly, after a steep ascent, there is a view of a steep slope below, where a lateral ravine comes down on the Sahid, green with crops of wheat and barley, poplars, willows, and a grove of fine walnuts, and more wonderful still, with an *imamzada* in good repair, and a village, also named Sahid, in which people live all the year. The glen is magnificent, and is the one spot that I have seen in Persia which suggests Switzerland.

It is a steep and difficult descent through a walnut grove to the village, and before I knew it I was on the roof of a house. The village is built in ten steps up the steep hillside, the posts which support one projecting roof resting on the back of the roof below.

The people were timid and suspicious, gave untrue replies to questions at first, said we were "doing talisman to take their country," and consulted in Aziz's and Mirza's hearing how they might rob us. It was even difficult to get them to bring fodder for the horses. They were fanatical and called us *Kafirs*. Some of the women

have never been out of their romantic mountain-walled
hole, in which they are shut up by snow for four months
every winter. Ten families live there, each one possess-
ing a step. They said they owned sixty-five goats and
sheep, five cows, and seven asses; that they sell their
wheat, and salt from a salt spring at the back of the
hill, and that their food is chiefly acorn flour made into
bread, curds, and wild celery.

This bread is made from the fruit of the *Quercus
ballota*, which is often nearly three inches long. The
acorns are not gathered, but picked up when they fall.
The women bruise them between stones to expel the
bitter juices. They are afterwards reduced to flour, which
is well washed to remove the remaining bitterness, and
dried in the sun. It is either made into thin cakes and
baked, or is mixed into a paste with buttermilk and water
and eaten raw. The baked cakes are not very unpalatable, but the paste is nauseous. Acorn flour is never
used from choice.

The grain is exchanged for blue cottons and tobacco.
It is not possible to imagine a more isolated life. Tihran
and Isfahan are names barely known to these people,
and the Shah is little more to them than the Czar.

Near the *imamzada* of Sahid is a burial-ground,
rendered holy by the dust of a *pir* or saint who lies
there. It has many headstones, and one very large gray
stone lion, on whose sides are rude carvings of a gun, a
sword, a dagger, a powder-flask, and a spear. On a few
low headstones a peculiar comb is carved, denoting that
the grave is that of a woman.

To several stones long locks of hair are attached, some
black and shining, others dead-looking and discoloured.
It is customary for the Bakhtiari women to sacrifice their
locks to the memory of their husbands and other near
male relatives.

I think that they have a great deal of conjugal and family affection, though their ways are rough, and that they mourn for their dead for a considerable time. On one grave a young woman was rocking herself to and fro, wailing with a sound like the Highland coronach, but longer and more despairing. She was also beating her uncovered bosom rhythmically, and had cut her face till the blood came. So apparently absorbed was she in her grief that she took no notice of a Feringhi and an Indian. She had been bereaved of her husband for a year, his life having been sacrificed in a tribal fight.

The next two days were occupied in what might well be called "mountaineering" on goat tracks; skirting great mountain spurs on shelving paths not always wide enough for a horse's two feet alongside of each other, with precipitous declivities of 1000 or 2000 feet; ascending on ledges of rock to over 9000 feet, then by frightful tracks descending 2000 or 3000 but to climb again; and at every descent always seeing in front dizzy zigzags surmounting the crest of some ragged ridge, only, as one knows, to descend again. *Screw* nearly fell over backwards with me once and again, and came down a smooth face of rock as mules sometimes come down a snow slide in Switzerland. I was told that I should "break my neck" many times, that no Bakhtiari had ever ridden over these tracks, or ever would, but my hurt knee left me no choice. These tracks are simply worn by the annual passage of the nomads and their flocks. They are frightful beyond all description. The worst paths in Ladak and Nubra are nothing to them.

Occasionally we traversed deep ravines with noisy torrents where the shade was dense, and willows, ash, walnut, cherry, elm, plum, and oak were crowded together, with the *Juniperus excelsa* in rifts above. With a moist climate it would be a glorious land, but even where the scenery is finest there is always something lacking. There is no atmosphere. All is sharp, colourless, naked. Even many of the flowers are queer, and some are positively ugly. Many have thorns, some are leather-like, others woolly, a few sticky. Inconspicuous flowers and large leathery leaves are very common. The seed-vessels of some are far prettier than the flowers, and brighter in colour. In several the calyx grows after the corolla has withered, and becomes bright pink or orange, like a very gay but only partially-opened blossom. *Umbelliferæ* predominate this month. *Compositæ* too are numerous. All, even bulbs, send down their roots very deep.

After leaving camp yesterday and crossing a high pass we descended into the earth's interior, only to ascend a second pass by a steep zigzag. Suddenly a wall of rock appeared as if to bar progress, but on nearing it a narrow V-shaped slit was seen to afford a risky passage, offering no other foothold than smooth shelving rock on the inside for a number of yards, with a precipice above on the right and below on the left. Ledges of slippery rock led up to it, and *Screw* was jumping and scrambling up these when the guides howled to me to stop, and I was lifted off somehow. The white Arab was rolling and struggling in the V, *Screw* following lost his footing, and the two presented a confusion of hoofs and legs in the air and bodies struggling and rolling through the slit till they picked themselves up with cut legs. The guides tried vainly to find some way by which the caravans which followed much later might avoid this risk, and the Agha went down the pass which had been so laboriously ascended to give directions for its passage.

The *charvadars* on reaching the difficulty made attempts to turn it but failed; some loads were taken off and carried by men, and each mule struggled safely through with one man at his head, and one or two supporting him by his tail. The passage of the V took the caravan an hour, but meantime there was the enjoyment of the sight of a confused mass of mountains, whitish precipitous ranges, sun-lit, with tremendous ravines between them, lying in the cool blue shadows of early morning; mountains with long straight summits, mountains snow-covered and snow-slashed, great spires of naked rock, huge ranges buttressed by huge spurs herbage-covered, with outcrops of barren rock,—a mighty, solitary, impressive scene, an uplifted wilderness without a camp.

The descent of 4000 feet from this summit consists of any number of zigzag tracks on the narrow top of the narrow ridge of one of the huge rocky buttresses of Gartak, both sides being precipitous. Even on the horse I was dizzy, and he went down most unwillingly, not taking any responsibility as to finding the safest way, and depending solely on my eye and hand. Mirza, being hampered with the care of his own mule, was useless, and otherwise I was alone. These thready zigzags ended on what appeared to be a precipice, from the foot of which human voices came up, shouting to me to dismount. I did so, and got down, hanging on to *Screw's* bridle, and letting myself down over the ledges by my hands for another hour, having to be careful all the time to avoid being knocked down by his slips and jumps. I could hardly get him to face some of the smooth broken faces of rock. A slide of gravel, a snow-bridge, worn thin, over a torrent, and some slippery rock ledges to scramble over by its side led to a pathless ascent through grass and bushes. The guides and Aziz roared to me from a valley below, by which roars I found my way down a steep hillside to the Gokun, a mountain river of a unique and most beautiful blue-green colour, abounding in deep pools from which it emerges in billows of cool foam.

I forded it by a broad ford where crystal-green water glides calmly over brown and red pebbles, with a willow-shaded margin, and as I crossed a flock of long-bearded goats swam and jumped from rock to rock from the other side, the whole scene an artist's dream. This valley has magnificent pasturage, hay not yet "sun cured," long grass, and abundant clover and vetches brightened by a profuse growth of a small *helianthus*.

The march over the Gokun Pass and down to the Gokun river is the worst I ever made. Had the track been in Ladak or Lahoul it would have been marked on the Government maps "impassable for laden animals." Yet Hadji's splendid mules, held at times by both head and tail, accomplished it, and only minor disasters occurred. One mule had his head gashed, Mirza had a bad fall, and broke my milk bottle, Hassan, leading his own horse, fell twenty feet with the animal and cut his arm, the ridge pole of my tent was broken, and is with difficulty bandaged so as to hold, and some of the other baggage was damaged. Hadji grumbles politely, and says that "in all time loaded mules were never taken over such tracks," and I believe him. Aziz says that I must be "tired of life," or I should never ride over them, and certainly *Screw* carried me at the peril of his life and mine.

The camps are pitched for Sunday at an altitude of 8000 feet, high above the river—mine under the befriending shade of a colossal natural sphinx, so remarkable that two photographs and a sketch by Mirza were taken of it. It confronted us in a startling way, a grand man's head with a flowing wig and a legal face, much resembling the photographs of Lord Chancellor Hatherley.

The mules have been poorly fed for the last few days, and it is pleasant to see them revelling in the abundant pasturage. After this tremendous nine hours' march they came in quite cheerily, Cock o' the Walk leading the caravan, with his fighting face on, shaking his grand mane, and stamping as if he had not walked a mile.

The Sunday has been a very quiet one, except for the fighting of the horses, which seem intent on murdering each other, the fussiness of Aziz about a cut which his mare got yesterday, and for which he expects my frequent attention, and the torment of the sand-flies, which revel in the heat which kills the mosquitos.

Kalahoma, July 11.—On Monday it was a pretty march from the shadow of the sphinx through a well-irrigated and cultivated valley with many camps, and by a high pass, to the neighbourhood of the Kuh-i-Shahan, on which I rested for some hours at a height of 12,010 feet, the actual summit being somewhat higher. On its north-east side the view was hideous, of scorched, rolling gravel hills and wide scorched valleys, with two winding streams, and some patches of wheat surrounding two scorched mud villages.

The descent to Camp Kamarun, a deep ravine with a rapid mountain stream, was blessed by a shower, which cooled the air, and resulted in the only grand, stormy, wild sunset that I have seen for months. This valley is blocked at the east end by Gargunaki, on the west by the Kala Kuh, and the rocky ranges of Faidun and the Kuh-i-Shahan close in its sides.

Long, long ago tradition says a certain great chief had eleven sons. They quarrelled and divided into hostile factions of four and seven, forming the still hostile groups of the Chahar Lang and the Haft Lang of to-day. For some time past the ruling dynasty has been of the Haft Lang division ; Aziz also belongs to it, and we have been almost entirely among its tribes hitherto. This ancient feud, though modified in intensity, still exists. At this camp we were among tribes of the Chahar Lang, and there was reason to apprehend robbery and a night attack; so careful arrangements were made, and the men kept guard by turns.

The following day's march, which was also pretty, included a long descent through a cultivated valley, with willows, plums, and walnuts growing along a stream, and a steep ascent and descent to the two villages of Masir on well-cultivated slopes, belonging to Taimur Khan, the chief of the powerful Magawe tribe, to whom the villagers pay what they call a moderate "rent" in sheep, goats, and grain. They are of the Chahar Lang, and deny that they are under the Ilkhani's rule. They had a fight with a tribe of the Haft Lang ten days ago, killed twelve men, had seven killed and wounded, and took some guns and horses. These, however, they have restored at the command of the Ilkhani, which contradicts their assertion.

They have a burial-ground with several very white lions rampant upon it, of most noble aspect, boldly carved, and with the usual bas-reliefs on their sides.

The camps were on a gravelly slope with a yellow glare, and the mercury reached 105°. The presence of villages in this country always indicates a comparatively warm climate, in which people can live throughout the winter. The Scripture phrase, "maketh the outgoings of the morning and evening to rejoice," has come to bear a clear and vivid meaning. In this country, in this fiery latitude, life is merely a struggle from the time the sun has been up for two hours until he sinks very low. "There is nothing hid from the heat thereof." One watches with dismay his flaming disc wheel into the cloudless sky, to blaze and scintillate mercilessly there for many terrible hours, scorching, withering, destroying, "turning a fruitful land into a desert," bringing eye diseases in his train. With sunset, but not much before, comes a respite, embittered by sand-flies, and life begins to be possible; then darkness comes with a stride and the day is done.

Among the many people who came to the *Hakīm* was a man who had received a severe sword cut in the recent fight. I disliked his expression, and remarked on it to Mirza. On the next day's march, though there were twelve men with the caravan, this man seized and made off with the handsome chestnut horse Karun, which was being led. The horse had a sore back and soon kicked off his rider and was recovered. On the same march Mujid was attacked, and under the threat of being stripped was obliged to give up all the money he had on his person. On the same day some women clamorously demanded bracelets, and when I did not give them two took hold of my bridle and one of my foot, and were dragging me off, when on Mirza coming up they let me go.

Marching among lower hills and broader valleys, irrigated and cultivated, with much wood along the streams and scattered on the lower slopes, we passed the inhabited villages of Tarsa and Sah Kala, surrounded by patches of buckwheat, vetches, and melons, and with much provision of *kiziks* for fuel on their roofs, and camped by the richly-wooded river Guwa, in a grove of fine trees, crossing its vigorous torrent the next morning by a wicker bridge, the Pul-i-Guwa. A long ascent among oaks, where the views of mountains and ravines were grand, an upland meadow where I found a white bee orchis, and a steep ascent among stones, brought us to the top of a pass 9650 feet in altitude. On its south-west side there is a very striking view of gorges of immense depth and steepness, through which the Guwa finds its way. To the northeast the prospect is of a very feeble country, which we entered by a tiresome gravelly descent, very open, composed of low hills with outcrops of rock at their summits, irrigated rolling valleys and plains, with deep rifts indicative of streams, and some Magawe villages.

Our route lay across the most scorched and gravelly part of the upper slopes of a wide valley, scantily sprinkled with blue *eryngiums* and a woolly species of *artemisia*, a very repulsive region, where herds of camels, kept for breeding purposes, were grazing. On the other side of this valley a spur of the fine mountain Jalanda projects, and on it are the two villages and fort of Kalahoma, the residence of Taimur Khan.

We halted below the hill while a spring was being searched for, and I was sitting on horseback eating my lunch, a biscuit in one hand and a cup in the other. I have mentioned the savagery of the horses, and especially of *Hakīm*, who has become like a wild beast. He was standing fully four horse-lengths away from me, with his tail towards me, and the guide had let go his bridle, when there was a roar or squeal, and a momentary vision of glaring wild-beast eyes, streaming mane, and open mouth rushing down upon me and towering above *Screw's* head, and the next thing I remember is finding myself on the ground with my foot in the stirrup and three men lifting me up.

I was a good deal shaken, and cut my arm badly, but mounted again, and though falling on my head has given me a sickish headache for two days, I have not absolutely required rest, and in camp there is no use in "making a fuss"—if indeed there ever is.

I shall not have pleasant memories of this camp. The tents were scarcely pitched before crowds assembled for medicine. I could get no rest, for if I shut the tent the heat was unbearable, and if I opened it there was the crowd, row behind row, the hindmost pushing the foremost in, so that it was 8 P.M. before I got any food. Yesterday morning at six I was awakened by people

all round the tent, some shaking the curtains and calling
" *Hakīm* ! *Hakīm* !" and though I kept it shut till
eleven, and raised the mercury to 115° by doing so,
there was no rest.

From eleven o'clock till 9 P.M., except for one hour,
when I was away at the Khan's, I was "seeing patients,"
wishing I were a real instead of a spurious *Hakīm*, for
there was so much suffering, and some of it I knew not
how to relieve. However, I was able (thanks to St.
Mary's Hospital, London) to open three whitlows and
two abscesses, and it was delightful to see the immediate
relief of the sufferers. "God is great," they all exclaimed,
and the bystanders echoed, "God is great." I dressed
five neglected bullet wounds, and sewed up a gash of
doubtful origin, and with a little help from Mirza prepared eye-lotions and medicines for seventy-three people.
I asked one badly-wounded man in what quarrel he had
been shot, and he replied that he didn't know, his Khan
had told him to go and fight.

In the afternoon several very distressed people were
brought from an Armenian village ten miles off, and were
laid by those who brought them at the tent door. At
five the crowd was very great and the hubbub inconceivable, and Mirza failed to keep order in the absence of
Aziz Khan, who had gone on a pilgrimage to a neighbouring *imamzada*. The mercury had never fallen below
100°. I had been standing or kneeling for six hours,
and had a racking headache, so I reluctantly shut up my
medicine chest and went by invitation to call on the
Khan's wives, but the whole crowd surrounded and followed me, swelling as it moved along, a man with a mare
with bad eyes, which had been brought ten miles for eye-
lotion, increasing the clamour by his urgency. " Khanum !
Khanum !" (lady) "Chashma !" (eyes) "Shikam !" (stomach)
were shouted on all sides, with " *Hakīm* ! *Hakīm* !" The

people even clutched my clothing, and hands were raised to heaven to implore blessings on me if I would attend to them.

The whole village of Kalahoma was out, thronging, pressing, and almost suffocating me, and the Khan's servants who came to meet me did not or could not disperse the people, though every man holds his life at the Khan's disposal. These villages, which are surrounded by opium fields, are composed of the rudest of human habitations, built of rough stones, the walls being only five feet high. There is much subterranean room for cattle. The stacks of such winter fodder as celery and *Centaurea alata*, and those of *kiziks* for fuel, are larger than the dwellings. The latter are of conical form, and many of them are built on the house roofs.

Taimur Khan's fort and *serai* are in the midst of all this, and are very poor and ruinous, but the walls are high, and they have a *balakhana*. As I approached the ladies came out to meet me, veiled in white cotton *chadars*. The principal wife took my hand and led me through a hole in the wall, not to be called a doorway, into a courtyard littered with offal and piled with stacked animal fuel, and up some high dilapidated steps, into a small dark room, outside of which are a very small "lobby" and a blackened ladder against the wall, leading to the roof, on which the ladies sleep in the hot weather. Some poor rugs covered the floor, and there were besides some poor cotton-covered bolsters. Everything, even the dress of the ladies, indicated poverty. The dark hot room was immediately packed with a crowd of women, children, and babies, all appallingly dirty. It was a relief when the Khan was announced in the distance, and they cleared out like frightened sheep, leaving only the four wives, who stood up at his approach, and remained standing till he was seated.

No " well-bred " Khan would pay me a visit in his
andarun without sending first with his " homage " to know
if I would receive him, nor did Taimur Khan violate this
rule or the other of remaining standing until I asked him
to be seated.   He is a tall, very melancholy-looking man,
with a Turkish cast of face, and is dressed in the usual
Persian style.   After a few ordinary commonplaces he
talked politics and tribal affairs, *apparently* frankly, but
who can say if truthfully ?   He knows that I have letters
from the Prime Minister, and he hoped that I might do
him some good at Tihran.   As soon as important subjects superseded trifles, the wives relapsed into complete
indifference, and stared into vacancy.

His tribe, the Magawe, is estimated at 500 families,
and has been powerful.   Taimur Khan is a staunch
adherent of the Ilkhani, but at this point there is a
change as to the tribute, half of which is paid to the
Ilkhani and half to the Governor of Burujird.   He has
many grievances, and complains most bitterly that he and
his tribe are being ground into poverty by exactions which,
he asserts, have this year raised the tribute from 700
to 4000 *tumans*.

He asks me to do something to help him, adding that
his house is in ruins, and that he is so oppressed that he
cannot build a new one, or have any surroundings suitable
to his rank.   I said that I could only send his statements
to the British " Vakil " in Tihran, and he at once asked
how many horses he should present him with.   I replied
that the " Vakil " would not accept anything, and that he
had lately declined a superb diamond setting in which
the Shah desired to send him his picture.   The Khan
raised his hands, with the exclamation " God is great ! "

Isfandyar Khan and Taimur Khan were at war some
years ago, and fought from mountain to mountain, and
Taimur Khan was eventually captured, taken to Buru-

jird, and sent to Isfahan, where he was kept in irons for
some years, the redoubtable Aziz Khan being one of his
captors. This accounts for the disappearance of Aziz on
"pilgrimage" to a neighbouring *imamzada*, and the consequent dulness of the camp.

Among a people at once simple and revengeful, it is
not unlikely that such severities may bear their legitimate
fruit if an occasion presents itself, such as the embroil-
ment of Persia with any other power. Another Khan
who was thrown into prison and irons by the Zil-es-
Sultan expressed himself strongly on the subject. "Five
years," he said, holding out his muscular wrists, on which
the marks of fetters are still visible, "I wore the chains.
Can I forget?" The Bakhtiaris do not love the Persians,
and are held, I think, by a brittle thread.

I have written of the extreme poverty of the surroundings of the Khaja Taimur or Taimur Khan. It is not a
solitary instance. Throughout this journey I am painfully
impressed with the poverty of the tribesmen. As compared with the wealth of those farther south when visited
by Sir A. H. Layard and the Baron de Bode, their condition is one of destitution. The Ilkhani and Ilbegi have
fine studs, but few of the Khans have any horses worth
looking at, and for some time past none at all have been
seen except a few belonging to the chiefs, and the men
either walk or ride very small asses.

Their cattle are few and small and their flocks insignificant when compared with those of the Arab tribes
west of the Tigris. Their tents and furnishings are likewise extremely poor, and they live poorly, many of them
only able to procure acorn flour for bread, and this though
they grow a great deal of grain, and every yard of land
is cultivated if water is procurable.

The hospitality which those two travellers mention as
a feature of the character of the more southerly Bakh-

tiaris does not exist among these people. They have, in fact, little to be hospitable with. They all speak of better days in the times of their fathers, when they had brood mares and horses to ride, much pastoral wealth and plenty of *roghan*, and when their women could wear jewels and strings of coins.

On this point I believe them, though there may possibly be exaggeration in Taimur Khan's statements. Persia has undoubtedly tightened her grip upon them, and she is sucking their life-blood out of them. This becomes very evident now that we have reached a point where the government of Burujird comes in, with the infinite unrighteousness of Persian provincial governors. It is not the tribute fixed by the Amin-es-Sultan which these Khans complain of, but the rapacious exactions of the local governors.

There is a " blood feud " between Taimur Khan and Aslam Khan, the chief of the Zalaki tribe, on whose territory we shall enter to-day. A nephew of Taimur killed a relation of Aslam, and afterwards Taimur sheltered him from legitimate vengeance. Just now the feud is very active, and cattle-lifting and other reprisals are going on. " Blood feuds " are of three degrees, according to the nature of the offence. In the first a man of the one tribe can kill a man of the other wherever he finds him. In the second he harries his cattle and goods. In the third he simply " boycotts " him and refuses him a passage through his territory. The Bakhtiaris have often been called " bloodthirsty." I doubt whether they are so, though life is of little account, and they are reckless about spilling blood.

They have a great deal of family devotion, which in lesser degree extends to the members of their tribe, and a Bakhtiari often spares the life of a man who has aggrieved him owing to his fear of creating a blood feud, which must be transmitted from father to son, and which must affect the whole tribe. As a deterrent from acts of violence it acts powerfully, and may account for the singular bloodlessness of some of the tribal fights. Few men, unless carried away by a whirlwind of fury, care to involve a tribe in the far-reaching consequences alluded to, and bad as the custom of blood feuds is, I think there can be no doubt that it acts as a curb upon the passions of these wild tribesmen. "There is blood between us and them," is a phrase often heard.

Punishments are simple and deterrent, well suited to a simple people. When a homicide is captured he is handed over to the relatives of the slain man, who may kill him, banish him, fine him, or pardon him. In point of fact, "blood-money" is paid to the family of the deceased person, and to save his life from their vengeance a homicide frequently becomes a mendicant on the other side of the mountains till he can gain the required sum. Moslem charity responds freely to a claim for alms to wipe out a blood stain. The Ilkhani has a right to fine a homicide. "Blood for blood" is a maxim very early inculcated.

The present feud between the Magawe and the Zalaki tribes is of the first degree. It is undoubtedly a part of the truly Oriental policy of Persia to foment tribal quarrels, and keep them going, with the object of weakening the power of the clans, which, though less so than formerly, is a standing menace to the central government.

On reaching camp after this visit I found a greater crowd than ever, and as "divers of them came from far," I tried to help them till nine o'clock, and as Aziz had returned the crowding was not so severe. He said, "You're very tired, send these people away, you've done enough." I answered that one had never done enough so long as one could do more, and he made a remark which led me to ask him if he thought a *Kafir* could reach Paradise? He answered "Oh no!" very hastily, but after a moment's thought said, "I don't know, God knows, *He doesn't think as we do*, He may be more merciful than we think. If Kafirs fear God they may have some Paradise to themselves, we don't know."

I. L. B.

LETTER XVIII (*Continued*) [1]

CAMP KALA KUH, *July 16.*

THE call to " Boot and Saddle " was at three, and I was
nearly too tired to pack in the sultry morning air. The
heat is overpowering. Khaja Taimur no doubt had
reasons for a difficulty in providing guides, which caused
delay. The track lay through pretty country, with
abounding herbage, to the village and *imamzada* of Mak-
hedi. There the guide said he dared not go any farther
for fear of being killed, and after some time another was
procured. During this delay a crowd of handsome but
hardship-aged women gathered round me, many of them
touching the handkerchiefs on their heads and then
tapping the palms of their hands, a significant sign,
which throughout Persia, being interpreted, means,
" Give me some money."

The Agha is in the habit of gathering the little girls
about him and giving them *krans* as from his own children,
a most popular proceeding usually ; but here the people
were not friendly, and very suspicious. Even the men
asked me clamorously, " Why does he give them money ?
it's poisoned, it's cursed, it's to make them blind." How-

[1] From Kalahoma for the rest of the route the predatory character of
the tribes, the growing weakness of the Ilkhani's authority, the "blood
feuds" and other inter-tribal quarrels, and the unsettled state of the Feili
Lurs, produced a general insecurity and continual peril for travellers, which
rendered constant vigilance and precautions necessary, as well as an alter-
ation of arrangements.

ever, avarice prevailed over fear. The people rarely see
money, and it is not used as a medium of exchange, but
they value it highly for paying the tribute and as ornaments for the women. Barter is the custom, and with
regard to "tradesmen," whether in camps or villages, it is
usual for each family to pay so much grain annually to
the blacksmith, the carpenter, the shoemaker—*i.e.* the man
who makes compressed rag or leather soles for *ghevas* and
unites the cotton webbing ("upper") to the sole—and
the *hammam* keeper, in the rare cases where there is
one. They were cutting wheat on July 12 there at an
altitude of 7000 feet. Where there are only camps the
oxen tread it out at once on the hard soil of the fields,
but where there is a village the sheaves are brought in on
donkeys' backs to a house roof of sun-dried clay, and are
there trodden out, the roofs being usually accessible from
the slope above.

We descended to a deep ford, crossed the river
Ab-i-Baznoi (locally known as Kakulistan, or "the curl,"
from its singular windings), there about sixty feet wide,
with clear rapid water of a sky-blue tint, very strong, and
up to the guide's waist, and entered a steep-sided stony
valley, where the heat was simply sickening. There the
second guide left us, saying he should be killed if he
went any farther, but another was willing to succeed him.
After a steep ascent we emerged on a broad rolling
upland valley, deeply gashed by a stream, with the grand
range of the Kala Kuh on the south side, and low bare
hills on the north. It is now populous, the valley and
hillsides are spotted with large camps, and the question
at once arose, "Hostile or Friendly?"

I was riding as usual with Mirza behind me, when a
man with a gun rushed frantically towards me from an
adjacent camp, waving his gun and shouting, "Who are
you? Why are you in our country? You're friends of

Khaja Taimur, you've given him presents, we'll rob you"!
With these and many similar words he pursued us, and
men started up as by magic, with long guns, running
alongside, the low spurs became covered with people in
no time, and there was much signalling from hill to hill,
" A-hoy-hoy-hoy-hoy," and sending of messengers. Mirza
pacified them by saying that we are friends of Isfandyar
Khan, and that I have presents for Aslam Khan, their
chief; but soon the shout of " Feringhis " was raised, and
from group to group along the knolls swelled the cry of
" Feringhis! Feringhis!" mixed with a few shouts of *Kafir*;
but without actual molestation we reached a steep and
uncomfortable camping-ground, Padshah-i-Zalaki, at an
altitude of 7800 feet, with an extensive view of the broad
green valley.

Before we halted Aslam Khan, a very fine-looking
man, and others met us, and performed feats of horsemanship, wheeling their horses in small circles at a
gallop, and firing pantomimically over their left shoulders
and right flanks. The Sahib came in later, so that our
party was a tolerably strong one.

The first thing the people did was to crowd into the
shelter-tent and lie down, staring fixedly, a thing which
never happened before, and groups steadily occupied the
tops of the adjacent spurs. After my tent was pitched
the people assembled round it in such numbers, ostensibly
desiring medicine, that the Khan sent two *tufangchis* to
keep order among them, and Karim, whose arm is now
well, was added as a protection. The Agha ordered that the
people should sit in rows at the sides and take their turn,
one at a time, to come into the verandah, but no sooner
were he and Aziz Khan out of sight than they began to
crowd, to shout, and to become unmanageable, scuffling
and pushing, the *tufangchis* pretending to beat them with
the barrels of their guns, but really encouraging them,

and at length going away, saying they could not manage
them.   Karim begged me to stop giving medicine, for he
was overpowered, and if he opposed them any more there
would be a fight.   They had said that if he " spoke
another word they would kill him."   They were perfectly
good-humoured all the time, but acted like complete
savages, getting under the *flys*, tugging at the tent ropes,
and trying to pull my blankets off the bed, etc.   At
last the hindmost gave a sudden push, sending the
foremost tumbling into the tent and over me, upsetting
a large open packet of sulphate of zinc, just arrived from
Julfa, which was on my lap.

I left the tent to avoid further mischief, but was
nearly suffocated by their crowding and tugging my dress,
shouting "*Hakīm*! *Hukīm*!"   The Sahib, who came to
the rescue, and urged them in Persian to depart, was
quite powerless.   In the midst of the confusion the Khan's
wives and daughter came to visit me, but I could only
show them the crowd and walk, followed by it, in the
opposite direction from the tent, till I met the Agha,
whose presence restored order.   That night nearly all
Hadji's *juls* or mule blankets and a donkey were stolen.

The Zalakis are a large and powerful tribe, predatory
by habit and ·tradition.   Aslam Khan himself directed
certain thefts from which we suffered, and quoted a passage from the Koran not only to extenuate but to warrant
depredations on the goods of " infidels."

Sunday was spent in the hubbub of a crowd.   I was
suffering somewhat from a fall, and yet more from the
fatigues of Kalahoma, and longed for rest, but the temperature of the tent when closed was 106°, and when
open the people crowded at the entrance, ostensibly for
medicine, but many from a pardonable and scarcely dis-
guised curiosity to see the " Feringhi *Hakīm*," and hear
her speak.

In the afternoon, with Mirza and Karim as a guard, I went somewhat reluctantly to the Khan's camp to return the abortive visit of the ladies. This camp consists of a number of black tents arranged in a circle, the Khan's tents only distinguishable from the rest by their larger size. Mares, dogs, sheep, goats, and fireholes were in the centre, and some good-looking horses were tethered outside.

The Khan's mother, a fine, buxom, but coarse-looking woman, met me, and took me to an open tent, fully forty feet long, the back of which was banked up by handsome saddle-bags. Bolsters and rugs were laid in the middle, on which the four legitimate wives and several inferior ones, with a quantity of babies and children crawling about them, were seated. Among them was a very handsome Jewish-looking girl of eighteen, the Khan's daughter, pleasing in expression and graceful in manner. She is married to a son of Taimur Khan, but he does not care for her, and has practically discarded her, which adds insult to the " blood feud " previously existing.

After I entered the tent the whole camp population, male and female, crowded in, pressing upon us with clamour indescribable. The Khan's mother slapped the wives if they attempted to speak and conducted herself like a ruling virago, occasionally shrieking at the crowd, while a *tufangchi* with a heavy stick belaboured all within his reach, and those not belaboured yelled with laughter.

The senior lady beckoned Mirza to lean towards her, and told him in a whisper that her handsome granddaughter is hated and despised by her husband, and has been sent back with a baby a year old, he having taken another wife, and that she wanted me to give her a " love philtre " that would answer the double purpose of giving her back his love and making her rival hateful in his eyes. During this whispered conference as many as could reach leant close to the speakers, like the "savages" that they are. I replied that I knew of no such philtres, that if the girl's beauty and sweetness could not retain her husband's love there was no remedy. She said she knew I had them, and that I kept them, as well as potions for making favourite wives ugly and odious to their husbands, in a leather box with a gold key! Then many headaches and sore eyes were brought, and a *samovar* and tea, and I distributed presents in a Babel in which anything but the most staccato style of conversation was impossible. When I left the crowd surged after me, and a sharp stone was thrown, which cut through my cloak.

Later, Aslam Khan, his brothers, and the usual train of retainers called. He is a very fine-looking man, six feet high, with a most sinister expression, and a look at times which inspired me with the deepest distrust of him. His robber tribe numbers 3500 souls, and he says that he can bring 540 armed horsemen into the field. He too asked for medicine for headache. Not only is there a blood feud between him and Khaja Taimur, but between him and Mirab Khan, through whose valley we must pass. In the evening the Khan's mother returned with several women, bent on getting the "love philtre." At night Hadji, who was watching, said that men were prowling round the tents at all hours, and a few things were taken.

On Monday morning early all was ready, for the three caravans from that day were to march together, and I was sitting on my horse talking with the Sahib, waiting for the Agha to return from the Khan's camp, when he rushed down the slope exclaiming, "There's mischief!" and I crossed the stream and watched it. About twenty men with loaded sticks had surrounded Mujid, and were

beating him and finally got him down. I leapt back to
my own camp, where Hassan and Karim were taking a
parting smoke, and ordered them to the rescue.   The
soldier rushed into the *mêlée*, armed with only a cane,
which was broken at once, and the Bakhtiaris got him by
his thick hair, and all but forced him down ; but he
fought like a bulldog, and so did Hassan, who was unarmed
and got two bad cuts.   Dashed too into the fray Hadji
Hussein, who fought like a bull, followed by his muleteers
and by Abbas Ali, who, being early knocked down, hung
on to a man's arm with his teeth.   The Sahib, who was
endeavouring to make peace, was untouched, possibly
because of his lineage and faith, and he yelled to Mirza
(who in a fight is of no account) to run for the Agha,
whose presence is worth fifty men.

Meanwhile a number of Zalakis, armed, two with
guns and the rest with loaded sticks, crowded round me,
using menacing gestures and calling me a *Kafir*, on
which I took my revolver out of the holster, and very
slowly examined the chambers, though I knew well that
all were loaded.   This had an excellent effect.   They fell
back, and were just dispersing when over the crest of the
hill cantered Aziz Khan, followed by the Agha, who, galloping down the slope, fired a revolver twice over the head
of a man who was running away, who, having stolen a
sheep, and being caught in the act by Mujid, had begun
the fray.   Aslam Khan followed, and, the men say, gave
the order to fire, but recalled it on finding that one of his
tribesmen had been the aggressor.   I thought he took the
matter very coolly, and he almost immediately told Mirza
to ask me for a penknife !

After this we started, the orders being for the caravans
to keep well together, and if we were absolutely attacked
to " fire."   After ascending a spur of the Kala Kuh we
left the track for an Ilyat camp on a steep hill among

oaks and pears, where I had promised to see a young creature very ill of fever.

Among the trees was a small booth of four poles, roofed with celery stalks, but without sides or ends, and in this, on a sheepskin, was a heap out of which protruded two white wasted arms. I uncovered the back of a head which turned slowly, and revealed, in a setting of masses of heavy shining hair, the white face of a young girl, with large brilliant eyes and very beautiful teeth. Her pulse was fluttering feebly, and I told the crowd that death was very near, for fear they should think I had poisoned her with the few drops of stimulant that she was able to swallow. Even here the death penalty sometimes follows the joy of maternity. She died in the evening, and now nothing remains of the camp but a heap of ashes, for these people always at once leave the camping-ground where a death has occurred.

Meanwhile the Agha was making friends with the people, and giving *krans* to the children, as is his habit. Scarcely had we left when he found that he had been robbed of a fine pair of binocular glasses, almost a necessity under the circumstances. English rifles, binoculars, and watches are all coveted by the Bakhtiaris. Aziz Khan became very grave, and full of dismal prophecies regarding the remainder of the journey.

After this divergence the scenery was magnificent. The Kala Kuh range is certainly finer than the Zard Kuh. It is more broken up into peaks of definite outline, and is more deeply cut by gorges, many of them the beds of torrents, densely wooded. In fact it is less of a *range* and more of a *group*. The route lay among huge steep mountains of naked rock, cut up by narrow, deep, and gigantic clefts, from whose depths rise spires of rock and stupendous, almost perpendicular cliffs. Green torrents flecked with foam boom through the shadows, or flash in the sunlight, margined wherever it is possible by walnuts, oaks, lilacs, roses, the *Lastrea dilatata*, and an entanglement of greenery revelling in spray.

A steep zigzag descent through oak and pear trees brought us to the vigorous torrent Ab-i-Sefid (white water), one of many of the same name, crossed by a natural bridge of shelving rock, slippery from much use. One of the Arabs so nearly fell on this that I dismounted, and just as I did so Abbas Ali's mule fell on his side, and *Screw* following did the same, breaking several things in the holster.

After crossing a deep ravine Abbas Ali sprang back down the steep to it, and the Sahib, who was behind, also ran down with three men to what was evidently a disaster. Mirza's mule had fallen over twenty feet, rolling over him three times with its load, hurting his knee badly. The Sahib said he never saw so narrow an escape from a broken neck. The loss of a bottle containing a quart of milk was the chief damage. A little farther up three men were tugging *Hakīm* up to the track by the tail. It was a very steep ascent by stony broken zigzags and ledges to the fairly level top of a spur of the Kala Kuh range, with a high battlemented hill behind, at the back of which dwell robber hordes, and many Seyyids, who pay no tribute, and are generally feared.

At this open, breezy height of 9200 feet the camps have been pitched for three days, and of the many camping-grounds which we have hitherto occupied I like it the best, so lofty is it, so lonely, so mysterious and unexplored. It has a glorious view of tremendous wooded ravines, down which green waters glide or tumble, of small lawn-like plateaux among woods, and of green peaks in the foreground, and on the other side of the narrow, sinuous valley, several thousand feet below, there is a confused mass of mountains, among which the snow-slashed southern faces of the peaks of the Zard Kuh and the grand bulk of a mountain of the Faidun range, are the most prominent.

Five thousand feet below, reached by a remarkable track, is Basnoi, a lonely depth, with successive terraces of figs, pomegranates, and walnuts, dense woods, and a luxuriant undergrowth of long grass and ferns. Among them are the remains of an ancient road of good width and construction, and of a very fine bridge of small blocks of carefully-dressed stone, with three arches, now ruined, with fine piers and stone abutments, the centre arch having a span of sixty feet. The roadway of the bridge is gone, and a crazy wicker framework is suspended in its place. The Bakhtiaris attribute these relics of an extinct civilisation to Shapur, one of the three kings of that name who reigned in the third and fourth centuries. All these green waters fall into the Ab-i-Diz.

Before sunset heads of men and barrels of guns were seen over the rocky cliff behind us. We had been warned against the outlaw tribes of that region, and had been told that they were preparing to rob the camp that night with thirty men, and had declared that if they failed they would dog us till they succeeded. This news was brought by Aslam Khan's brother in the afternoon. I asked Aziz with how much I should reach Burujird, and he answered, " It's well if you take your life there."

This and a whole crop of other rumours, magnified as they passed from man to man, produced a novel excitement in the lonely camps. Hadji buried his money, of which he had a large sum, and lay down upon it. Rifles and revolvers were cleaned and loaded, swords and knives sharpened, voices were loud and ceaseless, and those who were slightly hurt in the morning's fray recounted their adventures over and over again. All dispositions for safety were carefully made before night. Hassan, who has a horse, and large property in good clothes, wanted a revolver, but was wisely refused, on the ground that to arm undisciplined men indiscriminately would be to run a great risk of being ourselves shot in any confusion. There were then four men with rifles, five with revolvers, and Aslam Khan's brother and two *tufangchis* with guns.

About eight the Bakhtiari signal-call was several times repeated, and I wondered if it were foe or friend, till Aziz's answering signal rang out loud and clear, announcing that it was "friends of Isfandyar Khan." Shortly I heard, "the plot thickens," and the "friends" turned out to be another brother of Aslam Khan, with four *tufangchis* and a promise of eight more, who never arrived. According to these men reliable information had been received that Khaja Taimur, our friend of Kalahoma, was sending forty men to rob us on Aslam Khan's territory in order to get him into trouble.

This arrival increased the excitement among the men, who piled tamarisk and the gum tragacanth bush on the fires most recklessly, the wild, hooded *tufangchis* and their long guns being picturesque in the firelight. I am all but positively sure that the rumour was invented by Aslam Khan, in order to show his vigilant care of guests, and secure from their gratitude the much-coveted possession of an English rifle. Hadji came to my tent, telling me "not to be the least afraid, for they would not harm a lady." The Agha has a resource for every emergency, the Sahib is cool and brave, and besides that, I strongly suspected the whole thing to be a ruse of Aslam Khan, whom I distrust thoroughly. At all events I was asleep very early, and was only disturbed twice by Aziz calling to know if my servants were watching, and was only awakened at five by the Sahib and the Agha going past my tent, giving orders that any stranger approaching the camp was to be warned off, and was to be fired upon if he disregarded the warning.

A blissfully quiet day followed the excitement of the night before. The men slept after their long watch, and the fighting horses were at a distance. The Agha did not return, and for a day and night I was the only European in camp. Aziz Khan, with an English rifle, a hundred cartridges, and two revolvers in his belt, kept faithful watch, and to "make assurance doubly sure" I walked through the camp twice during the night to see that the men on guard were awake.

Before midnight there was a frightful "row" for two hours, which sounded as if fifty men were taking part in it. I have often wondered at the idiotic things that Hassan does, and at the hopelessly dazed way in which he sometimes stands. Now it has come out that he is smoking more and more opium, and has been supplying Karim with it.

Mujid, who was formerly the Agha's cook, has been promoted to be *major-domo*, rules the caravan on the march, heads it on a fine horse, keeps accounts, and is generally "confidential." Karim resents all this. He lately bought a horse because he could not bear to ride a baggage mule when the other man was well mounted, and being that night mad with opium, and being armed both with rifle and revolver, with which he threatened to kill Mujid, it was only by the united and long-continued efforts of all the men that bloodshed was prevented. The next day Hassan destroyed his opium pipe, and is trying to cure himself of the habit with the aid of morphia, but he complains of "agony in the waist," which is just the fearful craving which the disuse of the drug causes.

The Agha encountered very predatory Lurs in the lower regions. A mule was stolen by two Lurs, then

robbed from them by three, who in their turn were
obliged to surrender it to some passing Ilyats, from whom
he recovered it.   While he was resting at night he was
awakened by hearing some Lurs who had joined them dis-
cussing the practicability of robbing him, but when one
told the others that he had found out that "the Feringhi
has six shots," they gave it up.   At this camp we are only
a few days' march from classic ground, the ancient Elam
with its capital of Susa, and the remains of so fine a
bridge, with the unusual feature, still to be distinctly traced,
of level approaches, the adjacent ruins, and the tradition
of an old-world route, a broad road having followed the
river-bed to the plains of Lower Elam, all point to an
earlier and higher civilisation.   Overlooking the bridge on
the left bank of the Ab-i-Basnoi a large square enclosure,
with large stone slabs inside, was found, which had probably been used for a cistern, and outside there were
distinct traces of an aqueduct.

The "Sang Niwishta" (inscribed stone), which has
been talked about for a hundred miles, and promised to
be a great discovery, was investigated by a most laborious
march, and turned out a great disappointment.   It
was to be hoped, indeed it might have been expected,
that a journey through these, till now unexplored, regions
would have resulted in the discovery of additional records
of the past carved in stone, but such is not the case.

Still, it is something to have learned that even here
there was once a higher civilisation, and that in its day
there was great traffic along the Basnoi road, and that
every route through this Upper Elam, whether from
north, west, or east, from the Persian highlands to the
plains of Arabistan, and the then populous banks of the
Kerkhah, must have passed through the great gap below
Pul-i-Kul.

The Gokun, Sahid, Guwa, and any number of other

streams fall into this Ab-i-Basnoi, which is the channel for the drainage of far-off Faraidan, and after a full-watered course joins the Ab-i-Burujird, which drains the plain of Silakhor, the two forming the Ab-i-Diz, on which the now famous town of Dizful (lit. Pul-i-Diz or Bridge of Diz) is situated.

Gardan-i-Gunak, July 20.—On July 17 we retraced our steps to Padshah-i-Zalaki, and camped on a height above Aslam Khan's tents on ground so steep that the tent floor had to be cut into steps with a spade.   Aslam Khan and others came to meet us, again performing feats of horsemanship.   No sooner were the tents pitched than the crowd assembled, and it was another noisy and fagging day.   Among the things taken from my tent were an umbrella, knife, scissors, and most of my slender stock of underclothing.   The scissors and cotton were taken by a young sister-in-law of the Khan, while I was attending to a terrible hurt outside.   It turns out that Aslam Khan has got the Agha's binocular, and that he told his men to acquire a small but very powerful telescope which he coveted.   My milk bottle in a leather sling-case has a likeness to it, and this morning as I was giving a woman some eye-lotion her son withdrew this, almost under my eyes !

The Khan's face is a most faithful reproduction of that of Judas in Leonardo da Vinci's " Last Supper."   He is so fine-looking that one is surprised that he should condescend to do small mean things.   I sent him the knife he asked for, and soon he called and asked for a bigger one.   He passed off his handsome daughter, the wife of Taimur Khan's son, as his wife, in order to get, through her, a travelling-clock which he coveted.

They brought a woman to me who might have been produced from a London slum, ophthalmia in one eye, the other closed up and black, and behind it and through her nose a deep wound, gaping fully an inch, blood caked thick and black all over her face and matting her hair, her upper lip cut through, and two teeth knocked out— a regular hospital case. Her brother, they said, had quarrelled with her and had thrown stones at her only the day before, but they had already filled up the wounds with some horrible paste. I asked Sardah Khan why the Khan did not have the man thrashed for such a brutality, and he replied that no one would touch him, as he had killed three men last winter.

I spent two hours upon the poor creature, and the relief was so great that her gratitude was profuse, and the blessings invoked manifold. It was a great pleasure to me But many things were taken out of the tent while I sat outside attending to her. The Khan's brothers, *tufangchis* with their long guns, Seyyids with their green turbans and contemptuous scowl, women, and children were all pressing upon me, hindering and suffocating me in a temperature of nearly 100°. They seem to have no feeling for pain or shrinking from painful spectacles, and rather to enjoy the groans of the sufferer. Each time a piece of stone was taken out of the wounds they exclaimed "God is great!" Occasionally, when the crush interfered with what I was doing, a man beat them with his gun, or Aziz Khan threw stones at them, but it was useless.

The people tell our men that *Kafirs* have never before entered their valley, and that if we were not under the Shah's protection they would take all that we have. I imagine that the difficulties are far greater than I know, for the Agha, who minimises all danger, remarked last night that this is a most anxious time, and that he should be most thankful to get every one out of the country, for it was impossible to say what a day might bring forth. All idea of my returning to Julfa is now abandoned. Bad as it is it is safer to go on.

As the welcome darkness fell the hillsides near and far blazed with fires, and Aslam Khan's camp immediately below was a very picturesque sight, its thirty-one tents forming a circle, with the Khan's two tents in the middle, each having a fire in front. Supper was prepared in large pots; the men ate first, then the women, children, and dogs. The noise suggested pandemonium. The sheep and goats bleated, the big dogs barked, the men and women shouted and shrieked all together, at the top of their voices, rude musical instruments brayed and clanged, —it sounded diabolical. Doubtless the inroad of the Feringhis was the topic of talk. Savage life does not bear a near view. Its total lack of privacy, its rough brutality, its dirt, its undisguised greed, its unconcealed jealousies and hatreds, its falseness, its pure selfishness, and its treachery are all painful on a close inspection.

The following morning early we came up to the Gunak, the narrow top of a pass in the Kala Kuh range with an altitude of 10,200 feet, crossing on the way a steep and difficult snow-slide, and have halted here for two days. Marching with the caravan is a necessary precaution, but a most tedious and fatiguing arrangement. No more galloping, only a crawl at "caravan pace," about two and a half miles an hour for five, six, or seven hours, and though one is up at 2.45 it is fully five before the mules are under way, and meantime one is the centre of that everlasting crowd which, on some pretext or other, asks for medicine. If no ailment can be produced at present, then the request is, "Give me something from the leather box, I've a cough in the winter," or an uncovered copper bowl is brought, the contents of which would evaporate in a fortnight in this climate, with the plaint, "I've a brother," or some other relative, "who has sore eyes in spring, please give me some eye-lotion." Nothing is appreciated made from their own valuable medicinal herbs.

" Feringhi medicine " is all they care for, and in their eyes every Feringhi is a *Hakīm*.

I have often wondered that the Moslem contempt for women does not prevent even the highest chiefs from seeking a woman's medical help, but their own *Hakīms*, of whom there are a few, though I have never seen any, are mostly women, and the profession is hereditary. The men, they say, are too unsettled to be *Hakīms*. Some of these women are renowned for their skill as bullet extractors. If a father happens to have any medical knowledge he communicates it to his daughter rather than to his son. Aziz's grandmother learned medicine from a native Indian doctor in Fars, and his mother had a repute as a bullet extractor. A woman extracted the three bullets by which he has been wounded. The " fees " are very high, but depend entirely on the cure. A poor man pays for the extraction of a bullet and the cure of the wound from fifteen to twenty *tumans* (from £5 to £6 : 10s.), a rich man from forty to sixty. In all cases they only give medicine so long as they think there is hope of recovery, and have no knowledge of any treatment which can alleviate the sufferings of the dying. When death seems inevitable they stuff the nose with a paste made of aromatic herbs.

They dress wounds with an astringent paste made from a very small gall-nut found on one species of oak. For dyspeptic pains and " bad blood " they eat bitumen. For snake-bite, which is common, they keep the bitten person moving about and apply the back part of live hens to the wound till the hens cease to be affected, or else the intestines of a goat newly killed. For rheumatism, headache, and debility they have no remedies, but for fever they use an infusion of willow bark, which is not efficacious. They have great faith in amulets and charms, and in chewing and swallowing verses of the Koran in

case of illness. They are rigid "abstainers," and *arak* is
not to be procured in the Bakhtiari country. This
partly accounts for the extreme and almost startling
rapidity of the healing of surgical wounds.

Ophthalmia, glaucoma, bulging eyeballs, inflamed eyes
and eyelids, eczema, rheumatism, dyspepsia, and coughs
are the prevailing maladies, and among men, bad
headaches, which they describe as periodical and in-
capacitating, are common. The skin maladies and some
of the eye maladies come from dirt, and the parasites
which are its offspring. Among the common people the
clothes are only washed once a year, and then in cold
water, with the root of a very sticky soap wort. They
attribute all ailments but those of the skin and eyes to
"wind." Rheumatism doubtless comes from sleeping
in cotton clothing, and little enough of it, on the damp
ground.

There are no *sages femmes*. Every woman is supposed
to be able to help her neighbour in her hour of need.
Maternity is easy. The mother is often at work the
day after the birth of her child, and in less than a week
regains her usual strength.

Possession by bad spirits is believed in, and cowardice
is attributed to possession. In the latter case medicine is
not resorted to, but a *mollah* writes a text from the Koran
and binds the paper on the coward's arm. If this does not
cure him he must visit a graveyard on the night of the
full moon, and pass seven times under the body of one of
the sculptured lions on the graves, repeating an Arabic
prayer.

This pass gives a little rest. It is solitary, cold
(the mercury 48° at 10 P.M), and very windy. I appreciate the comparatively low temperature all the more
because the scenery beyond the Zalaki valley, in which
scorched valleys and reddish rocky ranges are repeated

ad nauseam, lies under a blazing sun and in a hot dust haze like that of the Indian plains. The ridge is only just wide enough for the camps, and falls down in abrupt descents to the source of the Ab-i-Sefid. Tremendous precipices and the naked peaks of the Kala Kuh surround us, and to the east the Zard Kuh and the long straight-topped range of the Kuh-i-Gokun (or Kainu ?), deeply cleft, to allow of the exit of the Ab-i-Gokun, wall in the magnificent prospect, woods and streams and blue and violet depths suggesting moisture and coolness. The ridge has a remarkably rich alpine flora.

Life is now only a "struggle for existence" on the lower altitudes, with their heat and hubbub; there is no comfort or pleasure in occupation under 9000 feet. Here there are only the sick people of the camps to attend to. The guides and guards all need eye-lotion, one bad wound needs dressing, and the Khan's brother has had fever severely, which is cured, and he offers me as a present a boy of five years old. Aslam Khan's face of Judas is not for nothing, but his brother is beautiful, and has the face of St. John.   I. L. B.

LETTER XIX

CAMP SHUTURUN, *July 25.*

AFTER that uplifted halt, which refreshed the Europeans but did not suit the health of the attendants, we descended, crossed the Zalaki valley and a low ridge, with populous camps, into the valley of the Mauri Zarin, where the nomads were busy harvesting, forded the river, and proceeded up its left bank to a dusty level on which a deep ravine opens, *apparently* blocked up by a castellated and nearly inaccessible rock of great height. At this place, where the Badush joins the Mauri Zarin, we were obliged to camp close to some Ilyat tents, which involved crowds, many demands, much noise, and much vigilance.

We were then in the territory of Mirab Khan, the chief of the Isawand tribe, between whom and Aslam Khan there is a blood feud, with most deadly enmity. He sent word that he was not well, and asked the Agha to go to see him, which he did, telling him that the *Hakīm* would also visit him. Later, taking Mirza and two guides, I forded and followed up the Ab-i-Arjanak for two miles by a most remarkable cañon. The lower part of its sides is steep and rocky, though not too steep for the growth of tamarisk scrub and much herbage, but above are prodigious conglomerate cliffs, and below, the river, which narrows to a stream, is concealed by enormous masses of conglomerate rock. This cleft must be fully 800 feet below the heights which surround it. A ridge runs across it at Arjanak, and the river passes underground.

The village and "Diz"[1] of Mirab Khan are reached by a frightfully steep ascent. Arjanak has been built for security on some narrow ledges below these colossal walls. It is a mere eyrie, a collection of rude stone hovels, one above the other, among which the Khan's house is distinguishable only by its *balakhana* and larger size. The paths on the dusty hillside are so narrow and shelving that I needed a helping hand as well as a stick to enable me to reach a small, oblong, rug-covered platform under some willow trees, where Mirab Khan received me, with a very repulsive-looking Seyyid scribe seated by him in front of a *samovar* and tea equipage, from which he produced delicious tea, flavoured with lime-juice. The Khan was courteous, *i.e.* he rose, and did not sit down till I did.

He is a most deplorable-looking man, very tall and thin, with faded, lustreless gray eyes, hollow, sallow cheeks, and a very lank, ugly, straight-haired beard, light brown in the middle. He and Khaja Taimur look more like decayed merchants than chiefs of "tribes of armed horsemen." I was very sorry for him, for he evidently suffers much, but then and afterwards he impressed me unfavourably, and I much doubt his good faith. He said he heard I should spend two or three days at Arjanak, and all he had was mine. He was not "like some people," he said, "who professed great friendship for people and then forgot all about them. When I make a friendship," he said, "it is for ever." I asked him if his tribe was at peace. "Peace," he replied sententiously, "is a word unknown to the Bakhtiaris." In fact he has more than one blood feud on hand. He complained bitterly of the exactions of Persia, and added

[1] A "Diz" is a natural fort believed to be impregnable.

the conjecture, expressed by many others, that England would shortly occupy Luristan, and give them equity and security. Another Khan of some power said to me that if England were to occupy south-west Persia, he would help her with 400 horsemen, and added, " An English fleet at Basrah, with an English army on board, would be the best sight which Bakhtiari eyes could see." [1]

I had to hear the long story of the Khan's complicated maladies, to look at many bad eyes, and at the wounds of a poor fellow suffering from snake-bite, who was carried on another man's back, and to promise to bring up my medicine chest the following day, the fame of the " leather box " having reached Arjanak.

On my way I had called at the *haram*, and the ladies accompanied me to the *durbar*, conduct which I think was not approved of, as they told me the next morning that they must not go there. After the Agha returned, the three wives and many other women clustered timidly round me. Two of them are very bright and pretty, and one, a Persian, very affectionate in her manner. She held my hand all the time. There was also a handsome daughter, with a baby, the discarded wife of a son of the next Khan. In winter, they said, they amuse themselves by singing, and playing with their children, and by making a few clothes, and the Persian embroiders boys' caps.

Aziz Khan has been irrepressible lately. His Arab mare is his idol, not because she is a lovable animal and carries him well, but because she is valuable property. He fusses about her ceaselessly, and if he were allowed

---

[1] To English people the Bakhtiaris profess great friendliness for England, and the opinion has been expressed by some well-informed writers that, in the event of an English occupation of the country, their light horse, drilled by English officers, would prove valuable auxiliaries. I am inclined, however, to believe that if a collision were to occur in south-west Persia between two powers which shall be nameless, the Bakhtiari horsemen would be sold to the highest bidder.

would arrange the marches and the camping-grounds with
reference solely to her well-being. She is washed from
her nose to the tip of her tail every evening, clothed, and
kept by the camp-fire. She is a dainty, heartless, frivolous
creature, very graceful and pretty, and in character much
like a selfish, spoilt woman.

Unfortunately, in one of the many attempted fights
among the horses, *Screw* kicked her on the chest and
fore-leg a few days ago, which has made a quarrel between
Hadji, *Screw's* owner, and Aziz. Now Aziz is making me
a slave to his animal. That night, after a tiring day, I was
sleeping soundly when I was awakened by Aziz saying
I must come to his mare or he would stay behind with
her the next day. This is his daily threat. So I had to
bring her inside my tent, and sleepily make a poultice and
bandage the hurt. I have very little vaseline, and after
putting it twice on the slight graze on her chest, which
it cured, I said, when he asked for it a third time, that I
must keep the rest for men. "Oh," he said, "she's of
more value than ten men." Lately he said, "I don't
like you at all, you give me many things, but you don't
give me money ; and I don't like the Agha, he doesn't give
me half enough. I'm going back to-morrow, and then
you'll be robbed of all your things, and you'll wish you
had given them to me."

When I do anything, such as opening a whitlow,
which he thinks clever, he exclaims, "May God forgive
your sins !" This, and "May God forgive the sins of
your father and mother !" are ejaculations of gratitude or
surprise. One day when I had been attending to sick
people for four hours, I asked him which was the more
"meritorious" act, attending to the sick or going on
pilgrimage ? He replied, "For a *Kafir* no act is good,"
but soon added, "*Of a truth God doesn't think as we do*, I
don't know."

Yesterday he came for plaster, and while I cut it he saw a padlock pincushion with a mirror front on my bed, and said, "You've given me nothing to-day, you must give me that because my mare kicked me." But I like him. He is a brave fellow, and with a large amount of the mingled simplicity and cunning of a savage has a great deal of thought, information, and ability, and a talk with him is worth having.

Mirab Khan had promised that not only guides but his son would accompany the Agha, but when I arrived at his eyrie the next morning it was evident that something was wrong, for the Agha looked gloomy, and Mirab Khan uncomfortable, and as I was dressing the wound of the snake-bitten man, the former said, " So far as I can see, we are in a perfect hornets' nest." Neither son nor guides were forthcoming. It was necessary to use very decided language, after which the Khan professed that he had withheld them in order to compel us to be his guests, and eventually they were produced.

I called again on the ladies, who received me in a sort of open stable, horses on one side and women on the other, in a crowd and noise so overpowering that I was obliged to leave them, but not before I had been asked for needles, scissors, love philtres, etc. Polygamy, besides being an atrocious system, is very hard on a traveller's resources. I had brought presents for four legitimate wives, but not for the crowd of women who asked for them. Each wife wanted to get her present unknown to the others. Later they returned my visit, and were most importunate in their requests.

When I went to say farewell to the Khan I found him on his knees, bowing his forehead to the earth upon a Mecca prayer-stone, and he concluded his prayers before he spoke—not like many of us, who would jump up ashamed and try to seem as if we never demeaned our-

selves by an act of devotion. His village, Diz Arjanak,
has a Diz, or stronghold, with a limited supply of water.
It is the *raison d'être* of his residence there. This Diz
consists of a few shelves or cavities, chiefly artificial,
scooped out in the face of the perpendicular cliff above
the village. They are only attainable by a very difficult
climb, have no internal communication, and would not
hold more than 150 people. In one cavity there is a
small perennial spring. The largest recess is said to be
twelve feet deep by about twenty long, and has a loop-
holed breastwork across the entrance. In case of attack
the Khan and the people provision this hiding-place, and
retire to it, believing it impregnable.

Mirab Khan on this and a later occasion complained,
and apparently with good reason, of grinding exactions
on the part of Persia. The Isawands, like the Magawes
and Zalakis, pay their tribute partly to Burujird and
partly to the Ilkhani. The sum formerly fixed and paid
was 150 *tumans*. It was raised to 300, which was paid
for two years. Now, he says, this year's demand (1890)
is for 500.

We left Diz Arjanak rather late in the afternoon,
ascended a valley which opens out beyond it, forded the
green bright waters of the Mauri Zarin, and crossed
beautiful open hillsides and elevated plateaux on its right
bank till we lost it in a highly picturesque gorge. Some
miles of very pleasant riding brought us to a rocky and
dangerous path along the side of a precipice above the
river Badush, so narrow as to involve the unloading of
several mules, and a bad slip and narrow escape on the
part of mine. The scenery is singularly wild and severe.
Crossing the Badush, and ascending a narrow ravine
through which it flows, we camped at its source at the
junction of two wild gullies, where the Sahib, after sundry
serious risks, had already arrived. We did not see a

single camp after leaving Arjanak, and were quite unmolested during a halt of two nights ; but it is an atmosphere of danger and possible treachery.

Camp Badush, at a height of 9100 feet, though shut
in by high mountains, was cool—a barren, rocky, treeless
spot. A great deal of bituminous shale was lying about,
which burned in the camp-fires fairly well, but with a
black heavy smoke and a strong smell.

The limestone fragments which lay about, on being
split, emitted a powerful odour of bitumen. Farther up
the gully there is a chalybeate spring, and the broken
fragments of the adjacent rocks are much stained with
iron. After a restful halt we retraced our route by a low
path which avoided the difficult precipices above the
Badush, forded it several times, crossed a low pass,
descended to the valley of the Mauri Zarin, forded the
river, and marched for some miles along its left bank, till
the valley opened on great grassy slopes, the skirts of the
rocky spurs which buttress the grand mountain Shuturun,
the " Camel Mountain," so called from its shape. It was
a very uninteresting march, through formless gravelly
hills, with their herbage all eaten down, nothing remaining but tamarisk scrub and a coarse yellow salvia. There
were neither camps nor travellers ; indeed, one need never
look for camps where there is no herbage.

This is a charming camping-ground covered with fine
turf, damp, I fear, and some of the men are " down "
with fever and rheumatism. There is space to see who
comes and who goes, and though the altitude is only
8400 feet, last night was quite cool. Ischaryar, Aziz
Khan's devoted young servant, the gentlest and kindest
Bakhtiari I have seen, became quite ill of acute rheumatism with fever, and felt so very ill and weak that he
thought he was going to die. I sent some medicine to
him, but he would not take it, saying that his master had

spoken unkindly to him, and he had no wish to live. However, this morbid frame of mind was overcome by firm dealing, and Aziz attended to him all night, and salol, etc., are curing him.

He is the one grateful creature that I have seen among these Orientals, and his gratitude is in return for a mere trifle. We were fording a stream one hot day, and seeing him scooping up water with difficulty in his hands, I took out my mug for him. Ever since he has done anything that he can for me. He brings tasteful little bouquets of flowers, gathers wild cherries, and shows the little courtesies which spring from a kindly nature. He said several times to Mirza, " It isn't only that the *Khanum* gave me the cup, but she took trouble for me." It may be imagined what a desert as to grateful and kindly feeling I am living in when this trifle appears like an oasis. Hard, cunning, unblushing greed is as painful a characteristic of the Bakhtiaris as it is of the Persians.

Hassan is now " down with fever" and the opium craving, and one of the *charvadars* with fever. The cold winds of Gunak were too much for them. All day shots have been heard among the near mountains. The Hajwands, a powerful tribe, and the Abdulwands are fighting about a recent cutting off of a cow's tail, but the actual cause of the feud is deeper, and dates farther back. Aziz Khan wants us to return to Diz Arjanak, fearing that we may become implicated, and the Agha is calling him a coward, and telling him to ride back alone. Bang! Bang! The firing is now close and frequent, and the dropping shots are varied by straggling volleys. With the glasses I can see the tribesmen loading and firing on the crests of the near hills. A great number are engaged. One tribe has put up a stone breastwork at our end of the valley, but the enemy is attacking the other.

3 P.M.—An hour ago Mirab Khan arrived with a number of armed horse and footmen. Before he left he spent, I may say wasted, nearly an hour of my time again on his maladies, and again wrote down the directions for his medicines. Volleys fired very near startled him into departing, and he rode hastily back to Arjanak, fearing, as he said, an attack. Nominally, he armed the guides and the men he left behind, but one of the guns has neither caps nor powder, and another has only three caps. All the animals have been driven in.

4 P.M.—A man with grimy arms bare to the elbow has just run down to the Agha's camp from the conflict. He says that his people, who are greatly inferior to the Hajwands in numbers, thought it was the camp of the Shah's revenue collector, and sent him to ask him to mediate. The Agha expressed his willingness to become a mediator on certain conditions. There is much excitement in camp, all the men who are well crowding round this envoy, who is guilty of saying that fifty men are to attack our camps to-night.

7.30 P.M.—The Agha, with the Sahib and Aziz Khan, three brave men mounted and armed with rifles and revolvers, went to mediate. I went to a knoll in the valley with some of our men, above which on either side were hills occupied by the combatants, and a large number of tribesmen crowned the crest of a hill lying across the ravine higher up. The firing was frequent, but at long range, and I was near enough to see that only one man fell.

Our party rode on till they reached the top of a low ridge, where they dismounted, reconnoitred, and then passed out of sight, being fired on by both parties. The tribesmen kept on firing irregularly from the hill crests, occasionally running down the slopes, firing and running into cover. The Sahib's *tufangchi*, who is of Cheragh

Ali's tribe, asked me, " Is this the way they fight in your country," I asked him if he would not like to be fighting ? and he replied, "Yes, if it were my quarrel." The sun was very bright, the sky very blue, and the smoke very white as it drifted over the lonely ravine and burst in clouds from the hill-tops. I saw the combatants distinctly without a glass, and heard their wild war-shouts. What a matter for regret is this useless tribal fighting, with its dreary consequences of wailing women and fatherless children ! " Why don't the English come and take us ? Why don't the English come and give us peace ? " are surely the utterances of a tired race.

After sunset the Agha returned, having so far succeeded in his mission that the headmen have promised to suspend hostilities for to-morrow, but still shots are fired now and then. I. L. B.

LETTER XX

LAKE IRENE, *July 27.*

YESTERDAY we marched through narrow defiles and along hillsides to this lake, without seeing a tent, a man, or even a sheep or goat, following a stream which bears several names and receives several torrents which burst, full grown, from powerful springs in the mountain sides —a frequent phenomenon in this country—from its source till its entrance into this lake. Its two sides differ remarkably. On the right bank rise the magnificent ranges which form Shuturun, broken up into precipices, deep ravines, and peaks, all rocky and shapely, and absolutely denuded of soil. The mountains on the left bank are great shapeless masses of bare gravel rising into the high but blunt summit of the Sefid Kuh, with only occasional outcrops of rock; here and there among the crevices of the rocky spurs of Shuturun the *Juniperus excelsa* plants itself; otherwise, on the sun-scorched gravel only low tamarisk bushes, yellow salvias, a few belated campanulas, and a very lovely blue *Tricho-desma mollis* remain.

On reaching the top of a very long ascent there was a unique surprise, for below, walled in by precipitous mountain sides, lies a lake of wonderful beauty, owing to its indescribable colour. Wild, fierce, and rocky are the high mountains in which this gem is set, and now verdureless, except that in some places where their steep sides enter the water willows and hawthorns find scanty roothold. Where the river enters the lake there is a thicket of small willows, and where it leaves it its bright waters ripple through a wood of cherry, pear, plum, and hawthorn. A broad high bank of gravel lies across a part of its lower end, and all seemed so safe and solitary that I pitched my camp here for Sunday at an unusual distance from the other camps.

"Things are not what they seem." Two armed Hajwands visited the camps, shots were heard at intervals this morning, and in the night some of the watch said they saw a number of men advancing towards us from under the bushes. I heard the sharp crack of our own rifles twice, and the Agha and Sahib calling on every one to be on the alert; the mules were driven in, and a great fire was made, but nothing came of it. To-night Mirab Khan's guides, who have been with us for some days, have gone back, journeying at night and hiding in caves by day for fear of being attacked.

This lovely lake, having no native name, will be known henceforward geographically as Lake Irene. Its waters lie in depths of sapphire blue, with streaks and shallows of green, but what a green! Surely without a rival on earth! Were a pea transparent, vivid, full of points and flashes of interior light, that would be the nearest approach to the colour, which changes never, while through the blazing hours the blue of the great depths in the centre has altered from sapphire to turquoise, and from turquoise to lapis-lazuli, one end and one side being permanently bordered round the margin with liquid emerald. The mountains have changed from rose to blue, from blue to gray, from gray to yellow, and are now flushing into pink. It is a carnival of colour, before the dusty browns and dusty grays which are to come.

Camp Sarawand, July 29.—To-day's march has been

a change from the grand scenery of the Bakhtiari mountains to low passes and gravelly spurs, which sink down
upon a plain.   A blazing hillside ; a mountain of gravel
among others of similar ugliness, sprinkled with camel
thorn and thistles ; a steep and long descent to a stream;
ripe wheat on some irrigated slopes ; above these the
hundred hovels of the village of Sarawand clinging one
above another to the hillside, their white clay roofs intolerable in the fierce light ; more scorched gravel hills breaking
off abruptly, and then a blazing plain, in a mist of dust
and heat, and low hills on the farther side seen through
a brown haze, make up the view from my tent.   The
plain is Silakhor in Persia proper, and, *nolens volens*,
that heat and dust must shortly be encountered in the
hottest month of the year.   Meanwhile the mercury is at
105° in the tent.

Outside is a noisy crowd of a mixed race, more
Persian than Lur, row behind row.   The *ketchuda* said
if I would stand outside and show myself the people
would be pacified, but the desired result was not
attained, and the crushing and pushing were fearful—
not that the people here or elsewhere are ever rude,
it is simply that their curiosity is not restrained by
those rules which govern ours.   The Agha tried to
create a diversion by putting a large musical box at a
little distance, but they did not care for it.   I attempted
to give each woman a card of china buttons, which they
like for sewing on the caps of their children, but the
crush was so overpowering that I was obliged to leave it
to Aziz.   Then came the sick people with their many
woes and wants, and though now at sunset they have all
gone, Aziz comes in every few minutes with the laugh of
a lost spirit, bringing a fresh copper bowl for eye lotion,
quite pleased to think of my annoyance at being constantly dragged up from my writing.

Camp Parwez, July 31.—We left early in the morning, *en route* for the fort of Yahya Khan, the powerful
chief of the Pulawand tribe, with a tall, well-dressed,
and very respectable-looking man, Bagha Khan, one of
his many fathers-in-law, the father of the present "reigning favourite," as guide. It was a very pretty track,
pursuing sheep-paths over steep spurs of Parwez, and
along the narrow crests of ridges, always with fine views.
On reaching an alpine valley, rich in flowers, we halted
till the caravan approached, and then rode on, the "we"
that day being the guide on foot, and the Agha, the Sahib,
Aziz Khan, Mirza, and myself on horseback in single
file. Three men looked over the crest of a ridge to the
left and disappeared abruptly, and I remarked to Mirza
that this was the most suspicious circumstance we had
yet seen. There was one man on the hill to the right,
with whom the guide exchanged some sentences in patois.

The valley opened out on the stony side of a hill,
which had to be crossed. As we climbed it was crested
with a number of men with long guns. Presently a
number of shots were fired at us, and the reloading of the
guns was distinctly seen. The order was given to "scatter"
and proceed slowly. When the first shot was fired Bagha
Khan, who must have been well known to all his tribesmen, dodged under a rock. Then came an irregular
volley from a number of guns, and the whistle and thud
of bullets over and among us showed that the tribesmen,
whatever were their intentions, were in earnest. To this
volley the Agha replied by a rifle shot which passed close
over their heads, but again they reloaded rapidly. We
halted, and Aziz Khan was sent up to parley with them.
No one could doubt his courage after that solitary ascent
in the very face of the guns.

Karim cantered up, anxious to fight, Mujid and
Hassan, much excited, dashed up, and we rode on slowly,

Hadji and his *charvadars* bringing up the caravan as steadily as if there were no danger ahead. Not a man showed the "white feather," though most, like myself, were "under fire" for the first time. When we reached the crest of the pass such a wild lot crowded about us, their guns yet hot from firing upon us. Such queer arms they had—one gun with a flint lock a century old, with the "Tower mark" upon it, loaded sticks, and long knives. With much talking and excitement they accompanied us to this camping-ground.[1]

The men varied considerably in their stories. They were frightened, they said, and fired because they thought we were come to harm them. At first I was sorry for them, and regarded them as merely defending their "hearths and homes," for in the alpine valley behind the hill are their black tents, their families, their flocks and herds—their world, in fact. But they told another story, and said they took us for a party of Hajwands. This was untenable, and the Agha told them that they knew that Hajwands do not ride on English saddles, and carry white umbrellas, and march with big caravans of mules. To me, when they desired my services, they said that had they known that one of the party was a *Hakīm* they never would have fired.

---

[1] This untoward affair ended well, but had there been bloodshed on either side, had any one of us been killed, which easily might have been, the world would never have believed but that some offence had been given, and that some high-handed action had been the cause of the attack. I am in a position to say, not only that no offence was given, but that here and everywhere the utmost care was taken not to violate Bakhtiari etiquette, or wound religious or national susceptibilities ; all supplies were paid for above their value ; the servants, always under our own eyes, were friendly but reserved ; and in all dealings with the people kindness and justice were the rule. I make these remarks in the hope of modifying any harsh judgments which may be passed upon any travellers who have died un-witnessed deaths at the hands of natives. There are, as in our case, absolutely unprovoked attacks.

Later, from Hadji and others I have heard what I think may be the true version of the affair. They knew that the party was a small one—only three rifles; that on the fifteen baggage-animals there were things which they specially covet, the value of which rumour had doubtless magnified a hundredfold; and that we had no escort. Behind were a number of the Sarawand men, and the Pulawands purposed, if we turned back or showed the "white feather" in any way, to double us up between the two parties and rob the caravan at discretion. The Agha was obliged to speak very severely to them, telling them that firing on travellers is a grave offence, and deserves as such to be represented to the Governor of Burujird. I cannot acquit the demure-looking guide of complicity in this transaction.

At this height of 9400 feet there is a pleasant plain, on which our assailants are camped, and our camps are on platforms in a gully near the top of Parwez. It is all very destitute of springs or streams, and we have only snow-water, and that only during the hot hours of the day, for ourselves and the animals.

The tribes among which we are now are powerful and very predatory in their habits. Their loyalty to the Ilkhani is shadowy, and their allegiance to the Shah consists in the payment of tribute, which cannot in all cases be exacted. Indeed, I think that both in Tihran and Isfahan there is only imperfect information as to the attitude of the Bakhtiari Lurs. Their unification under the rule of the Ilkhani grows more and more incomplete as the distance from Isfahan increases, and these tribes, which are under the government of Burujird nominally, are practically not under the Ilkhani at all. Blood feuds, predatory raids, Khans at war with each other, tribal disputes and hostilities, are nearly universal. It is not for the interest of Persia to produce by her misrule and intrigues such a chronic state of insecurity as makes the tribes desire any foreign interference which will give them security and rest, and relieve them from the oppressive exactions of the Persian governors.

On a recent march I was riding alone in advance of the caravan when I met two men, one mounted, the other on foot. The pedestrian could not have been passed anywhere unnoticed. He looked like a Sicilian brigand, very handsome and well dressed, walked with a long elastic stride, and was armed with a double-barrelled gun and two revolvers. He looked hard at me, with a jolly but not unfriendly look, and then seeing the caravan, passed on. This was Jiji, a great robber Khan of the Hajwand tribe, whose name inspires much fear. Afterwards he met Aziz Khan, and sent this picturesque message : " Sorry to have missed you in my own country, as I should have liked to have left you standing in your skins."

I went up the Kuh-i-Parwez with Bagha Khan, the guide of whom I have such grave suspicions, in the early morning, when the cool blue shadows were still lying in the ravines. Parwez, which on this side is an uninteresting mountain of herbage-covered gravelly slopes, falls down 4300 feet to the Holiwar valley on the other in a series of tremendous battlemented precipices of dark conglomerate rock.

The level summit of Parwez, though about 11,000 feet in altitude, is as uninteresting as the shapeless slopes by which we ascended it, but this dip on the southern side is wonderful, and is carried on to the gap of Bahrain, where it has a perpendicular scarp from its summit to the river of 5000 feet, and as it grandly terminates the Outer range, it looks like a glorious headland abutting on the Silakhor plain.

As a panoramic view it is the finest I have had from any mountain, taking in the great Shuturun range—the

wide cultivated plain of Silakhor, with its many villages;
the winding Ab-i-Diz, its yellow crops, hardly distinguishable from the yellow soil and hazy yellow hills whose
many spurs descend upon the plain—all merged in a
haze of dust and heat. The eye is not tempted to
linger long upon that specimen of a Persian summer
landscape, but turns with relief to the other side of the
ridge, to a confused mass of mountains of great height,
built up of precipices of solid rock, dark gray, weathered
into black and denuded of soil, a mystery of chasms, rifts,
and river-beds, sheltering and feeding predatory tribes,
but unknown to the rest of the world.

The chaos of mountain summits, chasms, and precipices is very remarkable, merging into lower and less
definite ranges, with alpine meadows at great heights,
and ravines much wooded, where charcoal is burned and
carried to Burujird and Hamadan. Among the salient
points of this singular landscape are the mighty Shuturun
range, the peak of Kuh-i-Kargun on the other side of the
Silakhor plain, the river which comes down from Lake
Irene, the Holiwar, with the fantastic range of the Kuh-
i-Haft-Kuh (seven peaks) on its left bank, descending
abruptly to the Ab-i-Zaz, beyond which again rises the
equally precipitous range of the Kuh-i-Ruhbar. Near
the Holiwar valley is a mountain formed by a singular
arrangement of rocky buttresses, surmounted by a tooth-
like rock, the Tuk-i-Karu, of which the guide told the
legend that in " ancient times " a merchant did a large
trade in a tent at the top of it, and before he died buried
his treasure underneath it.

A very striking object from the top is the gorge or
cañon, the Tang-i-Bahrain, by which the Ab-i-Burujird
leaves the plain of Silakhor and enters upon its rough
and fretted passage through ravines, for the most part inaccessible except to practised Ilyat mountaineers.

"Had I come up to dig for the hidden treasure of Tuk-i-Karu?" the guide asked. "Was I seeking gold? Or was I searching for medicine plants to sell in Feringhistan?"

The three days here have been rather lively. The information concerning routes has been singularly contradictory. There is a path which descends over 4000 feet to the Holiwar valley, through which, for certain reasons, it is desirable to pass. Some say it is absolutely impassable for laden mules, others that it can be traversed with precautions, others again that they would not take even their asses down; that there are shelving rocks, and that if a mule slipped it would go down to ———. Hadji with much force urges that we should descend to the plain, and go by a comparatively safe route to Khuramabad, leave the heavy baggage there, and get a strong escort of *sowars* from the Governor for the country of the Pulawands. There is much that is plausible in this plan, the Sahib approves of it, and the Agha, with whom the decision rests, has taken it into very careful consideration, but I am thoroughly averse to it, though I say nothing.

Hadji says he cannot risk his mules on the path down to the Holiwar valley. I could have filled pages with the difficulties which have been grappled with during the last few weeks of the journey as to guides, routes, perils, etc., two or three hours of every day being occupied in the attempt to elicit truth from men who, from either inherent vagueness and inaccuracy or from a deliberate intention to deceive, contradict both themselves and each other, but on this occasion the difficulties have been greater than ever; the order of march has been changed five times, and we have been obliged to remain here because the Agha has not considered that the information he has obtained has warranted him in coming to a decision.

Yesterday evening the balance of opinion was definitely against the Holiwar route, and Hadji was so vehemently against it that he shook a man who said it was passable. This morning the Sahib with a guide and Abbas Ali examined the road. The Sahib thought it was passable. Abbas Ali said that the mules would slip off the shelving rocks. All day long there have been Lur visitors, some saying one thing, and some another, but a dream last night reconciled Hadji to take the route, and the Agha after carefully weighing the risks all round has decided upon it.

All these pros and cons have been very interesting, and there have been various little incidents. I have had many visitors and "patients" from the neighbouring camp, and among them three of the men who fired upon us.

The trifle of greatest magnitude was the illness of Aziz's mare, the result of a kick from *Screw*. She had an enormous swelling from knee to shoulder, could not sleep, and could hardly eat, and as she belongs partly to Isfandyar Khan, Aziz Khan has been distracted about her, and has distracted me by constant appeals to me to open what seemed an abscess. I had not the courage for this, but it was done, and the cut bled so profusely that a pad, a stone, and a bandage had to be applied. Unfortunately there was no relief from this venture, and Aziz "worrited" me out of my tent three times in the night to look at the creature. Besides that, he had about twenty ailing people outside the tent at 6 A.M., always sending to me to "come at once."

He was told to wash the wound, but he would do nothing till I went out with my appliances, very grudgingly, I admit. The sweet animal was indeed suffering, and the swelling was much increased. A number of men were standing round her, and when I told Aziz to remove the clot from the wound, they insisted that she would bleed to death, and so the pros and cons went on till Aziz said, "The *Khanum* shall do it, these Feringhi *Hakīms* know everything." To be regarded as a *Hakīm* on the slenderest possible foundation is distressing, but to be regarded as a "vet" without any foundation at all is far worse.

However, the clot was removed, and though the wound was three inches long there was still no relief, and Aziz said solemnly, "Now do what you think best." Very gradual pressure at the back of the leg brought out a black solid mass weighing fully a pound. "God is great!" exclaimed the bystanders. "May God forgive your sins!" cried Aziz, and fell at my feet with a genuine impulse of gratitude. He insists that "a pound of flesh" came out of the swelling. The wound is now syringed every few hours, and Aziz is learning how to do this, and to dress it. The mare can both eat and sleep, and will soon be well.

This evening Aziz said that fifteen *tumans* would be the charge for curing his mare, and that, he says, is my present to him. He told me he wanted me to consider something very thoroughly, and not to answer hastily. He said, "We're a poor people, we have no money, but we have plenty of food. We have women who take out bullets, but in all our nation there is no *Hakīm* who knows the wisdom of the Feringhis. Your medicines are good, and have healed many of our people, and though a *Kafir* we like you well and will do your bidding. The Agha speaks of sending a *Hakīm* among us next year, but you are here, and though you are old you can ride, and eat our food, and you love our people. You have your tent, Isfandyar Khan will give you a horse of pure pedigree, dwell among us till you are very old, and be our *Hakīm*, and teach us the wisdom of the Feringhis."

Then, as if a sudden thought had struck him, he added, "And you can cure mules and mares, and get much money, and when you go back to Feringhistan you'll be very rich."

In nearly every camp I have an evening "gossip" with the guides and others of the tribesmen, and, in the absence of news from the larger world, have become intensely interested in Bakhtiari life as it is pictured for me in their simple narratives of recent forays, of growing tribal feuds and their causes, of blood feuds, and of bloody fights, arising out of trivial disputes regarding camping-grounds, right of pasture, right to a wounded bird, and things more trivial still. They are savages at heart. They take a pride in bloodshed, though they say they are tired of it and would like to live at peace, and there would be more killing than there is were it not for the aversion which some of them feel to the creation of a blood feud. When they do fight, "the life of a man is as the life of a sheep," as the Persian proverb runs. Mirza says that among themselves their talk is chiefly of guns and fighting. The affairs of the mountains are very interesting, and so is the keen antagonism between the adherents of the Ilkani and those of Isfandyar Khan.

Sometimes the conversation takes a religious turn. I think I wronged Aziz Khan in an earlier letter. He is in his way much more religious than I thought him. A day or two ago I was asking him his beliefs regarding a future state, which he explained at much length, and which involve progressive beatitudes of the spirit through a course of one hundred years. He laid down times and seasons very definitely, and was obviously in earnest, when two Magawe men who were standing by broke in indignantly, saying, "Aziz Khan, how dare you speak thus? These things belong to God, the Judge, He knows, we don't—we see the spirit fly away to judgment and we know no more. God is great, He alone knows."

Apparently they have no idea generally of a future except that the spirit goes either to heaven or hell, according to its works in the flesh. Some say that they are told that there is an intermediate place called *Barjakh*, known as the place of evil spirits, in which those who have died in sin undergo a probation with the possibility of beneficent results.

On asking what is meant by sin the replies all have the same tendency,—cowardice, breaches of the seventh commandment (which, however, seem to be so rare as scarcely to be taken into account, possibly because of the death penalty attaching to them), disobedience to a chief when he calls on them to go to war, fraternising with Sunnis, who are "accursed," betraying to an enemy a man of their own tribe, and compassing the death of another by poison or evil machinations.

On being asked what deeds are good, bravery is put first, readiness to take up a tribal quarrel, charity, *i.e.* kindness to the poor, undying hatred to the Caliph Omar, shown by ostracising the Sunnis, hatred of *Kafirs*, and pilgrimages, especially to Mecca.

Death in battle ensures an immediate entrance into heaven, and this is regarded as such a cause of rejoicing that not only is the *chapi* or national dance performed at a fighting man's grave, but if his death at a distance has been lawful, *i.e.* if he has been killed in fighting, they put up a rude temporary cenotaph with his gun, cap, knife, pipe, and other things about it, and dance, sing, and rejoice.

Otherwise their burial rites are simple. The corpse is washed seven times in water, certain Arabic formulas for the repose of the soul are recited, and the body, clothed and wrapped in a winding-sheet, is carried by four men to the burying-place on a bier extemporised out of tent-poles, and is buried in a shallow grave. It is not customary now to rejoice at the graves of women or old men, unless the latter have been distinguished warriors.

So far as I can learn, even in the case of the deaths of fighting men, when the *chapi* is danced at the grave, the women keep up the ordinary ceremonial of mourning, which is very striking. They howl and wail, beating their breasts rhythmically, keeping time with their feet, tearing their hair and gashing their faces with sharp flints, cutting off also their long locks and trampling upon them with piteous cries. This last bitter token of mourning is confined to the deaths of a husband and a first-born son, and the locks so ruthlessly treated are afterwards attached to the tombstone.

Mourning for a husband, child, or parent lasts a year, and the anniversary of the death is kept with the same ceremonies which marked the beginning of the period of mourning. In the case of a great man who has died fighting, the women of his tribe wail and beat their breasts on this anniversary for many subsequent years.

Nothing is buried with the corpse, and nothing is placed on the grave, but it is the universal custom to put a stone at the head of the body, which is always buried facing Mecca-wards. To this position they attach great importance, and they covet my compass because it would enable them at any point to find the position of the Kiblah. A comb or distaff rudely carved on a woman's headstone, and the implements of war or hunting on that of a man, are common, and few burial-places are without one or more of the uncouth stone lions to which frequent reference has been made.

The graveyards are very numerous, and are usually on small elevations by the roadside, so that passers-by, if they be Hadjis, may pray for the repose of the soul. It must be understood that prayer consists in the repetition of certain formulas in Arabic, which very few if any of these people understand.[1]

As to the great matter of their religion, on which I have taken infinite trouble to gain information, I can come to no satisfactory conclusion. I think that they have very little, and that what they have consists in a fusion of some of the tenets of Islam with a few relics of a nature worship, not less rude than that of the Ainos of Yezo and other aboriginal tribes.

They are Shiahs, that is, they hate the Sunnis, and though the belief in Persia that they compel any one entering their country to swear eternal hatred to Omar is not absolutely correct, this hate is an essential part of their religion. They hold the unity of God, and that Mohammed was His prophet; but practically, though they are not Ali Ilahis, they place Ali on as high a pedestal as Mohammed. They are utterly lax in observing the precepts of the Koran, even prayer at the canonical hours is very rarely practised, and then chiefly by Seyyids and Hadjis. It has been said that the women are devout, but I think that this is a mistake. Many of them have said to me, " Women have no religion, for women won't live again."

Those of the Khans who can read, and who have made pilgrimages to Mecca, such as the Hadji Ilkhani, Khaja Taimur, and Mirab Khan, observe the times of prayer and read the Koran, and when they are so engaged they allow of no interruption, but these are remarkable exceptions.

Pilgrimages and visits to *imamzadas* are lightly undertaken, either for the accumulation of merit, or to wash away the few misdeeds which they regard as sin, or in the hope of gaining an advantage over an enemy.

They regard certain stones, trees, hill-tops, and springs as " sacred," but it is difficult to define the very vague

[1] See Appendix A.

ideas which they attach to them. I am inclined to think that they look on them as the abodes of genii, always malignant, and requiring to be propitiated. In passing such places they use a formula equivalent to "May God avert evil," and it is common, as in Nubra and Ladak, to hang pieces of rag on such trees and stones as offerings to the *genius loci*.

They regard certain places as possibly haunted by spirits, always evil, and never those of the departed; but this can scarcely be termed a belief, as it is lightly held, and quite uninfluential, except in preventing them from passing such places alone in the darkness.

The opinions concerning God represent Him chiefly as a personification of a fate, to which they must bow, and as a Judge, to whom, in some mysterious way, they must account after death. Earthly justice appears to them as a commodity to be bought and sold, as among the Persians, or as it is among themselves, as severity solely, without a sentiment of mercy; and I have asked them often if they think that anything will be able to affect the judgment of the Judge of all, in case it should go against them. Usually they reply in the negative, but a few say that Ali, the Lieutenant of God, will ask for mercy for them, and that he will not be refused.

Of God as a moral being I think they have little conception, and less of the Creator as an object of love. Of holiness as an attribute of God they have no idea. Their ejaculation, "God is good," has really no meaning. Charity, under the term "goodness," they attribute to God. But they have no notion of moral requirements on the part of the Creator, or of sin as the breaking of any laws which He has laid down. They concern themselves about the requirements of religion in this life and about the future of the soul as little as is possible, and they narrow salvation within the limits of the Shiah sect.

After Mohammed and Ali they speak of Moses, Abraham, and Jesus as " Prophets," but of Moses as a lawgiver, and of Jesus as aught else but a healer, they seem quite ignorant.

And so they pass away, generation after generation, ignorant of the Fatherhood of God and the brotherhood of man, of the love to God and man which is alone the fulfilling of the law, and of the light which He, who is the resurrection and the life, has shed upon the destiny of the human spirit.

Generally I find them quite willing to talk on these subjects; but one man said contemptuously, "What has a *Kafir* to do with God?" The women know nothing, and, except among the sons of the leading Khans, there is no instruction in the Koran given to the children. If I have interpreted their views correctly they must be among the most ignorant of the races bound by the faith of Islam.

Khuramabad, August 6.—Leaving the camp on Parwez, and skirting the gravelly slopes on the north side of its ridge, a sudden dip over the crest took us among great cliffs of conglomerate, with steep gravelly slopes below, much covered with oaks growing out of scorched soil. Grooves, slides, broken ledges, and shelving faces of rock have to be descended. One part is awfully bad, and every available man and some passing Bakhtiaris (who wanted to be paid in advance for their services) went back to help the animals. The *charvadars* shouted and yelled, and the horses and some of the mules were taken by their heads and tails, but though nearly every man had a fall, horses, asses, mules, and a sheep which follows *Hakīm* got over that part safely. It was a fine sight, thirty animals coming down, what looked from below, a precipice, led by Hadji leading Cock o' the Walk, shaking his tasselled head, and as full of pride and fire as usual, and the mules looking wisely, choosing their way, and leaping dexterously upon and among the rocks. It is not a route for laden animals, but personally, as I had two men to help me, I did not find it so risky or severe as the descent of the Gokun Pass.

Below these conglomerate precipices are steep and dangerous zigzags, which I was obliged to ride down, and there we were not so fortunate, for Hadji's big saddle-mule slipped, and being unable to recover herself fell over the edge some hundred feet and was killed instant-aneously.

The descent of the southern face of Parwez, abrupt and dangerous most of the way, is over 4300 feet. The track proceeds down the Holiwar valley, brightened by a river of clear green water, descending from Lake Irene. Having forded this, we camped on its left bank on a gravelly platform at the edge of the oak woods which clothe the lower spurs of the grand Kuh-i-Haft-Kuh, with a magnificent view of the gray battlemented pre-cipices of Parwez. The valley is beautiful, and acres of withered flowers suggested what its brief spring loveli-ness must be, but its altitude is only 5150 feet, and the mercury in the shade was 104°, the radiation from the rock and gravel terrible, and the sand-flies made rest impossible. At midnight the mercury stood at 90°. There were no Bakhtiaris, but two or three patches of scorched-up wheat, not worth cutting, evidenced their occasional presence. Among these perished crops, revel-ling in blazing soil and air like the breath of a furnace, grew the blue *centaurea* and the scarlet poppy, the world-wide attendants upon grain; and where other things were burned, the familiar rose-coloured "sweet william," a white-fringed *dianthus*, and a gigantic yellow mullein audaciously braved the heat.

No one slept that night because of the sand-flies and

the need for keeping a vigilant watch. Indeed, the tents were packed shortly after sunset, and in a hot dawn we ascended to a considerable height above the valley, and then for many miles followed a stream in a wooded glen, where willows, planes, vines, rank grass, and a handsome yellow pea grew luxuriantly, looped together continually by the fragile *Clematis orientalis.* All that country would be pretty had it moisture and "atmosphere." The hillsides are covered with oaks and the *Paliurus aculeatus* on their lower slopes, rising out of withered flowers. All else is uncut sun-cured hay, and its pale uniform buff colour is soft, and an improvement on the glare of bare gravel.

Delays, occasioned by the caravan being misled by the guide, took us into the heat of the day, and before the narrow valley opened out into the basin surrounded by wooded spurs of hills in which Khanabad stands, it was noon. Men and animals suffered from the heat and length of that march. In the middle of this basin there is a good deal of cultivation, and opium, wheat, cotton, melons, grapes, and cucumbers grow well. Rice has already succeeded wheat, and will be reaped in November. Kalla Khanabad, the fort dwelling of Yahya Khan, with terraces of poplars, mulberries, pomegranates, and apricots below it, makes a good centre of a rather pretty view. Leaving it, on the right we turned up a narrow valley with a small stream and irrigation channels, and close to a spring and some magnificent plane trees camped for Sunday on a level piece of blazing ground where the mercury stood at 106° on both days. This spot was remarkable for some very fine *eryngiums* growing by the stream, with blossoms of a beautiful " French blue," the size of a Seville orange.

The Khan's son, a most unprepossessing young man, called on me, and I received him under the trees, a

number of retainers armed with long guns standing round
the edge of the carpet.   He was well dressed, but a
savage in speech and deportment.   As to the dress of
the Bakhtiaris, the ordinary tribesmen wear coarse cotton
shirts fastening at the side, but generally unfastened, blue
cotton trousers, each leg two yards wide, loose at the
bottom and drawn on a string at the top, webbing shoes,
worsted socks if any, woollen girdles with a Kashmir
pattern, and huge loose brown felt coats or cloaks with
long sleeves, costing from fifteen to twenty-five *krans* each,
and wearing for three or four years.   The Khans frequently have their *shulwars* of black silk, and wear
the ordinary Persian full-skirted coat, usually black, but
"for best" one of fine blue or fawn cloth.   All wear
brown or white felt skull-caps, and shave their heads for a
width of five inches from the brow to the nape of the
neck, leaving long side-locks.   The girdle supplies the
place of pockets, and in it are deposited knives, the pipe,
the tobacco-pouch, the flint and steel, and various etceteras.

Every man carries a long smooth-bore gun slung
from his left shoulder, or a stout shillelagh, or a stick
split and loaded at one end (the split being secured with
strong leather), or all these weapons of offence and defence
at once.

These very wide *shulwars*, much like the "divided
garment," are not convenient in rough walking, and on
the march a piece of the hem on the outer side is tucked
into the girdle, producing at once the neat effect of
knickerbockers.

The men are very well made.   I have never seen
deformity or lameness except from bullet wounds.   They
are not usually above the middle height, though that is
exceeded by the men of the Zalaki tribe.   They are
darker than the Persians.   As a general rule they have
straight noses, with very fully expanded nostrils, good

mouths, thin lips, straight or slightly curved eyebrows, dark gray or black eyes, hazel in a few instances, deeply set, and usually rather close together, well-developed fore-heads, small ears, very small feet, and small hands with tapering fingers. The limbs below the knee are remark-ably straight and well-developed, and the walk is always good.

It is not easy to say how the women are made, as their clothing gives no indications of form. They are long-limbed, and walk with a firm, even, elastic stride. They are frequently tall, and except when secluded are rarely stout. Their hands and feet are small. Their figures are spoilt (if they ever had any) by early maternity and hard work. At twenty a woman looks past forty. Many, perhaps it is not an exaggeration to say most, of them have narrowly escaped being handsome. Fine eyes, straight noses, and well-formed mouths with thin lips are the rule. The hair is always glossy and abundant, and the teeth of both sexes are white, regular, and healthy-looking, though toothache is a painfully common ailment.

The women's dress in the " higher classes " is much like that worn by the ordinary Persian women, with the exception of what I have elsewhere called " balloon trousers," but the hard-working tribesmen's wives are clothed in loose blue cotton trousers drawn in at the ankles, short open chemises, and short open jackets. A black or coloured kerchief covers the head, the ends hang-ing down behind or in front. They wear loose woollen shoes with leather soles. The dress is not pretty or picturesque, and is apt to be dirty and ragged, but it suits their lives and their hard work.

Both sexes stain the finger-nails and the palms of the hands with henna, and all wear amulets or charms suspended round the neck, or bound on the upper part of the arm. These consist of passages from the Koran, which are written on parchment in very small characters, and are enclosed in cases of silver or leather.

At night they merely take off the outer garment where they have two. The scanty ablutions are very curious. Each family possesses a metal jug of rather graceful form, with a long spout curiously curved, and the mode of washing, which points to an accustomed scarcity of water, is to pour a little into the palm of the right hand, and bathe the face, arms, and hands with it, soap not being used. They conclude by rinsing the mouth and rubbing the teeth either with the forefinger or with the aromatic leaf of a small pink salvia.

I called by appointment on the Khan's wives, sixteen in number. An ordinary tribesman marries as many wives as he can afford to house and keep. Poverty and monogamy are not allied here. Women do nearly all the work, large flocks create much female employment, and as it is " contrary to Bakhtiari custom " to employ female servants who are not wives, polygamy is very largely practised. On questioning the guides, who are usually very poor men, I find that they have two, three, and even four wives, the reverse of what is customary among the peasants of Turkey and Persia proper. The influence of a chief increases with the number of his wives, as it enlarges his own family connections, and those made by the marriages of his many sons and daughters. Large families are the rule. Six children is the average in a monogamous household, and the rate of infant mortality is very low.

The " fort " is really picturesque, though forlorn and dirty. It is built on the steep slope of a hill, and on one side is three stories in height. It has a long gallery in front, with fretwork above the posts which support the roof, round towers at two of the corners, and many irregular roofs, and steep zigzags cut in the rock lead up to it. The centre is a quadrangle. When I reached the gateway under the tower many women welcomed me, and led me down a darkish passage to the gallery aforesaid, which has a pretty view of low hills, with mulberries and pomegranates in the foreground. This gallery runs the whole length of the fort, and good rooms open upon it. It was furnished with rugs upon the floor, and two long wooden settees, covered with checked native blankets in squares of Indian yellow and madder red.

I had presents for the favourite wife, but as one man said this was the favourite, and another that, and the hungry eyes of sixteen women were fixed on the parcels, I took the safer course of presenting them to the Khan for the "ladies of the *andarun*." Yahya Khan sent to know if it would be agreeable to me for him to make his salaam to me, a proposal which I gladly accepted as a relief from the curiosity and disagreeable familiarity of the women. There was a complete rabble of women in the gallery, with crawling children and screaming babies — a forlorn, disorderly household, in which the component parts made no secret of their hatred and jealousy of each other.

I pitied the Khan as he came in to this Babel of intriguing women and untutored children — of women without womanliness and children without innocence — the lord and master of the women, but not in any noble sense their husband, nor is the house, or any polygamous house, in any sense a home.

The wife who, I was afterwards told, is the "reigning favourite" sat on the same settee as her lord, and he ignored the whole of them. Her father, Bagha Khan, asked me to give into his care the present for her, lest it should make the other wives jealous.

Yahya Khan rules a large part of the Pulawand tribe, 1000 families, and aspires to the chieftainship of its subdivisions, among which are the Bosakis, Hajwands, Isawands, and Hebidis, numbering 2800 families.[1]

He is a tall, big, middle-aged man with a very wide mouth, and a beard dyed auburn with henna——very

YAHYA KHAN.

intelligent, especially as regards his own interests, and very well off, having built his castle himself.

He asked me if I thought England would occupy south-west Persia in the present Shah's lifetime? Which

[1] I am inclined to estimate the Bakhtiari population at a higher figure than some travellers have given. I took forty-three men at random from the poorest class and from various tribes, and got from them the number of their families, wives and children only being included, and the average was eight to a household.

has the stronger army, England or Russia? Why England does not take Afghanistan? Did I think the Zil-es-Sultan had any chance of succeeding his father? but several times reverted to what seemed uppermost in his mind, the chances of a British occupation of Southern Persia, a subject on which I was unwilling to enter. He complained bitterly of Persian exactions, and said that the demand made on him this year is exactly double the sum fixed by the Amin-es-Sultan.

It is not easy to estimate the legitimate taxation. Probably it averages two *tumans,* or nearly fifteen shillings a family. The assessment of the tribes is fixed, but twenty, forty, and even sixty per cent extra is often taken from them by the authorities, who in their turn are squeezed at Tihran or Isfahan. Every cow, mule, ass, sheep, and goat is taxed. Horses pay nothing.

In order to get away from perilous topics, which had absolutely no interest for the women, I told him how interested I was in seeing all his people clothed in blue Manchester cottons, though England does not grow a tuft of cotton or a plant of indigo. I mentioned that the number of people dependent on the cotton industry in Britain equals the whole population of Persia, and this made such an impression on him that he asked me to repeat it three times. He described his tribe as prosperous, raising more wheat than it requires, and exporting 1000 *tumans'* worth of carpets annually.

It is curious that nomadic semi-savages should not only sow and harvest crops, and make carpets of dyed wool, as well as goat's-hair rugs and cloth, horse-furniture, *khūrjins,* and socks of intricate patterns, but that they should understand the advantages of trade, and export not only mules, colts, and sheep, but large quantities of charcoal, which is carried as far as Hamadan; as well as *gaz,* gallnuts, tobacco, opium, rice, gum mastic, clarified butter, the

skins of the fox and a kind of marten, and cherry sticks
for pipes.

Certainly the women are very industrious, rising at
daylight to churn, working all day, weaving in the intervals, and late at night boiling the butter in their big
caldrons.   They make their own clothes and those of
their husbands and children, except the felt coats, sewing
with needles like skewers and very coarse loosely-twisted
cotton thread.   They sew backwards, *i.e.* from left to
right, and seem to use none but a running stitch.   Everywhere they have been delighted with gifts of English
needles and thread, steel thimbles, and scissors.

When it is remembered that, in addition to all the
" household " avocations which I have enumerated, they
pitch and strike tents, do much of the loading and unloading of the baggage, and attend faithfully to their
own offspring and to that of their flocks and herds, it will
be realised that the life of a Bakhtiari wife is sufficiently
laborious.

We were to have left that burning valley at 11 P.M.,
and when I returned at dusk from the fort the tents
were folded and the loads ready for a moonlight march,
but Yahya Khan sent to say that for the ostensible
reason of the path being greatly obstructed by trees we
could not start till daylight.   Later he came with a
number of tribesmen and haggled noisily for two hours
about the payment of an escort, and the sheep a day which
it would require.   It was not a comfortable night, for the
sand-flies were legion, and we did not get off till 4.30,
when we were joined by Yahya Khan and his son, who
accompanied us to the Pul-i-Hawa.

The path from Kalla Khanabad runs at a considerable elevation on wooded hillsides and slopes of shelving rock, only descending to cross some curious ribs of
conglomerate and the streams which flow into the Ab-i-

Diz.   There are frequent glimpses of the river, which has the exquisite green colour noticeable in nearly all the streams of this part of Luristan.   At a distance of a few miles from Khanabad the valley, which has been pretty wide, and allows the river to expand into smooth green reaches, narrows suddenly, and the Ab-i-Diz, a full, strong stream, falls in a very fine waterfall over a natural dam or ledge of rock, which crosses it at its broadest part, and is then suddenly compressed into a narrow passage between cliffs and ledges of bituminous limestone, the lowest of which is a continuation of the path which descends upon it by some steep zigzags.

Below this gorge the river opens out into a smooth green stretch, where it reposes briefly before starting on a wild and fretted course through deep chasms among precipitous mountains, till it emerges on the plains above Dizful.   These limestone cliffs exude much bitumen, and there is a so-called bituminous spring.   Our men took the opportunity of collecting the bitumen and rolling it into balls for future use, as it is esteemed a good remedy for dyspepsia and " bad blood."

At the narrowest part of its channel the river is crossed by a twig bridge wide enough for laden animals, supported on the left bank by some tree-stems kept steady by a mass of stones.   In the middle it takes a steepish upward turn, and hangs on to the opposite cliff at a considerable elevation.   The path up from it to the top of the cliff is very narrow, and zigzags by broken ledges between walls of rock.   For loaded animals it is a very bad place, and the caravan took an hour and a half to cross, though only four mules were unloaded, the rest being helped across by men at their heads and tails. Several of them fell on the difficult climb from the bridge.   It would be bad enough if the roadway of osiers were level, but it shelves slightly to the south.

That gorge is a very interesting break in an uninteresting and monotonous region, and the broad fall
above the bridge is not without elements of grandeur.
The altitude of the river over which the Pul-i-Hawa hangs
is only 3800 feet, the lowest attained on this journey.

The popular nomenclature is adopted here, but it

A TWIG BRIDGE.

would be more accurate to call this stream the Ab-i-
Burujird, and to defer conferring the name of Ab-i-Diz
upon it till the two great branches have united far below
this point. These are the Ab-i-Burujird, rising to the
west of Burujird, which with the tributaries which enter
it before it reaches the Tang-i-Bahrain, drains the great
plain of Silakhor, and the Ab-i-Basnoi, a part of which
has been referred to under its local name of Kakulistan,
or " the Curl," which drains the upper part of the Persian

district of Faraidan, and receives the important tributaries of the Guwa and the Gokun before its junction with the Ab-i-Burujird. A tributary rising in the Kuh-i-Rang has been locally considered the head-water of the Ab-i-Diz.

Leaving the Ab-i-Diz, the path pursues valleys with streams and dry torrent-beds, much wooded with oak and hawthorn, with hills above, buff with uncut sun-cured hay, magnificent pasturage, but scantily supplied with water.

The *belut,* or oak, grows abundantly in these valleys, and on it is chiefly collected the deposit called *gaz,* a sweetish glaze upon the leaf, which is not produced every year, and which is rather obscure in its origin. When boiled with the leaves it forms a shiny bottle-green mass, but when the water is drained from them and carefully skimmed, it cools into a very white paste which, when made up with rose-water and chopped almonds, is cut into blocks, and is esteemed everywhere. It is mentioned by Diodorus Siculus.[1] The unwatered valleys are wooded with the *Paliurus aculeata* chiefly, and the jujube tree (*Zizyphus vulgaris*), which abounds among the Bakhtiari mountains.

The heat was frightful, and progress was very slow, owing to the low projecting branches of trees, which delayed the baggage and tore some of the tents. In places the path was further obstructed by a species of liana known in New Zealand as " a lawyer," with hooked thorns.

We passed by the steep ledgy village of Shahbadar, on the roofs of which I rode inadvertently, till the shouts of the people showed me my error, and encamped on the only available spot which could be found, a steep, bare prominence above a hollow, in which is a spring surrounded by some fine plane trees. The Shahbadar people live in their village for three winter months only,

[1] Book xvii. c. viii.

and were encamped above us, and there were two large camps below. Men from each of them warned us to beware of the others, for they were robbers, and there was a great deal of dexterous pilfering, which reduced my table equipments to a copper mug, one plate, and a knife and fork. My *shuldari* was torn to pieces, and pulled down over me, by a lively mule which cantered among the tent ropes.

The afternoon, with the mercury at 103°, was spent in entertaining successive crowds, not exactly rude, but full of untamed curiosity. I amused them to their complete satisfaction by letting them blow my whistle, fill my air-cushion, and put the whalebones into my collapsible basins. One of Milward's self-threading needles, which had luckily been found in my carpet, surprised them beyond measure. Every man and woman insisted on threading it with the eyes shut, and the *ketchuda* of one camp offered to barter a sheep for it. They said that my shabby tent, with its few and shabby equipments, was "fit for God!"

The camps passed on that day were constructed of booths made of stems of trees with the bark on, the roofs being made of closely-woven branches with the leaves on. These booths are erected round a square with mat walls, and face outwards, a sort of privacy being obtained by backs of coarse reed mats four feet high, and mat divisions between the dwellings. The sheep, goats, and cattle are driven into the square at night through a narrow entrance walled with mats.

Since leaving the Karun very few horses have been seen, and the few have been of a very inferior class. Even Yahya Khan, who has the reputation of being rich, rode a horse not superior to a common pack animal. The people we have been among lately have no horses or mares, the men walk, and the loads are carried on cows and asses.

In the greater part of this country I have not seen a mule, with the exception of some mule foals on a high pass near Ali-kuh. The Bakhtiaris breed mules, however, and sell them in Isfahan in the spring, but rarely use them for burden. They breed horses in some places, exporting the colts and keeping the fillies. Their horses are small and not good-looking, but are wiry and enduring, and as surefooted as mules. In fact they will go anywhere. One check on the breeding of good horses is that, when a man has a good foal, he is often compelled to make a present of it to any superior who fancies it.

The horses are shod, as in Persia proper, with thin iron plates covering nearly the whole hoof, secured by six big-headed nails. Reared in camps and among children, they are perfectly gentle and scarcely require breaking. A good Bakhtiari horse can be bought for £6 or £8. A good mule is worth from £7 to £11. Asses are innumerable, and are used for transporting baggage, equally with oxen and small cows. A good donkey can be bought for 30s.

The goats are very big and long-haired. The sheep, which nearly always are like the goats brown or black, and very tall, are invariably of the breed with the great pendulous tails, which sometimes weigh nearly eight pounds. They give a great deal of milk, and it is on this, not on cows' milk, that the people rely for the greater part of their food, their cheese, curds, *mast*, and *roghan*.

The goat-skins are invaluable to them. They use them for holding water and milk, and as churns for their butter. They make all their tents, their tent carpets, and their sacks for holding wool of goat's-hair, woven on rude portable looms.

The female costume changed at Shahbadar. The women now wear loose garments like nightgowns, open to the waist, and reaching from the neck to the feet, and red trousers, tight below the knee, but rarely visible below the outer dress. Their notion of ornament consists in having a branch or frond tattooed up the throat.

These tribes breed cattle extensively. One camp possessed over 300 young beasts. The calves are nourished by their mothers up to two years old. They have a few white angora goats of great beauty, but the majority are black and are valued chiefly for their milk and for their long coarse hair.

A march through fierce heat at a low level brought us at noon to the village of Imamzada-i-Mamil. The road, after continuing along the same wooded valley, which in a happier climate would be called a glen, emerges on scenery truly " park - like," softly - outlined hills covered with buff grass, and wooded on their gently-curved slopes with oak and hawthorn, fringing off into clumps and single trees. Smooth broad valleys, first of buff pasture, and then of golden wheat or green maize, lie among the hills. All is soft and lowland, and was bathed that day in a dreamy blue heat haze. Not a mountain rose above the gently-curved hills which were painted in soft blue on the sky of the distant horizon. The natural wood ceased. The surroundings underwent an abrupt change. Is it a change for the better, I wonder? Three months and a week have been spent in zigzagging among some of the loftiest mountains and deepest valleys of Persia, and they now lie behind, among the things that were. In fact, Khuramabad, from which I write, is not only out of the Bakhtiari country, but the Bakhtiari Lurs are left behind, and we are among the fierce and undisciplined tribes of the Feili Lurs.

The baggage animals were not dubious, as I am, as to the advantages of the change. When we reached the open, Cock o' the Walk threw up his beautiful head, knocked down the man who led him, and with a joyous neigh set off at a canter, followed by all the mules and horses, some cantering, some trotting, regardless of their loads, and regardless of everything, proceeding irresponsibly, almost knocking one out of the saddle by striking one with the sharp edges of *yekdans* and tent poles, till they were headed off by mounted men, after which some of them rolled, loads and all, on the soft buff grass. This escapade shows what condition they are in after three months of hard mountain work.

Reaching the village at noon, we halted till moonrise at midnight on an eminence with some fine plane and walnut trees upon it above a stream which issues from below an *imamzada* on a height, and passes close to a graveyard. Possibly this contaminates the water, for there has been a great outbreak of diphtheria, which has been very fatal. It is quite a small village, but thirteen children suffering from the most malignant form of the malady, some of them really dying at the time, were brought to me during the afternoon, as well as some people ill of what appeared to be typhoid fever. One young creature, very ill, was carried three miles on her father's back, though I had sent word that I would call and see her at night. She died a few hours later of the exhaustion brought on by the journey. The mercury that afternoon reached 103° in the shade.

Soon after midnight the mules were silently loaded, and we "stole silently away," to ride through the territory of the powerful Sagwands, a robber tribe, and reached this place in eight hours, having done twenty-two and a half miles. It was a march full of risk, through valleys crowded with camps, and the guide who rode in front was very much frightened whenever the tremendous barking of the camp dogs threatened to bring robbers down on us in the uncertain light. The caravan was kept in steady order, and the rearguard was frequently hailed by the leader. Nothing happened, and when day broke we were in open russet country, among low, formless gravelly hills, with the striking range of rocky mountains which hems in Khuramabad in front, under a hazy sky.

Later, fording the Kashgan, I got upon the Burujird caravan road, along which are telegraph poles, and on which there was much caravan traffic. Recrossing the Kashgan, but this time by a good two-arched bridge of brick on stone piers, the Yafta Kuh came in sight, and Khuramabad with its green gardens, its walls of precipitous mountains, and its ruined fort on an isolated and most picturesque rock in the centre of the town—a very striking view.

Khuramabad, before the fourteenth century, was called Diz Siyah, or the black fort, and was the capital of the Atabegs, the powerful kings who reigned in Luri-Kushuk from A.D. 1155 to about A.D. 1600. Sir H. Rawlinson does not regard any of its remains as earlier than the eleventh or twelfth century.

The camps are outside the town, on a stretch of burning gravel, with some scorched pasture beyond it, on which are Ilyat camps, then there are divers ranges of blackish and reddish mountains, with pale splashes of scorched herbage when there is any at all. Behind my tent are a clump of willows, an irrigating stream, large gardens full of fruit trees and melons, and legions of mosquitos.

Circumstances have changed, and the surroundings now belong to the showy civilisation of Persia. As I was lying under the trees, quite " knocked up " by the long and fatiguing night march and the great heat, I heard fluent French being spoken with a good accent. The *Hakīm* of the Governor had called. Cavalcades of Persians on showy horses gaily caparisoned dashed past

frequently. Ten infantrymen arrived as a guard and
stacked their arms under the willows, and four obsequious
servants brought me trays of fruit and sweetmeats put
up in vine leaves from the Governor.   Melons are a drug.
The servants are amusing themselves in the bazars.   It
is a bewildering transition.

The altitude is only 4050 feet, and the heat is awful—
the heat of the Indian plains without Indian appliances.
When the men took up stones with which to hammer the
tent pegs they dropped them "like hot -potatoes."   The
paraffin candles melt.   Milk turns sour in one hour.
Even night brings little coolness.   It is only heat and
darkness instead of heat and light.

I was too much exhausted by heat and fatigue to
march last night, and rested to-day as far as was possible,
merely going to pay my respects to the Governor of
Luristan, the Nizam-ul-Khilwar, and the ladies of his
haram.   The characteristics of this official's face are
anxiety and unhappiness.   There was the usual Persian
etiquette—attendants in the rear, scribes and *mollahs*
bowing and kneeling in front, and tea and cigarettes in
the pretty garden of the palace, of which cypresses, pomegranates, and roses are the chief features.   Mirza was
not allowed to attend me in the *andarun*, but a *munshi*
who spoke a little very bad French and understood less
stood behind a curtain and attempted to interpret, but
failed so signally that after one or two compliments I
was obliged to leave, after ascertaining that a really
beautiful girl of fourteen is the "reigning favourite."
The women's rooms were pretty, and the women themselves were richly but elegantly dressed, and graceful in
manner, though under difficulties.   After a visit to the
ruined fort, an interesting and picturesque piece of
masonry, I rode unmolested through the town and bazars.

Khuramabad, the importance of which lies in its

situation on what is regarded as the best commercial route
from Shuster to Tihran, etc., is the capital of the Feili
Lurs and the residence of the Governor of Luristan.
Picturesque at a distance beyond any Persian town that
I have seen, with its citadel rising in the midst of a
precipitous pass, its houses grouped round the base, its
fine bridge, its wooded gardens, its greenery, and the
rich valley to the south of the gorge in which it
stands, it successfully rivals any Persian town in its
squalor, dirt, evil odours, and ruinous condition. Two-
thirds of what was "the once famous capital of the
Atabegs" are now "ruinous heaps." The bazars are
small, badly supplied, dark, and rude; and the roads are
nothing but foul alleys, possibly once paved, but now
full of ridges, holes, ruins, rubbish, lean and mangy
dogs, beggarly-looking men, and broken channels of
water, which, dribbling over the soil in the bazars and
everywhere else in green and black slime, gives forth
pestiferous odours in the hot sun.

The people slouch about slowly. They are evidently
very poor, and the merchants have the melancholy
apathetic look which tells that "trade is bad." The
Feili Lurs, who render the caravan route to Dizful in-
cessantly insecure, paralyse the trade of what should
and might be a prosperous "distributing point," and the
Persian Government, though it keeps a regiment of
soldiers here, is unsuccessful in checking, far less in
curing the chronic disorder which has produced a nearly
complete stagnation in trade.

I am all the more disappointed with the wretched
condition of Khuramabad because the decayed state of
its walls is concealed by trees, and it is entered by a
handsome bridge 18 feet wide and 900 long, with
twenty-eight pointed arches of solid masonry, with a fine
caravanserai with a tiled entrance on its left side. The

Bala Hissar is a really striking object, its pile of ancient buildings crowning the steep mass of naked rock which rises out of the dark greenery and lofty poplars and cypresses of the irrigated gardens. This fort, which is in ruins, encloses within its double walls the Wali's palace and other official buildings, and a fine reservoir, 178 feet by 118, fed by a vigorous spring. In the gardens by the river, north of the fort, are some remains of the walls and towers of the ancient Atabeg capital, and there are also ruins of an aqueduct and of an ancient bridge, of which ten arches are still standing. The most interesting relic, however, is a round tower sixty feet high in fairly good preservation, with a Kufic inscription round the top.

It is said that there are 1200 houses in Khuramabad, which would give it a population of over 7000. It has been visited by several Englishmen for purposes of trade or research, and it has doubtless made the same impression upon them all as it does upon me.

Burujird, August 9.—A night march of twenty-two miles through perilous country brought us in blazing heat to an encampment of Seyyids of the Bairanawand tribe, fine-looking men, showing in their haughty bearing their pride in their illustrious lineage, but not above depriving us during the night of many useful articles. Their camp had three streets of tents, in front of which oxen were treading out wheat all day long. These Seyyids have much wealth in mares and oxen. Again we started at moonrise for what was regarded as a dangerous march, a party of Sagwands having gone on ahead, with hostile intentions, it was said.

However, nothing happened, and nothing was heard except the shouts of our own *charvadars* and the pandemonium made by the simultaneous barking of huge dogs in the many camps we passed but could not see. We rode through cultivated valleys full of nomads, forded the placid Bawali, and at dawn were at the foot of the grand pass of Handawan, 7500 feet in altitude, which is ascended by steep zigzags over worn rock ledges, and the dry boulder-strewn bed of a torrent. A descent of 2000 feet and a long ride among large formless hills took us to a narrow gorge or chasm with a fine mountain torrent, and thence to the magnificent Tang-i-Buzful, from which we emerged with some suddenness on the slopes of the low foot-hills on the north side of the plain of Burujird or Silakhor.

This very rich plain, about thirty miles long by from six to eight broad, has been described as "waterlogged," and the level of the water is only a foot below the surface. Certainly very numerous springs and streams rise along the hill slopes which we traversed and flow down into the plain, which is singularly flat, and most of it only relieved from complete monotony by the villages which, to the number of 180, are sprinkled over it, many of them raised on artificial mounds, at once to avoid the miasma from the rice-fields and as a protection from the Lurs. Above the south-eastern end rises the grand bulk of Shuturun Kuh, with a few snow-patches still lingering, and towards the other lies the town of Burujird, the neighbourhood of which for a few miles is well planted, but most of the plain is devoid of trees. It is watered by many streams, which flow into the Burujird river and the Kamand-Ab, which uniting, leave the plain by the magnificent Tang-i-Bahrain.

The first view, on emerging from the buff treeless mountains, was very attractive. The tall grass of the rich marshy pastures rippled in the breeze in wavelets of a steely sheen. Brown villages on mounds contrasted with the vivid green of the young rice. Towards Burujird, of which nothing but the gilding of a dome was visible, a mass of dark greenery refreshed the eyes. The charm

of the whole was the contrast between the "dry and
thirsty land where no water is" and abundant moisture,
between the scanty and scorched herbage of the arid
mountains and the "trees planted by the rivers of water,"
but I confess that the length and overpowering fatigue of
that thirty-three miles' march, much of it in blazing heat,
following on three nights without sleep, soon dulled
my admiration of the plain. Hour after hour passed
on its gravelly margin, then came melon beds, files of
donkeys loaded with melons in nets, gardens of cucumbers and gourds, each with its "lodge," irrigation channels,
dykes, apricot and mulberry orchards, lanes bordered
with the graceful *elœgnus*, a large and busy village, where
after a very uncertain progress we got a local guide, and
then a low isolated hill, crowned by a dwelling arranged
for security, and a liberally planted garden, a platform
with terraced slopes and straight formal walks, a terrace
with a fine view, and two tanks full of turtles (which
abound in many places) under large willows, giving a
pleasant shade. Between them I have pitched my
tents, with the lines of an old hymn constantly occurring
to me—

> "Interval of grateful shade,
> Welcome to my weary head."

Burujird, one and a half mile off, and scarcely seen
above the intervening woods, gives a suggestion of civilisation to the landscape. In the sunset, which is somewhat
fiery, Shuturun and the precipices of the Tang-i-Bahrain
are reddening.

The last three marches have been more severe than
the whole travelling of the last three months. Happy
thought, that no call to "boot and saddle" will break
the stillness of to-morrow morning!   I. L. B.

LETTER XXI

BURUJIRD, *Aug. 16.*

A WEEK has glided away since I sent my last diary letter, with only two events of direct personal interest, one being that I have bought a young, powerful little Bakhtiari horse, which has been in camp since we left the Karun river, a dark bay, with black points, big feet, a big ugly head, and big flopping ears, but otherwise passably good-looking, an unsuspicious animal, brought up in tent life, with children rolling about among his feet, and as yet quite ignorant that man can be anything but his friend. I intend to look after his well-being, but not to make a pet of him.

The other event occurred on the morning after our arrival, and took the place of the " boot and saddle " call, for I was awakened very early by a hubbub round my tent, the interpretation of which was that a packing case in three compartments, containing my cooking utensils, remaining table equipments, and stores, had been carried off before daylight, deposited in an adjacent plantation, broken open, and emptied.   Thus I was left with nothing, and have been unable to get anything in the bazars here except two cooking pots and a tin teapot of unique construction made to order.   The few other things which I still regard as absolute necessaries, a cup, plate, knife, fork, and spoon, have been lent me by the Agha. All my tea is gone, the worst loss of all.

Later in the day Hassan came in a quiet rage, saying that he would leave for Isfahan at once, because Mirza had accused him of not keeping an efficient watch, and shortly afterwards Mahomet Ali and his handsome donkey actually did leave.[1] Burujird bears a very bad reputation. Here, last year, a young English officer was robbed of his tents and horses, and everything but the clothes he wore.

The Governor, on hearing of the theft, said I should not have " camped in the wilderness," the " wilderness " being a beautifully kept garden with a gardener (who was arrested) and a house. For the last week a guard of six soldiers has watched by day and night.

The news received from the Bakhtiari country is rather startling. Mirab Khan, who looked too ill and frail for active warfare, sent a messenger with a letter to Khaja Taimur, urging him to join him in an attack on Aslam Khan. The letter was intercepted by this " Judas," and now the country from Kalahoma to Khanabad is in a flame. Serious troubles have broken out in this plain, all the Khans of the Sagwand tribe having united to rise against the payment of a tribute which they regard as heavy enough to " crush the life out of the people." The *Hākim* has telegraphed for troops, and the governor of Luristan is said to be coming with 500 men.

A " tribute insurrection," on a larger or smaller scale, is a common autumnal event. The Khans complain of being oppressed by " merciless exactions." They say that the tribute fixed by the Shah is " not too much," but that it is doubled and more by the rapacity of governors, and that the people are growing poorer every year. They complain that when they decline to pay more than the

---

[1] I have since heard that this youth was an accomplice of a Burujird man in this theft, and of an Armenian in a robbery of money which occurred in Berigun.

tribute fixed by the Amin-es-Sultan, soldiers are sent, who drive off their mares, herds of cattle, and flocks to the extent of three, four, and five times the sum demanded.

These few words contain the substance of statements almost universally made. There is probably another side, and they may be true in part only. The tribesmen of Silakhor state that they had protested and appealed in vain before they decided on resistance. Every Khan with whom I have conversed has besought me to lay his case before the " English Vakil " at Tihran.

This widely-diffused belief in England as the redresser of wrongs is very touching, and very palatable to one's national pride. All these people have heard of the way in which the cultivators in India have been treated, of " land settlements " and English " settlement officers," and they say, " England could make everything right for us." So she could, " an she would " ! As the governors pay large sums for offices from which they are removable at the Shah's pleasure, and as the lower officials all pay more or less heavily for their positions, we may reasonably infer that all, from the highest to the lowest, put on the screw, and squeeze all they can out of the people, over and above the tribute fixed at Tihran. Near views of Oriental despotisms are as disenchanting as near views of " the noble savage," for they contain within themselves the seeds of " all villainies," which rarely, if ever, fail of fructification.

Mirza Karim Khan, the Governor of Burujird, called a few days ago, a young harassed-looking man, with very fine features, but a look of serious bad health. He complained so much that the Agha asked his attendant, a very juvenile *Hakīm*, speaking a little scarcely intelligible French, if he would object to the Governor taking something from the famous " leather box," and the effect was so magical that the next day he looked a different man.

An arrangement was made for returning the visit, and he received us in a handsome tent in a garden, with the usual formalities, but only a scribe and the *Hakīm* were present. A *sowar*, sent from Burujird with a letter to the Sahib, was undoubtedly robbed of his horse, gun, and some of his clothing *en route*. Very quietly the Governor denied this, but as he did so I saw a wink pass between the scribe and *Hakīm*. It was a pitiable sight,—a high official sitting there, with luxuries about him, in a city with its walls, embankments, and gates ruinous, the brickwork in the palace gardens lying in heaps, his province partially disturbed, the people rising against what, at the least, are oppressive exactions, raising an enormous tribute, from which there is no outlay on province or city, government for the good of the governed never entering into his (as rarely into any other Oriental) mind.

This evening he has made a farewell visit on the terrace, attended by the *Hakīm*. Aziz Khan stood on the edge of the carpet, and occasionally interjected a remark into the conversation. I have before said that he has a certain gentlemanliness and even dignity, and his manner was neither cringing nor familiar. The *Hakīm*, however, warned him not to speak in presence of the Governor, a restraint which, though very different from the free intercourse of retainers with their chiefs among the Bakhtiari, was in strict accordance with the proprieties of Persian etiquette. Aziz stalked away, shaking his wide *shulwars*, with an air of contempt. "This governor," he afterwards said, "what is he? If it were Isfandyar Khan, and he were lying down, my head would be next to his, and twenty more men would be lying round him to guard his life with ours."

It seems as if Burujird were destitute of cavalry, at least of men who can be spared, though it has been stated that a whole cavalry regiment is in garrison.[1]

The Governor promised three escorts ; my modest request was for one *sowar*, and a very unmilitary-looking horseman has arrived for me, but now, within an hour of marching, the others are without even one !

Attended by the *Hakīm* and an escort, we rode yesterday through Burujird. To write that a third of it is in ruins is simply to write that it is a Persian town. It has crumbling mud walls, said to be five miles in circumference, five gates in bad repair, and a ditch, now partially cultivated.

It is situated in Lat. 33° 55′ N, and its Long. is 48° 55′ E. Its elevation is 4375 feet [Bell]. Its population is estimated at from 12,000 to 18,000, and includes a great many Seyyids and *mollahs*. It has a Persian Telegraph Office and Post Office, neither of them to be depended upon, six large and very many small mosques, a number of mosque schools, thirty-three public baths, and six caravanserais. It manufactures woollen goods, carpets, and the best *arak* to be found in Persia. It also produces dried fruits and treacle made from grapes.

The bazars are large, light, and well supplied with European goods, Russian and English cottons in enormous quantities, Austrian kerosene lamps of all descriptions and prices, Russian mirrors, framed coloured engravings of the Russian Imperial family, Russian *samovars*, tea-glasses and tea-trays, Russian sewing and machine cotton, American sewing machines, Russian woollen cloth, fine and heavy, Russian china,

[1] Throughout the part of Persia in which I have travelled I have observed a most remarkable discrepancy between the numbers of soldiers *said* to garrison any given place, and the number which on further investigation turned out to be actually there. It is safe to deduct from fifty to ninety per cent from the number in the original statement !

and Russian sugar-loaves, to the sale of which several shops are exclusively devoted.

Persian manufactures are chiefly represented by heavy cottons, dyed and stamped at Isfahan, carpets, saddles, horse and mule furniture, copper cooking utensils, shoes of all makes, pipes, *kalians*, rope, ornamented travelling trunks, *galon*, gimps, tassels of silk and wool, and "small wares" of all kinds, with rude pottery, oil jars, each big enough to contain a man, great water-jars, small clay bowls glazed roughly with a green glaze, guns, swords, pistols, long knives, and the tools used by the different trades.

Altogether the bazars look very thriving, and they were crowded with buyers. Possibly the people have rarely if ever seen a Feringhi woman, and they crowded very much upon me, and the escort drove them off in the usual fashion, with sticks and stones. Though much of Burujird lies in ruins it has a fair aspect of prosperity and some very good houses and new buildings. The roads are cobbled with great stones, and are certainly not worse than those of the older parts of Tihran. Water is abundant.

Nature evidently intends Burujird to be a prosperous city. The pasturage of the plain is magnificent, and the rich soil produces two crops a year. All cereals flourish. Wheat and barley ripen in July. Seven sorts of grapes grow, and ripen in August and September, and some of the clusters are finer than any of our hothouse produce. Water and musk melons, tobacco, maize, gourds and cucumbers, beans, the *bringal* or egg plant, peas, flax and other oil seeds, rice and cotton, apricots, walnuts, pomegranates, and peaches testify to the excellence of the soil and climate.

Not only is Burujird in the midst of an exceptionally fine agricultural district, but it is connected by caravan

routes with the best agricultural and commercial regions
of Persia to the north, east, and west by easy roads, never
snow-blocked, or at least they never need be if there were
traffic enough to keep them open.   It is only 130 miles
from rich Kirmanshah, 90 from the fertile district which
surrounds Hamadan, 60 from Sultanabad, the most important carpet-producing 'region of Western Persia, and
rich besides in grain and cotton, 140 from Kûm, on the
main road from Isfahan to Tihran, something about 230
from Tihran, and only 310 from Ahwaz.

These routes are all easy, though, so far as I know
them, very badly supplied with caravanserais, except on the
main road between the two capitals.   The southern road,
leading through Khuramabad to Dizful and Shuster, has
no great natural difficulties, though part of it lies through
a mountainous region.   Some blasting and much boulder-
lifting would, according to Colonel Bell, remedy the evils
of the fifty miles of it which he regards as bad.   But,
apart from this, the Shuster - Burujird route, the most
natural route for north and south-western Persian commerce to take to and from the sea, is at present useless
to trade from its insecurity, as the Feili Lurs, through
whose territory it passes, own no authority, live by
robbery when they have any one to rob, and are always
fighting each other.

There are no regular *charvadars* in Burujird, and
many and tedious have been the difficulties in the way
of getting off.   Up to last night I had no mules, and
Hadji said mournfully, " When you learn what other *charvadars* are like, you'll think of me."   I have taken leave
of Aziz Khan with regret.   He echoes the oft-repeated
question, " Why does not England come and give us
peace ?   In a few years we should all be rich, and not
have to fight each other."   " Stay among us for some
years," he said, " and you will get very rich.   What have

you to go back to in Feringhistan?"   He asked me for
a purse, and to put some *krans* in it for his children,
but not to give him any money.   He said that when he
asked for money and other things he was only in fun.
I do not know whether to believe him.

Mirza and my caravan started this morning, and now,
4 P.M., I am leaving with the *sowar*, with the mercury
at 90°, for the first march of a journey of 800 miles.

I. L. B.

LETTER XXII

HAMADAN, *Aug. 28.*

IT was as I thought. The *sowar* sent with me was only a harmless peasant taken from the plough, mounted on his own horse, and provided with a Government gun. The poor fellow showed the " white feather " on the first march, and I was obliged to assert the " ascendency of race " and ride in front of him. The villagers at once set him down as an impostor, and refused him supplies, and as his horse could not keep up with mine, and the road presented no apparent perils, I dismissed him at the end of three days with a *largesse* which gladdened his heart. He did not know the way, and the afternoon I left Burujird he led me through ploughed fields and along roadless hillsides, till at the end of an hour I found myself close to the garden from which I started.

The early part of the first march is over great bare gravelly slopes without water. Then come irrigation and villages. The hills have been eaten nearly bare. Nothing remains but a yellow salvia and the beautiful *Eryngium cœruleum*. There, as in the Bakhtiari country, the people stack the *Centaurea alata* for winter fodder. The road is good, and except in two places a four-wheeled carriage could be driven over it at a trot.

The camping - ground was outside Deswali, an unwalled village of 106 houses, with extensive cultivated lands and a " well-to-do " aspect. The people raise cereals, melons, cucumbers, grapes, and cotton, but in bad seasons have to import wheat.   There, as at every village since, the *ketchuda* has called upon me, and some of these men have been intelligent and communicative, and have shown such courtesies as have been in their power.   It is an unusual, if not an unheard-of, thing for a European lady, even if she knows Persian, to travel through this country without a European escort; but there has been no rudeness or impertinent curiosity, no crowding even; the headmen all seemed anxious for my comfort, and supplies at reasonable rates have always been forthcoming.

The heat at Deswali was overpowering, the mercury in my tent standing for hours on 17th August at 120°, the temperature in the shade being 104°.

It is vain to form any resolution against making a pet of a horse.   My new acquisition, " *Boy*," insisted on being petted, and his winning and enticing ways are irresistible. He is always tethered in front of my tent with a rope so long as to give him a considerable amount of liberty, and he took advantage of this the very first day to come into the tent and make it very apparent that he wanted me to divide a melon with him.   Grapes were his next *penchant*, then cucumber, bread, and biscuits.   Then he actually drank milk out of a soup plate.   He comes up to me and puts his head down to have his ears rubbed, and if I do not attend to him at once, or cease attending to him, he gives me a gentle but admonitory thump.   I dine outside the tent, and he is tied to my chair, and waits with wonderful patience for the odds and ends, only occasionally rubbing his soft nose against my face to remind me that he is there.   Up to this time a friendly snuffle is the only sound that he has made.   He does not know how to fight, or that teeth and heels are of any other use than to eat and walk with.   He is really the gentlest and most docile of his race.   The point at which he " draws the line " is being led. He drags back, and a mulish look comes into his sweet eyes. But he follows like a dog, and as I walk as much as I can I always have him with me. He comes when I call him, stops when I stop, goes off the road with me when I go in search of flowers, and usually puts his head either on my shoulder or under my arm. To him I am an embodiment of melons, cucumbers, grapes, pears, peaches, biscuits, and sugar, with a good deal of petting and ear-rubbing thrown in. Every day he becomes more of a companion. He walks very fast, gallops easily, never stumbles, can go anywhere, is never tired, and is always hungry. I paid £4 : 15s. for him, but he was bought from the Bakhtiaris for £3 : 14s. as a four-year-old. He is " up to " sixteen stone, jumps very well, and is an excellent travelling horse.

Redundant forelocks and wavy manes, uncut tails carried in fiery fashion, small noses, quivering nostrils, small restless ears, and sweet intelligent eyes add wonderfully to the attractiveness of the various points of excellence which attract a horse - fancier in Persia. A Persian horse in good condition may be backed against any horse in the world for weight-carrying powers, endurance, steadiness, and surefootedness, is seldom unsound, and is to his rider a friend as well as a servant. Generally speaking, a horse can carry his rider wherever a mule can carry a load, and will do from thirty to forty miles a day for almost any length of time.

The clothing of horses is an important matter. Even in this hot weather they wear a good deal—first a *parhan* or shirt of fine wool crossed over the chest; next the *jul*, a similar garment, but in coarser wool; and at night over all this is put the *namad,* a piece of felt half an inch thick, so long that it wraps the animal from head to tail, and so deep as to cover his body down to his knees. A broad surcingle of woollen webbing keeps the whole in place.

The food does not vary. It consists of from seven to ten pounds of barley daily, in two feeds, and as much as a horse can eat of *kah*, which is straw broken in pieces about an inch and a half long. While travelling, barley and *kah* are mixed in the nose-bag. No hay is given, and there are no oats. It is customary among the rich to give their horses an exclusive diet of barley grass for one month in the spring, on which they grow very fat and useless. Old horses are fed on dough-balls made of barley-flour and water. A grape diet is also given in the grape-producing regions in the autumn instead of *kah*. *Boy* eats ten pounds of grapes as a mere dessert.

I admire and like the Persian horse. His beauty is a constant enjoyment, and, ferocious as he is to his fellows, he is gentle and docile to man. I cannot now recall having seen a vicious horse in seven months. On the whole they are very well cared for, and are kindly treated. The sore backs of baggage horses are almost inevitable, quite so, indeed, so long as the present form of pack-saddle stuffed with *kah* is used. Mares are not ridden in Persia proper.

The march from Deswali to Sahmine is a pretty one, at first over long buff rolling hills and through large elevated villages, then turning off from the Kirmanshah road and descending into a broad plain, the whole of which for several miles is occupied by the trees and gardens of the eminently prosperous village of Sahmine, whose 500 families, though they pay a tribute of 2400 *tumans* a year, have "nothing to complain of."[1]

I was delighted with the oasis of Sahmine. It has abundant water for irrigation, which means abundant

[1] On this journey of 400 miles from Burujird to the Turkish frontier near Urmi, I never heard one complaint of the tribute which is paid to the Shah. All complaints, and they were many, were of the exactions and rapacity of the local governors.

fertility. Its walnut trees are magnificent, and its gardens are filled with noble fruit trees. The wheat harvest was being brought in, and within the walls it was difficult to find a place to camp on, for all the open spaces were threshing-floors, piled with sheaves of wheat and mounds of *kah*, in the midst of which oxen in spans of two were threshing. That is, they drew machines like heavy wood sleds, with transverse revolving wooden rollers set with iron fans at different angles, which cut the straw to pieces. A great heap of unbound sheaves is in the centre, and from this men throw down the stalked ears till they come up to the bodies of the oxen, adding more as fast as the straw is trodden down. A boy sits on the car and keeps the animals going in a circle hour after hour with a rope and a stick. The foremost oxen are muzzled. The grain falls out during this process.

On a windy day the great heaps are tossed into the air on a fork, the straw is carried for a short distance, and the grain falling to the ground is removed and placed in great clay jars in the living-rooms of the houses. All the villages are now surrounded with mounds of *kah* which will be stored before snow comes. The dustiness of this winnowing process is indescribable. I was nearly smothered with it in Sahmine, and on windy days each village is enveloped in a yellow dust storm.

Sahmine, though it has many ruinous buildings, has much building going on. It has large houses with *balakhanas*, a Khan's fort with many houses inside, a square with fine trees and a stream, and a *place* with a stream, where madder-red dyers were at work, and there are five small mosques and *imamzadas*. The gardens are quite beautiful, and it is indeed a very attractive village.

The people also were attractive and friendly. After the *ketchuda's* official visit the Khan's wives called, and

pressed me very hospitably to leave my tent and live
with them, and when I refused they sent me a dinner of
Persian dishes with sweetmeats made by their own hands.
The *kabobs* were quite appetising.   They are a favourite
Persian dish, made of pieces of seasoned meat roasted on
skewers, and served very hot, between flaps of very hot
bread.   Each bit of meat is rubbed with an onion before
being put on the skewer, and a thin slice of tail fat is
put between every two pieces.   The cooks show great
art in the rapidity with which they rotate a skewer full
of *kabobs* over a fierce charcoal fire.

In the evening, at the *ketchuda's* request, I held a
" reception " outside my tent, and it was a very pleasant,
merry affair.   Several of the people brought their children,
and the little things behaved most graciously.   It is very
pleasant to see the devotion of the men to them.   I told
them that in England many of our people are so poor
that instead of children being welcome they are regarded
ruefully as additional " mouths to feed."   " Ah," said the
ketchuda, a handsome Seyyid, " your land is then indeed
under the curse of God.   We would like ten children at
once, they are the joy of our lives."   Other men followed, expatiating on the delights of having children to
pet and play with on their return from work.

Sahmine not only dyes and prints cottons, but it exports wheat, barley, opium, cotton, and fruit, and appears
a more important and prosperous place than Daulatabad,
the capital of the district.

The fine valley between Sahmine and Daulatabad is
irrigated by a *kanaat* and canals, and is completely cultivated, bearing heavy crops of wheat, cotton, tobacco,
opium, *bringals,* and castor oil.   The wheat is now being
carried to the villages on asses' backs in great nets, lashed
to six-foot poles placed in front and behind, each pole
being kept steady by a man.

The heat on that march was severe. A heavy heat-haze hung over the distances, vegetation drooped, my mock *sowar* wrapped up his head in his *abba*, the horses looked limp, the harvesters slept under the trees, the buffaloes lay down in mud and water. Even the greenery of the extensive gardens in and around Daulatabad scarcely looked cool.

Daulatabad is a walled city of 4500 souls, has a fort, and is reputed to have a large garrison. The bazars, which contain 250 shops, are indifferent, and the five caravanserais wretched. It and its extensive gardens occupy the eastern extremity of a plain, and lie very near the steep rocky mountain Sard Kuh, through which, by the Tang-i-Asnab, the Tihran road passes. Another road over the shoulder of the mountain goes to Isfahan. The plain outside the walls has neither tree nor bush, and was only brought into cultivation two years ago. The harvest was carried, and as irrigation had been suspended for some weeks, there was nothing but a yellow expanse of short thin stubble and blazing gravel.

There was no space for camping in any available garden, and an hour was spent in finding a camping-ground with wholesome water on the burning plain before mentioned. I camped below a terraced and planted eminence, on which a building, half fort and half governor's house, has so recently been erected that it has not had time to become ruinous. It is an imposing quadrangle with blank walls, towers with windows at the corners, and a very large *balakhana* over the entrance. A winding carriage-drive, well planted, leads up to it, and there is a circular band-stand with a concrete floor and a fountain. The most surprising object was a new pair-horse landau, standing under a tree. Barracks are being built just below the house.

While my tent was being pitched, the Governor's

aide-de-camp, attended by a cavalry escort, called, and with much courtesy offered me the *balakhana*, arranged, he said, in European fashion.   The Governor was absent, but this officer said that it would be his wish to offer me hospitality.   As I felt quite unable to move he sent a skin of good water, some fruit, and a guard of four soldiers.

It was only 11 A.M. when the tents were pitched, and the long day which followed was barely endurable.   The mercury reached 124° inside my tent.   The servants lay in a dry ditch under a tree in the Governor's garden. *Boy* several times came into the shade of my verandah. The black flies swarmed over everything, and at sunset covered the whole roof of the tent so thickly that no part of it could be seen.   The sun, a white scintillating ball, blazed from a steely sky, over which no cloud ever passed. The heated atmosphere quivered over the burning earth. I was at last ill of fever, and my recipe for fighting the heat by ceaseless occupation failed.   It was a miserable day, and at one time a scorching wind, which seemed hot enough to singe one's hair, added to the discomfort.   " As the hireling earnestly desireth the shadow," so I longed for evening, but truly the hours of that day were " long drawn out."   The silence was singular.   Even the buzzing of a blue-bottle fly would have been cheerful. The sun, reddening the atmosphere as he sank, disappeared in a fiery haze, and then the world of Daulatabad awoke. Parties of Persian gentlemen on fiery horses passed by, dervishes honoured me by asking alms, the Governor's *major-domo* called to offer sundry kindnesses, and great flocks of sheep and goats, indicated by long lines of dust clouds, moved citywards from the hills.   Sand-flies in legions now beset me, and the earth, which had been imbibing heat all day, radiated it far into the morning. I moved my bed outside the tent and gave orders for an early start, but the *charvadar* who was in the city overslept himself, and it was eight the next day before I got away, taking Mirza with me.

The heat culminated on that day. Since then, having attained a higher altitude, it has diminished.[1] The road to Jamilabad ascends pretty steadily through undulating country with small valleys among low hills, but with hardly any villages, owing to the paucity of water. The fever still continuing, I found it difficult to bear the movement of the horse, and dismounted two or three times and lay under an umbrella by the roadside. On one of these halts I heard Mirza's voice saying in cheerful tones, " Madam, your horse is gone ! "　" Gone ! " I exclaimed, " I told you always to hold or tether him." " I trusted him," he replied sententiously. " Never trust any one or any horse, and least of all yourself," I replied unadvisedly. I sent him back with his horse to look for *Boy*, telling him when he saw him to dismount and go towards him with the nose-bag, and that though the horse would approach it and throw up his heels and trot away at first, he would eventually come near enough to be caught. After half an hour he came back without him. I asked him what he had done. He said he saw *Boy*, rode near him twice, did not dismount, held out to him not the nose-bag with barley but my " *courier bag*," and that *Boy* cantered out of sight ! For the moment I shared Aziz Khan's contempt for the " desk-bred " man.

Mirza is so good that one cannot be angry with him, but it was very annoying to hear him preach about " fate " and " destiny " while he was allowing his horse to grind my one pair of smoked spectacles into bits under his hoofs. I only told him that it would be time to fall back on *fate*

---

[1] North of Daulatabad, the route of last winter from Nanej to Kûm, the winter route from Kangawar to Tihran, was crossed. Although it is a "beaten track" for caravans, so far as I know the only information concerning it consists in two reports, not accessible to the public, in the possession of the Indian authorities.

and *destiny* when, under any given circumstances, such as these, he had exhausted all the resources of forethought and intelligence. My plight was a sore one, for by that time I was really ill, and had lost, as well as my horse and saddle, my food, quinine, writing materials, and needle-work. I got on the top of the baggage and rode for five hours, twice falling off from exhaustion. The march instead of being thirteen miles turned out twenty-two, there was no water, poor Mirza was so " knocked up " that he stumbled blindly along, and it was just sunset when, after a series of gentle ascents, we reached the village of Jamilabad, prettily situated on the crest of a hill in a narrow valley above a small stream.

To acquaint the *ketchuda* with my misfortune, and get him to send a capable man in search of the horse, promising a large reward, and to despatch Hassan with a guide in another direction, were the first considerations, and so it fell out that it was 10 P.M. before I was at rest in my tent, where I was obliged to remain for some days, ill of fever. The next morning a gentle thump, a low snuffle, and a theft of some grapes by my bedside announced that *Boy* was found, and by the headman's messenger, who said he met a Seyyid riding him to Hamadan. The saddle-cloth was missing, and all the things from the holsters, but after the emissary had been arrested for some crime the latter were found in his large pockets. Hassan returned late in the afternoon, having been surrounded by four *sowars*, who, under the threat of giving him a severe beating, deprived him of his watch.

When I was so far better as to be able to move, I went on to Mongawi, a large walled village at an elevation of 7100 feet, camped for two days on an adjacent slope, and from thence rode to Yalpand by a road on a height on the east side of a very wild valley on the west of which is Elwend, a noble mountain, for long an object of interest on the march from Kirmanshah to Tihran. A great number of the mountains of Persia are ridges or peaks of nearly naked rock, with precipices on which nothing can cling, and with bases small in proportion to their elevation. Others are "monstrous protuberances" of mud and gravel. Mount Elwend, however, has many of the characteristics of a mountain,—a huge base broken up into glens and spurs, among which innumerable villages with their surroundings of woods and crops are scattered, with streams dashing through rifts and lingering among pasture lands, vine-clothed slopes below and tawny grain above, high summits, snow-slashed even now, clouds caught and falling in vivifying showers, indigo colouring in the shadows, and rocky heights for which purple-madder would be the fittest expression.

In one of the loveliest of the valleys on the skirts of Elwend lies the large walled village of Yalpand on a vigorous stream. For two miles before reaching it the rugged road passes through a glen which might be at home, a water-worn ledgy track, over-arched by trees, with steep small fields among them in the fresh green of grass springing up after the hay has been carried. Trees, ruddy with premature autumnal tints and festooned with roses and brambles, bend over the river, of which little is visible but here and there a flash of foam or a sea-green pool. The village, on a height above the stream, has banks of orchards below and miles of grain above, and vineyards, and material plenty of all sorts. It was revelling in the dust storm which winnowing produces, and the *ketchuda* suggested to me to camp at some distance beyond it, on a small triangular meadow below a large irrigation stream. Hardly were the tents pitched when, nearly without warning, Elwend blackened, clouds gathered round his

crest and boiled up out of his corries, and for the first
time since the middle of January there were six hours
of heavy rain, with hail and thunder, and a fall of the
mercury within one hour from 78° to 59°. The coolness
was most delicious.

Hadji Hussein's prophecy that after I left him I should
"know what *charvadars* are" was not fulfilled on this
journey.   I had one young man with me who from having
performed the pilgrimage to Kerbela bears the name of
"Kerbelai" for the rest of his life. He owns the fine and
frisky animals he drives, and goes along at a good pace,
his long gun over his shoulder, singing as he goes.
Blithe, active, jolly, obliging, honest, kind-hearted, he
loads as fast as three ordinary men, and besides grooming
and feeding his animals well, he "ran messages," got the
water and wood, and helped to pitch and strike the
tents, and was as ready to halt as to march.   Hassan and
Mirza are most deliberate in their movements; nothing
can hurry them, not even the risk of being flooded out
of their tents; and when the storm came on Kerbelai
snatched the spade from them and in no time trenched
my tent and dug a channel to let the water out of the
meadow.

The next day was cloudless, and the sky, instead of
having a whitish or steely blue, had the deep pure tint
so often seen on a June day in England. The heat
returned, and it was a fatiguing and dusty march into
Hamadan, still mainly on the skirts of Elwend, among
villages surrounded by vineyards. After pursuing a by-
road from Jamilabad I joined the main road, two miles
from Hamadan, and the number of men on good horses,
of foot passengers, and of asses laden with fruit and
vegetables, indicated the approach to a capital as plainly
as the wide road, trenched on both sides and planted
with young willows.

The wall as is usual is of crumbling, rain-eaten, sun-dried bricks, and a very poor gateway admits the traveller into a network of narrow alleys, very ruinous, with infamous roadways, full of lumps, holes, slimy black channels, stout mangy dogs, some of them earless, tailless, and one-eyed, sleeping in heaps in the hot sun, the whole overwhelmingly malodorous.[1]

It was no easy matter to find the way to the American Mission House, even though the missionary *Hakīm* is well known and highly esteemed, and I rode through the filthy alleys of the city and its crowded bazars for more than an hour before I reached the Armenian quarter. The people were most polite. There was no shouting or crushing in the bazars, and in some cases men walked with me for some distance to show me the way, especially when I asked for the *Khanum's* house. Indeed they all seemed anxious to assist a stranger. Many of the children salaamed, as I thought, but I have since heard that they are fond of using to a Christian a word which sounds just like *salaam*, but which instead of meaning *Peace* is equivalent to " May you be for ever accursed !"

On reaching the Mission House I found it shut and that the missionaries were in the country, and after sending word that I had arrived I spent some hours in an Armenian house, where the people showed extreme hospitality and kindness.

They put a soft quilt down on the soft rugs, which covered the floor of a pretty whitewashed room, with

---

[1] Hamadan is the fourth city in the Empire in commercial importance. She has a Prince Governor, 450 villages in the district, raises revenue to the amount of 60,000 *tumans*, of which only 11,000 are paid into the Imperial Treasury, and, as the ancient Ecbatana, the capital of the Median kings, she has a splendid history, but the few lines in which I recorded my first impressions are not an exaggeration of the meanness and unsavouriness of her present externals.

many ornaments, chiefly Russian, and, finding that I was ill, they repeatedly brought tea, milk, and fruit instead of the heavy dinner which was at once cooked. The sight of several comely women dressed in shades of red, with clean white *chadars*, going about household avocations, receiving visitors and gracefully exercising the rites of hospitality in a bright clean house festooned with vines, was very pleasant to a dweller in tents. It is not Armenian custom for a daughter-in-law to speak in the presence of her mother-in-law, or even to uncover her mouth, or for young women to speak in presence of their elders. A wife cannot even address her husband in the presence of his mother, except in a furtive whisper. Owing to the custom of covering the mouth, which shows no symptom of falling into disuse, I did not see the face of a girl matron who, judging from her eyes, nose, and complexion, was the comeliest in the room.

Towards evening, as I lay trying to sleep, I was delightfully startled by a cheery European voice, and a lady bent over me, whose face was sunshine, and the very tone of her voice a welcome. Goodness, purity, love, capacity to lead as well as help, true strength, and true womanliness met in the expression of her countenance. Her spotless cambric dress, her becoming hat with its soft white *pagri*, the harmonious simplicity of her costume, and her well-fitting gloves and shoes were a joy after the slovenliness, slipshodness, and generally tumbling-to-pieces look of Oriental women. The Faith Hubbard School, one of the good works of the American Presbyterian Mission, was close by, and in half an hour Miss —— made me feel " at home." Blessed phrase !

I. L. B.

LETTER XXIII

I CAME for four days, and have been here nearly three weeks, which I would willingly prolong into as many months if the winter were not impending. Illness, the non-arrival of luggage containing winter clothing from Tihran, and the exceeding difficulty of finding a *charvadar* willing to go to Urmi by the route I wish to take, have all detained me. For some time I was unable to leave the house, and indeed have been out very little, and not outside the city at all.

I am disappointed both with Hamadan and its autumn climate. It stands at an elevation of 6156 feet [Schindler], and on the final slope of the Kuh-i-Hamadan, an offshoot of Mount Elwend, overlooking a plain about fifteen miles long by nine broad, populous and cultivated, bounded on the other side by low gravelly hills. At this altitude, and with autumn fairly begun, coolness might be expected, but the heat, which a fortnight ago seemed moderating, has returned in fury, with that peculiar faintness about it which only autumn gives. Mount Elwend attracts masses of clouds, and these tend to hang over the town and increase the stagnation of the air, about which there is a remarkable closeness, even in this high situation overlooking the plain. Intermittent fever and diphtheria are prevailing both in the city and the adjacent villages. Not only is the air close and still,

but the sun is blazing hot, and the mercury only varies
from 88° in the day to 84° at night. Brown dust-
storms career wildly over the plain, or hang heavily over
it in dust clouds, and the sand-flies are abundant
and merciless. In the winter the cold is intense, and
the roads are usually blocked with snow for several
weeks.

Water is abundant, and is led through open channels
in the streets. The plain too is well supplied, and the
brown villages, which otherwise would be invisible on the
brown plain, are denoted by dark green stains of willow,
poplar, and fruit trees. The town itself has fine gardens,
belonging to the upper classes, but these are only indicated by branches straying over the top of very high
walls.

My first impressions have received abundant confirma-
tion. Important as a commercial centre as Hamadan
doubtless is, it is as ruinous, filthy, decayed, and un-
prosperous-looking a city as any I have seen in Persia.
" Ruinous heaps," jagged weather-worn walls, houses
in ruins, or partly ruined and deserted, roofs broken
through, domes from which the glazed tiles have dropped
off, roadways not easy by daylight and dangerous at
night, water-channels leaking into the roads and often
black with slime, and an unusual number of very poor
and badly-dressed people going about, are not evidences
of the prosperity which, in spite of these untoward
appearances, really exists.

The high weather-worn mud walls along the alleys
have no windows, in order that the women may not see
or be seen by men. A doorway with a mounting-block
outside it, in " well-to-do" houses, admits into a vaulted
recess, from which a passage, dimly lighted, conducts into
the courtyard, round which the house is built, or into the
house itself. These courtyards are planted with trees

and flowers, marigolds and autumnal roses being now in the ascendant. Marble basins with fountains, and marble walks between the parterres, suggest coolness, and walnuts, apples, and apricots give shade. The men's and women's apartments are frequently on opposite sides of the quadrangles, and the latter usually open on *atriums*, floored with white marble and furnished with rugs and brocaded curtains. I have only seen the women's apartments, and these in the houses of rich traders and high officials are as ornamental as the exteriors are repulsive and destitute of ornament. Gilding, arabesques in colour, fretwork doors and panelling, and ceilings and cornices composed of small mirrors arranged so as to represent facets, are all decorative in the extreme. These houses, with the deep shade of their courtyards, the cool plash of their fountains, and their spacious and ex- quisitely-decorated rooms, contrast everywhere with the low dark mud hovels, unplastered and windowless, in which the poor live, and which the women can only escape from by sitting in the heaped and filthy yards on which they open, and which the inhabitants share with their animals. The contrast between wealth and poverty is strongly emphasised in this, as in all Persian cities, but one must add that the gulf between rich and poor is bridged by constant benevolence on the part of the rich, profuse charity being practised as a work of merit by all good Moslems.

The bazars are shabby and partially ruinous, but very well supplied with native produce and manufactures, English cottons, Russian merchandise, and "knick-knacks" of various descriptions. The presence of foreigners in the town, although they import many things by way of Baghdad, has introduced foreign articles of utility into the bazars, which are not to be found everywhere, and which are commending themselves to the people, " Peek

and Frean's" biscuits among them. The display of fruit
just now is very fine, especially of grapes and melons. The
best peaches, which are large and of delicious flavour, as
well as the best pears, come from the beautiful orchards
of Jairud, not far from Kûm. The saddlery and caravan
equipment bazars are singularly well supplied, as indeed
they should be, for Hamadan is famous for leather, and
caravans loaded with hides for its tanneries are met with
on every road. The bark and leaves of the pomegranate
are used for tanning. Besides highly ornamental leather
for book-bindings and women's shoes, the tanners prepare
the strong skins which, after being dyed red, are used
for saddles, coverings of trunks, and bindings for *khūrjins*.

Hamadan is also famous for *namads* or felts, which are
used as carpets and horse-coverings, and as greatcoats by
the peasants as well as by the Lurs. A good carpet felt
of Hamadan manufacture is an inch thick, but some made
at Yezd reach two inches. For rich men's houses they
are made to order to fit rooms, and valuable rugs are laid
over them. The largest I have seen is in the palace of
the Minister of Justice at Tihran, which must be fully
a hundred and twenty feet by eighty feet, and formed
fourteen mule-loads; but sixty by forty feet is not an
uncommon size, and makes eight mule-loads. These
carpet *namads*, the most delicious of floor-coverings, are
usually a natural brown, with an outline design in coloured
threads or in a paler shade of brown beaten into the
fabric. *Namads*, owing to their bulk and weight, are
never exported. The best, made at Hamadan, are about
20s. the square yard. Chairs spoil them, and as it is
becoming fashionable among the rich men of the cities
to wear tight trousers, which bring chairs in their train,
the manufacture of these magnificent floor-coverings will
probably die.

The felt coats, which protect equally from rain and

cold, are dark brown and seamless, and cost from 10s. to
20s. They have sleeves closed at the end to form a
glove, and with a slit below the elbow through which the
hand can be protruded and used. These coats are cloak-
like, the sleeve is as long as the coat, and they are often
worn merely suspended from the neck.

Hamadan is also famous for copper-work, and makes
and dyes cottons. The tanneries and the dye-works
between them create a stench which is perceptible for
miles. The neighbourhood produces much wine, white
like hock, and red like claret, both being harsh and the
first heady. The Armenians are the chief makers and
sellers of wine. I wish I could add that they are the only
people who get drunk, but this is not the case, for from
the Prince Governor downwards, among the rich Moslems,
intemperance has become common, and even many young
men are "going to wreck with drink," sacrificing the virtue
to which Moslems have been able to point with pride
as differentiating them from so-called Christians. I was
unable to return the Prince Governor's visit and courtesies
in accordance with the etiquette for a European lady
traveller, because of the helpless condition in which he and
a party of convivial friends were found by the messenger
sent by me to ask him to appoint an hour for my visit.
Raisins, treacle, and *arak* are also manufactured. The
rich prefer *cognac* to *arak*. It is spirit-drinking rather
than wine-drinking which is sapping the life of the
Moslems of Hamadan.

It is singular that in this Ecbatana, the capital of
Greater Media, there should be so very few remains of an
ancient greatness and splendour. Just outside the town
a low eminence called Musala is pointed out as the site
of the palace of the Median kings, but even this is
doubtful. Coins of an ancient date are both dug up and
fabricated by the Jews. Only two really interesting

objects remain, and the antiquity of one of these is not
universally accepted.   The tomb of Queen Esther and her
uncle Mordecai is the great show-place of Hamadan, and
is held in much veneration by the Jews of Turkey and
Persia, who resort to it on pilgrimage.   The Jews are
its custodians.

TOMB OF ESTHER AND MORDECAI.

This tomb consists of an outer and inner chamber,
surmounted by a mean dome about fifty feet in height.
The blue tiles with which it was covered have nearly all
dropped off.   The outer chamber, in which there are a
few tombs of Jews who have been counted worthy of
burial near the shrine, is entered by a very low door, and
the shrine itself by one still lower, through which one

is obliged to creep. The inner chamber is vaulted, and
floored with blue tiles, and having been recently restored
is in good order. Under the dome, which is lighted
with the smoky clay lamps used by the very poor, are
the two tombs, each covered with a carved wooden ark,
much defaced and evidently of great antiquity. There is
an entrance to the tombs below these arks, and each is
lighted by an ever-burning lamp. There is nothing in
the shrine but a Hebrew Old Testament and a quantity of
pieces of paper inscribed with Hebrew characters, which
are affixed by pilgrims to the woodwork. The tombs
and the tradition concerning them are of such great
antiquity that I gladly accept the verdict of those who
assign them to the beautiful and patriotic Queen and her
capable uncle.

On the dome is this inscription : " On Thursday the
15th of the month Adar in the year of the creation of
the world 4474 the building of this temple over the
tombs of Mordecai and Esther was finished by the hands
of the two benevolent brothers Elias and Samuel, sons of
Ismail Kachan."

The other object of interest, which has been carefully
described by Sir H. Rawlinson and Sir H. Layard, is
specially remarkable as having afforded the key to the
decipherment of the cuneiform character. It is in the
mountains above Hamadan, and consists of two tablets
six feet six inches by eight feet six inches (Layard) cut
in a red granite cliff which closes the end of a corrie.
There are other tablets near them, carefully prepared,
but never used. The three inscriptions are in parallel
columns in the three languages spoken in the once vast
Persian Empire—Persian, Median, and Babylonian, and
contain invocations to Ormuzd, and the high-sounding
names and titles of Darius Hystaspes and his son Xerxes.

Amidst the meanness, not to say squalor, of modern

Hamadan, no legerdemain of the imagination can re-create the once magnificent Ecbatana, said by the early Greek writers to have been scarcely inferior to Babylon in size and splendour, with walls covered with "plates of gold," and fortifications of enormous strength; the capital of Arbaces after the fall of Nineveh, and the summer resort of the "Great King," according to Xenophon.

The Jews are supposed to number from 1500 to 2000 souls, and are in the lowest state of degradation, morally and socially. That bad act of Sarah in casting out "the bondwoman and her son" is certainly avenged upon her descendants. They are daily kicked, beaten, and spat upon in the streets, and their children are pelted and beaten in going to and from the school which the Americans have established for them. Redress for any wrongs is inaccessible to them. They are regarded as inferior to dogs. So degraded are they that they have not even spirit to take advantage of the help which American influence would give them to get into a better position. The accursed vices of low greed and low cunning are fully developed in them. They get their living by usury, by the making and selling of wine and *arak*, by the sale of adulterated drugs, by peddling in the villages, and by doing generally the mean and dishonest work from which their oppressors shrink. Many of them have become Moslems, the law being that a convert to Islam can take away the whole property of his family. A larger number have, it is believed, joined the secret sect of the *Bābis*. I never heard such a sickening account of degradation as is given of the Hamadan Jews by those who know them best, and have worked the most earnestly for their welfare.

There are a number of Armenians in Hamadan, and several villages in the district are inhabited exclusively by them. There are also villages with a mixed Persian and Armenian population. They all speak Persian, and the men at least are scarcely to be distinguished from Persians by their dress. They are not in any way oppressed, and, except during occasional outbreaks of Moslem fanaticism, are on very good terms with their neighbours. They live in a separate quarter, and both Gregorians and Protestants exercise their religion without molestation. They excel in various trades, specially carpentering and working in metals. Their position in Hamadan is improving, and this may be attributed in part to the high-class education given in the American High School for boys, and to the residence among them of the American missionaries, who have come to be regarded as their natural protectors.

The population of Hamadan is "an unknown quantity." It probably does not exceed 25,000, and has undoubtedly decreased. Seyyids and *mollahs* form a considerable proportion of it, and it is one of the strongholds of the *Bábís*. It is usually an orderly city, and European ladies wearing gauze veils and properly attended can pass through it both by day and night. Several parts of it are enclosed by gates, as at Canton, open only from sunrise to sunset, an arrangement which is supposed to be conducive to security.   I. L. B.

LETTER XXIV

HAMADAN, *Sept. 14.*

I AM visiting the three lady teachers of the Faith Hubbard Boarding School for girls, and the visit is an oasis on my journey. It is a most cheerful house, a perfect hive of industry, each one being occupied with things which are worth doing. I cannot say how kind and how helpful they have all been to me, and with what regret I am leaving them.

The house is large, plain, airy, and thoroughly sanitary, very well situated, with an open view over the Hamadan plain. It is closely surrounded by the houses of the Armenian quarter, and all those domestic operations which are performed on the roofs in hot weather are easily studied, such as the drying of clothes and herbs, the cleaning of heads, the beating of children, the bringing out of beds at night, and the rolling them up in the morning, the " going to bed " of families much bundled up, the performance of the very limited ablutions which constitute the morning toilette, and the making and mending of clothes, the roof being for many months both living-room and bedroom.

At sunset, as in all Persian towns, a great hush falls on Hamadan. Only people who have business are seen in the streets, the bazars are closed, and from sunset to sunrise there would be complete silence were it not for the yelping and howling of the scavenger dogs and the long melancholy call to prayer from the minarets. If it is necessary to go out at night a person of either sex is preceded by a servant carrying a lantern near the ground. These lanterns have metal tops and bottoms, and waxed, wired muslin between, which is ingeniously arranged to fold up flat. They are usually three feet long, but may be of any diameter, and as your consideration is evidenced by the size of your lantern there is a tendency to carry about huge transparencies which undulate very agreeably in the darkness.

This is the Moharrem or month of mourning, for Hassan and Houssein, the slain sons of Ali, who are regarded by the Shiahs as the rightful successors of the Prophet and as the noblest martyrs in the Calendar. During this period the whole Persian community goes into deep mourning, and the streets and bazars are filled with black dresses only. In this month is acted throughout the Empire the *Tazieh* or Passion Play, which has for its climax the tragic deaths of these two men.[1]

I arrived in Hamadan on what should have been the first day of Moharrem, but there had been a difference of opinion among the *mollahs* as to the date, and it was postponed to the next day, for me a most fortunate circumstance, as no Christian ought to be seen in the streets at a time when they are filled with excited throngs frenzied by religious fanaticism. On the following day the quiet of the city was interrupted by singular cries, and by children's voices, high pitched, singing a chant so strange and weird that one both longs and dreads to hear it repeated. The Christians kept within their houses. Business was suspended. Bands of boys carrying black flags perambulated the town, singing one of the chants of

[1] For a detailed and most interesting account of these remarkable representations the reader is referred to Mr. Benjamin's *Persia and the Persians*, chap. xiii.

the Passion Play.   As night came on it was possible to feel the throb of the excitement of the city, and till the small hours the march of frenzied processions was heard, and the loud smiting on human breasts and the clash of the chains with which the dervishes beat themselves, were intermingled with a united rhythmic cry of anguish —*Ah Houssein!* *Wai Houssein!* (O Houssein! Woe for Houssein!) *Ya Houssein!* *Ya Hassan!* and in the flickering light of the torches black flags were waving, and frenzied men were seen beating their bare breasts.

In some of the cities these processions are a sickening spectacle.   Throngs move along the streets, escorting large troops of men either stripped to their waists or wearing only white shirts which expose the bosom.   Beating their breasts with their right hands in concert till they make them raw, gashing themselves on their heads with daggers, streaming with blood, and maddened by religious frenzy, they pass from street to street, and the yell rises from all quarters, *Ya Houssein!* *Wai Houssein!*   Occasionally men drop down dead from excitement, and others, falling from loss of blood, are carried away by their friends.   It is at the end of the month of mourning that these processions, called *testeh*, increase so much in frenzy and fanaticism as to be dangerous to the good order of cities, clashing with each other, and sometimes cutting their way through each other with loss of life.   To join in a *testeh* is to perform a " pious act," and atones for sin committed and to be committed.   The *Tazieh* or Passion Play itself, acted in splendour before the Shah, is repeated everywhere throughout Persia, lasting from ten to twelve days, the frenzy with which the different incidents are received culminating on the last day, when the slaughter of Houssein is represented.   On the whole the *Tazieh* is among the most remarkable religious phenomena of our age.

Under the rule of the present Prince Governor complete religious toleration exists in Hamadan, and the missionaries have a fair field, though it must never be forgotten that a *proselytising* Christian, rendering honour to Christ as God, by his mere presence introduces a disturbing element into a Moslem population. In consequence of this tolerant official spirit there are a few Moslem girls among the sixty boarders here. In addition there are a large number of day pupils.

The girls live in native fashion, and wear native dresses of red cotton printed with white patterns, white *chadars*, and such ornaments as they possess. They sit on the floor at their meals, at each of which one of the ladies is present. They have excellent food, meat once a day in summer and twice in winter, bread, tea, soup, curds, cheese, melons, cucumbers, pickles, and gourds. The winter supplies are now being laid in, and caravans of asses are arriving daily with firewood, cheeses, and melons. The elder girls cook, and all the washing, making, and mending are done at home, each elder girl in addition having a small family of young ones under her care. The only servant is the *bheestie* or water-carrier. The dormitories, class-rooms, eating-room, and *hammam* are large and well ventilated, but very simple.

A plain but thorough education of the " National School " type is given, in combination with an industrial training, fitted for girls whose early destiny is wifehood and maternity. Some of the teachers are men, but the religious instruction, on which great stress is laid, is given by the ladies themselves, and is made singularly interesting and attractive. Music and singing are regarded as among the recreations. The discipline is perfect, and the dirtiest, roughest, lumpiest, and most refractory raw material is quickly transformed into cleanliness, brightness, and docility, partly by the tone of the school and the influence of the girls who have been trained in it, but chiefly by the influence of love.

The respect with which the office of a teacher is regarded in the East allows of much more *apparent* familiarity than would be possible with us. Out of school hours the ladies are accessible at all times even to the youngest children. Many a little childish trouble finds its way to their maternal sympathies, and they are just as ready to give advice about the colour and making of dolls' clothes as about more important matters. The loving, cheerful atmosphere of an English home pervades the school. I write English rather than American because the ladies are Prince Edward Islanders and British subjects.

Some of the girls who have been trained here are well married and make good wives, and the school bids fair to be resorted to in the future by young men who desire companionship as well as domestic accomplishments in their wives. The ordinary uneducated Armenian woman is a very stupid lump, very inferior to the Persian woman. Of the effect of the simple, loving, practical, Christian training given, and enforced by the beauty of example it is easy to write, for not only some of the girls who have left the school, but many who are now in it show by the purity, gentleness, lovingness, and self-denial of their lives that they have learned to follow the Master, a lesson the wise teaching of which is, or should be, I think, the *raison d'être* of every mission school. Christianity thus translated into homely lives may come to be the disinfectant which will purify in time the deep corruption of Persian life.

The cost of this school under its capable and liberal management is surprising—only £3 : 15s. per head per annum! Its weak point (but at present it seems an inevitable blemish) is, that the board and education are gratuitous.

There is a High School for boys, largely attended, under the charge of Mr. Watson, the clerical missionary, with an Armenian Principal, Karapit, educated in the C. M. S. school in Julfa, a very able man, and he is assisted by several teachers. There is also a large school of Jewish girls, who are often maltreated on their way to and from it.

There are a flourishing medical mission and dispensary under Dr. Alexander's charge, with a hospital nearly finished for the more serious cases. There is another dispensary at Sheverin, and both there and here the number of patients is large. A small charge is made for medicines. Mirza Sa'eed, a medical student of mature years and remarkable capacities, occasionally itinerates in the distant villages, and, being a learned scholar in the Koran, holds religious disputations after his medical work is done. He was a Moslem, and having embraced Christianity preaches its doctrines with much force and enthusiasm. He is popular in Hamadan, and much thought of by the Governor in spite of his " perversion." He also gives addresses on Christianity to the patients who assemble at the dispensary. Any person is at liberty to withdraw during this religious service, but few avail themselves of the permission. Miss —— speaks on Christianity to the female patients at Sheverin, and befriends them in their own homes.

The day's work here begins at six, and is not over till 9 P.M. An English class for young men is held early, after which people on business and visitors of all sorts and creeds are arriving and departing all day, and all are welcome. On one day I counted forty-three, and there were many more than these. The upper class of Persian women announce their visits beforehand, and usually arrive on horseback, with attendants to clear the way. No man-servant must enter the room with tea or anything else during their visits. The Armenian women call at all hours, and the Jewish women in large bands without previous announcement. Tea *à la Russe* is provided for all, and Ibrahim goes to the door and counts the shoes left outside in order to know how many to provide for. "*Khanum*," he exclaimed one day after this inspection, "there are at least twenty of them!"

Some call out of politeness or real friendliness, others to see the *tamasha* (the sights of the house), many from the villages to talk about their children, and some of the Jewish women, who have become *Bābis*, ask to have the New Testament read to them in the hope of hearing something which they may use in the propagation of their new faith. A good many women have called on me out of politeness to my hostesses. Persian gentlemen invariably send the day before to know if a visit can be conveniently received, and on these occasions the ladies always secure the *chaperonage* of one of the men missionaries. The *concierge* has orders not to turn any one away, and it is a blessing when sunset comes and the stream of visitors ceases.

All meet with a genial reception, and the ladies usually succeed not only in lifting the conversation out of the customary frivolous grooves, but in awaking more or less interest in the religion which they are here to propagate. They are missionaries first and everything else afterwards, and Miss ——, partly because of her goodness and benevolence to all, and partly because of an uncompromising honesty in her religious beliefs which the people thoroughly appreciate, has a remarkable influence in Hamadan, and is universally respected. Her jollity and sense of humour are a great help. She thoroughly enjoys making people laugh.

I have never been in any place in which the relations with Moslems have been so easy and friendly. The

Sartip Reza Khan told me it would be a matter of regret to all except a few fanatics if the ladies were to leave the city. From the Prince Governor downwards courtesy and kindness are shown to them, and their philanthropic and educational work is approved in the highest quarters, though they never blink the fact that they are proselytisers.[1]

There is an Armenian Protestant congregation with a native pastor and a fine church, and nothing shows more plainly the toleration which prevails in Hamadan than the number of Moslems to be seen every Sunday at the morning service, which is in Persian. In this church total abstinence is a "term of communion," and unfermented wine is used in the celebration of the Eucharist.

This wine is very delicious, and has the full flavour and aroma of the fresh grape even after being three years in bottle. It is not boiled, as much "unfermented wine"

[1] Since I returned I have been asked more than once, "What are the results of missions in Hamadan?" Among those which appear on the surface are the spiritual enlightenment of a number of persons whose minds were blinded by the gross and childish superstitions and the inconceivable ignorance into which the ancient church of S. Gregory the Illuminator has fallen. The raising of a higher standard of morals among the Armenians, so that a decided stigma is coming to be attached to drunkenness and other vices. The bringing the whole of the rising generation of Armenians under influences which in all respects "make for righteousness." The elevation of a large number of women into being the companions and helps rather than the drudges of men. The bestowing upon boys an education which fits them for any positions to which they may aspire in Persia and elsewhere, and creates a taste for intellectual pursuits. The introduction of European medicine and surgery, and the bringing them within the reach of the poorest of the people. The breaking down of some Moslem prejudices against Christians. The gradually ameliorating influence exercised by the exhibition of the religion of Jesus Christ in purity of life, in ceaseless benevolence, in *truthfulness* and *loyalty to engagements*, in kind and just dealing, in temperance and self-denial, and the many virtues which make up Christian discipleship, and the dissemination in the city and neighbourhood of a higher teaching on the duties of common life, illustrated by example, not in fits and starts, but through years of loving and patient labour.

is here, but the grapes are put into a coarse bag, through which the juice drops without pressure. The gluten being retained by the bag, fermentation does not take place, and a bottle of the juice, even if left without a cork, retains its excellence till it dries up.

Hamadan, September 15.——" *Revenons à nos moutons* "—— the *moutons* in this instance being my travelling arrangements. Three roads go to Urmi from Hamadan, one, the usual caravan route *viâ* Tabriz, the commercial capital of Persia, and round the north end of Lake Urmi, very long, but safe ; another called the " Kurdistan route," which no *charvadar* will take by reason of its danger ; and a third by Sujbulāk, the capital of Persian Kurdistan, twenty marches, only five of which are reported as risky. I decided on the last, but it was only two days ago that I was able to get a *charvadar* willing to undertake the journey. " It is too late," they say, " there are robbers on the road," they " don't know the way," or " provender is dear," or " snow will come on " before they can return. Kerbelai, the excellent fellow who brought my loads from Burujird, wished to go, and I engaged him gladly, but afterwards his father came and declared he could not let him go, for he did not know the way, and would be robbed. Another man was engaged, but never reappeared.

Soon after I came a tall, well-dressed rich Turk, the owner of sixty mules, applied for the engagement, and we think that by certain underhand proceedings, familiar to the Persian mind, he has driven off other competitors, and made himself my last resource. I engaged him on Saturday, and the mules and Mirza went off this morning. An agreement was drawn up in Persian and English placing five mules *under my absolute control*, to halt or march as I desire, at thirteen pence a day each so long as I want them, with two men, " handing over the mules and men " to me till I reach Urmi, which arrival is to

suit my own convenience.   This was read over twice, and
the Turk sealed it in presence of four witnesses.   All his
other mules are going with loads to Urmi, and this
accounts for his great desire to send the five with me.   I
have expressly stipulated that I am to have nothing to
do with the big caravan, but am to take my own time.
This Turk has good looks and plausible manners, and
the animals have sound backs, but I distrust him.

The servant difficulty, which threatened to keep me
here indefinitely, is also adjusted.   Hassan left me when
I arrived, being unwilling to go to the north of Persia so
late, and he bought a new opium pipe, saying that he
cannot bear the pain and craving of being without it.
He was a fair travelling servant for a Persian, not un-
reasonably dishonest, and I am sorry to lose him.   In
the attempt to replace him a maze of lies, fraud, and
underhand dealing has been passed through.   I have at
last engaged Johannes, a strong-looking young Armenian,
speaking Turkish and Persian besides Armenian.   He
has never served Europeans, but has learned baking and
the wine trade.   He looks much of a cub.   For appearance sake I have armed him with a long gun.   He and
Mirza are alike incompetent to make any travelling arrangements or overcome any difficulties, to discover where
escorts are needed and where they may be dispensed
with, or to meet any emergencies, and as Persian will be
considerably replaced by Turki *en route* Mirza will be
of less and less use as an interpreter.   I cannot get any
recent information about the route, and very little at all.
I see endless difficulties ahead, and a prospect of illus-
trating in my own experience the *dictum* often dinned
into my ears, that "No lady ought to travel alone in
Persia."

This will be my last opportunity of posting a letter
for nearly a month.   The Persian post is only exceeded in

unreliability by the Persian telegraph.   To register letters
is the only way of securing their safe arrival, and it is
necessary to send a trustworthy man to the Post Offices,
who, after seeing the effacing stamp put upon the postage
stamp, will further insist upon seeing the postmaster put
the letters in the bag.   In Tihran the Europeans make
much use of the Legation bags, and the merchants
prefer to trust their letters to private *gholams* rather
than to the post, while at Isfahan people are often
glad to send their letters by the monthly telegraph
chapar rather than run a postal risk.   However, a foreign
letter, registered, is pretty safe.   The telegraph is worse ;
you often have to bribe the telegraph clerk to send the
message, and unless you see it sent it will probably be
destroyed.   Of five messages sent by me from Hamadan
one was returned because the British agent in Isfahan
was "not known" (!), two were slower than letters sent the
same day, the fourth took a week, and of the fifth there is
" no information."   Even in this important commercial
city the Post Office is only open for a short time on two
days in the week.   I. L. B.

LETTER XXV

GAUKHAUD, *Sept. 18*.

THIS is a difficult journey. The road is rarely traversed by Europeans, the marches are long, and I am really not well enough to travel at all, not having been able to shake off the fever. Cooler days and cold nights are, however, coming to the rescue.

My Hamadan friends gave me a *badraghah* (a parting escort)—Miss C. M——, Mr. Watson, Pastor Ovannes and his boy, all on horseback; Mrs. Watson and her baby on an ass; several servants on foot, and Miss M—— and Mrs. Alexander in a spidery American buggy with a pair of horses; Dr. Alexander, a man six feet two inches high and very thin, "riding postilion" on one of them to get the buggy over difficult places; Ibrahim, the ladies' *factotum*, with a gun slung behind him, follow-ing on horseback. Two of the ladies and the native pastor stayed at night. It was not a pleasant return to camp life, for Johannes is quite ignorant of it, and everything was at sixes and sevens. Nor was the first morning pleasant, for the head *charvadar*, Sharban, came speaking loud with vehement gesticulation, saying that if I did not march with the big caravan and halt when it did, they would only give me one man, and added sundry other threats. Miss M—— scolded him, re-minding them of their agreement, and Ibrahim told them that if they violated it in the way they threatened they

would have to " eat more wood than they had ever eaten
in their lives on going back to Hamadan." ("Eating
wood" is the phrase for being bastinadoed.)   A squabble
the first morning is a usual occurrence, and Miss M——
thought it would be all right, and advised me to go on
to Kooltapa, the first stage put down by the *charvadars*.

Cultivation extends over the eight miles from Hamadan
to Bahar.   There are streams, and willows, and various
hamlets with much wood, and Bahar is completely buried
in orchards and poplars.   It is a place of 1500 people,
and has well-built houses, small mosques, and *mollahs'*
schools.   It makes *gelims* (thin carpets), and grows
besides wheat, barley, cotton, and oil seeds, an immense
quantity of fruit, which has a ready market in the city.

Miss M—— and Pastor Ovannes escorted me for the
first mile, and, meeting the caravan on their way back,
gave Sharban a parting exhortation.   As soon as they
were out of sight he sent back one man, and, in spite
of Mirza's remonstrances, drove my *yabus* with the big
caravan—a grievance to start with, as his baggage animals
were so heavily loaded that they could not go even two
miles an hour, and I have taken five, though I only
need three, in order to get over the ground at three miles
an hour.   I am obliged to have Johannes with me, as
comparatively little Persian is spoken by the common
people along this road.

Beyond Bahar the road lies over elevated table-lands,
destitute of springs and streams, and now scorched up.
One or two small villages, lying off the track, and some
ruinous towers on eminences, built for watching robbers,
scarcely break the monotony of this twenty-four miles'
march.

At three, having ascended nearly 1000 feet, we
reached the small and very poor walled village of Kooltapa, below which are some reservoirs, a series of pools

connected by a stream, and the camping-ground, a fine
piece of level sward, much of which was already occupied
by two Turkish caravans, with 100 horses in each, and
a man to every ten. The loads were all carefully stacked,
covered with rugs, and watched by very large and fierce
dogs.

I lay down in the *shuldari*, feeling really ill. Four
o'clock, five o'clock, sunset came, but no caravan. Johannes
was quite ill, but went to the village to hire a *samovar*,
and to try to get tea and supplies. There was neither
tea nor *samovar*, and no supplies but horse food and
some coarse cheese and blanket bread, too sour and dirty
to be eaten. Long after dark they brought a little milk.
Boy was locked up in a house, and I rolled myself in his
blanket and the few wraps I had with me, and, making
the best of circumstances, tried to sleep ; but it was too
cold, and the position too perilous, and Johannes, who had
loaded his gun with ball, overcome with fatigue, instead
of watching was sound asleep. At eleven Mirza's voice,
though it said, " Madam, these *charvadars* won't do for
you, they are wicked men," was very welcome. They
had stopped half - way, and four of them, including
Sharban's father, had dragged him off his horse with
some violence, and had unloaded it. He appealed to
the village headman, who, after wrangling with them
for some hours, persuaded them to let him have a mule,
and come to Kooltapa with the servants' tent, my bed,
and other comforts, and sent two armed guides with him.

The larger tent was pitched and I went to bed, and
not having the nettings which hang from the roof of my
Cabul tent, and are a complete security against mere
pilferers, I put all I could under the blankets and
arranged the other things within reach of my hand in
the middle of the tent. I also burned a light, having
learned that Kooltapa is a dangerous place. At mid-

night the Turkish caravans started with noise inconceivable, yells of *charvadars*, shouts of village boys, squeals of horses, barking of big dogs, firing of guns, and jangling of 200 sets of bells, all sobering down into a grandly solemn sound as of many church steeples on the march.

I went out to see that all was right, found my servants sleeping heavily and had not the heart to awake them, found the mercury a degree below the freezing point, and lay down, covering my head with a blanket, for the shivering stage of fever had come on. The night was very still, and after some time I heard in the stillness the not uncommon noise of a dog (as I thought) fumbling outside my tent. I took no notice till he seemed getting in, when I jumped up with an adjuration, saw the floor vacant, and heard human feet running away. I ran out and fired blank cartridge several times in the direction of the footsteps, hoping that the flashes would reveal the miscreant, but his movements had been more agile than mine. Mirza ran into the village and informed the *ketchuda*, but he took it very quietly and said that the robbers were Turks, which was false. I offered a large reward, but it was useless.

When daylight came and I investigated my losses I found myself without any of the things which I have come to regard as indispensable. My cork helmet, boots, gloves, sun umbrella, stockings, scanty stock of underclothing, all my brushes, towels, soap, scissors, needles, thread, thimble, the strong combination knife which Aziz coveted and which was used three or four times every day, a large silk handkerchief a hundred years old which I wore as a protection from the sun, my mask, revolver case, keys, pencils, paint brushes, sketches, notes of journeys, and my one mug were all gone. If anything could be worse, my gold pen, with which I have written for the last eighteen years, had also disappeared. Furthermore, to

relieve the tedium of the long wait during the pitching of
my tent, and of the hour's rest which I am obliged to
take on my bed after getting in, I was "doing" a large
piece of embroidery from an ancient Irish pattern,
arabesques on dark, apricot-coloured coarse silk in low-
toned greens, pinks, and blues, all outlined in gold. This
work has been a real pleasure to me, and I relied on it
for recreation for the rest of my journey. Gone too,
with all the silks and gold for finishing it! Now I have
nothing to do when the long marches are over, and as I
can scarcely write with this pen and have also lost my
drawing materials, a perspective of dulness opens out
before me. If Sharban had not disobeyed orders and
stayed behind with my tent all this would not have happened. I now realise what it is to be without what to a
European are "the necessaries of life," and I can scarcely
replace any of them for three weeks.

The caravan came in at nine, and I soon got into my
tent and spent much of the day in making a head-cover
by rolling lint and wadding in handkerchiefs and sewing
them up into a sort of turban with a leather-needle and
packthread obtained from Mirza. I was able to get from
a villager a second-hand pair of *ghevas*,—most serviceable shoes, with "uppers" made of stout cotton webbing
knitted here by the women and among the Bakhtiaris by
the men, and with soles of rag sewn and pressed tightly
together and tipped with horn. These and the "uppers"
are connected with very stout leather brought to a point
at the toe and heel. *Ghevas* are the most comfortable,
and for dry weather and mountain-climbing the most
indestructible of shoes. Thus provided I have to face
the discomfort caused by the other losses as best I may.
"It's no use crying over spilt milk!"

The day before, when the *charvadars* pulled Mirza off
his mule and he threatened them with the agreement,

they replied that it was false that they had made any
agreement except to take me to Urmi in twenty days,
and that they were not afraid of the Prince Governor of
Hamadan, "for he is always asleep, and the Feringhi is
only a Khanum." I sent to them that I wished to leave
Kooltapa at noon. They replied that they were not going
to move. I was in their power, for they had received
advance pay for seven days, and I said no more about
moving. However, at noon I sent Mirza to read the
agreement to them, and Sharban and his father could not
deny the authenticity of the seal, and a superior villager,
who could read, testified that Mirza had read it correctly.

They then saw that they had put themselves into a
"tight place," and sent that they desired to humble themselves, saying, "your foot is on our eyes," a phrase of
humility. I took no notice of them all day, but at
sunset sent for Sharban, and telling Mirza not to soften
down my language, spoke to him in few words. "You
have broken your agreement, and you will have to take
the consequences. Your conduct is disgraceful and
abominable, so cowardly that you don't deserve to be
called a man, it is only what one would expect from a
pidar sag. Do you mean to keep your agreement or
not?" He began to whine, and threw himself at my feet,
but I reluctantly assumed a terrific voice, and saying
"*Khamosh! Bero!*" (Be silent! Begone!), shut the tent.

Bijar, September 21. — No Persian ever believes
your word, and these poor fellows did not believe that
I had letters to the governors *en route.* They are now
terribly frightened, and see that a Feringhi, even though
"*only a Khanum,*" cannot be maltreated with impunity.
When I arrived here, even before I sent my letter of
introduction, the Governor sent a *farash-bashi* with
compliments and offers of hospitality, and afterwards a
strong guard. Then Sharban piteously entreated that I

would not take him before the Governor, and would not make him " eat wood," and his big caravan at last has chimed away on its northward journey to be seen no more. Thus, by acting a part absolutely hateful to me, the mutiny was quelled, and things are now going on all right, except that Sharban avails himself of small opportunities of being disobliging. I do sincerely detest the cowardliness of the Oriental nature, which is probably the result of ages of oppression by superiors.

It is so vexing that the policy of trust which has served me so well on all former journeys has to be abandoned, and that one of suspicion has to be substituted for it. I am told by all Europeans that from the Shah downwards no one trusts father, brother, wife, superior, or inferior. Every one walks warily and suspiciously through a maze of fraud and falsehood. If one asks a question, or any one expresses an opinion, or tells what passes for a fact, he looks over each shoulder to see that no one is listening.[1]

A noble Persian said to me, " Lying is rotting this country. Persians tell lies before they can speak." Almost every day when one is wishing to be trustful, kind, and considerate, one encounters unmitigated lying, cowardly bluster, or dexterously-planned fraud, and the necessity of being always on guard is wearing and repulsive.

Here is another specimen of the sort of net which is woven round a traveller. At Kooltapa, after the theft, I sent to the *ketchuda* for a night-watchman, and he

[1] Apparently it was always thus, for on a tablet at Persepolis occurs a passage in which the vice of lying is mentioned as among the external dangers which threatened the mighty empire of the Medes and Persians. "Says Darius the king: May Ormuzd bring help to me, with the deities who guard my house ; and may Ormuzd protect this province from slavery, from decrepitude, *from lying* ; let not war, nor slavery, nor decrepitude, *nor lies* obtain power over this province."

replied that he could not give one without an order, and that as he knew only Turki, my letter in Persian from the Prince Governor of Hamadan was nothing to him.   Later, a *sowar*, who said he was also a "road-guard," came and said that he only was responsible for the safety of travellers, and that I could not get a watchman from the *ketchuda*, as no one could pass the gates after sunset without his permission.   I already knew that there were no gates.   He said he was entitled to five *krans* a night for protecting the tents.   (The charge is one *kran*, or under exceptional circumstances two.)   I told him we were quite capable of protecting ourselves. Late in the evening an apparently respectable man came and warned us to keep a good look-out, as this *sowar* and another had vowed to rob our tents out of revenge for not having been employed.   These men, acting as road-guards, are a great terror to the people.   They levy blackmail on caravans and take food for their horses and themselves, "the pick of everything," without payment.   The people also accuse them of committing, or being accessory to, the majority of highway robberies.   The women who came to condole with me on my losses accused these men of being the thieves, but it was younger feet which clattered away from my tent.

Sharban, thoroughly subdued for the time, and his servant watched, and to show that they were awake fired their guns repeatedly.   The nightly arrangement now is to secure a watchman from the *ketchuda*; to walk round the camp two or three times every night to see that he is awake, and that *Boy* is all right; to secure the *yekdan* to my bed with a stout mule-chain, and to rope the table and chair on which I put my few remaining things also to the bed, taking care to put a tin can with a knife in it on the very edge of the table, so that if the things are tampered with the clatter may awake me.

After leaving Kooltapa, treeless country becomes bushless, and nothing combustible is to be got but animal fuel. Manure is far too precious for this purpose to be wasted on the fields. Men with asses follow caravans and collect it in bags. The yards into which the flocks and herds are driven at night have now been cleaned out, and in every village all the women are occupied in moulding the manure into *kiziks* or cakes fully a foot long and four inches thick. These, after being dried in the sun, are built up into conical stacks, often exceeding twenty feet in height, and are plastered with a layer of the same material. The making of this artificial fuel is one of the most important industries of Persia, and is exclusively in the hands of women. The preparation of the winter stock takes from six to fourteen weeks, and is very hard wet work. The fuel gives out a good deal of heat, but burns fast. Its combustible qualities are increased by an admixture of cut straw. At this season, between the colossal black stacks of fuel and the conical piles of winter " keep " upon the roofs, the villages are almost invisible.

The march to Gaukhaud was over twenty miles of rolling scorched table-lands—baked mud, without inhabitants. Gaukhaud and the villages for fifty miles farther are unwalled, but each house, with its cattle-yard and upper and underground folds, has a massive mud wall sloping slightly inwards, with an entrance closed by a heavy wooden gate, strengthened with iron. The upper sheep-folds have thick stone doors three feet square. Each house is a fortress, and nothing is to be seen above its walls but a quantity of beehive roofs and a number of truncated cones of winter fodder on a central platform.

The female costume is also different. The women, unveiled, bold-faced, and handsome in the Meg Merrilees

style, wear black sleeveless jackets vandyked and tasselled,
red skirts, and black handkerchiefs rolled round their heads.
Little Persian is spoken or even understood, and everything indicates that the limit of Persia proper, *i.e.* the
Persia of Persians, has been passed.   Gaukhaud is a village
of 350 houses, grows wheat, barley, grapes, and melons ;
and though a once splendid caravanserai on a height is
roofless and ruined, and the village has no better water
than an irrigation ditch, it is said to be fairly prosperous.

The march to Babarashan is for twenty miles along a
featureless irrigated valley about a mile wide, with grass
and stubble, several beehive villages, and mud hills never
over 150 feet high on either side.   Crossing a brick
bridge over a trifling stream, and passing through the
large village of Tulwar, where men who were burying a
corpse politely laid fried funeral-cakes flavoured with
sesamum on my saddle-bow, we ascended over low
scorched hills, much ploughed for winter sowing, to the
beehive village of Babarashan, of 180 houses, abundantly
supplied with water, where we camped close to some
tents of the Kara Tepe and a large caravan.   The dust
blown across the camp from the threshing-floors was ob-
noxious but inevitable.   The " sharp threshing instruments
having teeth " are not used in this region, but mobs of
animals, up to a dozen, tied together, oxen, cows, horses,
and asses, are driven over the wheat.

I am finding the disadvantages of having an untrained
servant.   Johannes that evening ran hither and thither
without method, never finished anything, spent an hour
in bargaining for a fowl, failed to get his fire to burn,
consequently could not cook or make tea, and I went
supperless to bed.   The same confusion prevailed the
next morning, but things have been better since.   No
life is so charming as camp life, but incompetent servants
are a great drawback.

Another uninteresting march of twenty miles over high table-lands and through a valley surrounded by mud hills, with quaint outcrops of broken rock on their summits, and a pass through some picturesque rocky hills brought us into a basin among mountains, in which stands the rather important town of Bijar in the midst of poplars, willows, apricots, and vines. Bijar is said to have 5000 inhabitants. It has a Governor for itself and the surrounding district, and a garrison of a regiment of infantry and 100 *sowars* to keep the turbulent frontier Kurds in order. It has ruinous mud walls, no regular bazars, only shops at intervals; fully a third is in ruins, and most of the houses and even the Governor's palace are falling into decay. It is, however, accounted a thriving place, and is noted for *gelims* and carpenters' work. It has four caravanserais, hardly habitable, however, seven *hammams*, and a few mosques and *mollahs'* schools. It has an air of being quite out of the world. I have been here two days, and as foreigners are very rarely seen, the greater part of the population has strolled past my tent.

I camped as usual outside the walls, near a small spring, and soon a *farash-bashi* came from the Governor, with a message expressive of much annoyance at my having "camped in the wilderness when I was their guest, and they would have given me a safe camping-ground in the palace garden." Mirza took my introduction to him, and he sent a second message saying that the next three marches were "very dangerous," and appointed an hour for an interview. Soon eight infantrymen, well uniformed and set up, with rifles and fixed bayonets, arrived and mounted guard round my tent, changing every six hours. This completed Sharban's discomfiture.

Various difficulties arose on Sunday, and much against my will I had to call on the Governor. He received me in a sort of *durbar*. A great number of men, litigants and others, crowded the corridors and reception-rooms. He looked bloated and dissipated, and seemed scarcely sober. He sat on cushions on the floor, with a row of scribes and *mollahs* on his right, and many *farashes* and soldiers stood about the door. Seyyids, handsome and haughty, glanced at me contemptuously, and the drunken giggle of the Khan and the fixed scowl of the motionless row of scribes were really overpowering. Tea was produced, but the circumstances were so disagreeable that I did not wait for the conventional third cup. The Khan said that the ladies are in the country a few miles off, and hoped I would visit them, that some marches on the road are unsafe, and that he would give me a letter which would be useful in procuring escorts after I left his jurisdiction, and he has since sent it. He was quite courteous, as indeed all Persians of the upper classes are, but I hope never again to pass through the ordeal of calling upon a Moslem without a European escort.

Later, the principal wife of the military commander of the district called with a train of shrouded women, followed by servants bringing an abundant dinner, with much fruit. She came to ask me to take up my quarters in the very handsome house which is her husband's, very near my tent. After a good deal of intelligent conversation she asked if I had a husband and children, and on my replying in the negative she expressed very kindly sympathy, but added, " There are things far worse, things which can never be where, as among you, there is only one wife. One may have a husband and children, and yet, God knows, be made nearly mad by troubles," and she looked as if indeed her sorrows were great. Doubtless a young wife has been installed as favourite, or there is a divorce impending.

Takautapa, September 24. — This is a great grain-

growing region, and by no means unprosperous, but it
only yields one crop a year, the land is ploughed immediately after harvest, and the irrigation is cut off
until sowing-time. Consequently nothing can exceed the
ugliness of the aspect of the country at this time. There
is not one redeeming feature, and on the long marches
there is rarely anything to please or interest the eye.
On the march from Bijar there was not a green thing
except some poplars and willows by a stream, not a
blade of grass, not a green "weed,"—nothing but low
mud hills, with their sides much ploughed and the
furrows baked hard, and unploughed gravelly stretches
covered sparsely with scorched thistles.

Eight miles of an easy descent of 1500 feet brought
us to the Kizil Uzen, a broad but fordable stream, on the
other side of which is Salamatabad, a village consisting
chiefly of the large walled gardens and houses of the
Governor of Bijar. A little higher up there is a solid
eight-arched stone bridge, over 300 feet long. This
Kizil Uzen is one of the most important streams in north
Persia. It drains a very large area, and after a long and
devious course enters the Caspian Sea under the name of
the Sefid Rud. Eleven miles from this place I crossed
the lofty crest of the ridge which divides the drainage
basins of the Kizil Uzen and Urmi. A number of
sowars came out and escorted me through a gateway down
a road with high walls and buildings on both sides to an
inner gateway leading to the Khan's *andarun*. Here we
all dismounted, but the next step was not obvious, for the
heavy wooden gate which secludes the *andarun* was
strongly barred, and showed no symptoms of welcome.
An aged eunuch put his melancholy head out of a hole
at the side, and said that the ladies were expecting me
and that food was ready for the animals and the servants,
but still the gate moved not. I asked if Mirza could go

with me to interpret, the *sowars* suggesting that he could
be screened behind a curtain, quite a usual mode of dis-
posing of such a difficulty.   The eunuch returned, and
with him the Khan's mother, a fiendish-looking middle-
aged woman, who looked through the peep-hole, but on
seeing a good-looking young man drew back, and said very
definitely that no man could be admitted, especially in the
absence of the Khan.   All the men were warned off, and
the door was opened so as just to allow of my entrance
and no more.

The principal wife received me in a fine lofty room
with fretwork windows opening on a courtyard with a
fountain in it and a few pomegranates, and a crowd of
Persian, Kurdish, and negro women, with all manner of
babies.   The lady is from Tihran, and her manners have
some of the ease and polish of the capital.   It is still
the Moharrem, and she was enveloped in a black *chadar*,
and wore as her sole ornament a small diamond-studded
watch as a locket.   Her mother-in-law, who, like many
mothers-in-law in Persia, fills the post of *duenna* to the
establishment, frightened me by the expression of her
handsome face and her sneering, fiendish laugh.   It must
be admitted that there was much to amuse her, for
my slender stock of badly-pronounced Persian is the
Persian of muleteers rather than of polite circles, and
she mimicked every word I uttered, looking all the time
like one of Michael Angelo's "Fates."

The room was very prettily curtained, and furnished
with Russian materials, they told me, and the lithographs,
the photographs and their frames, and the many "knick-
knacks" which adorned the tables and recesses were all
Russian.   They showed me several small clocks and very
ingenious watches, all Russian also.   They said that the
goods in the shops at Bijar are chiefly Russian, and
added, "The English don't try to suit our taste as the

Russians do." The principal lady expressed a wish for greater liberty, though she qualified it by saying that men who love their wives could not let them go about as the English ladies do in Tihran. Dinner had been prepared, a huge Persian dinner, but they kindly allowed me to take tea instead, and produced with it *gaz* (manna) and a cake flavoured with asafœtida. When I came to an end of my Persian, and they of their ideas, I said farewell, and was followed to the gate by the mocking laugh of the *duenna*.

The *sowars* asserted that the next *farsakh* was " very dangerous," so we kept together. Wild, desolate, rolling, scrubless open country it is, the spurs of the Kurdish hills. The *sowars* were very fussy and did a great deal of galloping and scouting, saying that bands of robber horsemen are often met with on this route, who, being Sunnis, would rejoice in attacking Shiahs. Doubtless they magnified the risk in order to enhance the value of their services. In the early afternoon we reached the Kurdish village of Karabulāk, sixty mud hovels, on the flaring mud hillside, the great fodder stacks on the flat roofs alone making the houses obvious. The water is very bad and limited in quantity, and of milk there was none. The people are very poor and unprosperous, and a meaner set of donkeys and oxen than those which were treading out the corn close to my tent I have not seen.

Though most of the inhabitants are Kurds, there are some Persians and Turks, and each nationality has its own *ketchuda*. Towards evening the *sowars* came to me with the three *ketchudas*, who, they said, would arrange for a guard, and for my escort the next day. I did not like this, for the *sowars* had good double-barrelled guns, and were in Persian uniform, and had been given me for three days, but there was no help for it. The *ketchudas* said that they could not guarantee my safety that night with less than ten men, and I saw in the whole affair a design on my very slender purse. A monetary panic set in before I reached Hamadan : the sovereign had fallen from thirty-four to twenty-eight *krans*, the Jews would not take English paper at any price, I could not cash my circular notes, and it was only through the kindness of the American missionaries that I had any money at all, and I had only enough for ordinary expenses as far as Urmi. I told them that I could only pay two men, and dismissed the *sowars* with a present quite out of proportion to the time they had been with me.

During these arrangements the hubbub was indescribable, but the men were very pleasant. Three hours later the *sowars* returned, saying that after riding eight miles they had met a messenger with a letter from the Khan, telling them to go on another day with me. I asked to see the letter, and then they said it was a verbal message. They had never been outside of Karabulāk ! I tell this in detail to show how intricate are the meshes of the net in which a traveller on these unfrequented roads is entangled.

Later, ten wild-looking Kurds with long guns, various varieties of old swords, and long knives, lighted great watch-fires on either side of my tent; and put *Boy* between them. This pet likes fires, and lies down fearlessly among the men, close to the embers.

A little below my camp was a solitary miserable-looking melon garden with a low mud wall. At midnight I was awakened by the loud report of several guns close to my tent, and confused shouts of men, with outcries of women and children. The watchmen saw two men robbing the melon garden, shot one, and captured both. I gave a present to the guards in the morning, and the *ketchudas* took half of it.

The march to Jafirabad is over the same monotonous

country, over ever-ascending rolling hills, with small plateaux among them, very destitute of water, and consequently of population, the village of Khashmaghal, with 150 houses, and two ruined forts, being the one object of interest.

On the way to Jafirabad is the small village of Nasrabad, once a cluster of semi-subterranean hovels, inhabited by thieves. Some years ago the present Shah halted near it on one of his hunting excursions, and observing the desolation of the country, and water running to waste, gave money and lands to bribe a number of families to settle there. There are now sixty houses surrounded by much material wealth. The Shah still divides 100 *tumans* yearly among the people, and takes a very small tribute. Nasr-ed-Din has many misdeeds to answer for, many despotic acts, and some bloodshed, but among the legions of complaints of oppression and grinding exactions which I hear in most places, I have not heard one of the tribute fixed by him—solely of the exactions and merciless rapacity of the governors and their subordinate officials.

Jafirabad, a village of 100 houses in the midst of arable land, has one of those camping-grounds of smooth green sward at once so tempting and so risky, and we all got rheumatism in the moist chilliness of the night. The mercury is still falling slowly and steadily, and the sun is only really hot between ten and four. Jafirabad is a prosperous village, owned, as many in this region are, by the Governor of Tabriz, who is merciful as to tribute.

Everything was wet, even inside my tent. It was actually cold. In the yellow dawn I heard Mirza's cheerful voice saying, " Madam, they think your horse is dead ! " The creature had been stretched out motionless for two hours in the midst of bustle and packing. I told them to take off his nose-bag, which was nearly full, but

still he did not move. I went up to him and said
sharply, " Come, get up, old *Boy*," and he struggled slowly
to his feet, shook himself, and at once fumbled in my
pockets for food, thumping me with his head as usual
when he failed to find any. He was benumbed by
sleeping on the damp ground in the hoar-frost. The
next night he chose to sleep under the verandah of my
tent, snoring loudly. He has became quite a friend and
companion.

The *sowars* finally left me there, and I was escorted
by the *ketchuda*, a very pleasant intelligent man of
considerable property, with his two retainers. The
next stage has the reputation of being " very dangerous,"
and many people anxious to go to the next village
joined my caravan. My tents were guarded by eight
wild-looking village Kurds, armed with clubbed sticks
and long guns. I asked the *ketchuda* if two were not
enough, and he said that I should only pay for two,
the others were there for his satisfaction, that two might
combine to rob me, but that more would watch each
other, and that the robbers of this region do not pilfer in
ones and twos, but swoop down on tents in large parties.

The next march is chiefly along valleys among low
hills. The *ketchuda* did much scouting, not without
good reason, and we all kept close together. A party of
well-mounted men rode down upon us and joined us.
Mirza sidled up to me, and in his usual cheery tones
said " Madam, these are robbers." They were men of a
well-known band, under one Hassan Khan. They spoke
Persian, and Mirza kept me informed of what they were
saying. They said they had been out a night and a day
without success, and they must take my baggage and
horse—they wanted horses badly. The *ketchuda*, to
whom they were well known, remonstrated with them,
and the parley went on for some time, they insisting, and

he threatening them with the regiment from Bijar, but
all he said was of no use, till he told them that I was
the wife of the Governor of Tabriz, that I had been
paying a visit to Hamadan, and was then going to be the
guest of the ladies of Hadji Baba, Governor of Achaz,
that I had been committed to him, and that he was
answerable for my safety.   " You know I am a man of
my word," was the conclusion of this brilliant lie, which
served its purpose, for they said they knew him, and
would not rob me *then*.

They rode with us for some miles, in fact the leader,
a sinister-looking elderly man, in a turban and brown
abba like an Arab, rode so close to me that the barrel
of his gun constantly touched my saddle.   They carried
double-barrelled guns besides revolvers.   On coming to
a part of the country where the *ketchuda* said the road
became safe, I sent the caravan on with the servants, the
band having gone in another direction, and halted for two
hours.   Riding on again, and turning sharply round a large
rock, there they all were, dismounted, and rushed out upon
us.   A *mêlée* ensued, and as I then had only two men they
were two to one, and would certainly have overpowered
my escort had not several horsemen appeared in the
distance, when they mounted and rode away.   One of
the horses was scratched, and I got an accidental cut on
my wrist.   They believed that I had a considerable sum
of money with me.   The *ketchuda* of Takautapa said
that they had robbed his village of some cattle a few
days before.

Takautapa is a village of thirty-five houses, with two
shops, and a gunsmith who seemed to drive a " roaring
trade."   For three days I have scarcely seen an unarmed
man.   Shepherds, herdsmen, ploughmen, travellers, all
carry arms.   Mirza went to the Governor of Achaz, six
miles off, with my letter from the Governor of Bijar, and

he was most courteous. He sent his secretary to ask me
to spend a day or two at his house, and told him, in case
I could not, to remain for the night to arrange for my
comfort and safety, an order very efficiently carried out.[1]

He sent word also that if I could not accept his
hospitality I was still to be his guest, and not to pay for
anything—a kindness which, for several reasons, I never
accept. He added, that though the road was safe, he
should send three *sowars* " to show the *Khanum* honour,"
and they had received strict orders not to accept any
present. The men who attempted to rob my caravan
spent the night here, and, as they had robbed them
before, the villagers were very glad of the protection of
the Governor's scribe and my *sowars*.

Sujbulāk, October 2.—Having been "courteously entreated," I sent on the caravan and servants at daybreak, and, having the *sowars* with me, was able to make
the march to Geokahaz at a fast pace. The *sowars*
were three wild-looking Kurds, well mounted, and in
galloping *Boy* had to exert himself considerably to keep
up with them, and they obviously tried to force his pace.

The day was cool, cool enough for a sheepskin coat,
and the air delightful. The halcyon season for Persian
travelling has come, the difficulties are over, and the
fever has left me. Brown, bare, and bushless as are the
rolling hills over which the road passes, it would be im-

---

[1] I have very great pleasure in acknowledging a heavy debt of gratitude
to Persian officials, high and low, for the courtesy with which I was
uniformly treated. It is my practice in travelling to make my arrangements very carefully, to attend personally to every detail, and to give
other people as little trouble as possible, but in Persia, when off the beaten
track, the insecurity of some of the roads, the need of guards at night
when one is living in camp, and the frequent insubordination and
duplicity of *charvadars* render a reference to the local authorities occasionally imperative ; and not only has the needed help been given, but it
has been given *courteously*, and I have always been treated as respectfully
as an English lady would expect to be in her own country.

possible not to enjoy the long gallops over the stoneless soil, the crisp, bracing air, the pure blue of the glittering sky, and the changed altitude of the sun, which, from having been my worst foe is now a genial friend. True, the country over which I pass is not interesting, but, as everywhere in Persia, craggy mountains are in sight, softened by a veil of heavenly blue, and the country, though uninteresting, suggests pleasant thoughts of fertility, an abundant harvest, and an industrious and fairly prosperous people.[1] Turki is now almost exclusively spoken.

The whole of that day's route was an ascent, and the halting-place was nearly 9000 feet in altitude. I crossed the Sarakh river by a three-arched brick bridge, and afterwards the Gardan-i-Tir-Machi, from which there is an extensive view, and reached Geokahaz by a rough path on the hillside frequently dipping into deep gulches, now dry. The wettest of these is close to the village, and is utilised for a flour-mill. Springs abound, and as Persian soil brings forth abundantly wherever there is water, the village, which is Kurdish, confessed to being extremely prosperous. Its seven threshing-floors were in the full tide of winnowing with the fan, and so complete is the process that nothing but the wheat is left on the firm,

[1] The general verdict of travellers in Persia is, that misrule, heavy taxation, the rapacity and villainy of local governors, and successive famines have reduced its small stationary population to a condition of pitiable poverty and misery, and this is doubtless true of much of the country, and of parts of it which I have traversed myself. But I can only write of things as I found them, and on this journey of 300 miles from Hamadan to Urmi I heard comparatively little grumbling. Many of the villages are contented with their taxation and landlords, in others there are decided evidences of prosperity, and everywhere there is abundance of material comfort, not according to our ideas, but theirs. As to *clothing and food*, the condition of the cultivators of that part of western Persia compares favourably with that of the *rayats* in many parts of India. But just taxation and a complete reform in the administration of justice are needed equally by the prosperous and unprosperous parts of Persia.

hardened gypsum floor, recalling the Baptist's words,
Whose fan is in his hand, and he will throughly
purge his floor." The wheat was everywhere being
gathered " into the garner "—the large upright clay receptacles holding twenty bushels each with which every
house is supplied.

This village of only 200 houses owns 7000 sheep
and goats, 60 horses and mares, and 400 head of cattle,
and its tribute is only 230 *tumans*. It and very many
other villages belong to Haidar Khan, Governor of
Achaz, of whom the villagers speak as a lenient lord.
Apricot and pear orchards abound, and on a piece of
grass in one of these I found my camp most delectably
pitched. The *ketchuda* and several other men came to
meet me ; indeed, the *istikbal* consisted of over twenty
Kurdish horsemen. The village was absolutely crowded
with men and horses, 200 pilgrims being lodged there
for the night.

The road at intervals all day had been enlivened by
long files of well-mounted men in bands of 100 each on
their way to the shrines of Kerbela, south of Babylon, to
accumulate " merit," receive certificates, and be called
Kerbelai for the remainder of their lives. Superb-looking
men in the very prime of life most of them are, cheerful
and ruddy, wearing huge black sheepskin caps shaped like
mushrooms, high tan-leather boots, gaily embroidered,
into which their full trousers are tucked, and brown
sheepskin coats covering not only themselves but the
bodies of their handsome fiery horses. A few elderly
unveiled women were among them. They ride mostly
on pads with their bedding and clothing under them, and
their *kalians* and cooking utensils hanging at the sides.
All are armed with guns and swords. I met over
1000 of them, most of them Russian subjects, and those
who had occasion to pass in front of my tent vindicated

their claim to be the subjects of a civilised power by
bowing low as often as they saw me. They are really
splendid men, and had many elements of the picturesque.

The 200 who halted in Geokahaz were under the
command of a Seyyid who, before starting, beat about
for recruits, and levied from them about five *krans* per
head. On the journey he receives great honour as a
descendant of the Prophet. He has a baggage mule and
a tent, and the " pilgrims " under his charge gratefully
cook his food, wait on him, groom his animal, water the
dusty ground round his tent, shampoo his limbs, keep
the flies from him, and are rewarded for the performance
of all menial offices by being allowed to kiss his hand.
On his part he chooses the best stations and the most
fortunate days for starting, and he pledges himself to
protect his flock from the woful plots of malignant genii
and the effects of the evil eye. On the journey he both
preaches and recites tales.

The Seyyid in charge of this party was a man of commanding *physique* and deadly pallor of countenance.
As frigid as marble, out of which his statuesque face
might well have been carved, he received the attention
paid to him with the sublime indifference of a statue of
Buddha. The odour of an acknowledged sanctity hung
about him, and pride of race and pride of asceticism
dwelt 'upon his handsome features. He spent the
evening in preaching a sermon, and, by a carefully-
arranged exhibition of emotion, studied to perfection,
wound up his large audience to a pitch of enthusiasm.
The subject was the virtues of Houssein, and what preacher
could take such a text without enlarging finally upon the
martyrdom of that " sainted " man ? Then the auditors
wept and howled and beat their breasts, and long after
I left the singular scene, trained " cheers " for the Prophet,
for Ali, and for the martyred Hassan and Houssein, led

by the Seyyid, rang out upon the still night air. At midnight, and again at four, a solitary bell-like voice proclaimed over the sleeping village, "There is but one God, and Mohammed is His prophet, and Ali is His lieutenant"; and 200 voices repeated grandly in unison, "There is but one God, holy and true, and Mohammed is His prophet, and Ali is His lieutenant." The addition of the words "holy and true" to the ordinary formula is very striking, and is, I believe, quite unusual. The Seyyid preached in Persian, and the pilgrims speak it.

In such caravans a strictly democratic feeling prevails. All yield honour to the Seyyid, but otherwise all are equal. No matter what the social differences are, the pilgrims eat the same food, lodge in the same rooms, sit round the same bivouac fire, and use towards each other perfect freedom of speech—a like errand and a like creed constituting a simple bond of brotherhood.

Geokahaz is the first Kurdish village in which I have really mixed with the people. I found them cordial, hospitable, and in every way pleasant. The *ketchuda's* wife called on me, and later I returned the visit. Each house or establishment has much the same externals, being walled round, and having between the wall and house an irregular yard, to which access is gained by a gate of plaited osiers. Within are very low and devious buildings, with thick mud walls. The *atrium*, an alcove with plastered walls, decorated with circles and other figures in red, is the gathering-place of the men, with their guns and pipes.

It is necessary to stoop very low to enter the house proper, for the doorway is only three feet high, and is protected by a heavy wooden door strengthened by iron clamps. The interior resembles a cavern, owing to the absence of windows, the labyrinth of rooms not six feet high, the gnarled, unbarked trees which support the roofs, the dimness, the immense thickness of the mud walls, the rays of light coming in through protected holes in the roof, the horses tethered to the tree-trunks, and the smoke. The "living-room" is a small recess, rendered smaller by a row of clay receptacles for grain as high as the roof on one side, and a row of oil-jars, each large enough to hold a man, on the other. A fire of animal fuel in a hole in the middle of the floor emitted much pungent smoke and little heat. A number of thick wadded quilts were arranged for me, and tea was served in Russian glass cups from a Russian *samovar*.

The wife was handsome, and never in any country have I seen a more beautiful girl than the daughter, who might have posed for a Madonna. They told me that for the five months of winter the snow comes "as high as the mouth," and that there is no egress from the village. The men attend to the horses and stock, and the women weave carpets, but much of the time is spent by both in sleep.

Accompanied by this beautiful girl, who is graceful as well as beautiful, and an old servant, I paid many visits, and found all the houses arranged in the same fashion. I was greatly impressed by their scrupulous cleanliness. The floors of hardened clay are as clean as sweeping can make them, and the people are clean in dress and person. The women, many of whom are very handsome, are unveiled, and do not even wear the *chadar*. The very becoming head-dress is a black coronet, from which silver coins depend by silver chains. A red kerchief is loosely knotted over the back of the head, on which heavy plaits of hair are looped up by silver pins. This girl passed with me through the crowds of strange men unveiled, with a simplicity and maidenly dignity which were very pleasing. It was refreshing to see the handsome faces, erect carriage, and firm, elastic walk of these

Kurdish women after the tottering gait of the shrouded, formless bundles which pass for Persian women. The men are equally handsome, and are very manly-looking.

These Kurdish villagers are Sunnis, and are on bad terms with their neighbours, the Shiahs, and occasionally they drive off each other's cattle.

On leaving this pleasant place early next morning the *ketchuda* and a number of men escorted me for the first *farsakh*, and with my escort of *sowars* increased by four wild-looking "road-guards," riding as it seemed good to them, in front or behind, sometimes wheeling their horses at a gallop in ever-narrowing circles, sometimes tearing up and down steep hills, firing over the left shoulders and right flanks of their horses, lunging at each other with much-curved scimitars, and singing inharmonious songs, we passed through a deep ravine watered by a fine stream which emerges through gates of black, red, and orange rock into a long valley, then up and up over long rolling hills, and then down and down to a large Ilyat camp beside a muddy and nearly exhausted stream, where they feasted, and I rested in my *shuldari*.

Two or three times these "road-guards" galloped up to shepherds who were keeping their flocks, and demanded a young sheep from each for the return journey, and were not refused. The peasants fear these men much. They assert that, so far from protecting caravans and travellers, they are answerable for most of the robberies on the road, that they take their best fowls and lambs without payment, and ten pounds of barley a day for their horses, and if complaints are made they quarter themselves on the complainant for several days. For these reasons I object very strongly to escorts where they are not absolutely needed for security. I pay each man two *krans* a day, and formerly gave each two *krans* daily as "road money" for himself and his horse, but finding

that they took the food without paying for it, I now pay
the people directly for the keep of the men and horses.
Even by this method I have not circumvented the rapacity
of these horsemen, for after I have settled the " bill "
they threaten to beat the *ketchuda* unless he gives them
the money I have given him.

The Ilyat women from the camp crowded round me
with a familiarity which, even in savages, is distressing,
a contrast to the good manners and unobtrusiveness of
the women of Geokahaz.

On the way to Sanjud, a Kurdish village in a ravine
so steep that it was barely possible to find a level space
big enough for my tent, there is some very fine scenery,
and from the slope of Kuh Surisart, on the east side of
the Gardan-i-Mianmalek, the loftiest land between Hamadan and Urmi, the view is truly magnificent.   The
nearer ranges stood out boldly in yellow and red ochre,
in the valleys indigo shadows lay, range beyond range
of buff-brown hills were atmospherically glorified by
brilliant cobalt colouring, and the hills which barred the
horizon dissolved away in a blue which blended with the
sky.   In that vast solitude the fine ruins of the fortress
palace of Karaftu, where the fountain still leaps in the
deserted courtyard, are a very conspicuous object.

From the Mianmalek Pass there is a descent of 5000
feet to the Sea of Urmi, and the keen edge of the air
became much blunted ere we reached Sanjud.   Nearly
the whole of the road from Hamadan has been extremely
solitary.   We have not met or passed a single caravan,
and on this march of seven hours we did not see a human
being.   Yet there are buff-brown villages lying in the
valleys among the buff-brown hills, and an enormous
extent of country is under tillage.   In fact, this region
is one of the granaries of Persia.

Sanjud is a yellow-ochre village of eighty houses built

into a yellow-ochre hillside, above which rises a high hill
of red mud. It is not possible to give an idea of the
aspect of the country at this season. Sheep and goats
certainly find pickings among the rocks, but the visible
herbage has all been eaten down. The thistles and other
fodder plants have been cut and stacked in the villages.
Most of the streams are dry, and the supplies of drinking water are only pools, much fouled by cattle. The
snows which supply the sources of the irrigation channels
have all melted, and these channels are either dry or
stopped. There has scarcely been a shower since early
April, and for nearly six months the untempered rays of
the Persian sun have been blazing upon the soil. The
arable land, ploughed in deep furrows, has every furrow
hardened into sun-dried brick. Villages of yellow or
whitish baked mud, supporting on their dusty roofs buff
stacks of baked fodder, are hardly distinguishable from
the baked hillsides. The roads are a few inches deep in
glaring white dust. Over the plains a brown dust haze
hangs.

This rainless and sun - scorched land lives by the
winter snows, and the snowfall of the Zagros ranges is
the most interesting of all subjects to the cultivator of
Western Persia. If the country were more populous,
and the profits of labour were secure, storage for the
snow-water would be an easy task, and barren wastes
might sustain a prosperous people; for the soil, when
irrigated, is prolific, and the sun can always be relied
upon to do his part. The waste of water is great, as
considerably more than half the drainage of the empire
passes into *kavirs* and other depressions. The average
rainfall on the central plateau is estimated by Sir Oliver
St. John at five inches only in the year.

My arrival at Sanjud was not welcome. The *ketchuda*
sent word that he was not prepared to obey the orders of

the *Sartip* of Achaz.   I could buy, he said, what I could get, but he would furnish neither supplies nor guards for the camp.   I did not wonder at this, for a traveller carrying an official letter is apt to be palmed off on the villagers as a guest, and is not supposed to pay for anything.

I went to see the *ketchuda*, and assured him that I should pay him myself for all supplies, and a night's wages to each watchman, and the difficulty vanished. Many of the handsome village women came to see me. The *ketchuda* made me a feast in his house, and when I bade him farewell in the morning he said solemnly, " We are very glad you have been our guest, we have suffered no loss or inconvenience by having you, we should like to be protected by the great English nation." This polite phrase is frequently used.

The Persian Kurds impress me favourably as a manly, frank, hospitable people.   The men are courteous without being cringing, and the women are kind and jolly, and come freely and unveiled to my tent without any obtrusiveness.

The *ketchuda* sent eight guards to my camp at night, saying it was in a very dangerous place, and he did not wish his village disgraced by a stranger being robbed so near it.   He added, however, that six of these men were sent for his own satisfaction, and that I was only to pay for the two I had ordered.

My journey, which is through a wild and little frequented part of Persia, continues to be prosperous.   The climate is now delightful, though at these lower altitudes the middle of the day is rather hot.

It was a fertile and interesting country between Sanjud and Sain Kala, where I halted for Sunday.   The road passes through the defiles of Kavrak, along with the deep river Karachai, from the left bank of which rises pre-

cipitously, at the narrowest part of the throat, the fine
mountain Baba Ali. A long valley, full of cultivation
and bearing fine crops of cotton, a pass through the red
range of Kizil Kabr, and a long descent brought us
to a great alluvial plain through which passes the river
Jagatsu on its way to the Dead Sea of Urmi. Broad
expanses of shingle, trees half-buried, and a number of
wide shingly water-channels witness to the destructive-
ness of this stream. A severe dust storm rendered the
end of the march very disagreeable, as the path was
obliterated, and it was often impossible to see the horses'
ears. In winter and spring this Jagatsu valley is completely flooded, and communication is by boats. There
are nearly 150 villages in the district, peopled almost
entirely by Kurds and Turks, and there are over 200
nomad tents. The Jagatsu is celebrated for its large fish.

When the storm abated we were close to Sain Kala,
a picturesque but ruinous fort on a spur of some low
hills, with a town of 300 houses at its base. In the
eastern distance rises the fine mountain Pira Mah, and
between it and Sain Kala is a curious mound—full of
ashes, the people said—a lofty truncated cone, evidently
the site of an *Atash-Kardah*, or fire-temple. This town
is in the centre of a very fertile region. Its gardens and
orchards extend for at least a mile in every direction,
and its melons are famous and cheap—only 6d. a dozen
just now.

It is a thriving and rising place. A new bazar is
being built, with much decorative work in wood. The
junction of the roads to Tabriz from Kirmanshah
and Hamadan, with one route to Urmi, is in the
immediate neighbourhood, and the place is busy with
the needs of caravans. It looks much like a Chinese
Malay settlement, having on either side of its long narrow
roadway a row of shops, with rude verandahs in front.

Among the most prominent objects are horse, mule, and ass shoes; pack-saddles, *khurjins*, rope, and leather. Fruiterers abound, and melons are piled up to the roofs. Russian cottons and Austrian lamps and mirrors repeat themselves down the long uncouth alley.

The camping-ground is outside the town, a windy and dusty plain. Here my eight guards left me, but the *ketchuda* shortly called with a message from the *Sartip* commanding a detachment of soldiers and the town, saying that a military guard would be sent before sunset. Sain Kala is in the government of Sujbulāk, and its people are chiefly Kurds with an admixture of Turks, a few Persians, mainly officials, and the solitary Jew dyer, who, with his family, is found in all the larger villages on this route.

An embroidery needle was found sticking in my *dhurrie* a few days ago, and I had the good fortune not only to get some coarse sewing-cotton but some embroidery silks at Sain Kala, and having a piece of serge to work on, and an outline of a blue centaurea, I am no longer destitute of light occupation for the mid-day halt.

Truly "the Sabbath was made for man"! Apart from any religious advantages, life would be very grinding and monotonous without the change of occupation which it brings. To stay in bed till eleven, to read, to rest the servants, to intermit the perpetual *driving*, to obtain recuperation of mind and body, are all advantages which help to make Sundays red-letter days on the journey; and last Sunday was specially restful.

In the afternoon I had a very intelligent visitor, a *Hakīm* from Tabriz, sent on sanitary duty in consequence of a cholera scare—a flattering, hollow upper-class Persian. He introduced politics, and talked long on the relative prospects of Russian or English

ascendency in Asia. England, he argued, made a great
mistake in not annexing Afghanistan, and his opinion, he
said, was shared by all educated Persians. " You are a
powerful nation," he said, " but very slow. The people,
who know nothing, have too much share in your government. To rule in Asia, and you are one of the greatest of
Asiatic powers, one must not introduce Western theories
of government. You must be despotic and prompt, and
your policy must not vibrate. See here now, the Shah
dies, the Zil-i-Sultan disputes the succession with the
Crown Prince, and in a few days Russia occupies Azir-
bijan with 200,000 men, captures Tihran, and marches
on Isfahan. Meanwhile your statesmen talk for weeks
in Parliament, and when Russia has established her
prestige and has organised Persia, then your fleet with a
small army will sail from India ! Bah ! No country
ruled by a woman will rule in Asia."

In the evening the *ketchuda* and two other Persian-
speaking Kurds hovered so much about my tent that I
invited them into the verandah, and had a long and
pleasant talk with them, finding them *apparently* frank
and full of political ideas. They complained fiercely of
grinding exactions, which, they said, " keep men poor all
their lives." " The poorest of men," they said, " have to
pay three *tumans* (£1) a year in money, besides other
things ; and if they can't pay in money the tax-gatherer
seizes their stock, puts a merely nominal value upon it,
sells it at its real value, and appropriates the difference."
They did not blame the Shah. " He knows nothing."
They execrated the governors and the local officials.[1]   If

[1] The truth is that since Persia broke the power of the Kurds ten
years ago, at the time of the so-called Kurdish invasion, she has kept a
somewhat tight hand over them, and her success in coercing them indicates pretty plainly what Turkey, with her fine army, could do if she were
actually in earnest in repressing the disorder and chronic insecurity in
Turkish Kurdistan.

they keep fowls, they said, they have to keep them underground or they would be taken.

At the Shah's death, they said, Persia will be divided between Russia and England, and they will fall to Russia. "Then we shall get justice," they added. I remarked that the English and the Kurds like each other. They said, "Then why is England so friendly with Turkey and Persia, which oppress us, and why don't travellers like you speak to the Sultan and the Shah and get things changed." They said that at one time they expected to fall under English rule at the Shah's death, "but now we are told it will be Russia."

After a long talk on local affairs we turned to lighter subjects. They were much delighted with my folding-table, bed, and chair, but said that if they once began to use such things it would increase the cost of living too much, "for we would never go back to eating and sleeping among the spiders as Mohammedans do." They said they had heard of Europeans travelling in Persia to see mines, to dig among ruins for treasure, and to collect medicinal herbs, but they could not understand why I am travelling. I replied that I was travelling in order to learn something of the condition of the people, and was interested likewise in their religion and the prospects of Christianity. "Very good, it is well," they replied; "Islam never recedes, nor can Christianity advance."

LETTER XXV (*Continued*)

THE following morning the *Sartip* turned out in my honour all the road-guards then in Sain Kala to the number of twelve to escort me to the castle of Muhammad Jik, a large village, the residence and property of the *Naib Sartip*. This was the wildest escort I have had yet. These men were dressed in full Kurdish finery, and besides guns elaborately inlaid with silver and ivory, and swords in much-decorated scabbards, they carried daggers with hilts incrusted with turquoises in their girdles. They went through all the usual equestrian performances, and added another, which consists in twirling a loaded and clubbed stick in a peculiar manner, and throwing it as far ahead as possible while riding at full gallop, the one who picks it up *without dismounting* being entitled to the next throw. Very few succeeded in securing it in the regulation manner, and the scrimmage for this purpose was often on the point of becoming a real fight. They worked themselves up to a pitch of wild excitement, screamed, yelled, shouted, covered their horses with sweat and foam, nearly unhorsed each other, and used their sharp bits so unmercifully that the mouth of every horse dripped with blood.

After they received *bakhsheesh* they escorted me two miles farther " to honour the *Khanum*," fired their guns in the air, salaamed profoundly, and with shrieks and yells left me at a gallop.

The village of Muhammad Jik has a well-filled bazar
and an aspect of mixed prosperity and ruin.   The castle,
a large, and, at a distance, an imposing pile, a square fort
with flanking towers, is on an eminence, and has a fine
view of the alluvial plain of the Jagatsu, studded with
villages and cultivated throughout.

Here, for a rarity, the *Seigneur* lives a stately life
among those who are practically his serfs in good old
medieval fashion.   Large offices are enclosed within an
outer wall, and are inhabited by retainers.   Rows of
stables sheltered a number of fine and well-groomed horses
from the sun.   Bullocks were being brought in from
ploughing; there were agricultural implements of the best
Persian type, fowls, ducks, turkeys, angora goats; negroes
and negresses, grinning at the stranger; mounted messengers with letters arriving and departing; scribes in white
turbans and black robes lounging—all the paraphernalia
of position and wealth.

It was nearly nine, and the great man had not risen,
but he sent me a breakfast of tea, *kabobs*, cracked wheat,
curds, *sharbat*, and grapes.   The courtyard is entered by
a really fine gateway, and the castle is built round a
quadrangle.   The *andarun* and its fretwork galleries are
on one side, and on another is what may be called a hall
of audience, where the *Sartip* hears village business and
decides cases.

He offered me a few days' hospitality, paid the usual
compliments, said that no escort was needed from thence
to Sujbulāk, where my letter to the Governor would procure me one if " the roads were unsettled," hoped that I
should not suffer from the hardships of the journey, and
offered me a *kajaveh* and mule for the next marches.

A level road along the same prosperous alluvial plain
leads to Kashava, a village of 100 houses embosomed in
fruit trees and surrounded by tobacco and cotton.   It

has an old fort, a very fine spring, and a " resident proprietor," who, as soon as he heard of my arrival, sent
servants with melons and tea on silver trays, stabled
my horse, and provided me with a strong guard, as the
camping-ground was much exposed to robbers. Such
attentions, though pleasant, are very expensive, as the
greater the master the greater are the expectations of the
servants, and the value of such a present as melons must
be at least quadrupled in *bakhsheesh.*

While halting the next day the horses eagerly ate
the stalks and roots of a strongly-scented bulb which
lay almost on the surface of the ground, and were simul-
taneously seized with a peculiar affection. Their hair
stood out from their bodies like bristles, and they threw
their heads up and down with a regular, convulsive, and
apparently perfectly involuntary motion, while their eyes
were fixed and staring. This went on for two hours,
Boy following me as usual ; but owing to this most distressing jerk, over which he had no control, he was
unable to eat the dainties which his soul loves, and
which I hoped would break up the affection—a very
painful one to witness. After the attack both animals
perspired profusely. The water literally ran off their
bodies. The jerks gradually moderated and ceased, and
there were no after effects but very puffy swellings about
the throat. Both had barley in their nose-bags, but
pawed and wriggled them off in order to get at this
plant, a species of *allium.*

When *Boy* was well enough to be mounted we
descended into an immense plain, on which were many
villages and tracks. This plain of Hadji Hussein is
in fact only another part of the alluvial level of the
Jagatsu, which, with a breadth of from four to ten miles,
extends for nearly forty miles, and is fertile and populous
for most of its length. At the nearest village all the

men were busy at the threshing-floor, and they would not give me a guide; at the next the *ketchuda* sent a young man, but required payment in advance.

After crossing the plain, on which villages occur at frequent intervals on gravelly islands surrounded by rich, stiff, black soil, we forded the broad Jagatsu and got into the environs of, not an insignificant village, as I expected, but an important town of 5000 people. A wide road, planted and ditched on both sides, with well-kept irrigated gardens, shaded by poplars, willows, and fruit trees, runs for a mile from the river into the town, which is surrounded by similar gardens on every side, giving it the appearance of being densely wooded. The vineyards are magnificent, and the size and flavour of the grapes quite unusual. Melons, opium, tobacco, cotton, castor oil, sesamum, and *bringals* all flourish.

Miandab is partly in ruins, but covers a great extent of ground with its 1000 houses, 100 of which are inhabited by Jews and twenty by Armenians. People of five tribes are found there, but unlike Sain Kala, where Sunnis and Shiahs live peaceably, the Mussulmans are all Shiahs, no Sunni having been allowed to become a permanent inhabitant since the Kurdish attack ten years ago, when Sunnis within the city betrayed it into the hands of their co-religionists.

It has several mosques, a good bazar with a domed roof, a part of which displays very fine copper-work done in the town, and a garrison of 100 men. I saw the whole of Miandab, for my caravan was lost, and an hour was spent in hunting for it, inquiring of every one if he had seen a caravan of four *yabus*, but vainly, till we reached the other side, where I found it only just arrived, and the men busy tent-pitching in a lonely place among prolific vineyards. Sharban had lost the way, and after much marching and counter-marching had reached the

ford of the Jagatsu, which I had been told to avoid,
where the caravan got into deep strong water which
carried the *yabus* off their feet, and he says that they and
the servant were nearly drowned.   Mirza had to go back
into the town to obtain a guard from an official, as the
camping-ground was very unsafe, and it was 11 P.M.
before dinner was ready.

The next day I was ill, and rode only twelve miles,
for the most part traversing the noble plain of Hadji
Hussein, till the road ascends by tawny slopes to the
wretched village of Amirabad—seventeen hovels on a
windy hill, badly supplied with water.   Partly sunk
below ground, this village, at a short distance off, is only
indicated by huge stacks of the *Centaurea alata* and tall
cones of *kiziks*, which, being neatly plastered, are very
superior in appearance to the houses which they are
intended to warm.

The western side of the great plain was studded with
Ilyat camps of octagonal and umbrella-shaped tents with
the sides kept out by stout ribs.   Great herds of camels,
and flocks of big fat-tailed sheep, varying in colour from
Vandyke brown to golden auburn, camels carrying fodder,
and tribesmen building it into great stacks, round which,
but seven feet off, they place fences of a reed which is
abundant in swampy places, gave life and animation.
Ilyat women brought bowls of milk and curds, and offered
me the hospitality of their tents.

As I passed through a herd of grazing camels, an
ancient, long-toothed, evil-faced beast ran at *Boy* with
open mouth and a snarling growl.   Poor *Boy* literally
gasped with terror (courage is not his strong point) and
dashed off at a gallop ; and now whenever he sees camels
in the distance he snorts and does his best to bolt to one
side, showing a cowardice which is really pitiable.

It was very cold when I left Amirabad the next

morning at 6.30, and hoar-frost lay on the ground. The
steadiness with which the mercury descends at this
season is as interesting as its steady ascent in the spring,
and its freedom from any but the smallest fluctuations in
the summer. The road to Sujbulāk passes over uplands
and hill-slopes, tawny with sun-cured grass, and after
crossing some low spurs, blue with the lovely *Eryngium
cœruleum*, descends into a long rich valley watered by the
river Sanak. This valley, in which are situated Inda
Khosh and other large villages, is abundantly irrigated,
and is cultivated throughout. Well planted with fruit
trees, it is a great contrast to the arid, fiery slopes which
descend upon it.

Long before reaching Sujbulāk there were indications
of the vicinity of a place of some importance, caravans
going both ways, asses loaded with perishable produce,
horsemen and foot passengers, including many fine-looking
Kurdish women unveiled, and walking with a firm mascu-
line stride, even when carrying children on their backs.

A few miles from the town two *sowars* met me, but
after escorting me for some distance they left me, and
taking the wrong road, I found myself shortly on a slope
above the town, not among the living but the dead.
Such a City of Death I have never seen. A whole hour
was occupied in riding through it without reaching its
limits. Fifty thousand gravestones are said to stand on
the reddish-gray gravel between the hill and the city wall,
mere unhewn slabs of gray stone, from six inches to as
many feet in height, row beyond row to the limit of vision
—300,000 people, they say, are buried there. There is
no suggestion of "life and immortality." Weird, melancholy, and terribly malodorous, owing to the shallowness
of the graves, the impression made by this vast cemetery
is solely painful. The tombs are continued up to the
walls and even among the houses, and having been much

disturbed there is the sad spectacle of human skulls and bones lying about, being gnawed by dogs.

The graveyard side of Sujbulāk is fouler and filthier than anything I have seen, and the odours, even in this beautiful weather, are appalling. The centre of each alley is a broken channel with a broken pavement on each side. These channels were obviously constructed for water, but now contain only a black and stagnant horror, hardly to be called a fluid, choked with every kind of refuse. The bazars are narrow, dark, and busy, full of Russian commodities, leather goods, ready-made clothing, melons, grapes, and pop-corn. The crowds of men mostly wore the Kurdish or Turkish costume, but black-robed and white-turbaned Seyyids and *mollahs* were not wanting.

Sujbulāk, the capital of Northern Persian Kurdistan, and the residence of a governor, is quite an important *entrepôt* for furs, in which it carries on a large trade with Russia, and a French firm, it is said, buys up fur rugs to the value of several hundred thousand francs annually. It also does a large business with the Kurdish tribes of the adjacent mountains and the Turkish nomads of the plains, and a considerable trade in gall-nuts. It has twenty small mosques, three *hammams*, some very inferior caravanserais, and a few coffee-houses. Its meat bazar and its grain and pulse bazars are capacious and well supplied.

It has a reputed population of 5000 souls. Kurds largely predominate, but there are so many Turks that the Turkish Government has lately built a very conspicuous consulate, with the aspect of a fortress, and has appointed a consul to protect the interests of its subjects. There are 120 Armenians, who make wine and *arak*, and are usurers, and gold and silver smiths. The Jews get their living by money-lending, peddling drugs, dyeing cotton goods, selling groceries, and making gold and silver lace.

There is a garrison, of 1000 men nominally, for the town and district are somewhat turbulent, and a conflict is always imminent between the Kurds and Turks, who are Sunnis, and the small Persian population, which is Shiah. The altitude of Sujbulāk is 4770 feet. Here I have come upon the track of Ida Pfeiffer, who travelled in the Urmi region more than forty years ago, when travelling in Persia was full of risks, and much more difficult in all respects than it is now.

KURD OF SUJBULĀK.

The Sanak, though clear and bright, is fouled by many abominations, and by the ceaseless washing of clothes above the town; there are no pure wells, and all people who care about what they drink keep asses constantly bringing water from an uncontaminated part of the river, two miles off. Even the Governor has to depend on this supply.

Sujbulāk looks very well from this camp, with the bright river in the foreground, and above it, irregularly grouped on a rising bank, the façade, terraces, and towers of the Governor's palace, the fort-like Turkish consulate, and numbers of good dwelling-houses, with *balakhanas* painted blue or pink, or covered with arabesques in red, with projecting lattice windows of dark wood, and balconies overhanging the water.

This shingle where I am encamped is the Rotten Row of the town, and is very lively this evening, for numbers of Kurds have been galloping their horses here, and performing feats of horsemanship before the admiring eyes of hundreds of promenaders, male and female, most of the latter unveiled. As all have to cross the ford where the river is some inches above a man's knees, the effect is grotesque, and even the women have no objection to displaying their round white limbs in the clear water. The ladies of the Governor's *andarun* sent word that food and quarters had been prepared for me since noon, but I excused myself on the plea of excessive fatigue. This message was followed by a visit from the Governor's foster-mother, an unveiled jolly woman, of redundant proportions, wearing remarkably short petticoats, which displayed limbs like pillars. A small woman attended her, and a number of Kurd men, superbly dressed, and wearing short two-edged swords, with ebony hilts ornamented with incrustations of very finely-worked filigree silver. These weapons are made here. The lady has been to Mecca, and evinces much more general intelligence than the secluded women. She took a dagger from one of the attendants, and showed me with much go how the thrusts which kill are made.

All were much amused with *Boy's* gentle ways. He had been into the town for supplies, and, as usual, asked me to take off his bridle by coming up and putting his ears under my chin, when, if I do not attend to him at once, he lifts his head and gives me a gentle push, or rubs his nose against my cheek. The men admired his strong, clean limbs, which are his best points. Last night I heard snoring very near me, and thinking that the watchmen were sleeping under the *flys*, I went out to waken them, and found the big beast stretched out fast asleep in the verandah of the tent, having retired there for warmth. I accompanied my visitors to the ford, followed by *Boy*, to their great amusement, as it was to mine to see the stout lady mount nimbly on a Kurd's back, and ride him " pickaback " through the water!

This has not been a comfortable afternoon. The Governor has been out all day hunting, and his deputy either at the bath or a religious function. Milk can only be got in the Jewish quarter, where smallpox is prevailing; the Sanak water is too foul to be used for tea, and no man will go two miles so late for a pure supply. Johannes, who is most disobedient as well as incompetent, has brought no horse food, and poor *Boy* has been calling for it for two hours, coming into my tent, shaking the bag in which the barley is usually kept, and actually in his hunger clearing the table of melons and grapes. These, however, are only among the very small annoyances of travelling.

9 P.M.—The Governor has returned, and has sent a guard of twenty-five soldiers, with an invitation to visit the ladies before I start to-morrow. I. L. B.

LETTER XXVI

TURKMAN, *Oct. 6*.

RISING very early on Friday morning to keep my appointment with the ladies of the Governor of Sujbulāk, as well
as to obtain a letter from him, I reached the palace
entrance a little after sunrise, the hour agreed upon.
The walls and gateway are crumbling, the courtyard is in
heaps, the glass windows of the façade and towers are much
broken, the plaster is mangy—a complete disappointment.
The Kurdish guard slept soundly at the entrance; only
a big dog, more faithful than man, was on the alert.
The Governor was not yet awake, nor the ladies. It would
be an " intolerable crime," the sentry said, to waken them.
He looked as if he thought it an "intolerable crime"
that his own surreptitious slumbers had been disturbed.
It is contrary to Persian etiquette to waken persons of
distinction till they please. I waited at the entrance for
half an hour and then reluctantly departed, very sorry
not to give the ladies the opportunity they ardently
desired of seeing a European woman. They had sent
word that they had only once in their lives seen one!

The march to the poor village of Mehemetabad was
over uninteresting low rounded hills and through a
valley without habitations, opening upon a fine plain, at
the south-east end of which the village stands. The
camping-ground was a green fallow near some willows
and a stream. After marching for some hours under

a glittering sky and a hot sun over scorched, glaring yellow soil, a measure of greenness just round the tent is most refreshing to eyes which are suffering from the want of the coloured glasses which were ground under a *yabu's* hoofs a fortnight ago.

The Khan of the village was very courteous, and sent a tray of splendid grapes, and six watchmen. Buffalo bulls of very large size were used there for burden. Buffaloes are a sure sign of mitigated aridity, for they must bathe, *i.e.* lie down in water three times daily, if they are to be kept in health, and if the water and mud are not deep enough for this, boys go in along with them and pour water over them with a pannikin. In these regions they are almost exclusively used for burdens, draught, and milk, and everywhere their curved flat horns and sweet, calm, silly faces are to be seen above the water of the deep irrigation ditches. The buffalo, though usually mild enough to be driven by small children, has an uncertain temper, and can be roused to frightful ferocity. In Persian Kurdistan, if not elsewhere, this is taken advantage of, and in the spring, when the animals are in good condition after the winter's rest, the people have buffalo fights, in which cruel injuries would be inflicted were it not for the merciful provision of nature in giving these animals flat incurved horns.[1]

As I sat at my tent door a cloud of dust moved along the road towards the village, escorting an indefinite something which loomed monstrously through it. I have not seen a cart for nine months, and till the unmistak-

[1] While I was sleeping in a buffalo stable in Turkey two buffaloes quarrelled and there was a terrible fight, in which the huge animals interlocked their horns and broke them short off, bellowing fearfully. It took twenty men with ropes, or rather cables, two and a half inches in diameter, which are kept for the purpose, to separate them ; and their thin skins, sensitive to insect bites and all irritations, were bleeding in every direction before they could be forced apart.

able creak of wooden wheels enlightened me I could not
think what was approaching. Actually every village on
these plains has one or more buffalo-carts, with wooden
wheels without tires, and hubs and axles of enormous
size and strength, usually drawn by four buffaloes. A man
sits on the front of the cart and drives with a stick, and
a boy *facing backwards* sits on the yoke between the two
foremost beasts. He croons a perpetual song, and if this
ceases the buffaloes stop. For every added pair (and on
the next plain I saw as many as six yoke) there is an
additional boy and an additional song.

This apparition carried a light wooden frame, which
was loaded to a preposterous height with the strong reeds
which are used to support the mud roofs, heavily weighted
as these are with stacks of fodder.

One would think one was in the heart of the Bakhtiari country and not on a caravan route, from the
difficulty of getting any correct guidance as to the road,
distance, safety, or otherwise, etc. Sharban has never
been this way, and is the prey of every rumour. Between his terror of having to "eat wood" on his return,
and his dread of being attacked and robbed of his *yabus*,
he leads an uneasy life, and when, as at Mehemetabad,
there is no yard for his animals, he watches all night in
the idea that the guards are the "worst robbers of all."
I think he has all the Mussulman distrust of arrangements made by a woman! Hitherto the guards have
been faithful and quiet. I always ask them not to talk
after 8 P.M., and I have not once been disturbed by
them; and when I walk as usual twice round the camp
during the night I always find them awake by their big
watch-fires.

The village Khan, an intelligent man, spent some time
with me in the afternoon. The fields of his village are
not manured at all, and the yield is only about tenfold.

Willows are grown for the sake of the osiers, which are a necessity, and not for fuel, and the whole of the manure is required for cooking and heating purposes. He said that his village becomes poorer annually owing to the heavier exactions of the officials and the larger sums demanded to "buy off robbers." The latter is a complaint often made in the villages which are near the Turkish frontier, a boundary which from all accounts needs considerable "rectification." The people say that Kurds cross the border, and that unless they bribe them they drive off their sheep and cattle and get over it again safely, but I doubt the truth of these statements.

I got away at sunrise for a march of nominally fourteen miles, but in reality twenty-four. Sharban not only stated the distance falsely but induced others to do the same thing, and when he passed me at midday, saying the halting-place was only two miles ahead, he went on for twelve miles, his desire being to rejoin that bugbear, the "big caravan," which he heard had reached Urmi. The result is that I have had to rest for two days, and he has gained two days' pay, but has lost time

After some serious difficulties in crossing some swampy streams and a pitiable display of cowardice on *Boy's* part, we embarked on the magnificent plain of Sulduz, where Johannes, with a supreme self-confidence which imposed on me, took the wrong one of two tracks, and we rode west instead of east, to within a few hours' journey of a pass into Turkey through the magnificent range of the Zibar mountains, which even at this advanced season are in some places heavily patched with last winter's snow.

To regain the caravan route we had to cross the greater part of this grand plain, which I had not then seen equalled in Persia for fertility and population. It possesses that crown of blessings, an abundant water supply, indeed so abundant that in the spring it is a swamp, and the spring sowing is delayed till May. It has several large villages, slightly raised and well planted, a few of them with the large fortified houses of resident proprietors overtopping the smaller dwellings. Evidences of material prosperity meet the eye everywhere, a prosperity which needs to be guarded, however, for every shepherd, cowherd, ploughman, and buffalo-driver goes about his work armed.

Large herds of mares with mule foals, of big fat cattle, and of buffaloes, with plenty of mud to wallow in, stacks of real hay and of fine reeds, buffalo carts moving slowly near all the villages carrying the hay into security, grass uncut and unscorched, eighteen inches high, a deep, black, stoneless soil, impassable at certain seasons, towering cones of animal fuel, for export as well as use, an intensely blue sky above, a cool breeze, and the rare sight of cloud-shadows drifting over waving grass and flecking the cobalt sides of the Zibar mountains, combined to form a picture I would not willingly have missed, impatient as I was for the first view of the Sea of Urmi.

Beyond there are low stony hills, which would be absolutely bare now but for the *Eryngium cœruleum* and the showy spikes of a great yellow mullein, a salt lake, most of which is now a salt incrustation, mimicking ice from beneath which the water has been withdrawn, but with an odour which no ice ever has, then a gradual ascent to a windy ridge, and then—the Dead Sea of Urmi or Urumiya.

Dead indeed it looked from that point of view, and dead were its surroundings. It lay, a sheet of blue, bluer even than the heavens above it, stretching northwards beyond the limits of vision, and bounded on the east, but very far away, by low blue ranges, seen faintly through a blue veil. On the west side there are

mountains, which recede considerably, and descend upon
it in low rounded buff slopes or downs, over which the
track, keeping near the water, lies.　There was not a
green thing, not a bush, or house, or flock of sheep, or
horseman, or foot passenger along the miles of road
which were visible from that point.　The water lay in
the mocking beauty of its brilliant colouring, a sea without a shore, without a boat, without a ripple or flash of
foam, lifeless utterly, dead from all time past to all time
to come.　Dead, too, it is on closer acquaintance, and its
odour, which can be discerned three miles off, is that
odour of corruption known to science as sulphuretted
hydrogen.　Now and then there is a shore, a shallow
bay or inlet, in which the lake, driven by the east wind,
evaporates, leaving behind it a glaring crust of salt,
beyond which a thick, bubbly, blackish-green scum lies on
the blue water.　In such places only the expressive old-
fashioned word *stench* can describe the odour, which was
strong enough nearly to knock over the servants and
charvadars.　No description can give an idea of the
effluvium which is met with here and there beside this
great salt lake, which has a length of eighty miles and
an average breadth of twenty-four.

A few miles from Dissa the lake-water is brought into
tanks and evaporated, and many donkeys were being loaded
with the product, which, like all salt which is sold in
Persia, is impure, and for European use always requires
a domestic and tedious process of purification.

After a solitude of several miles villages appear, lying
off the road in folds of the hills, which gradually recede
so far as to leave a plain some miles broad and very
fertile.　At the end of an eleven hours' march we reached
the important village of Dissa, with large houses and
orchards, abundant water, a detachment of soldiers as a
garrison, a resident proprietor's house, to which in his

absence I was at once invited by his wife, and so surrounded by cultivation that a vacant space could only be found for the camp in a stubble-field.

The caravan had only just come in, and there was neither fuel nor drinking water within easy reach. I was so completely worn out that I was lifted off the horse and laid on the ground in blankets till the camp was in order late at night. Sharban, knowing that his deception was discovered, had disappeared with his *yabus* without helping as usual to pitch my tent. Mirza, always cheerful and hard-working, though always slow, and Johannes did their best, but it is very hard on servants who are up before five not to bring them in till sunset, when their work is scarcely over till near midnight, and has to be done in the dark. The next day there were a succession of dust storms and half a gale from noon to sunset, but my tent stood it well, and the following day this was repeated. These strong winds usually prevail in the afternoon at this season.

Urmi, October 8. — A march over low and much-ploughed hills, an easy descent and a ford brought us down upon the plain of Urmi, the "Paradise of Persia," and to the pleasant and friendly hamlet of Turkman, where I spent the night and made the half-march into Urmi yesterday morning. This plain is truly "Paradise" as seen from the hill above it, nor can I say that its charm disappears on more intimate acquaintance. Far from it!

I have travelled now for nine months in Persia and know pretty well what to expect—not to look for surprises of beauty and luxuriance, and to be satisfied with occasional oases of cultivation among brown, rocky, treeless hills, varied by brown villages with crops and spindly poplars and willows, contrasting with the harsh barrenness of the surrounding gravelly waste.

But beautiful Urmi, far as the eye can reach, is one oasis. From Turkman onwards the plain becomes more and more attractive, the wood-embosomed villages closer together, the variety of trees greater. Irrigation canals shaded by fruit trees, and irrigation ditches bordered by reeds, carry water in abundance all through the plain. Swampy streams abound. Fair stretches of smooth green sward rejoice the eye. Big buffaloes draw heavy carts laden with the teeming produce of the black, slimy, bountiful soil from the fields into the villages. Wheat, maize, beans, melons, gourds, potatoes, carrots, turnips, beets, capsicum, chilis, *bringals*, lady's fingers, castor-oil (for burning), cotton, madder, salsify, scorzonera, celery, oil-seeds of various sorts, opium, and tobacco all flourish. The orchards are full of trees which almost merit the epithet noble. Noble indeed are the walnuts, and beautiful are the pomegranates, the apricots, the apples, the peach and plum trees, and glorious are the vineyards with their foliage, which, like that of the cherry and pear, is passing away in scarlet and gold. Nature has perfected her work and rests. It is autumn in its glories, but without its gloom.

Men, women, and children are all busy. Here the wine-press is at work, there girls are laying clusters of grapes on terraces prepared for the purpose, to dry for raisins; women[1] are gathering cotton and castor-oil seeds, little boys are taking buffaloes to bathe, men are driving and loading buffalo-carts, herding mares, ploughing and trenching, and in the innumerable villages the store-houses are being filled; the herbs and chilis are hanging from the roofs to dry, the women are making large cakes of animal fuel (of which they have sufficient for export), and are building it into great conical stacks, the crones are spinning in the sun, and the swaddled infants bound

[1] Christian women and girls share the work of the fields with the men.

in their cradles are lying in the fields and vineyards, while the mothers are at work. This picture of beauty, fertility, and industry is framed by the Kurdistan mountains on the one side, and on the other by long lines of poplars, through which there are glimpses of the deep blue waters of the Urmi Sea. These Kurdistan mountains, a prolongation of the Taurus chain, stern in their character, and dwarfing all the minor ranges, contrast grandly with the luxuriant plains of Sulduz and Urmi.

As I passed northwards the villages grew thicker, the many tracks converged into a wide road which was thronged with foot passengers, horsemen, camel and horse caravans, and strings of asses loaded with melons and wood. Farther yet the road passes through beautiful orchards with green sward beneath the trees ; mud walls are on both sides, and over them droop the graceful boughs and gray-green foliage of an *elægnus*, with its tresses of auburn fruit.

At the large village of Geog-tapa a young horseman overtook me, and said in my native tongue, " Can you speak English ? " He proved to be a graduate of the American College at Urmi, and a teacher in *Shamasha Khananeshoo's* school (known better to his supporters in England as Deacon Abraham). He told me that I was expected, and shortly afterwards I was greeted by the son of the oldest missionary in Urmi, Dr. Labaree.

The remaining four miles were almost entirely under the shade of fine trees, past the city walls and gates, put into tolerable repair after the Kurdish invasion ten years ago, and out into pretty wooded country, with the grand mountains of the frontier seen through the trees, where a fine gateway admitted us into the park in which are the extra-mural buildings of the American Presbyterian Mission, now more than half a century old. These are on high ground, well timbered, and the glimpses through the trees of the mountains and the plain are enchanting.

Through the kindness of my friends at Hamadan, who had written in advance, I am made welcome in the house of Dr. Shedd, the Principal of the Urmi College.[1]

Within two hours of my arrival I had the pleasure of visits from Canon Maclean and Mr. Lang of the English Mission, and from Dr. Labaree and the ladies of the Fiske Seminary, the English, French, and American missionaries being the only European residents in Urmi.

I. L. B.

[1] It is a pleasant duty to record here the undeserved and exceeding kindness that I have met with from the American, Presbyterian, and Congregational missionaries in Persia and Asia Minor. It is not only that they made a stranger, although a member of the Anglican Church, welcome in their refined and cultured homes, often putting themselves to considerable inconvenience in order to receive me, but that they ungrudgingly imparted to me the interests of their work and lives, helping me at the cost of much valuable time and trouble with the complicated and often difficult arrangements for my farther journeys, showing in every possible way that they "know the heart of a stranger," being themselves "strangers in a strange land." Specially, I feel bound to acknowledge the kindness and hospitality shown to me by the Presbyterian missionaries in Urmi, who were aware that one object of my journey through North-West Persia was to visit the Archbishop of Canterbury's Assyrian Missions, which work on different and, I may say, opposite lines from their own.

NOTES ON PROTESTANT MISSIONS IN URMI [1]

A SKETCH of Urmi would present few features of general interest if it did not embrace an outline of the mission work which is carried on there on a large scale, first by the numerous agents, lay and clerical, male and female, of the American Presbyterian Board of Foreign Missions, and next by the English Mission clergy and the Sisters of Bethany, who form what is known as " The Archbishop of Canterbury's Mission to the Assyrian Christians."

Besides these there is a Latin Mission of French Lazarists, aided by Sisters of St. Vincent de Paul, which has been at work in Urmi and on the plain of Salmas for forty years.

Urmi, the reputed birthplace of Zoroaster, and in past ages the great centre of Fire Worship, was made the headquarters of the American Mission to the Nestorians in 1834, which, with the exception of the C. M. S. Mission in Julfa, was the only Protestant Mission in Persia up to the year 1885.

At present there are four ordained American missionaries, several ladies, and a medical missionary working in Urmi. Under their superintendence are thirty ordained and thirty-one licentiate pastors, ninety-three native helpers, and three Bible-women. The number of Nestorians or Syrians employed as teachers in the

[1] The name of the town and lake is spelt variously Urmi, Urumi, Urumiya, Ourmia, and Oroomiah. The Moslems call it Urumi, and the Christians Urmi, to which spelling I have adhered.

College and the Fiske Seminary for girls, as translators, as printers, and as medical assistants, is very considerable.

The whole plain of Urmi, with its innumerable villages, and the eastern portion of the Kurdish mountains, with its Syrian hamlets, are included within the sphere of Mission work.

This Mission has free access to Syrians, Armenians, and Jews, but for Moslems there can be no public preaching or teaching, nor can a Moslem openly profess Christianity, or even frequent the Syrian services, without being a marked man. Hence, while all opportunities are embraced of conversation with Mohammedans, and of circulating the Bible among them, the mission work is chiefly among nominal Christians.

The Americans own a very large amount of property at Urmi. The Fiske Seminary—a High School, in which a large number of girls receive board as well as education—is within the city walls, as well as some of the houses of both clerical and lady missionaries. About a mile outside they have acquired a beautiful and valuable estate of about fifteen acres, plentifully wooded and watered, and with some fine avenues of planes. On this are the large buildings of the Urmi College, the professors' houses, the Dispensary, and the Medical Mission Hospitals for the sick of both sexes.

A very high-class education is given in the Urmi College, and in addition to the general course there are opportunities for both theological and medical education. Last year there were 151 students, of which number eighteen graduated.

The education given is bringing about a result which was not anticipated. The educated Syrian and Armenian young men, far from desiring generally to remain in their own country as pastors and teachers, and finding no opportunities of " getting on " otherwise, have of late been seized with a craze for leaving Persia for America, Russia, or any other country where they may turn their education to profitable account. It is hardly necessary to add that the admirable training and education given in the Fiske Seminary do not produce a like restlessness among its "girl graduates." The girls marry at an early age, make good housewives, and are in the main intelligent and kindly Christians.

Possibly the education given in the Urmi College is too high and too Western for the requirements of the country and the probable future of the students. At all events similar regrets were expressed in Urmi, as I afterwards heard, regarding some of the American Mission Colleges in Asia Minor. The missionaries say that the directly religious results are not so apparent as could be desired, that the young men are not ready to offer themselves in any numbers for evangelistic work, and that the present tendency is to seek secular employment and personal aggrandisement.

Though this secular tendency comes forward strongly at this time, a number of evangelistic workers scattered through Persia, Turkey, and Russia [1] owe their education

[1] At the present time, when the persecution of the *Stundists* in Russia is attracting considerable attention, it may interest my readers to hear that one of the earliest promoters of the *Stundist* movement was Yacub Dilakoff, a Syrian, and a graduate of the Old American College. He went to Russia thirty years ago, and was so horrified at the ignorance and gross superstition of the peasantry that he studied Russian in the hope of enlightening them, and to aid his purpose became an itinerant hawker of Bibles. The "common people heard him gladly," and among both the Orthodox and the Lutherans prayer unions were formed, from which those who frequented them received the name by which they are known, from *stunde*, hour.

Dilakoff, whom the *Stundists* love to call "our Bishop," has been thrown into prison several times, but on his liberation began to teach among the sect of the *Molokans* in the Crimea and on the Volga with such success that sixteen congregations have been formed among them. His zeal has since carried him to the *Molokan* colonies on the Amoor, where he has been preaching and teaching for three years with such remarkable results as to have received the title of "a Modern Apostle."

and religious inspiration to the teachings of the Urmi College. At present a few of the young men have banded themselves together to go forth as teachers and preachers with the object of carrying the Gospel to all, without distinction of nationality. The hopefulness of this movement is that it is of native origin, and that the young men are self-supporting. A capable Syrian physician and a companion are also preaching and healing at their own cost, only accepting help towards the expense of medicines.

The Medical Mission at Urmi, with its well-equipped Dispensary and its two admirable Hospitals, is of the utmost value, as such missions are all the world over.

Dr. Cochrane, from his courtesy and attention to the niceties of Persian etiquette, is extremely acceptable to the Persian authorities, and has been entrusted by them more than once with missions involving the exercise of great tact and ability. He is largely trusted by the Moslems of Urmi and the neighbourhood, and mixes with them socially on friendly and easy terms.

He and some of the younger missionaries were born in Persia, their fathers having been missionaries before them, and after completing their education in America they returned, not only with an intimate knowledge of etiquette and custom, as well as of Syriac and Persian, but with that thorough sympathy with the people whom they are there to help and instruct, which it is difficult to gain in a single generation, and through languages not acquired in childhood. Dr. Cochrane has had many and curious dealings with the Kurds, the dreaded inhabitants of the mountains which overhang the beautiful plain of Urmi, and a Kurd, who appears to be in perpetual " war-paint," is the gatekeeper at the Dispensary. One of the most singular results of the influence gained over these fierce and predatory people by the " Missionary *Hakīm* " occurred in 1881, when Obeidullah Khan, with 11,000 Kurds, laid siege to Urmi.

Six months previously, at this Khan's request, Dr. Cochrane went up a three days' journey into the mountains, where he remained for ten days, during which time he cured the Khan of severe pneumonia, and made the acquaintance of several of the Kurdish chiefs. Before the siege began Obeidullah Khan sent for Dr. Cochrane, saying that he wished to know his residence and who his people were, so as to see that none of them suffered at the hands of his men. Not only this, but he asked for the names of the Christian villages on the plain, and gave the *Hakīm* letters with orders that nothing should be touched which belonged to them. The mission families were assembled at the College, and 500 Christians, with their cattle and horses, took refuge in the College grounds, which were close to the Kurdish lines. The siege lasted seven weeks, with great loss of life and many of " the horrors of war," as time increased the fury of both Kurds and Persians. But Obeidullah kept his word, and for the sake of the *Hakīm* and his healing art, not only was not a hair on the head of any missionary touched, but the mixed multitude within the gates and the herds were likewise spared.

Mrs. Cochrane, the widow of the former medical missionary, superintends the food and the nursing in the hospitals, and I doubt whether the most fanatical Kurd or Persian Moslem could remain indifferent to the charm of her bright and loving presence. The profession of Dr. Cochrane opens to him homes and hearts everywhere. All hold him as a friend and benefactor, and he has opportunities, denied to all others, of expounding the Christian faith among Moslems. A letter from him is a safe - conduct through some parts of the Kurdish mountains, and the mere mention of his name is a passport to the good-will of their fierce inhabitants.

The work of the mission is not confined to the city of Urmi. Among the villages of the plain there are eighty-four schools, taught chiefly in Syriac, seven of which are for girls only. The mission ladies itinerate largely, and are warmly welcomed by Moslem as well as Christian women, and even by those families of Kurds who, since their defeat in 1881, have settled down to peaceful pursuits, some of them even becoming Christians.

In fifty years the American missionaries have gained a very considerable and wide-spread influence, not only by labours which are recognised as disinterested, but by the purity and righteousness of their lives; and the increased friendliness and accessibility of the Moslems of Urmi give hope that the purer teachings of Christianity and the example of the life of our Lord are regarded by them with less of hostility or indifference than formerly.

The history of the mission is best given in the words of Dr. Shedd, one of its oldest members.[1]

[1] In twenty-eight years after its establishment a conference of bishops, presbyters, and deacons, all of whom had received ordination in the Old Church, with preachers, elders, and missionaries, met and deliberated. "This conference adopted its own confession, form of government, and discipline—at first very simple. Some things were taken from the canons and rituals of the Old Church, others from the usages of Protestant Churches. The traditions of the Old Church were respected to some extent ; for example, no influence has induced the native brethren to remit the diaconate to a mere service in temporalities. The deacons are a preaching order."

Of the subsequent history of this church the same authority writes as follows :—

"The missionaries in 1835 were welcomed by the ecclesiastics and people, and for many years an honest effort was made to reform the old body " (the Syrian Church) "without destroying its organisation. This effort failed, and a new church was gradually formed for the following reasons—

"(1) *Persecution.* The patriarch did all in his power to destroy the Evangelical work. He threatened, beat, and imprisoned the teachers and

The communicants of the "Evangelical Syriac Church," which might be termed, from its organisation and creed, the *Presbyterian Syriac Church*, numbered 216 in 1857 and 2003 in 1887.

converts, and made them leave his fold. (2) *Lack of discipline.* The converts could no longer accept unscriptural practices and rank abuses that prevailed, and it became evident that there was no method to reform them. At every effort the rent was made worse. (3) *Lack of teaching.* The converts asked for better care, and purer and better teaching and means of grace than they found in the dead language, rituals, and ordinances of the Old Church.

"The missionaries were slow in abandoning the hope that the Nestorian Church would become reformed and purified ; but their hope was in vain, their efforts therefore have been not to proselytise, but to leaven the whole people with Christian truth. The separation was made in no spirit of hostility or controversy. There was no violent disruption. The missionaries have never published a word against the Old Church ecclesiastics or its polity.

"The ordination of the Old Church has always been accepted as valid. The missionaries and the evangelical bishops have sometimes joined in the ordination services, and it would be difficult to draw the line when the Episcopal ordination ceased and the Presbyterian began in the Reformed body.

"The relation of the Presbyterian mission work to the old ecclesiastics is thus something different from that found among any other Eastern Christians. The Patriarch in office fifty years ago was at first very friendly to the missionaries, and personally aided in superintending the building of mission houses. Subsequently he did all in his power to break up the mission. The Patriarch now in office has taken the attitude of neutrality, with frequent indications of fairness and friendliness toward our work.

"The next in ecclesiastical rank is the Mattran (Syriac for Metropolitan), the only one left of the twenty-five Metropolitans named in the thirteenth century. The present incumbent recently made distinct overtures to our Evangelical Church to come to an understanding by establishing the scriptural basis of things essential, and allowing liberty in things non-essential. He fails, perhaps, to understand all the scriptural issues between us, but he has a sincere desire to walk uprightly and to benefit his people.

"Of the bishops, three have been united with the Reform, and died in the Evangelical Church. The three bishops in Kurdistan are friendly, and give their influence in favour of our schools.

"A large majority of the priests or presbyters of the Old Church, in Persia at least, joined the Reform movement, and as large a proportion of the deacons. In all, nearly seventy of the priests have laboured with the

Apart from the results of Christian teaching and example, there can be, I think, no doubt that the residence of righteous foreigners in Urmi for over half a century has had a most beneficial effect on the condition of the Nestorians. At the time when the first American missionaries settled in Urmi the yoke of Islam was hardly bearable. The Christians were oppressed and plundered, their daughters were taken by violence, and they were scarcely allowed to practise the little religion left to them. The Persian Government, sensitive as it is to European opinion, has gradually remedied a state of matters upon which the reports of the missionaries were justly to be dreaded, and at the present time the Christians of Urmi and the adjacent plain have comparatively very little to complain of.

At the same time the Syriac Church was at its lowest ebb, absolutely sunk in ignorance and superstition. It had no exposition of the Bible, and all worship was in the ancient Syriac tongue, then as now " not understanded of the people." It had no books or any ability to establish schools. Bibles were scarce, and a single copy of the Psalms could not be bought for less than 32s. The learned nuns and deaconesses of the early days were without successors. Women were entirely neglected, and it was regarded as improper for the younger among them to be seen at church. In Urmi not a woman could read, and in the whole Nestorian region they were absolutely illiterate, with the exception of the Patriarch's sister and two or three nuns.

mission as teachers, preachers, or pastors, and more than half of these continue, and are members of our Synod. In some places the Reform has gathered nearly all the population within its influence. In many places it is not unusual to find half the population in our winter services. On the other hand, there are many places where the ecclesiastics are immoral and opposed, and ignorance and vice abound, and the Reform moves very slowly."

The translation of the Bible into modern Syriac, a noble work, now undergoing revision; the College; the Female Seminary; the translation and publication of many luminous books; the circulation of a periodical called *Rays of Light*, together with fifty years of intercourse with men and women whose chief aim is the religious and intellectual elevation of the people among whom they dwell, have wrought a remarkable change, though that the change is menaced with perils, and is not an absolutely unmixed good, cannot be gainsaid.

It is for the future to decide whether the Reform movement in Umri or elsewhere could survive in any strength the removal of the agency which inaugurated it, and whether a Church without a ritual and with a form of government alien to the genius of the East and the traditions of the fathers, can take root in the affections of an eminently conservative people.

The Mission, founded by the present Archbishop of Canterbury at the request of the *Catholicos* of the East, Mar Shimun, the Patriarch of the Syrian Church, arrived in Urmi in the autumn of 1885. At the time of my visit it consisted of five mission priests, graduates of Oxford and Cambridge Universities, and an ordained Syrian, four of whom were at the headquarters in Urmi, one in the Kurdish mountains, and one on the Urmi Plain. Four Sisters of Bethany arrived in the spring of 1890 for the purpose of opening a boarding-school for girls and instructing the women.

It is hardly necessary to say that the lines on which the Anglican and American missions proceed are diametrically different, and the modes of working are necessarily in opposition. The one is *practically* a proselytising agency, and labours to build up a Presbyterian Church in Persia; the other purposes to "bring back an ancient church into the way of truth, and so prepare it for its union with its mother church, the Orthodox Church of the East." The objects of the latter and its ecclesiastical position are stated briefly in the note below.[1]

The actual work to be done by the Mission is thus summed up by its promoters : "The work of the Mission is in the first place to train up a body of literate clergy ; secondly, to instruct the youth generally in both religious and secular knowledge ; and thirdly, to print the very early liturgies and service-books, to which the Assyrians are much attached, which have never been published in the original, and of which the very primitive character is shown by their freedom from doubtful doctrine. The Mission in no way seeks to Anglicanise the Assyrians on the one hand, nor, on the other, to condone the heresy which separated them from the rest of Christendom or to minimise its importance."

The English clergy are celibates, receive no stipends, and live together, with a common purse, each receiving £25 per annum for personal expenses.

---

[1] "By God's help : (1) To raise up and restore a fallen Eastern Church to take her place again amongst the Churches of Christendom. (2) To infuse spiritual life into a church which the oppression of centuries has reduced to a state of weakness and ignorance. (3) To give the Chaldæan or Assyrian Christians (a) a religious education on the broad principles of the Holy Catholic and Apostolic Church ; (b) a secular education calculated to fit them for their state of life, the common mistakes and dangers of over-education and of Europeanising education being most carefully guarded against. (4) To train up the native clergy, by means of schools and seminaries, to be worthy to serve before God in their high vocation, and to rise to their responsibilities as leaders and teachers of the people in their villages. (5) To build schools, of which at present there are none, owing to the extreme poverty and misery of the people. (6) To aid the Patriarch and Bishops by counsel, by encouragement, and by active support. (7) To reorganise the Chaldæan Church upon her ancient lines, to set in motion the ecclesiastical machinery now rusty through disuse, and to revive religious discipline amongst clergy and laity. (8) To print the ancient Chaldæan service-books. They are now only in MS., and the number of copies is totally insufficient for the supply of the parish churches."

It is not a proselytising mission. It teaches, trains, and prints. It has one High School at Urmi for boys under seventeen, and two upon the Urmi Plain, but the work to which these may be regarded as subsidiary is the Urmi Upper School for priests, deacons, and candidates for holy orders. In these four establishments there are about 200 pupils, mostly boarders. There are also seventy-two village day-schools, and the total attendance last year was—boys 1248, girls 225. Seventy-six deacons and young men above seventeen are in the Upper School at Urmi.

The education given in the ordinary schools is on a level with that of our elementary schools. In the school of St. Mary and St. John, which contains priests, deacons, and laymen, some being mountaineers, the subjects taught are Holy Scripture, catechism, Scripture geography, universal history, liturgy, preaching, English, Persian, Osmanli Turkish, arithmetic, and Old Syriac.[1] Preaching is taught practically. A list of 100 subjects on a systematic theological plan has been drawn up, and each week two of the deacons choose topics from the list and write sermons upon them.

In 1887 the Mission clergy drew up a catechism containing between 200 and 300 questions, with "Scripture proofs," which the scholars in all their schools are obliged to learn by heart.

The boys of the Urmi High School and of the Upper School board in the mission house, and are under the constant supervision of the clergy. Their food and habits of living are strictly Oriental. All imitations of Western manners and customs are forbidden, the policy of the Mission being to make the Syrians take a pride in their national customs, which as a rule are adapted to their

---

[1] "*Old Syriac* as a lesson means reading portions of Holy Scripture, and translating them into modern Syriac."

circumstances and country, and to look down upon those who ape European dress and manners. Denationalisation is fought against in every possible way.

A year and a half ago work among women was begun by four ladies of the community of the Sisters of Bethany. The position of Syrian women, in spite of its partial elevation by means of the Fiske Seminary, is still very low, and within the Old Church there is an absolute necessity for raising it, and through it the tone of the home life and the training of children. These ladies have thirty boarders in their school between the ages of eight and sixteen, a previous knowledge of reading acquired in the village schools being a condition of admission. The daily lessons consist of Bible teaching, the catechism before referred to, ancient and modern Syriac, geography, arithmetic, and all ·branches of housework and needle-work. Due regard is paid to Syrian customs, and the picturesque Syrian costume is retained.

Since these ladies have acquired an elementary know-ledge of Syriac they have been itinerating in the Urmi villages, holding Bible classes, giving instruction, and dis-tributing medicines among the sick. The ignorance and superstition of the Christian women are almost past belief. One great difficulty which the " sisters " have to encounter arises from the early marriages of the girls, child-brides of eleven and twelve years old being quite common. It may reasonably be expected that the presence and influ-ence, the gentleness and self-sacrifice of these refined and cultured Christian ladies will tell most favourably upon their pupils, and strengthen with every month of their residence in Urmi. The Moslems understand and respect the position of voluntarily celibate women, and speak of them as " those who have left the world."

The Mission clergy of late have striven to instruct the adult Syrian population of the Urmi Plain by preaching among them systematically, explaining in a very elementary manner the principles of Christianity, and their application to the life of man. They have also set up a printing press, and have already printed in Syriac type a number of school books, the Catechism, the *Liturgy of the Apostles*, the most venerable of the Syrian Liturgical documents, the *Second* and *Third Liturgies*, the *Baptismal Office*, ancient and modern Syriac grammars, and a Lectionary.

It is the earnest hope of the promoters of this Mission that if this ancient Oriental church, once the first mission agency in the world, can be reformed and enlightened, she may yet be the means of evangelising the two great sects of Moslems by means of missionaries akin to them in customs, character, and habits of thought— " Orientals to Orientals."

The subject of Christian missions in Persia is a very interesting one, and many thoughtful minds are asking whether Christianity is likely to be a factor in the future of the Empire ? As things are, no direct efforts to convert Moslems to Christianity can be made, for the death penalty for apostasy is not legally abolished, and even if it were, popular fanaticism would vent itself upon proselytes. It must be recognised that the Christian missionary is a disturbing element in Persia. He is tolerated, not welcomed, and tolerated only while his efforts to detach people from the national faith are futile. Missions have been in operation in Persia for more than fifty years, and probably at the present time there are over seventy-five missionaries at work in the country. If the value of their work were to be judged of by the number of Moslem converts they have made it must be pronounced an *absolute failure*.

The result of the impossibility of making any direct attack upon Islam is that these excellent men and women are at present ostensibly engaged in the attempt to purify the faith and practice of the Syrian and Armenian churches, to enlighten their members religiously and intellectually, and to Christianise the Jews, waiting patiently for the time when an aggressive movement against Islam may be possible. In the meantime the Holy Scriptures are being widely disseminated; the preacher of Christianity itinerates among the villages, the Christian religion is greatly discussed, and missionary physicians, the true pioneers of the faith, are modifying by their personal influence the opposition to the progress of the missionaries with whom they are associated.

On the whole, and in spite of slow progress and the apparently insurmountable difficulties presented by hostility or indifference, I believe that Christian missions in Persia, especially by their educational agencies and the circulation of the Bible, are producing an increasing under-current, tending towards secular as well as religious progress, and are gaining an ever-growing influence, so that, lamentably slow as the advance of Christianity is, its prospects cannot justly be overlooked in considering the probable future of Persia.[1]

[1] The absolute fact, however, is that Christian nations have not shown any zeal in communicating the blessings of Christianity to Persia and Southern Turkey. England has sent two missions—one to Baghdad, the other to Julfa. America has five mission stations in Northern and Western Persia, but not one in Southern Turkey or Arabia.

The populous shores of the Persian Gulf, the great tribes of the plains of the Tigris and Euphrates, the Ilyats of Persia, the important cities of Shiraz, Yezd, Meshed, Kashan, Kûm, Kirmanshah, and all Southern, Eastern, and Western Persia (excepting Hamadan and Urmi), are untouched by Christian effort! Propagandism on a scale so contemptible impresses intelligent Moslems as a sham, and is an injury to the Christianity which it professes to represent.

LETTER XXVII

URMI, *Oct. 14.*

VERY few European travellers visit Urmi and its magnificent plain, the " Paradise of Persia," though it is only 112 miles from Tabriz.   Gardens come up to the city walls, and the plain, about fifty miles long by eighteen broad, is cultivated throughout, richly wooded, very populous, and bounded on the east not by a desert with its aridity, but by the blue waters of the Urmi Sea, and on the west by the magnificent mountains of Kurdistan.   The city is some miles to the west of the lake.

Urmi is on the whole very pretty and in good repair. The Christian quarter is almost handsome, well built and substantial, and the houses are generally faced with red bricks.   The bazars are large and well supplied, and trade is active.   The walls and gateways are in good repair, and so is the deep ditch, which can be filled with water, which surrounds them.   Every gate is approached by an avenue of noble *elægnus* and other fruit trees.   The gardens within the walls are very fine, and orchards and vineyards, planes and poplars testify to the abundance of water and the excellent method of its distribution. The altitude is stated at 4400 feet.   The estimate of the population varies from 12,000 to 20,000.

Though the Sea of Urmi receives fourteen rivers, some of them by no means insignificant, and has no known outlet, it recedes rather steadily, leaving bare a soil of exceeding richness, and acres of dazzling salt. It has very few boats, and none suited for passenger traffic. Its waters are so salt that fish cannot live in them.

The antiquarian interests of Urmi consist in the semi-subterranean Syrian church of Mart-Mariam, said to have been built by the Magi on their return from Bethlehem! a tower and mosque of Arab architecture seven centuries old, and some great mounds outside the walls, from sixty to one hundred feet in height, composed entirely of ashes, marking the site of the altars at which the rites of one of the purest of the ancient faiths were celebrated. As the birthplace of Zoroaster, and for several subsequent ages the sacred city of the Fire Worshippers and the scene of the restoration of the Mithraic rites, Urmi must always remain interesting.

The Christian population of the city is not very large, though it is estimated that there are 20,000 Syrian Christians in the villages of the plain. The city Syrians are mostly well-to-do people, who have come into Urmi to practise trades. The best carpenters, as well as the best photographers and tailors, are Syrians, and though in times past the Moslems refused to buy from the Christians on the ground that things made by them are unclean, the prejudice is passing away.

There is a deputy-governor called the *Serperast*, whose duty it is to deal with the Christians. The office seems to have been instituted for their protection at the instigation of the British Government, but the Europeans regard it simply as a means of oppression and extortion, and desire its abolition. Canon Maclean goes so far as to say, " The multiplication of judges in Persia means the multiplication of injustice, and of the number of persons who can extort money from the unfortunate people." The *Serperast* depends chiefly for his living and for keeping up a staff of servants on what he can get out of the Christians in the way of fines and bribes, and consequently he foments quarrels and encourages needless litigation on all hands, the Syrians being by all accounts one of the most litigious of peoples.

I write of the Christians of Urmi and its plain as Syrians because that is the name by which they call themselves. We know them at home as *Nestorians*, but this is a nickname given to them by outsiders, and I know of no reason why we should use a nomenclature which attaches to a nation the stigma of an ancient "heresy." They are sometimes called Chaldæans,[1] and the present Archbishop of Canterbury has brought into currency the term "Assyrians," which, however, is never used by themselves, or by any Orientals in speaking of them. The Moslems apply the name Nasara (Nazarenes) solely to the Syrian Christians. They claim that Christianity was introduced among them by the Magi on their return from Bethlehem. The highest estimate of their numbers is 120,000, and of these more than 80,000 are in Turkey. The Persian Syrians inhabit the flat country, chiefly the plains of Urmi and Salmas, where the fertile lands are most carefully cultivated by their industry.

In my last letter I remarked upon the prosperity and garden-like appearance of the Urmi Plain. Its 20,000 Syrian inhabitants usually live in separate villages from the Kurds, Persians, and Armenians, and are surrounded on all sides by Moslems of the Shiah sect. The landlords or Aghas of their villages are generally Moslems, who govern their tenants in something of feudal style. Land is a favourite investment in Persia, and owing to the industrious habits of the Syrians, the "Agha-ship" of their villages commands a high price. The Aghas often oppress the peasants, but the tenure of houses is fairly secure, and according to Canon Maclean, to whom I am indebted for

---

[1] A name usually applied to the Roman Uniats at Mosul.

my information, a system much like the Scotch feuing system (though without feu charters) is in force. If a man wishes to build a house he takes a present of a few sugar-loaves or a few *krans* with him, and applies to an Agha for a site. After it is granted he pays an annual ground rent of 4s. 9d., but he can build his house as he pleases, and it cannot be taken from him so long as he pays his ground rent. Moreover, he can sell the house and give a title-deed to the purchaser, with the sole restriction that the new possessor must become a vassal of the Agha.

In addition to the payment of the ground rent, the tenant is taxed annually by the Agha for every female buffalo 2s., for every cow 1s., and for every ewe and she-goat 6d., after they have begun to bear young. The Agha also receives from each householder annually two fowls, a load of *kiziks*, some eggs, three days' labour or the price of it, and a fee on every occasion of a marriage. Each house pays also a tax of 8d. a year and gives a present of firewood to the *Serperast* of Urmi, the Mussulman governor of the Christians. In his turn the Agha pays to the Shah from a third to a half of the total taxation.

A village house, even when built of sun-dried bricks, rarely costs more than £35, and often not the half of that sum.[1] The great feature of a Syrian dwelling is what is called emphatically "the house"; the combined living-room, bedroom, smoking-room, kitchen, bakery, and work-room of one or more families. This room cannot possess a *balakhana*, as its openings for light and air are in the roof. A stable, store-rooms, and granary are attached to it.

Vineyards are the chief reliance of the Syrians of the Urmi Plain, their produce, whether as grapes, raisins, or wine, being always marketable. They are held on the

[1] The mode of building mud houses was described in Letter VI. vol. i. p. 149.

same tenure as the houses, and as long as the vine-stocks
remain in the ground, and the ground rent, which is
7s. a year for the *tanap*, a piece of ground 256 yards
square, is paid, the tenant cannot be evicted. Where
vineyards are sub-let for a year a fair rent is from 10s.
to 12s. a *tanap*. If a tenant buys a property from an
Agha the yearly taxation is 5s. a *tanap*; grass fields and
orchards are held on the same tenure as vineyards, and
at the same rent. With ploughed land the case is
different. If the tenant provides the seed, etc., he gives
the Agha a third of the produce, and if the Agha provides
seed the tenant returns two-thirds. The tenant of
ploughed land may be changed annually.

This paying the rent in kind is going on just now in
every village, and the Aghas secure themselves against
dishonesty by requiring that the grain shall be threshed
on their floors. In addition, their servants watch night
and day by turns, in an erection similar to the " lodge in
a garden of cucumbers " or melons, an arbour of boughs
perched at a height of seven or eight feet upon four
poles. The landlord's *nasr* appears at intervals to take
away his master's share of the grain. It is all delightfully
primitive.

The arrangements sound equitable, the taxes are
moderate, and in some respects the Christians are not
more victimised by their landlords than are their Mohammedan neighbours. The people acknowledge readily
that as regards oppression they are much better off
than they were, and that in this respect the presence of
the American missionaries in Urmi has been of the
greatest advantage to them, for these gentlemen never
fail to represent any gross case of oppression *which can
be thoroughly substantiated* to the Governor of Urmi, or
in the last resort to the Governor of Azerbijan. The
oppressions exercised by the Aghas consist in taking extra

taxes, demanding labour without wages, and carrying off Christian girls for their *harams*. The laws which affect Christians specially and injuriously are—

1. That the evidence of a Christian is not received against a Mussulman.

2. That if any member of a Christian family becomes a Moslem, he or she becomes entitled to claim the whole property of the " house," which as often as not consists of two or three families. The apostatising member of a household is usually a girl, who either falls in love with or is carried off by a young Mohammedan, who declares truly or falsely that she has embraced his creed. A good governor is careful in these matters, and in some cases gives the girl only her share of the family property, but a bad governor may at any time carry out the law, or use it as a means for extorting ruinous bribes.[1]

Every Christian man above the age of sixteen pays a poll tax of 3s. annually for exemption from military service, but from this impost the headman of a village, who is at once its tax-gatherer and its spokesman, is

[1] Dr. Labaree, whose experience stretches back for thirty years, writes of the races under Persian rule in the Province of Azerbijan in the following terms: "The Nestorians and Armenians of Persia in common with their Mohammedan neighbours suffer from the evil forms of society and government which have been bequeathed to them from the earliest dawnings of history. Landlordism in its worst forms bears sway. The poor *rayat* or tenant must pay his landlord one-half or two-thirds of all the produce of his farm. Aside from his poll tax he must pay a tax on his house, his hayfields, and his fruit trees, and on all his stock with the exception of the oxen with which he tills the soil. But this is not all. He is virtually at the mercy of his Agha, which translated literally means master, a word which most correctly describes the relation of the landlord to his peasants. By law he may require from each of his *rayats* three days of labour without pay. In reality he makes them work for him as much as he sees fit. He helps himself to what he pleases whenever he makes them a visit. He sells them grain and flour above the market price. He ties them up and beats them for slight offences. And to all this and much else must the poor peasant submit for fear of worse persecutions if he complains. In these respects Moslem, Christian, and Jew suffer alike."

free. He ranks next to the priest, and is treated by the villagers with considerable respect. I have found the Syrian *kokhas* as polite and obliging as the Persian *ketchudas*.

Although the Persian Government has been tolerably successful in subduing the Kurds within its territory, the Christians of the slopes of the Urmi Plain are exposed to great losses of sheep and cattle from Kurdish mountaineers, who (it is said) cross the Turkish frontier, and return into Turkey with their booty.[1]

The American and English missionaries do not paint the Syrians *couleur de rose*, though the former during their long residence in the country must have lifted up several hundreds to the blessings of a higher life, and these in rising themselves must have exercised an unconscious influence on their brethren. Since I came I have seen several women whose tone would bear comparison with that of the best among ourselves, and who owe it gratefully to the training and influence of the Fiske Seminary. I like the women much better than the men.

The Christians complain terribly of the way in which "justice" is administered, and doubtless nothing can be worse, but the Europeans say that the people bring much of its hardship upon themselves by their frightful litigiousness, and their habit of going to law about the veriest trifles. Intense avarice seems to be a characteristic of the Syrians of the Persian plains, and they fully share with other Orientals in the failings of untruthfulness and untrustworthiness. They are said to be very drunken as well as grossly ignorant and superstitious, and the abuses and unutterable degradation of their church perpetuate all that is bad in the national

---

[1] Later, I heard the same accusation brought against the Persian Kurds by a high official in Constantinople.

character. The women are spoken of as chaste, and some of the worst forms of vice are happily unknown among the Syrians, though they are practised by the Moslems around them. Their hospitality, their sufferings for the faith, and their family attachment are justly to be reckoned among their virtues, but on the whole I think that the extraordinary interest attaching to them, and which I feel very strongly myself, is due rather to their Past than to their Present.

On this plain the dress of the men is much assimilated to that of the Persians, but the women wear their national costume. The under-garment is a coloured shirt, over which is worn a sleeved waistcoat of a different colour, and above this is an open-fronted coat reaching to the knees. Loose trousers, so full as to look like a petticoat, are worn, and frequently an apron and a heavy silver belt are added. The head-dress is very becoming, and consists of a raised cap of cloth or silk, embroidered or jewelled, with a white muslin veil over it and the head, but the face is exposed, except in the case of married women, who draw a part of the veil over the mouth. It is not proper that the hair should be seen.

There is something strikingly Biblical about their customs and speech. At dinner at Geog-tapa I noticed that it is a mark of friendship for a man to dip a piece of bread (a sop) into the soup and give it to another, a touching reminiscence. A priest is greeted with " Hail, Master," a teacher is addressed as " Rabban," the saluta-tation is " Peace be with you," and such words as *Talitha cumi* and *Ephphatha* occasionally startle the ear in the midst of unintelligible speech, suggesting that the Aramaic of our Lord's day was very near akin to the old Syriac, of which the present vernacular is a development. As among the Moslems, pious phrases are common. A Syrian receiving a kindness often replies, " May God give you

the kingdom of Heaven," and when a man makes a purchase, or enters on a new house, or puts on a new garment,
it is customary to say to him, "May God bless your
house, your garment," etc. A child learning the letters
of the alphabet is taught to say at the close, " Glory to
Christ our King." A copyist begins his manuscript by
writing within an ornamental margin, " In the strength
of our Lord Jesus Christ we begin to write," and a man
entering on a piece of work honours the Apostolic command by saying, " If the Lord will I shall accomplish it." [1]
My friends tell me that I shall find the Syrians of
the mountains a different people, and a mountaineer is
readily recognised in the streets by the beauty and
picturesqueness of his dress.

The eight days in Urmi have been a very pleasant
whirl, a continual going to and fro between the College
and the Fiske Seminary, the English clergy house and
the Sisters' house, receiving Syrian visitors at home and
holding a reception for them in the city, calling on
the Governor, visiting the English upper school, where
deacons, in the beautiful Syrian costume, with daggers
in their girdles, look more like bandits than theological
students, and spending a day at Geog-tapa, where I saw
Shamasha Khananeshoo's (Deacon Abraham's) orphanage,
dined with him and his charming wife, and a number
of other Syrians in Syrian style, and went to the
crowded Geog-tapa church, where the part of the floor
occupied by the women looked like a brilliant tulip-bed.
Here, in the middle of the service, the *Qasha* or priest
said that the people, especially the women, were very
anxious to know for what reason I was travelling, to
which evidence of an enlightened curiosity I returned a

---

[1] The national customs of the Syrians are endless, and in many ways
very interesting. They are treated very fully in a scarce volume called
Residence in Persia among the Nestorians, by Dr. Justin Perkins.

reply through an interpreter, and reminded them of the glories of their historic church and its missionary fervour.

Geog-tapa (*cerulean hill*) possesses one of the largest of the Zoroastrian mounds of ashes. It is a pity that these are not protected, and that the villagers are allowed to carry away the soil for manure, and to break up the walls and cells (?) which are imbedded in them for building materials. This vandalism has brought to notice various curious relics, such as earthenware vessels of small size and unique shape, and a stone tomb containing a human skeleton, with several copper spikes from four to five inches long driven into its skull. In another mound, at some distance from this one, a large earthen sarcophagus was discovered, also containing a skeleton with long nails driven into its skull.

Deacon Abraham's work is on the right lines, being conducted entirely by Syrians. It is most economically managed, and the children are trained in the simple habits of Syrian peasants. The religious instruction is bright and simple. The boys receive an elementary education, a practical training in agriculture on some lands belonging to the Orphanage, and in various useful handicrafts. As much of the money for the support of this work is raised in England, it is satisfactory to know that the accounts are carefully audited by the American missionaries.

The days have flown by, for, in addition to the social whirl, I have been occupied in attempts, only partially successful, to provide myself with necessaries for the journey, and in an endeavour, altogether unsuccessful, to replace Johannes by a trustworthy servant. The kind friends here have lent me a few winter garments out of their slender stock, and have helped me in every way.

It has been most difficult to get *charvadars*. The country on the other side of the frontier is said to be " unsettled," no Persians will go by the route that I wish to take, and two sets of Kurds, after making agreements to carry my loads, have disappeared. Various Syrians have come down from the mountains with stories of Kurdish raids on their sheep and cattle, but as such things are always going on, and the impression that " things are much worse than usual " does not rest on any ascertained basis, my friends do not advise me to give up the journey to Kochanes, and I am just starting *en route* for Trebizond.   I. L. B.

FAREWELL IMPRESSIONS OF PERSIA

In the letters by which this chapter is preceded few general opinions have been expressed on Persia, its government, and its people, but now that I contemplate them with some regard to perspective, and have reversed some of my earlier and hastier judgments, I will, with the reader's permission, give some of the impressions formed during a journey extending over nine months, chiefly in the western and south-western portions of the Empire.

On the pillared plain of Persepolis, on the bull-flanked portals which tower above the Hall of Xerxes, the Palace of Darius, and the stairways with the sculptured bas-reliefs, which portray the magnificence, the military triumphs, and the religious ceremonial of the greatest of the Persian monarchs, runs the stately inscription: " I am Xerxes the King, the Great King, the King of Kings, the King of the many-peopled countries, the Upholder of the Great World, the son of Darius the King, the Achæmenian " ; and on the tablets on the rock of Besitun is inscribed in language as august the claim of Darius the Mede to a dominion which in his day was regarded as nearly universal.

The twenty-four centuries which have passed since these claims were made have seen the ruin of the Palace-Temples of Persepolis, the triumph of Islam over Zoroastrianism, the devastating sweep of the hordes of Taimurlane and other semi-barbaric conquerors, the destruction of ancient art and frontiers, and the compression of the Empire within comparatively narrow limits.

Still, these limits include an area about thrice the size of France, the sovereign has reassumed the title of King of Kings, Persia takes her own place—and that not a low one—in the comity of nations, and the genuine Persians retain vitality enough to compel the allegiance of the numerically important tribes included within their frontiers, though scarcely more than 30,000 soldiers are with the colours at any given time.

Still, under a land system fourteen centuries old, Persia produces cereals enough for home consumption with a surplus for export; her peasants are thrifty and industrious, and their methods of tillage, though among the most ancient on earth, are well adapted to their present needs and the conditions of soil and climate.

Her merchants are able and enterprising, and her sagacious liberality in the toleration of Christians and Jews has added strength to her commercial position.

Though she has lost the high order of civilisation which she possessed centuries before Christ, she has in no sense relapsed into barbarism, and on the whole good order and security prevail.

The condition of modern Persia has to be studied along with that of the configuration of the country.   The traveller through Khorasan and Seistan, from the Gulf to Yezd, or from Bushire to Tihran, views it as a sparsely-peopled region—a desert with an occasional oasis, and legitimately describes it as such.   The traveller through the " Bakhtiari mountains," and from Burujird through Western Persia up to the Sea of Urmi, seeing the superb pasturages and perennial streams of the Zard-Kuh, the Sabz-Kuh, and the Kuh-i-Rang, and the vast area of careful cultivation, sprinkled with towns and villages, which extends from a few miles north of Burujird to the walls of Urmi and far beyond, may with equal fidelity describe it as a land of abounding waters, a peopled and well-watered garden.

The direction of my journey has been fully indicated. It is only from the descriptions of others that I know anything of the arid wastes of Eastern Persia or of the moist and malarious provinces bordering on the Caspian Sea, with their alluvial valleys and rice grounds, and their jungle and forest-covered mountains, or of the verdureless plains and steppes of Kerman and Laristan.

Persia proper, the country which has supplied the race which has evinced such a remarkable vitality and historic continuity, may be described as a vast plateau from 3500 to 6000 feet in altitude, extending on the east into Afghanistan, on the north-west into Armenia, and overlooking the Caspian to the north, and the Persian Gulf and the vast levels of Mesopotamia to the south and south-west.

To reach this platform from the south, lofty ranges, which include the *kotals* of Shiraz, must be crossed. From the Tigris valley on the west it is only accessible by surmounting the Zagros chain and lesser ranges ; and to attain it from the north the traveller must climb the rocky pathways of the Elburz mountains. This great " Iranian plateau," except in Eastern Persia, is intersected both by mountain ranges and detached mountain masses, which store up in their sunless hollows the snowfall on which all Persian agriculture depends, the rainfall being so scanty as to be of little practical value.

Thus the possibility of obtaining supplies of water from the melting snows dictates the drift of population, and it seems unlikely that the plains of Eastern Persia, where no such supplies exist, were ever more populous than now. It was otherwise with parts of Central Persia, now lying waste, for the remains of canals and *kanaats* attest that a process of local depopulation has been going on. It is the configuration of the country rather than anything else which accounts for the unpeopled wastes in some directions, and the constant succession of towns and populous villages in others.

Of the population thus distributed along hill slopes and on the plains at the feet of the ranges, there is no accurate record, and the total has been variously estimated at from six to nine millions. Estimates of the urban and village populations were in most cases supplied to me by the Persian local officials, but from these I am convinced that it is necessary to make a very liberal deduction. General Schindler, a gentleman for some years in the Persian Government service, who has travelled over a great part of Persia with the view of ascertaining its resources and condition, in the year 1885 estimated its population at 7,653,000. In his analysis the Christian and the Bakhtiari and Feili Lur populations are, according to present information, greatly under-estimated.

If I may venture to hazard an opinion, after travelling over a considerable area of Western Persia, it would be that the higher estimate is nearest the mark, for the natural increase in time of peace, as accepted by statists, is three-quarters per cent per annum, and Persia has had peace and freedom from famine for very many years.[1]

The country population consists of *rayats* or permanent cultivators, and Ilyats or nomadic pastoral tribes. Coal - fields and lead and iron may hereafter produce commercial centres, but the industry of Persia at present may be said to be nearly altogether agricultural.

[1] On this subject there can be no better authority than the Hon. George N. Curzon, M.P., who after careful study has estimated the total population of Persia at over nine millions.

The settled peasant population, so far as I am able to judge, is well fed and fairly well clothed, and the habitations suit the climate. The people are poor, but not with the poverty of Europe—that is, except in famine years, there is no scarcity of the necessaries of life, with the single exception of fuel.

The wages of the agricultural labourer vary from 5d. a day with food to 9d. without; a skilled mason earns 1s. 6d., a carpenter 1s. 4d. Men-servants get from 17s. to £2 per month, nominally without board, but with *modakel* and other pickings; female servants much less. Prices are, however, low. Clothing, tea, coffee, and sugar cost about the same as in Europe. The cotton worn by the poor is very cheap. Wheat, which is sold by weight, costs at harvest-time from 7s. 6d. to 15s. per load of 320 lbs. I have been told by several cultivators that a man can live and bring up an average family on something under £6 a year.

I did not see anything like "grinding poverty" in the villages. If it existed, the old and helpless could scarcely be supported by their relatives, and the women, in spite of the seclusion of custom and faith, would be compelled to work in the fields, a "barbarism" which I never saw in Persia among Moslems.

In both town and country the working classes appeared to me to be as comfortable and, on the whole, as happy as people in the same condition in life in most other countries, with the exception, and that not a small one, of their liability to official exactions. The peasants are grossly ignorant, hardy, dirty, bigoted, domestic, industrious, avaricious, sober, and tractable, and ages of misrule have developed in them many of the faults of oppressed Oriental peoples. Of the country outside of the district in which they live they usually know nothing, they detest the local governors, but to the

Shah they willingly owe, and are ready to pay, a right loyal allegiance.

My impression of the Persians of the trading and agricultural classes is that they are thoroughly unwarlike, fairly satisfied if they are let alone, unpatriotic, and apparently indifferent to the prospect of a Russian " occupation." Their bearing is independent rather than manly; their religious feelings are strong and easily offended; their sociability and love of fun come out strongly in the freedom of their bazars. Europeans do not meet with anything of the grovelling deference to which we are accustomed in India. If there be obsequiousness in stereotyped phraseology, there is none in manner. We are treated courteously as strangers, but are made to feel that we are in no wise essential to the well-being of the country, and a European traveller without introductions to the Provincial authorities finds himself a very insignificant person indeed.

Governors and the governed are one. They understand each other, and are of one creed, and there is no ruling alien race to interfere with ancient custom or freedom of action, or to wound racial susceptibilities with every touch. Even the traditional infamies of administration are expected and understood by those whom they chiefly concern.

The rich men congregate chiefly in the cities. It is very rare to find any but the poorer Khans, Aghas or proprietors of villages, men little removed from the peasants around them, living on their own properties. The wealthy *Seigneur*, the lord of many villages, resides in Tihran, Kirmanshah, or Isfahan; pays a *nasr*, who manages his estate and fleeces his tenants, and spends his revenues himself on urban pleasures. The purchase of villages and their surrounding lands is a favourite investment. This system of absenteeism not only prevents that friendly contact between landowner and peasant which is such a desirable feature of proprietorship, but it leaves the villages exposed to the exactions of the *nasr*, and without a semblance of protection from the rapacious demands of the provincial authorities. It is noteworthy that fortunes made in trade are seeking investment in land.

The upper classes in Persia appear to me to differ widely from Orientals, as they are supposed to be, and often really are. They love life intensely, fill it with enjoyment, and neither regard existence as a task to be toiled through nor as a burden to be got rid of. Handsome, robust, restless, intelligent, imaginative, accumulative, vivacious, polished in manner and speech, many of them excellent linguists, well acquainted with their own literature, especially with their poets; lavish, alike in expenditure on personal luxuries and in charity to the poor; full of artistic instincts, and loving to surround themselves with the beautiful; inquisitive, adaptable; addicted to sport and out-of-doors life, untruthful both from hereditary suspiciousness and excess of courtesy—the Persian gentleman has an individuality of his own which is more nearly akin to the French or Russian than to the Oriental type.

My impressions of the morals both of the Persian peasantry and the Bakhtiari Lurs are, as to some points, rather favourable than the reverse, and I think and hope that there is as much domestic affection and fidelity as is compatible with a religion which more or less effectually secures the degradation of woman. The morals of the upper classes are, I believe, very easy. In various carefully written papers, one of them at least official, very painful glimpses have been given incidentally into the state of Persian upper-class morality, and undoubtedly the intrigues of the *andarun* are as unfavourable to purity as they are to happiness.

For the traveller the greater part of Persian territory is absolutely safe. I have ridden on horseback through it at every season of the year, in some regions without an escort, in others with Persian or Kurdish guards supplied by the local authorities, and was never actually the victim of any form of robbery, except the pilfering from an unguarded tent. Though travelling with only an Indian servant, I found the provincial authorities everywhere courteous, and ready to aid my journey by every means within their power, though in Persia as elsewhere I never claimed, and indeed never received, any special favour on the ground of sex.

A few darker shadows remain to be put in. There is no education truly so called for Persians, except in Tihran, and under the existing system the next generation is not likely to be more enlightened than the present. · All the towns and the larger villages possess mosque schools, in which the highest education bestowed is a smattering of Arabic and a knowledge of the tales of *Saadi*. The Persian characters are taught, and some attention is paid to caligraphy, for a man who can write well is sure to make a fair living. The parrot-like reading of the Koran in Arabic is the *summum bonum* of the teaching. Very few of the boys in the village schools learn to write, but if a clever lad aspires to be a *mirza* or secretary· he pays great attention to the formation of the Persian characters, and acquires that knowledge of compliment, phrase, and trope which is essential to his proposed calling.

Reading, writing, and the elements of arithmetic are usual among the bazar class and merchants, but with the rest the slight knowledge of reading acquired in childhood is soon forgotten, and the ability to repeat a few verses from the Koran and a few prayers in Arabic is all that remains of the mosque school " education."

School discipline is severe, and the rope and pulley and bastinado are used as instruments of punishment.

A few young men in the cities, who are destined to be *mollahs*, *hakīms*, or lawyers, proceed to the *Medressehs* or Colleges, where they acquire a thorough knowledge of Arabic, do some desultory reading, and "hang on" to their teachers, at whose feet they literally sit on all occasions, and after a few years have been spent in rather a profitless way they usually find employment.

Government *employés*, courtiers, the higher officers in the army, diplomats, and sons of wealthy Khans receive the rudiments of a liberal education in the College at Tihran, where they frequently acquire a very creditable knowledge of French.

The admirable schools established by the American and English missionaries at Urmi, Tihran, Tabriz, Hamadan, and Julfa affect only the Armenians and Syrians and a few Jews and Zoroastrians. Outside of these there is neither intellectual nor moral training, and even the simplest duties of life, such as honesty, truthfulness, and regard for contract, are never inculcated.

It may be supposed that in conformity with the Moslem axiom, "not to open the eyes of a woman too wide," the bulk of Persian women are not thought worthy of any education at all. A few of the daughters of rich men can read the Koran, but without comprehending it, and can both read and recite poetry.

Throughout the country, law, that is the *Urf* or unwritten law, a mass of precedents and traditions orally handed down and administered by secular judges—is not held in any respect at all, and while the rich can override it by bribery, the poor regard it only as a commodity which is bought and sold, and which they are too poor to buy.

The other department of Persian law, the *Shāhr*,

which is based upon the Koran, and is administered by
religious teachers, takes cognisance chiefly of civil cases,
and its administration is nearly as corrupt as that of the
Urf. Law, in the sense in which we understand it, as the
avenger of wrong and the sublimely impartial protector
of individual rights and liberties, has no existence at all
in Persia.

The curse of the country is venal mal-administration.
It meets one at every turn, and in protean shapes.
There is no official conscience, and no public opinion
to act as a check upon official unscrupulousness. Of
Government as an institution for the good of the
governed there is no conception. The greed, which is
among the most painful features of Persian character,
finds its apotheosis in officialism. From the lowest to
the highest rounds of the official ladder unblushing
bribery is the *modus operandi* of promotion.

It is very obvious that the Shah himself is the
Government. He is an absolute despot, subject to no
controlling influences but the criticisms of the European
press, and the demands of the European Legations. He
is the sole executive. His ministers are but servants of
the highest grade, whose duties consist in carrying out
his orders. The lives and properties of all his subjects
are held only at his pleasure. His sons are but his tools,
to be raised or degraded at his will, and the same may
be said of the highest personages in the Empire. The
Shah is the State,—irresponsible and all-powerful.

Nasr-ed-Din is a most diligent ruler. No pleasures,
not even the chase, to which he is devoted, divert his
attention from business. He takes the initiative in
all policy, guides with a firm hand the destinies of
Persia, supervises every department, appoints directly to
all offices of importance, and by means known to absolute
rulers has his eyes in every part of his dominions. He

is regarded as a very able man,—his European travels have made him to some extent an enlightened one.

His reign of forty-two years has been disfigured, especially in its earlier portion, by some acts which we should regard as great crimes, but which do not count as such in Oriental judgment; neither are the sale of offices, the taking of bribes under the disguise of presents, the receiving of what is practically *modakel*, or exactions upon rich men, repugnant in the slightest degree to the Oriental mind.

Remembering the unwholesome traditions of his throne and dynasty, we must give him full credit for everything in which he makes a new departure. Surrounded by intrigue, hampered by the unceasing political rivalry between England and Russia, thwarted by the obstructive tactics of the latter at every turn, and with the shadow of a Russian occupation of the northern provinces of the Empire looming in a not far distant future, any step in the direction of reform taken by the Shah involves difficulties of which the outer world has no conception, not only in braving the antagonism of his powerful neighbour, and her attempted interference with the internal concerns of Persia, but in overcoming the apathy of his people and the prejudices of his co-religionists.

As it is, under him Persia has awakened partially from her long sleep. The state of insecurity described by the travellers of thirty and forty years ago no longer exists. Far feebler than Turkey, Persia, through the resolute will of one man, has eclipsed Turkey altogether in suppressing brigandage, in subduing the Kurds and other nomadic tribes, in securing safety for travellers and caravans even on the remoter roads, and in producing tolerable contentment among the Armenian and Nestorian populations.

Under him the authority of the central Government

has been consolidated, the empty treasury has been filled, the semi-independence of the provincial governors has been broken, Persia has been re-created as a coherent Empire, certain roads have been made, posts and telegraphs have been inaugurated, an Imperial Bank with branches in some of the principal towns has been formed, foreign capital has been encouraged or at least permitted to enter the country, a concession for the free navigation of the Karun has been granted, and the *Nasiri* Company, the most hopeful token of native progress, has received Imperial favour.

But under all this lies the inherent rottenness of Persian administration, an abyss of official corruption and infamy without a bottom or a shore, a corruption of heredity and tradition, unchecked by public opinion or the teachings of even an elementary education in morals and the rudiments of justice. There are few men pure enough to judge their fellows or to lift clean hands to Heaven, and power and place are valued for their opportunities for plunder.

In no part of Persia did I hear any complaint of the tribute levied by the Shah. It is regarded as legitimate. But in most districts allegations concerning the rapacity and exactions of the provincial governors were universal, and there is unfortunately great reason for believing them well founded. The farming of the taxes, the practical purchase of appointments, the gigantic system of bribery by which all offices are obtained, the absence of administrative training and supervision, the traditions of office, and the absolute dependence of every official on the pleasure of a Sovereign surrounded by the intrigues of an Oriental court, are conditions sufficient to destroy the virtue of all but the best of men.

Where all appointments are obtained practically by bribery, and no one has any security in the tenure of an office of which slander, bribery, or intrigue at Court may at any moment deprive him, it is natural that the most coveted positions should be those in which the largest perquisites can be made, and that their occupants should feel it their bounden duty to "make hay while the sun shines,"—in other words, to squeeze the people so long as there is anything left to squeeze. The great drawback of the Persian peasant's life is that he has no security for the earnings of labour. He is the ultimate sponge to be sucked dry by all above him. Every official squeezes the man below him, and the highest is squeezed by the Crown.

Little, if any, of the revenue drawn from the country is spent on works of public utility, and roads, bridges, official buildings, fortifications, and all else are allowed to fall into disrepair. In downright English the administration of government and law is execrable, and there can be little hope of a resurrection for Persia until the system under which she is impoverished be reformed or swept away.

But who is to cleanse this Augean stable? Who will introduce the elementary principles of justice? Are tools of the right temper to work with to be found among the men of this generation? Is the dwarfing and narrowing creed [1] of Islam to be replaced or in any way to be

---

[1] In *The Caliphate, its Rise, Decline, and Fall*, a valuable recent work, its author, Sir W. Muir, K.C.S.I., dwells very strongly on the narrowing influence of Islam on national life, and concludes his review of it in the following words : "As regards the spiritual, social, and dogmatic aspect of Islam, there has been neither progress nor material change. Such as we found it in the days of the Caliphate, such is it also at the present day. Christian nations may advance in civilisation, freedom, and morality, in philosophy, science, and the arts, but Islam stands still. And thus stationary, so far as the lessons of its history avail, it will remain." In a chapter at the end of his book he deals with polygamy, servile concubinage, temporary marriages, and the law of divorce, as cankering the domestic life of Mohammedan countries, and *infallibly neutralising all civilising influences.*

modified by Christianity? It looks very much as if the men to initiate and carry out administrative and financial reforms are not forthcoming, and that, unless the Shah is willing to import or borrow them, the present system of official corruption, mendacity, bribery, and obstruction may continue to prevail.

The inherent weakness of Persia lies in her administrative system rather than in her sparse population and paucity of fuel and water, a paucity arising partly out of misgovernment. In the felt evils of this system, and in the idea that law, equitable taxation, and security for the earnings of labour are distinctively European blessings, lies a part of the strength of Russia in Persia. I have elsewhere remarked upon the indifference with which Russian annexation is contemplated. A reformed system of administration, by giving the Persian people something to live for and die for, would doubtless evoke the dormant spirit of patriotism, and render foreign conquest, or acquisition without conquest, a less easy task.

After living for ten months among the Persian people, and fully recognising their faults, I should regret to see them absorbed by the "White Czar" or any other power. A country which for more than 2000 years has maintained an independent existence, and which possesses customs, a language, a civilisation, and a nationality of its own, and works no injury to its neighbours, has certainly a *raison d'être*.

My early impressions of Persia were of effeteness and ruin, but as I learned to know more of the vitality, energy, and industry of her people, and of the capacities of her prolific soil, I have come to regard her resurrection under certain circumstances as a possibility, and cordially to echo the wish eloquently expressed by the Marquis of Salisbury on the occasion of the Shah's last visit to England: "We desire above all things that

Persia shall not only be prosperous, but be strong,—strong in her resources, strong in her preparations, strong in her alliances,—in order that she may pursue the peaceful path on which she has entered in security and tranquillity."   I. L. B.

LETTER XXVIII

KOCHANES, *Oct. 23*.

THE Kurdish *katirgis* turned out very badly.   They came at twelve instead of eight, compelling me to do only a half-day's march.   Then they brought six horses instead of the four which had been bargained for, and said they would " throw down the loads " if I did not take them. Each night they insisted on starting the next morning at daybreak, but no persuasions could get them off before eight.   They said they could not travel with a Christian except in broad daylight.   They would only drive a mile an hour, and instead of adhering to their contract to bring me here in four days, took four to come half-way.   On the slightest remonstrance they were insolent and violent, and threatened to " throw down the loads " in the most inconvenient places, and they eventually became so mutinous that I was obliged to dismiss them at the half-way halt at the risk of not getting transport any farther.[1]

The " throw on the road " from Urmi was a very large one, and consisted of nearly all the English and American Mission clergy and two Syrians, all on screaming, biting, kicking horses.   It was a charming ride through fruitful country among pleasant villages to Anhar.   The wind was strong and bracing.   Clouds were drifting grandly

---

[1] I have since heard that these Kurds, a short time afterwards, betrayed some Christian travellers into the hands of some of their own people, by whom they were robbed and brutally maltreated.

over the splendid mountains to the west, the ranges to the north were glorified by rich blue colouring, purple in the shadows ; among mountains on the east the Urmi sea showed itself as a turquoise streak, and among gardens and vineyards in the middle distance rose Zoroastrian cones of ashes, and the great mound, which tradition honours as the scene of the martyrdom of St. George.

When all my kind friends left me, and I walked alone in the frosty twilight on the roof of my comfortable room in the *Qasha's* house, and looked towards the wall of the frontier mountains through which my journey lay, I felt an unwonted feeling of elation at the prospect before me, which no possible perils from Kurds, or from the sudden setting-in of winter could damp, and thus far the interest is much greater even than I expected.

The next morning I was joined by *Qasha*——, a Syrian priest, a man of great learning and intelligence, a Turkish subject and landed proprietor, who knows everybody in this region, and speaks English well. He is fearfully anxious and timid, partly from a dread of being robbed of his splendid saddle mule, and partly from having the responsibility of escorting an English lady on a journey which has turned out full of peril.

On the long ascent from Anhar a bitter wintry wind prevailed, sweeping over the tattered thistles and the pale belated campanulas which alone remain of the summer flora, but the view from the summit was one of rare beauty. The grandly drifting clouds of the night before had done their work, and had draped the Kurdish mountains half-way down with the first snows of winter, while the valley at their feet, in which Merwana lies, was a smiling autumn scene of flowery pasturage and busy harvest operations under the magic of an atmosphere of living blue.

Merwana is a village of 100 houses, chiefly Christian,

though it has a Kurdish *ketchuda*. It is a rich village,
or was, being both pastoral and agricultural. The
slopes are cultivated up to a great height, and ox sleds
bring the sheaves to the threshing-floor. The grain is
kept in great clay-lined holes under ground, covered with
straw and earth. I write that the village *was* rich.
Lately a cloud of·Kurds armed with rifles swooped down
upon it towards evening, drove off 900 sheep, and killed
a man and woman. The villagers appealed to Government, after which Hesso, a redoubtable Kurdish chief in
its pay, went up with a band of men to Marbishu, a
Christian village in Turkey, drove off 1460 sheep, and
offered to repay Merwana with the stolen property. As
matters now stand 700 of the poorest of the sheep have
been restored to Marbishu, Merwana loses all, and Hesso
and his six robber brothers have gained 760. The sole
hope of the plundered people of both villages is in the
intercession of Dr. Cochrane with the Governor of
Azerbijan.[1]

As I reached Merwana at 10 A.M., and the *katirgis*,
after raging for an hour, refused to proceed, I took Mirza
and *Qasha* Bardah, the priest under whose hospitable roof
I lodged, with me, and went up the valley to Ombar,
the abode of Hesso, with the vague hope of "doing something" for the poor people. The path lay among bright
streams and flowery pastures, the sun was warm, the air
sharp, the mountains uplifted their sunlit snows into a
heaven of delicious blue, the ride was charming. Hesso's
village, consisting of a few very low rough stone houses,
overshadowed by great cones of *kiziks*, is well situated on
a slope above a torrent issuing from a magnificent cleft
in the mountain wall, at the mouth of which is a square
keep on a rock.

---

[1] I give the story as it was repeatedly told to me. It was a very shady
and complicated transaction throughout.

Hesso's house is just a "but and a ben," with a door which involves stooping. Its rough stone walls are unplastered, and the only light admitted comes from a hole in the roof, which serves to let out the smoke. I confess

HESSO KHAN.

to a feeling of trepidation when I asked to see the Kurdish chief, and I felt the folly of my errand. A superbly-dressed Kurd took us into a room dense with tobacco smoke, which, from its darkness, the roughness of its walls, and the lowness of its rude roof, resembled a

cave rather than a house.   Yet Hesso receives £200 a
year from the Persian Government, and has apparently
unlimited opportunities for plunder.

There were some coarse mats on the floor, and a
samovar with some Russian glass tea-cups.   Two Persian
officials and a number of well-armed and splendidly-
dressed Kurds, with jewelled *khanjars* and revolvers in
their girdles and rifles by their sides, sat or reclined
against the wall.   Hesso himself leaned against a roll of
bedding at the upper end of the room, and space was
made for us on the floor at his left hand.   A superb
stage brigand he looked, in fitting surroundings, the
handsomest man I have seen in Persia, a large man,
with a large face, dark prominent eyes, a broad brow, a
straight nose, superb teeth, a fine but sensual mouth, a
dark olive complexion, and a false smile.   A jewelled
Kurdish turban with much crimson, a short jacket and
full trousers of a fine cream-coloured woollen fabric, an
embroidered silk shirt, socks of an elaborate pattern, a
girdle of many yards of Kashmir stuff, with eight knots,
one above another, in the middle, and a *khelat* or coat of
honour of rich Kerman brocade formed his striking
costume.   In his girdle he wore a *khanjar*, with an ebony
hilt and scabbard ornamented with filigree gold knobs
incrusted with turquoises, attached to the girdle by a
silver chain two yards long, of heavy filigree balls, a
beautiful piece of work.   Hesso's brothers, superb men,
most picturesquely dressed, surrounded him.   The Kurds
who handed round the tea and the jewelled *kalians* looked
fantastic brigands.   The scene was a picture.

Of course my errand failed.   I could not speak about
the sheep through the priest of the robbed village, and
Hesso said that he could not speak on any " political "
subject before the Persians who were present.   The
conversation was not animated, and *Qasha* Bardah was

very nervous till Hesso turned round, and with an
awakened expression of face asked how it was that
"England had allowed Turkey to grow so feeble that her
frontier and Armenia are in a state of anarchy"? Hesso's
handsome face is that of a villain. He does not look
more than thirty. He has 200 well-mounted marksmen
at his disposal. The father of this redoubtable Kurdish
chief died in prison, where he was confined by order of the
Shah, and the son revenged himself by harrying this part
of the Shah's dominions, and with sixty men, including his
six brothers, successfully resisted a large Persian force
sent against him, and eventually escaped into Turkey,
doing much damage on his way. Hesso on arriving in
Kerbela obtained a letter from the Sheikh, or chief *Mollah*
there, saying that he offered his submission to the Shah,
and went to Tihran, where after seeing the Shah's
splendour he said that if he had known it before, he
would not have been in rebellion.

Before this the Persians took a strong castle from the
Kurds, and garrisoned it with an officer and a company
of soldiers. Up to it one day went Hesso boldly, keeping
the six men who went with him out of sight, and
thumped upon the gate till it was opened, saying he was
a bearer of despatches. He first shot the sentry dead,
and next the officer, who came to see what the disturbance was about. Meantime the six men, by climbing on
each other's shoulders, scaled the castle wall, and by confused shouts and dragging of the stone roller to and fro
over the roof they made the garrison believe that it was
attacked by a large force, and it surrendered at discretion.
The lives of the soldiers were spared, but they were marched
out in their shirts, with their hands above their heads.

The Merwana threshing-floor was guarded at night
by ten men. The following morning we were to have
started an hour before daylight, but the *katirgis* refused

to load, and the Kurdish *ketchuda*, with his horsemen, declined to start till an hour after sunrise, because he could not earlier "tell friends from foes." The ground was covered with hoar-frost, and the feathery foliage of the tamarisk was like the finest white coral.

Turning into the mountains, we spent nine hours in a grand defile, much wooded, where a difficult path is shut in with the Marbishu torrent. The Kurds left us at Bani, when two fine fellows became our protectors as far as a small stream, crossing which we entered Turkey. At a Kurdish semi-subterranean village, over which one might ride without knowing it, a splendidly-dressed young Khan emerged from one of the burrows, and said he would give us guards, but they would not go farther than a certain village, where two of his men had been killed three days before. "There is blood between us and them," he said. After that, for five hours up to Marbishu, the scenery is glorious. The valley narrows into a picturesque gorge between precipitous mountains, from 2000 to 4000 feet above the river, on the sides of which a narrow and occasionally scaffolded path is carried, not always passable for laden mules. Many grand ravines came down upon this gorge, their dwarf trees, orange, tawny, and canary-yellow, mingled with rose-red leafage. The rose bushes are covered with masses of large carnation-red hips, the bramble trailers are crimson and gold, the tamarisk is lemon-yellow. Nature, like the dolphin, is most beautiful in dying.

The depths were filled with a blue gloom, the needle-like peaks which tower above glittered with new-fallen snow, the air was fresh and intoxicating—it was the romance of travel. But it soon became apparent that we were among stern and even perilous realities. A notorious robber chief was disposed to bar our passage. His men had just robbed a party of travellers, and were spread over the hill. They took a horse from Johannes, but afterwards restored it on certain conditions. Farther on we met a number of Kurds, with thirty fat sheep and some cattle, which they were driving off from Marbishu. Then the *katirgis* said that they would go no farther than the village, for they heard that robbers were lying in wait for us farther on!

In the wildest part of the gorge, where two ravines meet, there is fine stoneless soil, tilled like a garden; the mountains fall a little apart—there are walnuts, fruit trees, and poplars; again the valley narrows, the path just hangs on the hillside, and I was riding over the roofs of village houses for some time before I knew it. The hills again opened, and there were flourishing breadths of turnips, and people digging potatoes, an article of food and export which was introduced by the missionaries forty years ago. The glen narrowed again, and we came upon the principal part of Marbishu—rude stone houses in tiers, burrowing deeply into the hills, with rock above and rock below on the precipitous sides of a noisy torrent, crossed by two picturesque log bridges, one of the wildest situations I have ever seen, and with a wintry chill about it, for the sun at this season deserts it at three. Rude, primitive, colourless, its dwellings like the poorest cow-sheds, its church like a Canadian ice-house, clinging to mountain sides and spires of rock, so long as I remember anything I shall remember Marbishu.

Steep narrow paths and steep rude steps brought us to a three-sided yard, with a rough verandah where cooking and other operations were going on, and at the entrance we were cordially welcomed by *Qasha* Ishai, the priest. After ascertaining that it would be very dangerous to go farther, I crossed the river to the church, which is one of the finest in the country, and a place of pilgrimage. The village is noted for its religious faith-

fulness. The church is said to be 850 years old—a
low, flat-roofed, windowless stone building. Either it
was always partially subterranean, or the earth has
accumulated round it, for the floor is three feet below
the ground outside. The entrance is by a heavy door
two feet six inches high. Inside it is as nearly dark as
possible. Two or three circular holes at a great height
in the enormously thick wall let in as many glimmers,
but artificial light is necessary. There are several small
ante-chapels. In two are rude and ancient tombs of
ancient bishops, plain blocks of stone, with crosses upon
them. In another is a rough desk, covered with candle
droppings, on which the *Liturgy of the Apostles* lay
open, and on it a cross, which it is the custom to kiss.
A fourth is used for the safe keeping of agricultural implements. Two are empty, and one of these serves the
useful purpose of a mortuary chapel. The church proper
is very small and high. The stone floor has been worn into
cavities by the feet of worshippers ; the walls, where not
covered with lengths of grimy printed cotton, are black
with the candle smoke of ages. The one sign of sacred
use is a rude stone screen at the east end, at openings
in the front of which the people receive the Eucharist.
Behind this is the sanctuary, into which the priest alone,
and he fasting, may enter. Old brass lamps and candelabra, incrusted with blackened tallow, hang from the
roof, and strings of little bells from wall to wall, which
are plucked by each recipient of the sacred elements as
he returns to his " stand."

In this gloomy vault-like building prayers are said, as
in all Nestorian churches, at sunrise and sunset by the
priest in his ordinary clothing, the villagers being summoned by the beating of a mallet on a board.[1]

[1] Dr. Cutts, in his interesting volume, *Christians Under the Crescent in
Asia*, gives the following translation of one of the morning praises, which

The church is a place of refuge when a Kurdish attack is expected. Nine years ago the people carried into it all their movables that they valued most, believing it to be secure, but the Kurds broke in in force and took all they wanted. The few sacred treasures of the village and the Eucharistic leaven are hidden in an elevated recess in the wall. The graveyard, which contains only a few flat slabs imbedded in the soil, is the only possible camping-ground; but though it is clean and neat, it looked so damp and felt so cold that I preferred to accept a big room with walls six feet thick in the priest's house, even though it overhangs the torrent with its thunder and clash.

forms part of the daily prayer. The earlier portion is chanted antiphonally in semi-choirs—

"*Semi-choir*—1*st.* At the dawn of day we praise Thee, O Lord : Thou art the Redeemer of all creatures, give us by Thy mercy a peaceful day, and give us remission of our sins.

"2*d.* Cut not off our hope, shut not Thy door against our faces, and cease not Thy care over us. O God, according to our worthiness reward us not. Thou alone knowest our weakness.

"1*st.* Scatter, O Lord, in the world love, peace, and unity. Raise up righteous kings, priests, and judges. Give peace to the nations, heal the sick, keep the whole, and forgive the sins of all men.

"2*d.* In the way that we are going may Thy Grace keep us, O Lord, as it kept the child David from Saul. Give us Thy mercy as we are pressing on, that we may attain to peace according to Thy will. The Grace which kept the prophet Moses in the sea, and Daniel in the pit, and by which the companions of Ananias were kept in the fire, by that Grace deliver us from evil.

" *Whole choir.*—In the morning we all arise, we all worship the Father, we praise the Son, we acknowledge the Holy Spirit. The grace of the Father, the mercy of the Son, and the hovering of the Holy Spirit, the Third Person, be our help every day. Our help is in Thee. In Thee, our true Physician, is our hope. Put the medicine of Thy mercy on our wounds, and bind up our bruises that we be not lost. Without Thy help we are powerless to keep Thy commandments. O Christ, who helpest those who fulfil Thy will, keep Thy worshippers. We ask with sighing, we beseech Thy mercy, we ask forgiveness from that merciful One who opens His door to all who turn unto Him. Every day I promise Thee that to-morrow I will repent : all my days are past and gone, my faults still remain. O Christ, have mercy upon me, have mercy upon me."

Many a strange house I have seen, but never anything so striking as the dwelling of *Qasha* Ishai. Passing through the rude verandah, and through a lofty room nearly dark, with a rough stone dais, on which were some mattresses, and berths one above another, I stumbled in total darkness into a room seventy feet by forty, and twenty feet or more high in its highest part. It has no particular shape, and wanders away from this lofty centre into low irregular caverns and recesses excavated in the mountain side. Parts of the floor are of naked rock, parts of damp earth. In one rocky recess is a powerful spring of pure water. The roofs are supported on barked stems of trees, black, like the walls, wherever it was possible to see them, with the smoke of two centuries. Ancient oil lamps on posts or in recesses rendered darkness visible. Goat-skins, with the legs sticking out, containing butter, hanging from the blackened crossbeams, and wheat, apples, potatoes, and onions in heaps and sacks, piles of wool, spinning-wheels, great wooden cradles here and there, huge oil and water jars, wooden stools, piles of bedding, ploughs, threshing instruments, long guns, swords, spears, and gear encumbered the floor, while much more was stowed away in the dim caverns of the rock.

I asked the number of families under the roof. " Seven ovens," was the reply. This meant seven families, and it is true that three generations, seventy-two persons, live, cook, sleep, and pursue their avocations under that patriarchal roof.

The road is a bad one for laden beasts, and very dangerous besides, and the few travellers who visit Kochanes usually take the caravan route from Urmi *viâ* Diza, and the fact of an English person passing through Marbishu with a letter to the Turkish authorities was soon " noised abroad," and I was invited to spend the evening in this most

picturesque house. All the inmates were there, and over
a hundred of the villagers besides; and cooking, baking,
spinning, carding wool, knitting, and cleaning swords and
guns went on all the time. There were women and girls
in bright red dresses; men reclining on bedding already
unrolled on the uneven floor, or standing in knots in
their picturesque dresses leaning on their long guns,
with daggers gleaming in their belts; groups seated round
the great fire, in the uncertain light of which faces
gleamed here and there in the dim recesses, while the
towering form of *Qasha* Ishai loomed grandly through
the smoke, as the culmination of the artistic effect.

The subject discussed was equally interesting to the
Syrians and to me,—the dangers of the pass and the
number of guards necessary. We talked late into the
night, and long before I left the female and juvenile part
of the family had retired to their beds. Again I heard of
Hesso's misdeeds, of the robbery of 1400 sheep; of the
driving off on the previous morning of thirty sheep
which they were about to barter for their winter supply
of wheat; of the oppressive taxation, 100 *liras* (nearly
£100) on 100 houses; of the unchecked depredations of
the Kurds, which had increased this summer and autumn,
leaving them too poor to pay their taxes; of a life of
peril and fear and apprehension for their women, which
is scarcely bearable; of the oppression of man and the
silence of God. Underlying all is a feeling of bitter
disappointment that England, which "has helped the
oppressed elsewhere, does nothing for us." They thought,
they said, " that when the English priests came it was the
beginning of succour, and that the Lord was no longer
deaf, and our faces were lightened, but now it is all dark,
and there is no help in God or man."

I now find myself in the midst of a state of things of
which I was completely ignorant, and for which I was

utterly .unprepared, and in a region full of fear and danger, in which our co-religionists are the nearly helpless prey of fanatical mountaineers, whose profession is robbery.

Looking round on the handsome men and comely women, who would greet the sunrise with Christian prayer and praise, and whose ancestors have worshipped

A SYRIAN FAMILY.

Christ as God for fourteen centuries in these mountain fastnesses, I wondered much at my former apathy concerning them.   It is easier to *feel* them our fellow-Christians on the spot than to put the feeling into words, but writing here in the house of their Patriarch, the *Catholicos* of the East, I realise that the Cross signed on their brows in baptism is to them as to us the symbol of triumph and of hope; that by them as by us the Eucharistic emblems are received for the life of the soul, " in remembrance of Christ's meritorious Cross and

Passion "; that through ages of accumulating wrongs and almost unrivalled misery, they like us have worshipped the crucified Nazarene as the crowned and risen Christ, that to Him with us they bend the adoring knee, and that like us they lay their dead in consecrated ground to await through Him a joyful resurrection.

There were five degrees of frost during the night, and as I lay awake from cold the narratives I had heard and the extraordinary state of things in which I so unexpectedly found myself made a very deep impression on me. There, for the first time in my life, I came into contact with people grossly ignorant truly, but willing to suffer " the loss of all things," and to live in " jeopardy every hour" for religious beliefs, which are not otherwise specially influential in their lives. My own circumstances, too, claimed some consideration, whether to go forward, or back to Urmi. It is obvious from what I hear that the bringing my journey to Erzerum to a successful issue will depend almost altogether on my own nerve, judgment, and power of arranging, and that at best there will be serious risks, hardships, and difficulties, which will increase as winter sets in. After nearly coming to the cowardly decision to return, I despised myself for the weakness, and having decided that some good to these people might come from farther acquaintance with their circumstances, I fell asleep, and now the die is cast.

We were ready at daybreak the next morning, but for the same reasons as those given at Merwana did not start till seven for an eleven hours' march. I took two armed horsemen and six armed footmen, all fine fellows used to the work of reconnoitring and protecting. Three of them scouted the whole time high up on the sides of the pass, not with the purposeless sensational scouting of Persian *sowars*, but with the earnestness of men who

were pledged to take us safely through, and who live
under arms to protect their property and families.

After five hours of toiling up the Drinayi Pass, taking
several deep fords, and being detained by a baggage
horse falling fifty feet with his load, we crossed the
summit, and by a long descent through hills of rounded
outlines covered with uncut sun-cured hay, reached the
plain of Gawar, where the guards left us. On the way we
passed the small Christian hamlet of Eyal, which was
robbed of its sheep with the sacrifice of the shepherd's
life the following night. At the village of Yekmala on the
plain the Kurdish *katirgis* by a shameful exaction got
us into great trouble, and there was a fight, in which
Johannes's gun was wrested from him, and some of my
things were taken, the Kurds meantime driving off their
animals at a fast trot. The aspect of affairs was so very
bad and the attack on my men so violent that I paid the
value of the Kurdish depredations, and we got away. A
little farther on the *katirgis* were extremely outrageous,
and began to fulfil their threat of "throwing down their
loads," but I persuaded *Qasha* ——, who was alarmed and
anxious, to leave them behind, and they thought better
of it.

The mountain-girdled plain of Gawar is a Paradise
of fertility, with abundant water, and has a rich black
soil capable of yielding twenty or thirtyfold to the cultivator. On it is the town of Diza, chiefly Armenian,
which is a Turkish customs station, a military post, and
the residence of a Kaimakam. There are over twenty
Christian as well as some Moslem villages on Gawar,
and a number of Kurdish hamlets and "castles" on the
slopes and in the folds of the hills above it.

The sun was sinking as we embarked on the plain,
and above the waves of sunset gold which flooded it rose
the icy spires and crags of the glorious Jelu ranges and

the splintered Kanisairani summits. The plain has an altitude of over 6000 feet, and there was a sharp frost as we dismounted at the village of Pirzala and put up at the house of the *Malek* David, having been eleven and a half hours in the saddle. After consulting with him and other village worthies I dismissed the *katirgis* and paid them more than their contract price. The next morning they swore by the Prophet's beard, and every other sacred thing, that they had not been paid, and when payment was proved by two respectable witnesses, they were not the least abashed. Poor fellows! They know no better and are doubtless very poor. I was glad to get rid of their sinister faces and outbreaks of violence, but for some days it was impossible, being harvest-time, to obtain transport to Kochanes, though I was able to leave Pirzala for other villages.

The next day mists rolled down the mountains, and a good cold English rain set in, in which I had a most pleasant ride to Diza, which was repeated the following day in glorious weather, the new-fallen snow coming half-way down the mountain sides. I was surreptitiously on Turkish soil, and it was necessary to show my passport to the Diza officials, get a permit to travel, and have my baggage examined. Ishu, the present *Malek* of the plain, through whom all business between the Christians and the Government is transacted, accompanied us to the Mutessarif of Julamerik.

Diza is an unwalled town on an eminence crowned by barracks. The garrison of 200 men was reduced to six during the summer. The Kurds evidently took the reduction as a hint to them to do what they liked, and they have mercilessly ravaged and harried the plain for months past.[1] An official assured me that 15,000 sheep have

[1] About Christmas 1890 in Constantinople I had an opportunity of laying the state of the Gawar Christians and the reduction of the garrison

been driven off from the Gawar Christian villages between the middle of June and the 17th of October, partly by the nomad Herkis.   There are now sixty soldiers at Diza, and the Mutessarif of Julamerik is there, having come down to capture Abdurrahman Bey, one of the great oppressors of the Christians,—an attempt rendered abortive (it is said) by a bribe given by the Bey to the commanding officer of the troops.

I was interested in my first visit to a Turkish official. His room was above a stable, with a dark and difficult access, and the passages above were crowded with soldiers. The Mutessarif sat on a divan at the upper end of a shabby room, an elderly man much like Mr. Gladstone, very courteous and gentlemanly, with plenty of conversation and *savoir-faire*.   He said that the letter I carry is "a very powerful document," that it supersedes all the usual formalities, that my baggage would not even be looked at, and that I should not require a *teskareh* or permit.   By his advice I called on the Kaimakam, and in each room a soldier brought in delicious coffee.   The Kaimakam was also very courteous, and talked agreeably and intelligently, both taking the initiative, as etiquette demands.

In this and in the general tone there was a marked difference between Persian and Turkish officialdom.   The Persian Governor is surrounded by civilians, the Turkish by soldiers, and in the latter case the manner assumed by subordinates is one of the most profound respect.

of Diza before His Highness Kiamil Pasha, then Grand Vizier.   He appeared deeply interested, and said that it was the purpose of his Government to send troops up to the region as soon as the roads were open. Since then I have heard nothing of these people, but to-day, as this sheet is going to press, I have received the following news from Dr. Shedd of Urmi: "You will be glad to know that Gawar is very much changed for the better.   The Turkish Governor has been removed, and another of far better character and ability has the post.   The Kurdish robbers have been arrested, and their leader, Abdurrahman Bey, killed."—*November* 2, 1890.

The sealing of my passport took a considerable time, during which, with *Qasha* ——, I paid several visits, was regaled with Armenian cookery, tried to change a *mejidieh* at the Treasury, but found it absolutely empty, and went to see a miracle-working New Testament, said to be of great antiquity, in an Armenian house. It was hanging on the wall in a leather bag, from which depended strings of blue and onyx beads. Sick people come to it even from great distances, as well as the friends of those who are themselves too ill to travel. The bag can only be opened by a priest. The power of healing depends on a sum of money being paid to the priest and the owners. The sick person receives a glass bead, and is forthwith cured.

On Gawar Plain I lodged in the village houses, either in semi-subterranean hóvels, in which the families live with their horses and buffaloes, or in rooms over stables. Very many sick people came to me for medicines, and others with tales of wrong for conveyance to "the Consul" at Erzerum. No one seemed to trust any one. These conversations were always held at night in whispers, with the candle hidden "under a bushel," the light-holes filled up with straw, the door barred or a heavy stone laid against it, and a watch outside.

The Gawar Christians are industrious and inoffensive, and have no higher aspiration than to be let alone, but they are the victims of a Kurdish rapacity which leaves them little more than necessary food. Their villages usually belong to Kurdish Aghas who take from them double the lawful taxes and tithes. The Herkis sweep over the plain in their autumn migration "like a locust cloud," carrying off the possessions of the miserable people, spoiling their granaries and driving off their flocks. The Kurds of the neighbouring slopes and mountains rob them by violence at night, and in the day by exactions made under threat of death.   The latter mode of robbery is called "demand."   The servants of a Kurdish Bey enter and ask for some jars of oil or *roghan,* a Kashmir shawl, women's ornaments, a jewelled dagger, or a good foal, under certain threats, or they show the owner a bullet in the palm of the hand, intimating that a bullet through his head will be his fate if he refuses to give up his property or informs any one of the demand.

In this way (among innumerable other instances) my host at ———,[1] a much-respected man, had been robbed of five valuable shawls, such as descend from mother to daughter, four handsome coats, and 300 *krans* in silver. In the last two years ten and fifteen loads of wheat have been taken from him, and four four-feet jars filled with oil and *roghan.*   Four hundred and fifty sheep have likewise been seized by violence, leaving him *with only fifteen*; and one night while I was at his house fifty-three of the remaining village sheep, some of which were his, were

[1] The complaints to which I became a listener were made by *maleks,* bishops, priests, headmen, and others.   Exaggerations prevail, and the same story is often told with as many variations as there are narrators. I cannot vouch for anything which did not come under my own observation.   Some narratives dissolved under investigation, leaving a mere nucleus of fact.   Those which I thought worthy of being noted down —some of which were published in the *Contemporary Review* in May and June in two papers called *The Shadow of the Kurd*—were either fortified by corroborative circumstances, or rest on the concurrent testimony as to the main facts of three independent narrators.

In some cases I was asked to lay the statements before the British Consul at Erzerum, with the names of the narrators as the authority on which they rested, but in the greater number I was implored not to give names or places, or any means of identification.   "We are in fear of our lives if we tell the truth," they urged.   Sometimes I asked them if they would abide by what they told me in the event of an investigation by the British Vice-Consul at Van.   "No, no, no, we dare not !" was the usual reply. Under these circumstances, the only course open to me is to withhold the names of persons and places wherever I was pledged to do so, but as a guarantee of good faith I have placed the statements, confidentially, with the names, in the hands of Her Majesty's Principal Secretary of State for Foreign Affairs.

driven off in spite of the guards, who *dare not fire.* I
was awakened by the disturbance, and as it was a light
night I saw that the Kurds who attacked the sheepfold
were armed with modern guns. The *reis* of that village
and this man's brother have both been shot by the
Kurds.

Testimony concurred in stating that the insecurity of
life and property has enormously increased this summer,
especially since the reduction of the Diza garrison; that
" things have grown very much worse since the Erzerum
troubles;" that the Kurds have been more audacious in
their demands and more reckless of human life; and that
of late they have threatened the Christians *as such*, saying
that the Government would approve of " their getting rid
of them." Very little of any value, the people said, was
left to them, and the extreme bareness of their dwellings,
and the emptiness of their stables and sheepfolds, while
surrounded with possibilities of pastoral and agricultural
wealth, tend to sustain their statements. " The men of
Government," they all said, " are in partnership with the
Kurds, and receive of their gains. This is our curse."

Many women and girls, especially at Charviva and Vasivawa, have been maltreated by the Kurds. A fortnight
ago a girl, ten years old, going out from ——, to carry
bread to the reapers, was abducted. It became known
that two girls in —— were to be carried off, and they
were hidden at first in a hole near ——. Their hiding-
place last week was known only to their father, who
carried them food and water every second night. He
came to me in the dark secretly, and asked me to bring
them up here, where they might find a temporary asylum.
Daily and nightly during the week of my visit Gawar
was harried by the Kurds, who in two instances burned
what they could not carry away, the glare of the blazing
sheaves lighting up the plain.

The people of Gawar express great anxiety for teachers. The priests and deacons must work like labourers, and cannot, they say, go down to Urmi for instruction. A priest, speaking for two others, and for several deacons who were present, said, " Beseech for a teacher to come and sit among us and lighten our darkness before we pass away as the morning shadows. We are blind guides, we know nothing, and our people are as sheep lost upon the mountains. When they go down into the darkness of their graves we know not how to give them any light, and so we all perish."

This request was made in one of the large semi-subterranean dwellings, which serve for both men and beasts in Kurdistan. The firelight flickered on horses and buffaloes, receding into the darkness, and the square mud-platform on which we sat was framed by the long horns and curly heads of mild-eyed oxen.

I answered that it would be very difficult to raise money for such an object in England. " But England is very rich," the priest replied. I looked round, and the thought passed across my mind of Him " who though He was rich yet for our sakes became poor," whose life of self-denial from the stable at Bethlehem to the cross on Calvary is the example for our own, and whose voice, ringing down through ages of luxury and selfishness, still declares that discipleship involves a love for our brethren equal to His own. Yes, " England is very rich," and these Syrians are very poor, and have kept the faith through ages of darkness and persecution.

This plain, the richest in Kurdistan, is also most beautiful. In winter a frozen morass, it is not dry enough for sowing till May, and even June. This accounts for the lateness of the harvest. The Jelu mountains, the highest in Central Kurdistan,—a mass of crags, spires, and fantastic parapets of rock, with rifts and abysses of

extraordinary depth,—come down almost directly upon
it. There is no wood. The villages are all alike, surrounded just now by piles of wheat and straw on their
threshing-floors, with truncated cones of fodder, and high
smooth black cones of animal fuel. These are often the
only signs of habitations. One may ride over the roofs
without knowing that houses are below.

Being entirely baffled by the difficulty of obtaining
transport, I went on to Gahgoran, and put up at the
house of the parish priest, where the subterranean granary
allotted to me was so completely dark that I sat all day
in the sheepfold in order to be able to write and work,
shifting my position as the sun shifted his. A *zaptieh*
had been sent from Diza, who guarded me so sedulously
that *Qasha* —— dared not speak to me, lest the man
should think he was giving me information.

Gahgoran was full of strangers. The Patriarch had
come down from Kochanes, and occupied the only room
in the village, whither I went to pay my respects to
him. The room was nearly dark, and foggy with
tobacco smoke, but a ray of light fell on Mar Gauriel,
Bishop of Urmi, a handsome full-bearded man in a
Nestorian turban, full trousers, a madder-red frock with
a bright girdle in which a *khanjar* glittered, and a robe
over all, a leader of armed men in appearance. I had
met him in Urmi, and he shook hands and presented me
to Mar Shimun, a swarthy gloomy-looking man. In his
turn he presented me to Mar Sergis, Bishop of Jelu, a
magnificent-looking man with a superb gray beard, the
beau-ideal of an Oriental ecclesiastic. *Maleks* and headmen of villages sat round the room against the wall, not
met for any spiritual conclave but for stern business
regarding the taxes, for the Patriarch is a salaried official
of the Turkish Government. All rose when I entered,
and according to a polite custom stood till I sat down.

They held out no hope of getting baggage animals, and I returned to the sheepfold.

It was a long day. The servants did not arrive till night, and Kochanes receded hourly! Many people came for medicine, and among them a very handsome man whose house was entered by Kurds a month ago, who threatened him with death unless he surrendered his possessions. After this he and his brothers fled and hid among the wheat, but fearing to be found and killed, they concealed themselves for a fortnight in the tall reeds of a marsh. He is now subject to violent fits of trembling. "My illness is fear," the poor fellow said. Three hundred sheep had been taken from him and twenty-five gold *liras*; his grass had been burned, "and now," he said, "the oppressor Hazela Bey says, 'give me the deeds of your lands, if not I will kill you.'" He had been a *Malek*, and was so rich that he entertained travellers and their horses at all times. Now his friends have to give him wheat wherewith to make bread.

The house of *Qasha* Jammo has granaries at each side of the low door, a long dark passage leading into a subterranean stable with a platform for guests, and a living-room, on a small scale, like the one at Marbishu. A space was cleared in the granary for my bed among wheat, straw, ploughs, beetles, starved cats, osier grain-tubs coated with clay, six feet high, and agricultural gear of all sorts. It was a horrid place, and the door would not bolt. After midnight I was awakened by a sound as if big rats were gnawing the beams. I got up and groping my way to the door heard it more loudly, went into the passage, looked through the chinks in the outer door, and saw a number of Kurds armed with guns. I retreated and fired my revolver in the granary, which roused the dogs, and the dogs roused the twenty strangers who were receiving the priest's hospitality. In the stable were fourteen horses, including my own two, and several buffaloes. The Kurds had dug through the roof of the granary opposite mine, and through its wall into the stable, and were on the point of driving out the horses through the common passage when the hardy mountaineers rushed upon them. The same night, though it was light and clear, another house in Gahgoran was dug into, and a valuable horse belonging to a man in the Patriarch's train was abstracted. A descent was also made on the neighbouring village of Vasivawa, which has suffered severely. Eight *zaptiehs* employed by the villagers at a high price to watch the threshing-floor, and my own *zaptieh* escort, were close at hand.

Horses having at last been obtained from a Kurdish Bey, I left on Tuesday, the Gahgoran people being stupefied with dismay at the growing audacity of the Kurds. The mountain road was very dangerous, but I travelled with Mar Gauriel and his train, thirteen well armed and mounted men, besides armed servants on foot. The ice was half an inch thick, but the sun was very hot. The mountain views were superb, and the scenery altogether glorious, but the passes and hillsides are not inhabited. We were ten hours on the journey, owing to the custom of frequent halts for smoking and talking.

In the afternoon a party of Syrians with some unladen baggage mules came over the crest of a hill, preceded by a figure certainly not Syrian. This was a fair-complexioned, bearded man, with hair falling over his shoulders, dressed in a girdled cassock which had once been black, tucked up so as to reveal some curious nether garments, Syrian socks, and a pair of rope and worsted shoes, such as the mountaineers wear in scaling heights. On his head, where one would have expected to see a college " trencher," was a high conical cap of white felt with a *pagri* of black silk twisted into a rope, the true

Tyari turban.   This was Mr. Browne, one of the English Mission clergy, who, from living for nearly four years among the Syrians of the mountains, helping them and loving them, has almost become one of them.   He was going to Diza to get winter supplies before his departure for one of the most inaccessible of the mountain valleys, but with considerate kindness turned back to Kochanes with me, and remains here until I leave.   This fortunate *rencontre* adds the finishing touch to the interest of this most fascinating Kurdistan journey.

Crossing the Kandal Pass, we descended on the hamlet of Shawutha, superbly situated on a steep declivity at the head of a tremendous ravine leading to the Zab, blocked apparently by mountains violet-purple against a crimson sky, with an isolated precipitous rock in the foreground, crowned by an ancient church difficult of access.   Below the village are fair shelving lawns, with groups of great walnut trees, hawthorn, and ash, yellow, tawny, and crimson—a scene of perfect beauty in the sunset, while the fallen leaves touched the soft green turf with ruddy gold.   The camping-grounds were very fair, but the villagers dared not let me camp.   The Kurds were about, and had exacted a ewe and lamb from every house.   Owing to the influx of strangers, it was difficult to get any shelter, and I slept in a horse and ox stable, burrowed in the hillside, the passage to the family living-room, without any air holes, hot and stifling and used my woollen sheets for curtains.   The village is grievously smitten by the "cattle plague."   In telling me of the loss of "four bulls" within three days, my host used an expression which is not uncommon here, "By the wealth of God, and the head of Mar Shimun."

Yesterday we descended 1500 feet, alongside of a torrent fringed with scarlet woods, and halted where the Shawutha, Kochanes, and Diz valleys meet at the fords

of the Zab, here known as " the Pison, the river of Eden."
The Zab, only fordable at certain seasons, is there a fast-
flowing dark green river, fully sixty yards wide, deep
enough to take the footmen up to their waists, and strong
enough to make them stagger, with a lawn bright with
autumnal foliage below the savage and lofty mountains
on its right bank.

From the Zab we ascended the gorge of the Kochanes
water by a wild mountain path, at times cut into steps
or scaffolded, and at other times merely a glistening track
over shelving rock, terminating in a steep and difficult
ascent to the fair green alp on which Kochanes stands at
the feet of three imposing peaks of naked rock—Quhai-
balak, Qwarah, and Barchallah.

Thus I beheld at last the goal of my journey from
Luristan, and was not disappointed.   Glorious indeed is
this Kurdistan world of mountains, piled up in masses of
peaks and precipices, cleft by ravines in which the Ashirets
and Yezidis find shelter, every peak snow-crested, every
ravine flaming with autumn tints; and here, where the
ridges are the sharpest, and the rock spires are the most
imposing, on a spur between the full-watered torrents of
the Terpai and the Yezidi, surrounded on three sides
by gorges and precipices, is this little mountain village,
the latest refuge of the Head of a Church once the most
powerful in the East.

Kochanes consists of a church built on the verge of a
precipice, many tombs, a grove of poplars, a sloping lawn,
scattered village houses and barley-fields extending up
the alp, and nearly on the edge of a precipitous cliff the
Patriarch's residence, a plain low collection of stone
buildings, having an arched entrance and a tower for
refuge or defence.   The houses of his numerous relations
are grouped near it.   Everything is singularly picturesque.
The people, being afraid of an attack from the Kurds,

would not suffer me to pitch my tent on their fair meadow, and Sulti, the Patriarch's sister, has installed me in a good room in the house, looking across the tremendous ravine of the Terpai upon savage mountains, the lower skirts of which are clothed with the tawny foliage of the scrub oak, and their upper heights with snow.

I. L. B.

LETTER XXIX

KOCHANES, *Oct. 27.*

AFTER two days the Patriarch arrived from Gahgoran with nearly forty persons. To realise what this house is like, one must go back four centuries, to the mode of living of the medieval barons of England. Mar Shimun is not only a spiritual prince, but the temporal ruler of the Syrians of the plains and valleys, and of the Ashirets or tribal Syrians of the mountains of Central Kurdistan, as well as a judge and a salaried official of the Turkish Government. He appoints the *maleks* or lay rulers of each district, where the office is not hereditary, and possesses ecclesiastical patronage. For over four centuries the Patriarch has been of the family of Shimun, which is regarded as the royal family ; and he is assisted in managing affairs by a " family council." Kochanes is thus the ecclesiastical and political metropolis of the Syrian nation, and the innumerable disputes which arise among the people of this region are brought here for judgment and arbitration.

It is a crowded life. From sunrise to sunset the pavement outside the rude hall of entrance, the great room, like that at Marbishu, where Sulti presides, and the guest-chambers, are always thronged with men waiting to be received by the Patriarch, sleeping on the big settle in the hall, or cleaning swords and guns, or wrestling, performing feats of horsemanship, playing chess,

and eating.   Sixty persons more or less are guests here.
Every one coming into the valley is received, and horses
are stabled while men are fed.   Outside, sheep and
fowls are being continually killed, two or three sheep
being required daily; mules are departing for Diza for
stores, or are returning with flour and sugar; oxen are
bringing in hay, and perpetual measuring and weighing
are going on.   The cost of provisioning such an army of
guests is enormous, and presses heavily on the Patriarch's
slender resources.   Intrigues are rife.   In some ways
every man's hand is against his fellow, and the succession to the Patriarchate, although nominally settled, is
a subject of scheming, plotting, rivalries, and jealousies.
Then there are various appointments, secular and spiritual,
to be wrangled for, the difficult relations with Turkey to
be managed, and such a wavering policy to be shaped
towards Rome and American Presbyterianism as shall
absolutely break with neither.

Among the guests who come and go as they please,
unquestioned, are refugees from the barbarities of the
Kurds, among the most pitiable of whom is Mar ——,
Bishop of ——, bereft under threat of death of his
Episcopal seal, and a fugitive from his diocese, which
is almost destroyed by violence and exactions.   Few
hours pass in which some fresh tale of bloodshed, or
the driving off of flocks, or the attacking of travellers,
or the digging into houses, is not brought up here.   A
piteous state of alarm prevails.   Mar Shimun, naturally
feeble and irresolute, and his family council are helpless.
His dual position aggravates his perplexities.   Counsels
are divided and paralysed.   No one knows where to turn
for help on earth, and "the Lord is deaf," some of the
people say.

On entering the house by an archway, where the
heavily-bossed door stands always open, a busy scene is

to be witnessed in the hall, which is roughly paved with irregular slabs of stone. On the rude stone settle men are sitting or sleeping, or a carpenter is using it as his bench, or a sheep is being cut up on it. At the end of a passage is the "house," a high, big, blackened room, with shelving floors of earth and rock, ovens in the floors, great *quaraghs* holding grain, piles of wood, men sawing logs, huge pots, goat-skins of butter hanging from the rafters, spinning-wheels, a loom, great roughly-cut joints of meat, piles of potatoes, women ceaselessly making blankets of bread, to be used as tablecloths before being eaten, preparations for the ceaseless meals involved by the unbounded hospitality of the house, and numbers of daggered serving-men, old women, and hangers-on. This room is only lighted from the doors and from a hole in the roof. Nearly opposite is a low dark lobby, from which open my room, sixteen feet square, with walls three feet thick, and Mar Shimun's room, about the same size, which serves him for sleeping, eating, reception-room, and office.

On the same side of the hall are two guest-rooms, now packed to their utmost capacity, and a large room in which Ishai, the Patriarch's half-brother, a young man of exceeding beauty, lives, with his lovely wife, Asiat, and their four children. In a ruinous-looking tower attached to the main building Mr. Browne has his abode, up a steep ladder. Below there are houses inhabited by the Patriarch's relations, one of whom, Marta, is a dignified and charming woman, and the mother of Mar Auraham, the Patriarch-designate, whose prospective dignity is the subject of much intrigue.

The presiding genius of the Patriarch's household is his sister Sulti, a capable woman of forty, who has remained unmarried in order to guide his house, and who rules as well as guides. When she sleeps I know not.

She is astir early and late, measuring, weighing, directing, the embodiment of Proverbs chap. xxxi. No little
brain-power must be required for the ordering of such a
household and the meeting of such emergencies as that
of to-day, when twenty Jelu men arrived unexpectedly.

The serving-men all look like bandits. The medieval
Jester is in existence here, Shlimon, a privileged person,
who may say and do anything, and take all manner of
liberties, and who, by his unlimited buffooneries, helps
the Patriarch and his family through the dulness of the
winter days. He and another faithful fellow, said to be
equally quick with his tongue and his dagger, are Mar
Shimun's personal servants. At fixed hours the latter
carries food to his lord in tinned copper bowls on a large
round tray, knives and forks not having penetrated to
Kochanes.

The routine of the day is as follows. The Patriarch
rises very early, and says prayers at dawn, after which
those who have the *entrée* are served with pipes and coffee
in his room, and talk *ad libitum*. Business of all sorts
follows ; a *siesta* is taken at mid-day, then there is business
again, and unlimited talk with unlimited smoking till five,
when the Patriarch goes to prayers at church, after which
everybody is at liberty to attend his *levée*, and talking
and smoking go on till 9 or 10 P.M. It is a life without
privacy or quiet. The affairs of the mountains, litigation,
tribal feuds, the difficulty of raising the tribute, the
gossip of the village, and just now, above all else, the
excesses of the Kurds, form the staple of conversation, as
I understand from *Qasha* ——, who, as a personal friend,
spends much of the day in the Patriarch's room. In
winter, when Kochanes is snowed up, chess and the pranks
and witticisms of the Jester fill up the time.

The curious little court, the rigid etiquette, the clank
of arms, the unbounded hospitality, and the political and

judicial functions exercised by the Patriarch, with the
rude dwelling and furnishings, combine to re-create the
baronial life as it might have been lived in Roslin or
Warkworth Castles.

Though I had half-seen Mar Shimun at Gahgoran, I
was only formally presented after his arrival here. It is
proper for a woman to cover her head before him, and
I put on my hat and took off my shoes. His room
is well paved, the plaster is newly coloured, and there is
a glazed window with a magnificent prospect. There
were rugs at one end, on which the Patriarch was seated,
with two chairs at his left hand. He rose to receive me,
and, according to custom, I kissed his hand. He took
my letter of introduction, and put it under a cushion, as
etiquette demanded, and asked me to be seated. On the
floor along the walls were bishops, priests, deacons, Jelu
and Tyari mountaineers, lowlanders from Urmi, and men
of the Shimun family, all most picturesquely dressed and
smoking long wooden pipes. On each subsequent occasion, when I paid my respects to him, he was similarly
surrounded. Mr. Browne acted as interpreter, but
nothing but very superficial conversation was possible
when there was the risk that anything said might be
twisted into dangerous use. Mar Shimun is a man about
the middle height, with large dark eyes, a sallow complexion, a grizzled iron-gray beard, and an expression of
profound melancholy, mingled with a most painful look
of perplexity and irresolution. He cannot be over fifty,
but the miseries and intrigues around him make him
appear prematurely old. When I approached the subject
of the anarchy of the country he glared timidly and
fearfully round, and changed the subject, sending me
a message afterwards that *Qasha* ―― and Kwaja
Shlimon, a Chaldæan educated in Paris, are in possession
of all that he could tell me, and would speak for him.

He and his family are very proud both of ancestry and position. Within limits his word is law; a letter from him is better than any Government passport or escort through the nearly inaccessible fastnesses of the Ashirets; "By the Head of Mar Shimun," and "By the House of Mar Shimun" are common asseverations, but he and his are exposed constantly to indignities and insults from minor Turkish officials and from Kurdish chiefs, and the continual disrespect to his person and office is said to be eating into his soul.

He wears a crimson *fez* with a black *pagri*, a short blue cloth jacket with sleeves wide at the bottom and open for a few inches at the inner seam, blue cloth trousers of a sailor cut, a red and white striped satin shirt, the front and sleeves of which are very much *en évidence*, and a crimson girdle, but without the universal *khanjar*.

This is the man who is the head at once of a church and nation, the temporal and spiritual ruler of the Syrian people, the hereditary Patriarch, the *Catholicos* of the East, whose dynastic ancestors ranked as sixth in dignity in the Catholic Church in its early ages. It was not, however, till the early part of the fifth century, when the Church of the East threw in her lot with Nestorius, after his condemnation in 431 by the Council of Ephesus for "heretical" views on the nature of our Lord, that the *Catholicos* of the East assumed the farther title of Patriarch. As I look on Mar Shimun's irresolute face, and see the homage which his people pay to him, I recall the history of a day when this church, which only survives as an obscure and hunted remnant, planted churches and bishoprics in Persia, Central Asia, Tartary, and China; its missionaries, full of zeal and self-sacrifice, brought such legions into its fold that in the sixth century the ecclesiastical ancestor of this Patriarch, then resident at Baghdad, ruled over twenty-five metropolitical provinces extending from Jerusalem to China; and when in the fourteenth century it was not only the largest communion in Christendom, but outnumbered the whole of the rest of Christendom, east and west, Roman, Greek, and other churches put together. It is truly a marvel not only that Baghdad, Edessa, and Nisibis possessed Nestorian schools of divinity and philosophy, but that Christian colleges, seminaries, and theological schools flourished in Samarcand, Bokhara, and Khiva! How this huge church melted away like snow, and how the tide of Christianity ebbed, leaving as a relic on its high-water mark within the Chinese frontier a stone tablet inscribed with the Nestorian creed, and how Taimurlane pursued the unfortunate Christian remnant with such fury that the *Catholicos* himself with a fugitive band was forced to fly into these mountains, are matters of most singular historic interest. Most fascinating indeed is it to be here. Each day seems but an hour, so absorbing are the interests, so deep the pathos, so vivid the tableaux, so unique the life in this hamlet of Kochanes, on its fair green alp at a height of 6000 feet among these wild mountains of Kurdistan, musical with the sound of torrents fed by fifty snow-drifts, dashing down to join " the Pison, the river of Eden " (as the Patriarch calls the Zab), on its way to the classic Tigris.

The afternoon I arrived, Sulti, Marta, Asiat, and several other women courteously visited me, and the next day I returned their visits in their simple pleasant houses. These formalities over, I have enjoyed complete liberty, and have acquainted myself with the whole of Kochanes, and with many of the people and their interests, and have had small gatherings of men in my room each evening, *Qasha* —— or Mr. Browne interpreting their tales of strife or wrong.

" Fear is on every side," the fear of a people practically

unarmed, for their long guns, some of them matchlocks,
are of no use against the rifles of the Kurds, *nor dare
they fire in self-defence.*   Travelling is nearly suspended.
A company of people whose needs call them to Urmi
dare not run the risk of the journey till they can go down
with Mar Gauriel and his large escort.   It is evident
that the Patriarch and his people hoped for a British
protectorate as one result of " the Archbishop of Canterbury's Mission," and that they are bitterly disappointed
that their condition is growing worse.

   " How can we listen to teaching," say some of them,
" when we have no rest ?   How can we believe in God
when He lets these things happen to us ?   The Almighty
is deaf, and we cease to pray.   Can we hear teaching
when the wolf is on us by night and day ?   If we let go
the Cross we might be rich and safe.   Night by night
we ask, ' Shall we see the morning ? ' for our oppressors
wax fiercer daily."

   Mar ——, Bishop of ——, mentioned previously as a
fugitive from his diocese, is a fine, pleasant-looking middle-
aged man, more like a sailor than an ecclesiastic.   Late one
night, in a whisper, with a trusty watch at the door, he told
his story, through *Qasha* ——, in the following words:

   " I fled, fearing for my life, because many times I had spoken
against the oppressions.   The Kurds have carried away most of
the sheep and goats, besides taking all they wished to have, and
they entered through the houses, plundering everything, and burning two in ——.   Their words are ' give or die.'   I petitioned
Government regarding the oppressions, and Mohammed Bey came,
and by threat of death he got my seal, and wrote in my name a
letter, saying it was all false, there were no oppressions, and he was a
very good man, and he signed it with my seal, and it went to Stamboul.   My seal has now been for one year in the hands of Mohammed Bey, who has killed about thirty Christians in Berwar.   Three
months ago I fled to save my life.

"Seventeen years the oppressions have begun; but it was ten years ago when we could easily keep ourselves and raise our bread—now we cannot. In ——, five years ago, all had plenty of dress and bread, and every family kept two cows and two hundred or more of sheep. But now, when I visited them, I would shame to look at the female persons, so naked were they, and so did they hide themselves for shame in the dark parts of their houses, for their dress was all in pieces, so that their flesh was seen. I was thirsty and asked for milk, and they made reply, 'Oh, we have not a cow, or a sheep, or a goat: we forget the taste of milk!' And most of their fine fields were gone out of their hands by oppressions, for they could no longer find money wherewith to pay taxes, and they sold them for a vile price.

"K—— was the best village in Sopana, and more wealthy than any village of Kurds or Christians. There I went and asked for some milk. They said, 'Never a goat, or a sheep, or a cow have we.' I ask of all the families their condition, and they make reply, with many tears, 'All that we have has left our hands, and we fear for our lives now. We were rich, now we have not bread to eat from day to day.' Seventeen years ago the village of B—— had fifty families of wealthy villagers, but now I only find twelve, and those twelve could scarcely find bread. I had asked bread, but I could not find it. By day their things were taken by force out of their houses: at night their sheep and cattle were driven off. They could keep nothing. Our wheat, our sheep, our butter is not our own. The chief, Mohammed Bey, and his servants ask of us, saying, 'Give, or we will kill you.'"

This is a sample of innumerable tales to which I listen daily. Some are probably grossly exaggerated, others, and this among them, are probably true in all essential particulars. Daily, from all quarters, men arrive with their complaints of robbery and violence, and ask the Patriarch to obtain redress for them, but he is powerless.

My favourite walk is down the fair green lawn outside the village, on which is a copse of poplars, with foliage of reddening gold. Beside it, on the verge of the

DESIGNS ON TOMBS AT KOCHANES.

precipitous heights above the Terpai, is a bold group of rocks, on which the church dedicated to Mar Shalita is built.   The ruins of a former church, dedicated to Mart Mariam, are higher up the alp.   Below the rocks are a great number of tombstones, with incised ornaments upon them bearing the general name of crosses.   The

church has nothing speci-
ally ecclesiastical in its
appearance.   It has some
resemblance to a keep with
out-buildings, and its irregular form seems to have
been dictated by the con-
figuration of the rock.   It
has no windows, and the
cruciform slits at a great
height look like loopholes.
It is indeed the ultimate
refuge of the Patriarch

SYRIAN CROSS.

and the villagers in case of a descent of the Kurds. I walked all round it, through the poplar grove, with its mirthful waters, among the tombs, and back by the edge of the ravine to the west side without finding a door.   In truth the only entrance is up a rude and very steep ladder, about ten feet high, with a rude door at the top six inches thick, but only three feet high. How old and infirm people get up and down I cannot tell. So difficult is the access that I was glad to avail myself of the vigorous aid of Mar Gauriel, who, having visited England, is ready on all occasions with courteous atten- tions to a lady.   The reason of the low doors is said to be that all may bow their heads on entering the house of God, and that the Moslems may not stable their cattle in the church.   The entrance harmonises with the obvious pervading motive of the design, which is *inaccessibility*.

The door opens into a small courtyard, partly protected by a wooden roof. At its farther end, in a recess in its massive wall, is a small altar. Its west wall is pierced so that the approach can be commanded. In this courtyard the daily prayers are frequently said during the warm weather. A few steps lead from this into a building of two stories, a rude little house in fact, once occupied by one of the Patriarchs, and latterly by the late Rabban Yonan, a holy man, almost a hermit, whose reputation for sanctity has extended far beyond the limits of Kurdistan.

Removing our shoes, we entered the church through a sort of porch, the lintel of which is ornamented with bas-reliefs consisting of a cross in knot-work and side ornaments of the same, very rudely executed. The threshold is elevated, and the lintel of the door only three feet four inches high, so that the worshipper must bend again before entering. It was a gloomy transition from the bright October sunshine to the dark twilight within, and even with the aid of candles the interior was only dimly seen. It consists of a nave, about thirty-four feet long, with a sanctuary, and a sacristy which also serves as the baptistery, at the east end. The nave is lofty and without seats. The worshippers stand during divine service, even the aged and infirm only rest by leaning on their cross-handled staffs. In the nave, below the screen of the sanctuary, are three altars. On one, the " altar of prayers," the anthem books are laid ; on another, the " altar of the Gospels," is a copy of the Gospels wrapped in a cloth, on which is a cross, which it is customary to kiss ; on the third there is also a cross. A very thick wall separates the nave from the eastern chamber, which in its turn is divided unequally into two parts. This wall is pierced by a narrow chancel arch, and there is a narrow platform behind the altars of prayer, etc., ascended by three steps, at which the people receive the Eucharistic elements. Through the arch is dimly seen the altar, over which is a stone canopy, or *baldáchino*, supported on four pillars. In the sacristy is a narrow but deep font, in which the infant is baptized by being dipped in the water up to the knees at the name of the Father, up to the waist at the name of the Son, and wholly immersed at the name of the Holy Ghost, the priest repeating, " Thou art baptized in the name of the Father, Amen, and of the Son, Amen, and of the Holy Ghost, Amen." Before the rite the infant's forehead is anointed with oil in the church, and it is completely anointed in the baptistery before being plunged into the font. Every infant has two god-parents, who act as sponsors at its subsequent marriage. These persons by undertaking this office are placed in a relationship of affinity close enough to be a bar to marriage. After the baptism the child is confirmed in the nave with oil and the imposition of the priest's hands, and after being very tightly bound up in its swaddling clothes is handed to the god-parents. Infant communion is the rule of the Church, but the elements are rarely received at the time of baptism.

Baptism is only valid when celebrated by a priest and in a consecrated church. Private baptisms are unlawful, but there is a form of prayer appointed for use if a child is dangerously ill, during which the priest signs a basin of water with the sign of the Cross, saying, " In the strength of our Lord may this water be of blessing in the name," etc. The mother afterwards bathes the child in the water, and if it dies they " trust it to the mercy of God." If it recovers it must be taken to church to be baptized in the usual manner. The Holy Communion, the *Kourbana*, ought by rule to precede baptism in the very early morning, and the baptismal rite ought to be administered on the eighth day, but it is often postponed till the annual village festival, at which the *Kourbana* is always celebrated.[1]

The whole interior of the church of Kochanes is covered by a plain vaulted stone roof. At the west end of the nave is a row of oblong stone tombs, four feet high, in which several of the patriarchs are buried; and a steep narrow stone stair leads from these to a small door high up in the north wall, which gives access to a small chamber in which the priest prepares and bakes the bread for the Holy Communion. The flour for this purpose is preferably of wheat which has been gleaned by girls. It is ground in a hand-mill and is mixed with "holy leaven," handed on from sacrament to sacrament. The bread is made into round cakes, a quarter of an inch thick and two and a half inches in diameter, which are stamped with a cross. Great importance is attached to the elements, and the water used for mixing with the sacramental wine is always brought from the purest spring within reach.[2]

On one side of this upper chamber, at a height of four feet, there is the mouth of a sort of tunnel which runs between the flat exterior roof and the vaulted ceiling of the nave. This is used for concealing the Liturgies and the other poor valuables of the church in times of peril. Secret as this hiding-place is, the Kurds discovered it some years ago, and carried off and de-

---

[1] For the correction of my very imperfect investigations into the religious customs of the Syrians, I am indebted to a very careful and learned paper by Canon Maclean, *Some Account of the Customs of the Eastern Syrian Churches*, originally published in the *Guardian*, and now to be obtained at the office of "The Archbishop of Canterbury's Mission to the Assyrian Christians, 2 Deans Yard, Westminster."

[2] A singular legend is told regarding the origin of the sacred leaven and the sacred oil.

The Syrians say that as our Lord went up out of the Jordan after His baptism John the Baptist collected in a phial the baptismal water as it dropped from His sacred person, giving it before his death to St. John the

stroyed whatever of value had been hidden, including a *firman* and a knife which (it is said) were given by Mohammed to a former *Catholicos*, and which are now in Stamboul.

The general arrangement of the church is a pathetic protest against chronic insecurity and persecution. The interior, and especially the sanctuary, are as black as smoke can make them, although very few candles are ordinarily used, the clergy holding rolls of thin wax taper in their hands when they require light on the Liturgies and Gospel. There is little architectural ornament except some sculptured stones, and two recesses with scallop-shell roofs at the sides of the chancel arch. The church is in good repair, for if any rain gets into a sacred building it has to be reconsecrated.

Towards five o'clock the sounding-board is beaten, and the Patriarch, the two bishops, and some other men, all in secular dress, saunter down to evening prayers, which are usually said by the Patriarch himself, and consist of a few prayers, a short lesson, and some psalms. The custom is for the people on entering to kiss the Cross, the Gospels, and the Patriarch's hand, and to lay their daggers in the church porch. Clerical vestments are not worn at these services. The Liturgies and Gospels are magnificent specimens of caligraphy, and the Syriac characters are in themselves beautiful.

Evangelist. At the Last Supper (the legend runs) our Lord gave to John two loaves, putting it into his heart to preserve one. At the Cross, when this same apostle saw the "blood and water," he took the phial from his bosom and added the water from the pierced side to the water of baptism, dipping the loaf at the same time in the blood. After the Day of Pentecost the disciples, before going forth to "disciple" the nations, ground John's blood-dyed loaf to powder, mixed it with flour and salt, divided it among themselves, and carried it forth to serve as leaven for ever for the bread of remembrance. In like manner they took of the mingled water of the phial, and mixing it with oil of unction, divided it, and preserved it for the perpetual sanctification of the waters of baptism.

It is appointed that the whole Psalter be recited in three days, and though I imagine that some abridgment is made, the priests and people, contrary to rule, are apt to sit on the floor during the antiphonal singing of the psalms, owing to their extreme length. The chanting is very discordant, as each man adopts the key which suits himself.

The " kiss of peace " is an interesting and decorous feature of the daily worship, and is always given at the beginning, even if it should be omitted at the close. On entering the church the priest crosses himself and kisses the Cross, which always lies on the altar on the north side, saying, " Glory be to God in the highest." After this the people come forward and kiss first the Cross and then the priest's hand, and each passing on touches the hands of those who before him have kissed the sacred emblem and raises his own hand to his lips. It is the custom always to kiss the hand of a bishop or priest on meeting him in the road or elsewhere, and the salutation is performed in a reverential manner.

The church furniture and vestments show the great poverty of the people. The altar cloth is figured white cotton. Two tarnished and battered candlesticks stand on the altar, and a very sordid cross in the recess behind it. The chalice is a silver bowl, tarnished, almost blackened, by neglect, and the paten is a silver tray in the same state. There are a bronze censer, an antique, with embossed scripture figures upon it, and a branched lamp-stand surmounted by a bird, both of the rudest construction, and greatly neglected. Dust and cobwebs of ancient date, droppings from candles and bits of candle wicks offend Western eyes in the sacristy and elsewhere.

The clerical dress is very simple and of the poorest

materials. The priest wears an alb, a girdle, and a stole crossed over the breast, and at the *Kourbana* a calico square with crosses in coloured cotton sewn upon it, thrown over the shoulders, and raised at times to cover the head, or to form a screen between him and the congregation. The deacon wears an alb or "church shirt" with coloured cotton crosses on the breast and back, a blue and white girdle, and a stole which is crossed over the right shoulder and has its ends tucked into the girdle. The only difference in the dress of a bishop is that he wears a stole reaching to the ankles and not crossed upon the breast. The ordinary attire of the clergy and laity is the same, and the same similarity pervades their occupations. Even bishops may be seen hard at work in the fields. The sanctuary is held in great reverence, and Mar Gauriel, who is more like a jolly sailor than a priest, put on a girdle and stole before entering it when he showed it to me. Strange to say, the priests and deacons officiating at the Holy Communion retain their shoes and remove their turbans. The graves round the church are very numerous, and are neatly kept. One burial has taken place since I came. The corpse, that of a stranger, was enclosed in a rough wooden coffin, and the blowing of horns, beating of drums, carrying of branches decorated with handkerchiefs and apples, and the wailing of the women and other demonstrations of grief, such as men jumping into the grave, beating their breasts and uttering cries of anguish, distressing scenes which are usual at Syrian funerals, were consequently absent. The burial service is very striking and dramatic, and there are different "orders" for bishops, priests, deacons, laymen, women, and children. The whole, if recited at full length, takes fully five hours! Besides prayers innumerable both for the departed and the survivors, there are various dialogues between the mourners and the departed, and between the departed and the souls of those already in Hades.[1]

In spite of the perils around, "marrying and giving in marriage" go on much as usual. Mar Gauriel, Bishop of Urmi, has come up on nothing less important than a matrimonial errand, to ask for the hand of the Patriarch's niece, a small child of eight years old, the daughter of Ishai and Asiat, for his nephew, a boy of fourteen. Girls may marry at twelve, and the beautiful Asiat, the child's mother, is only twenty. I was invited to tea when the proposals were made in a neutral house, where Mr. Browne interpreted the proceedings for me. Mar Gauriel, handsomely dressed in red, with a *khelat* or "coat of honour" given him by the Shah over his usual clothes, looked as blithe and handsome as a suitor should. He sat on one side of the floor with a friend to help his suit, and on the other were seated Sulti, Asiat, and the child.

Conversation was general for a time; then the Bishop, with a change of face which meant business, produced a small parcel, and laid on the floor, with a deliberate pause between the articles, carbuncle and diamond rings, gold-headed pins, gold bracelets, a very fine pink coral neck-

---

[1] A portion of one of the latter follows :—

The newly dead.—"Hail, my brethren and friends who sleep. Open the door that I may enter in and see your ranks."

Those in Hades.—"Come, enter and see how many giants are sleeping here, and have been made dust and rust and worms in the bosom of Sheol. Come, enter and see, O child of death, the race of Adam : see and gaze where thy kind dwells. Come, enter and see the abundance of the bones and their commingling. The bone of the king and the bone of the servant are not separated. Come, enter and see the great corruption we are dwelling in."

The mourners.—"Wait for the Lord, who will come and raise you by His right hand."

Translations of the Liturgies are to be found in Dr. Badger's valuable book, *The Nestorians and their Rituals.*

lace, with a gold and turquoise pendant, and finally a long chain of hollow balls of massive filigree silver, beautiful enough to " fetch " any woman. The mother and aunt sat rigidly, assumed stony faces, and would not admire. But Mar Gauriel had other weapons in his armoury, and produced from a large bundle articles of dress of full size, among which were Constantinople gauze gowns sprigged with gold, a green silk gown covered with embroidery, and lastly a sort of coat of very rich cloth of gold, a costly thing. The child's eyes sparkled at this. The Bishop looked up from it at the two women, but a look of contempt alone flitted across their stony faces.

Then he began his plea, which was loud and eloquent. He said he could get a hundred brides for his nephew, who would be good workers, but the daughter of Asiat should be a princess, and have servants to wait upon her, and have nothing to do. He said he would wait four years for her, he only wanted a promise. He was not tactful. He set forth the advantages of an alliance with himself too strongly for a suitor. The house of Mar Shimun is very proud and its connection is courted by all, and the ladies were obdurate and literally frowned on his plea, looking with well-acted contempt upon the glittering display on the floor. Two days later the Patriarch himself rejected Mar Gauriel's suit, saying, " It would be a shame for the House of Mar Shimun—it would be a shameful example to betroth so young a girl." There the matter must rest, for a time at least.

An actual marriage is arranged, and this time the bride, Sanjani, is a handsome and very attractive girl of fourteen years old, with a strong will and individuality. She has been several times to see me, and I have become quite interested in her. Yesterday a number of men were seen descending the dizzy zigzags which lead from Jelu down the mountain on the other side of the Terpai ravine, and

later, after a few shots had been fired, a party of Jelu
mountaineers superbly dressed came up into Kochanes,
also on a matrimonial errand.   Some of these men are
quite blond.   They came on behalf of a youth of high
position in Jelu, and the bargaining was keen, for the
girl is of the House of Mar Shimun.   Eventually they
gave twenty *liras*, a mule, a gun, thirty sheep, and a revolver for her, as well as presents to the negotiators.   She
wept most bitterly at the prospect of leaving Kochanes.
The money is spent on the *trousseau*, and the bride's
parents give a present to the bridegroom.

Shortly after the betrothal, Mar Sergis, Bishop of
Jelu, arrived, with fifty Jelu men, the young bridegroom,
and some matrons.   The Bishop, who is a grand-looking
man, was dressed in a robe, red *shulwars*, and a turban ;
the other men were in silks and gold embroideries, and
carried jewelled *khanjars*, revolvers, and long guns with
the stocks curiously inlaid with ivory and silver.   As
they climbed up through the bushes of the ravine they
simulated an attack by skirmishers, firing guns and
revolvers.   A few Kochanes men fired as if in defence,
but most of the people decided not to show this " sign of
joy," because news had come that the Kurds had driven
off the sheep of the father of Asiat.   So with this feint
of attack and capture the brilliant throng reached the
top of the ascent, Mar Sergis and others riding mules,
musicians playing a drum and flageolets, and five or six
men with drawn swords in their right hands and leather
shields on their left arms escorting the bridegroom to
the hospitalities of the Patriarch's house.   The roofs
were crowded with villagers, but the bride was hidden
in her father's house.   The father had beaten her on
her head with a long wooden spoon, and she was lying
down !

On that and the two following evenings there was

dancing in the house late into the night, and the days were spent in feasting, sword-dances, and masquerading. It is regarded as a very "good" marriage for Sanjani. The marriage ceremony, which is private, was performed in the church at sunrise on the fourth day. There were present Mar Sergis the bridegroom's uncle, the bridegroom, "the bridegroom's friend," and Sanjani and her mother, who were preceded to the church by a fifer. The marriage service, which took half an hour, was performed at the west end of the nave. At the conclusion wine and water (but not as a Eucharistic symbol), mixed with a little earth from the church precincts, were administered to the married couple. The ring is used as with us. The most curious part of the ceremony is that while the service or "Blessing," as it is called, is proceeding, the groomsman holds up a light wooden frame, to which fruits are attached. This is also hung over the bridegroom's head at the father-in-law's house, and is carried with him when he goes out to dance. It is broken on the last day of the feasting, and the pair and their friends eat the fruit. The festivities were prolonged for three days more, after which the bride, with music and firing of guns, was taken away in charge of the matrons to her husband's house in Jelu, where there were to be rejoicings and feastings for other seven days. As the bride's procession passes, the bridegroom, attended by his young men-friends, takes his place on a roof, with a store of apples beside him, which, after signing himself with the Cross, he throws among the crowd, the hitting of the bride being regarded as a sign of good luck.

Bishops are not allowed to marry, but to priests after their ordination both first and second marriages are permitted. The law of divorce is very lax, even according to the Church canons, and Canon Maclean says that the practice is very bad, and that it is a great temptation to the bishops, several of whom are very poor, to grant divorces for the sake of the fees.

Friday was a severe fast in the Patriarch's household, as in all others. The fasts of the Syrian Church, it has been said, " can only be described as prodigious." A Syrian fast means serious self-denial, for it involves not only abstinence from meat, but from fish, honey, eggs, milk, butter, cheese, and all animal products, and the Syrian eats nothing but rice cooked in walnut oil, raisins, walnuts, treacle, beans, plain potatoes, and bread. All Wednesdays and Fridays in the year this strict *regimen* is adhered to, and the members of the Old Church also fast for fifty days in Lent, and twenty-five in Advent, and keep the very severe three days' fast of the Ninevites. Most adults keep also the fast of St. Mary, the first fourteen days of August. No religious observance is more rigidly adhered to by the nation than these severe and prolonged abstinences, and it is difficult for the Syrians to believe in the piety of any who do not, by the same methods, mortify the body and bring it into subjection.

Mar Auraham, son of Marta, a man of twenty-six, Patriarch-designate, and a bishop without a diocese, has returned, and spent part of yesterday evening in my room. He looks delicate, but has a bright, intelligent, charming face, and his conversation was thoughtful and interesting. He really cares about his church and its discipline, is regarded as honourable and straight-forward in a marked degree, and as preferring the spiritual to the temporal interests of his nation. He is apparently a warm friend of the English Mission, and if he should succeed to the chair of Mar Shimun great progress might be expected; but intrigues are surging round him, and the patriarchal family is not without its ambitions, to which he may possibly be sacrificed.

The succession to the Patriarchate and Episcopate is

the subject of a peculiar arrangement, which makes these offices practically hereditary. In the Mar Shimun family there has been provided for more than three centuries a regular succession of youths called *Nazarites*, who have never eaten meat or married, and whose mothers ate no meat for many months before they were born. One of these is chosen by the Patriarch as his successor, and then some of the disappointed youths take to eating meat like other men. At the present time, though Mar Auraham has been designated, there are one or two boy-relatives of the Patriarch who are being brought up not to eat meat. The same prohibition applies to a bishop. He also usually has one or more *Nazarites*, frequently nephews or cousins, who have been brought up by him not to eat meat, one of whom, if there be more than one, he chooses as his successor. If he neglects to make a choice, the Bishopric at his death falls like a fief to the Patriarch, who has an enormous diocese, while three of the Bishops have only a few villages to look after.

Bishops, priests, and deacons are very poor. Occasion-ally a church has a field or two as an endowment, or the villagers contribute a small sum annually, or plough the priest's fields, or shear his sheep, but the fees given for baptisms, marriages, and other occasional offices would be his sole dependence unless he followed some secular calling. In some places there is a plethora of supernumerary priests, and it is shrewdly said that these obtain holy orders from the Bishops for the sake of the loaves of sugar paid as fees. There are great abuses connected with ordination. One of the present bishops was consecrated when quite a young boy, and deacons are often ordained at sixteen, and even much earlier. Mar Auraham must have been consecrated before he was twenty. The only qualification for ordination is the ability to read old Syriac. The gaily-dressed and fully-armed young mountaineers whom

I have seen as representing the diaconate look far more
like bandits than deacons.   In one large village there are
at present fifty deacons and fifteen priests attached to one
church !!

The *Kourbana* cannot be celebrated without the

SYRIAN PRIEST AND WIFE.

assistance of a deacon.   It is almost entirely confined to
the great festivals and the feast of the patron saint of
each village.   After the making of the bread with the
"holy leaven," and certain preliminaries by the clergy,
the congregation comes into church, summoned by blows
on the wooden sounding-board.   The men stand in front,
the women behind, all taking off their shoes and kissing

the Cross. When the elements are to be received the priest advances to the door of the sanctuary, and a deacon, completely enveloped by the curtain before the entrance, holds the paten while the priest gives the bread to the men first, then to the women and to the little children, held up either by father or mother. The adults receive the cup in order from the deacon, who passes it through a hole in a wall about six feet high, which runs parallel with the wall of the sanctuary, but at a little distance from it. On leaving the church after communion each person takes a piece of ordinary bread from a tray near the door. The priests and deacons communicate after the people when the sanctuary veil has again been drawn. The Eucharist is always celebrated at or before daybreak, except in the case of certain fast days and at funerals, when it is considered a devotional act to fast till mid-day. During parts of the communion service one deacon swings a censer and another " clangs " a cymbal.

The *Kourbana* as celebrated in the Syrian villages reminds me both of the great communion gatherings of the Scottish Highlands and the Church service which, in my childhood, ushered in the revelry of the village wake or feast. The festivals which, as in England, fall on the feast of the patron saint of the village are the great gaieties of Syrian life, and even the Kurd cannot altogether overshadow them. After the celebration of the *Kourbana* at dawn, when the crowds are frequently so great that the church is filled by several successive congregations of communicants, the day is spent in visiting, and in every house fruit, sweetmeats, and tea are provided for all comers, and *arak*, if it be obtainable, forms a part of the entertainment. Dances and games are kept up all day, and at its close many are drunk and disorderly. These are the occasions when fighting with the Moslems is apt to take place.

Men and women, of course, dance separately, and the women much in the background. The dancing, as I have seen it, is slow and stately. A number of either sex join hands in a ring, and move round to slow music, at times letting go each other's hands for the purpose of gesticulation and waving of handkerchiefs. It is not unlike the national dance of the Bakhtiaris. The women not only keep in retirement on this but on all occasions. They never sit at meat with the men, but take their food afterwards in private—indeed, I strongly suspect that they eat the leavings of their superiors. It is not, however, only the women who occupy a subordinate position. Young men treat not only their fathers but their elder brothers with extreme respect ; and when there are guests at table the sons do not sit down with the fathers, but wait on the guests, and take their own meals, like the women, afterwards.

The Syrians call Easter " The Great Feast " and Christmas " The Little Feast." At the former, eggs coloured red are lavishly bestowed. The festival of the Epiphany also receives great honour, but it is curious that a people who believe that they owe their Christianity to the Wise Men should not keep this feast so much in commemoration of them as of our Lord's baptism. So much does the latter view preponderate, that the Urmi Christians call it by a name which means " The New Waters." Here in the mountains, however, it is called " The Brightness." During the night before the celebration of the *Kourbana* on the Feast of the Epiphany it is customary to plunge into frozen pools ! " One Lord, one faith, one baptism " they hold with us, and it is of great interest to recognise this fact in the midst of many superstitions and even puerilities.

It is impossible by any language to convey an idea of the poverty and meanness, the blackness and accumulations of dust, the darkness and the gloom of the Syrian churches, of which this one is a favourable specimen, typi-fying, I fear, too truly the gross ignorance, indifference, and superstition in which bishops, priests, and people are buried. And yet they are "faithful unto death." My daily wonder is that people who know so little will for that little suffer the loss of all things. Apostasy would be immediate emancipation from terror and ruin, but it is nearly unknown. Their churches are like the catacombs. Few things can be more pathetic than a congregation standing in the dark and dismal nave, kissing the common wooden cross, and passing from hand to hand the kiss of peace, while the priest, in dress like their own, with girdle and stole of the poorest material, moves among the ancient Liturgies in front of the dusty sanc-tuary, leading the worshippers in prayers and chants which have come down from the earliest ages of Chris-tianity; from the triumphant Church of the East to the persecuted remnant of to-day.   I. L. B.

LETTER XXIX (*Continued*)

WHO is or is not in this house it is hard to say.   Mirza tells me that there are 115 guests to-day!   Among them are a number óf Tyari men, whose wild looks, combined with the splendour of their dress and arms, are a great interest.   Their chief man has invited me to visit their valley, and they say if I will go to them they will give me "a fine suit of clothes."   I need it much, as doubtless they have observed!   Their jackets are one mass of gold embroidery (worked by Jews), their shirts, with hanging sleeves, are striped satin; their trousers, of sailor cut, are silk, made from the cocoons of their own silkworms, woven with broad crimson stripes on a white ground, on which is a zigzag pattern; and their handsome jack-boots are of crimson leather.   With their white or red peaked felt hats and twisted silk *pagris*, their rich girdles, jewelled daggers, and inlaid pistols, they are very imposing.   Female dress is very simple.

These Tyari men come from one of the wildest and most inaccessible valleys of Central Kurdistan, and belong to those Ashirets or tribal Syrians who, in their deep and narrow rifts, are practically unconquered by the Turks and unmolested by the Kurds, and maintain a fierce semi-independence under their *maleks* (lit. kings) or chiefs.   They are wild and lawless mountaineers, paying taxes only when it suits them; brave, hardy, and warlike, preserving their freedom by the sword; fierce, quarrelsome among themselves, and having little in common with the *rayahs* or subject Syrians of the plains except their tenacious clinging to their ancient Church, with its Liturgies and rites, and their homage to our Lord Jesus as divine. They and their priests, many of whom cannot even read, are sunk in the grossest ignorance. They love revenge, are careless of human life, and are wilder and more savage than their nominal masters. It is among these people, who purchase their freedom at the cost of absolute isolation, that Mr. Browne is going to spend the coming winter, in the hope of instructing their priests and deacons, to whom at present guns are more than ordinances. He has been among them already, and has won their good-will.

A SYRIAN GIRL.

These Ashirets, of whom the Tyari guests are specimens, are quite unlike the Syrian lowlanders, not only in character but in costume and habits. As they have naturalised numbers of Kurdish words in their speech, so their dress, with its colour, rich materials and embroideries, and lavish display of decorated and costly arms, is almost altogether

Kurdish. If report speaks truly their fierce tribal feuds and readiness with the dagger are Kurdish also. Their country is the country of the hunted. Its mountains rise nearly perpendicularly to altitudes of over 12,000 feet, and the valleys, such as Tyari, Tkhoma, Baz, Diz, and Jelu, are mere slits or gashes, through which furious tributaries of the greater Zab take their impetuous course. Above these streams the tribes have built up minute fields by raising the lower sides on stone walls a few feet above the rivers, the upper being the steep hill slope. So small are these plots that it is said that the harvest of some of them would only fill a man's cap! Occasionally heavy floods sweep away the rice and millet cultivation of a whole district, and the mountaineers are compelled to depend for their food entirely on the produce of their flocks.

If they could sustain themselves and their animals altogether within their own fastnesses, they would be secure from molestation either from Kurds or Turks, for the only possible entrances to their valleys are so narrow and ruggedly steep as scarcely to be accessible for a pack-horse, and ten men could keep any number at bay. But unfortunately the scanty herbage of their mountains is soon exhausted, and they have to feed their flocks outside their natural fortifications, where the sheep are constantly being carried off by the Kurds, who murder the shepherds and women. The mountaineers are quick to revenge themselves ; they carry off Kurdish sheep, and savage warfare and a life under arms are the normal condition of the Ashirets. The worst of it is, that they are disunited among themselves, and fight and spoil each other as much as they fight the Kurds, even at times taking part with them against their Christian brethren. Travellers are scarcely safer from robbery among them than among the Kurds, but fierce, savage, and quarrelsome as they are, and independent both of Turk and Kurd, they render a sort of obedience to Mar Shimun, who rules them, through their *maleks*. There is not only enmity between tribe and tribe, but between village and village, and, as in parts of the Bakhtiari country, guides refuse to conduct travellers beyond certain spots, declaring that " blood " bars their farther progress.

Besides the Kurdish and Ashiret inhabitants of these mountains of Kurdistan there are Yezidis, usually called devil-worshippers, and a few Jews and Armenians. Probably there is not a wilder population on the face of the earth, or one of whose ideas, real beliefs, and ways Europeans are so ignorant. What, for instance, do we really know of the beliefs which underlie the religious customs of the Kizilbashes and Yezidis, and of the Christianity to which these semi-savage Ashirets are so passionately attached ?

If I were to leave Mr. Browne unnoticed I should ignore the most remarkable character in Kochanes. Clothed partly as a Syrian and living altogether like one,—at this time speaking Syriac more readily than English ; limited to this narrow alp and to the narrower exile of the Tyari valley ; self-exiled from civilised society; snowed up for many months of the year ; his communications even with Van and Urmi irregular and precarious ; a priest without an altar ; a teacher without pupils ; a hermit without privacy; his time at the disposal of every one who cares to waste it ; harassed by Turkish officialism and obstruction, and prohibited by the Porte from any active " mission work," it yet would be hard to find a sunnier, more loving, and more buoyant spirit. He has lived among these people for nearly four years as one of themselves, making their interests completely his own, suffering keenly in their persecutions and losses, and entering warmly even into their most trivial concerns, till he has become in fact a Syrian among Syrians. He sits on the floor in

native fashion; his primitive and unpalatable food, served
in copper bowls from the Patriarch's kitchen, is eaten with
his fingers; he is nearly without possessions, he sleeps on
the floor "among the spiders" without a mattress, he
lives in a hovel up a steep ladder in a sort of tower
out of repair—Syrian customs and etiquette have become second nature to him.

He has no "mission work" to report. He is himself the mission and the work. The hostility of the
Turkish Government and the insecurity of the country
prevent him from opening schools, he cannot even
assemble a few boys and teach them their letters; he got
a bit of land and the stones for erecting a cottage, but is
not allowed to build; his plans are all frustrated by
bigotry on one side and timidity on the other, and he is
even prevented from preaching by the blind conservatism
of the patriarchal court. It has not been the custom to
have preaching at Kochanes. "Sermons were dangerous
things that promoted heresy," the Patriarch said. But
Mr. Browne is far from being idle. People come
to him from the villages and surrounding country for
advice, and often take it. They confide all their concerns
to him, he acts effectively the part of a peacemaker in
their quarrels, he is trusted even by the semi-savage
chiefs and priests of the mountain tribes, and his medical skill, which is at the service of all, is largely resorted
to at all hours of the day. Silenced from preaching and
prohibited from teaching, far better than a sermon
is his own cheery life of unconscious self-sacrifice, truth,
purity, and devotion. This example the people can
understand, though they cannot see why an English-
man should voluntarily take to such a life as he leads.
His power lies in his singular love for them, and in
his almost complete absorption in their lives and interests.

His room is most amusing. It is little better than a

Kerry hovel. He uses neither chair, table, nor bed; the uneven earthen floor is covered with such a litter of rubbish as is to be seen at the back of a "rag and bone" shop, dusty medicine bottles predominating. There is a general dismemberment of everything that once was serviceable. The occupant of the room is absolutely unconscious of its demerits, and my ejaculations of dismay are received with hearty laughter.[1]

Humbly following his example, I have become absorbed in the interests of the inhabitants of Kochanes, and would willingly stay here for some weeks longer if it were not for the risk of being blocked in by snow on the Armenian highlands. The cattle plague is very severe, in addition to other misfortunes. The village has already lost 135 of its herd, and I seldom go out without seeing men dragging carcasses to be thrown over the cliff. The people believe that the men will die next year.

My future journey and its safety are much discussed. If I had had any idea of the "disturbed" state of the region that I have yet to pass through I should never have entered Turkey, but now I have resolved to go *via* Bitlis to Erzerum. If the road is as dangerous as it is said to be, and if the rumours regarding the state of the Christians turn out to have much truth in them, the

---

[1] In the winter of 1887 and the spring of 1888 every effort was made by Fikri Pasha, the Turkish Governor of this district, but a Kurd by race, to dislodge Mr. Browne from his position in the mountains. "Soldiers were continually sent to inquire into his plans; he was accused of practising without a diploma as a medical man, because he gave a few simple remedies to the natives in a country destitute of physicians, and his position became well-nigh intolerable when he found that his host, Mar Shimun, was being insulted and punished for harbouring him, and that the native Christians were being made to suffer for his residence among them. The Patriarch, however, stood firm. 'Your presence here,' said he to Mr. Browne, 'may save us from a massacre; and as for these troubles we must put up with them as best we can.' These words were verified a few months afterwards."—Mr. Athelstan Riley's *Report on the Archbishop of Canterbury's Mission to the Assyrian Christians*, 1888.

testimony of a neutral observer may be useful and helpful. At all events the risk is worth running. My
great difficulty is that *Qasha* —— must leave me here
to return to Urmi with Mar Gauriel's escort, and that I
have no competent man with me in case of difficulty.
Mirza not only does not speak Turkish, but has no "back-
bone," and Johannes, besides having the disadvantage
of being an Armenian, is really half a savage, as well
as disobedient, bad-tempered, reckless, and quarrelsome.
He fought with a Turk at Yekmala, and got me into
trouble, and one of his first misdemeanours here was to
shoot the church doves, which are regarded as sacred,
thereby giving great offence to the Patriarch.

It is most difficult to get away. The Julamerik
muleteers are afraid of being robbed on the route I wish
to take, and none of them but a young Kurd will undertake my loads, and though he arrived last night the
zaptiehs I applied for have failed me. They were to have
been here by daylight this morning, and the loads were
ready, but nine o'clock came without their appearance.
I wanted to take armed men from Kochanes, but Mar
Shimun said that twelve Christians would be no protection against the Kurds, and that I must not go without
a Government escort, so things were unpacked. Late
this evening, and after another messenger had been sent
to Julamerik, one *zaptieh* arrived with a message that
they could not spare more, and the people protest against
my leaving with such insufficient protection.

Another difficulty is the want of money. Owing to
the "boom" in silver in Persia, and the semi-panic which
prevailed, the utmost efforts of my friends in Urmi could
only obtain £10 for a £20 note, and this only in silver
mejidiehs, a Turkish coin worth about 4s. As no money
is current in the villages change cannot be procured, and
on sending to Julamerik for small coins, only a very

limited quantity could be obtained—Russian *kopecks* locally
current at half their value, Turkish coins the size of a
crown piece, but so debased that they are only worth 1s.,
a number of pieces of base metal the size of sixpences,
and "groats" and copper coins, miserably thin.   It took
me an hour, even with Mr. Browne's help, to count 8s.
in this truly execrable money.   The Julamerik *shroff* sent
word that the English sovereign is selling at 16s. only.

So, owing to these delays, I have had another day
here, with its usual routine of drinking coffee in houses,
inviting women to tea in my room, receiving mountaineers
and others who come in at all hours and kiss my hand,
and smoke their long pipes on my floor, and another
opportunity of walking in the glory of the sunset, when
the mountain barriers of beautiful Kochanes glow with a
colouring which suggests thoughts of "the land which is
very far off."   Good Mr. Browne makes himself one with
the people, and is most anxious for me to identify everybody, and say the right thing to everybody—no easy task,
and as I hope and fear that this is my last evening, I
have tried to "leave a pleasant impression" by spending
it in the great gathering-place, called pre-eminently the
"house"!   Mirza says that the people talk of nothing
but "guns, Kurds, the harvest, and the local news," but the
conversation to-night had a wider range, and was often
very amusing, taking a sombre turn only when the risks
of my journey were discussed, and the possible misconduct
of my Kurdish *katirgi*.   Ishai, who describes him as "a
very tame man" (not at all my impression of him), has
told him that "if he gives any trouble the House of Mar
Shimun will never forget it."

Nothing could exceed the picturesqueness of the
"house" to-night.   There were doubtless fifty people
there, but the lamps, which look as old as the relentless
sweep of Taimurlane, hanging high on the blackened

pillars, only lighted up the central group, consisting of Sulti and Marta in the highest place, the English priest in his turban and cassock, the grotesque visage of Shlimon the Jester, and the beautiful face and figure and splendid dress of Ishai the Patriarch's brother, as proud as proud can be, but sitting among the retainers of his ancient house playing on a musical instrument, the hereditary familiarity of serf and lord blending with such expressions of respect as " your foot is on my eyes," and the favourite asseveration, " by the Head of Mar Shimun." The blackness in which the lofty roof was lost, the big ovens with their busy groups, the rows of men, half-seen in the dimness, lounging on natural ledges of rock, and the uphill floor with its uncouth plenishings, made up such a picture as the feudalism of our own middle ages might have presented.

My letter[1] from the Turkish Ambassador at Tihran was sent to Julamerik this afternoon, and has produced another *zaptieh*, and an apology !   I. L. B.

---

[1] Translation of a letter given to the author by His Excellency the Turkish Ambassador to the Court of Tihran.

" Among the honoured of English ladies is Mrs. Bishop. On this tour of travel she has a letter of recommendation from the Exalted Government of England, issued by the English Embassy in Tihran, and earnest request is made that in her passage through the Imperial Territory she be well protected. As far as *zaptiehs* are necessary let them be given for her safety, all necessary provision for her most comfortable travel be perfected, and all her requests from the High Government of the Osmanlis be met.

" That all courtesy and attention be shown to this distinguished lady, this letter is given from the Embassy at Tihran."

As various statements purporting to be narratives of attacks made upon me in Turkey have appeared in Russian and other papers, I take this opportunity of saying that they are devoid of any foundation. I was never robbed while in the dominion of His Majesty the Sultan: courtesy was shown me by all the Turkish officials between the Persian frontier and Erzerum, and efficient escorts of steady and respectful *zaptiehs* were readily supplied.

LETTER XXX

KOTRANIS, KURDISTAN, *Oct. 28*.

HERE, in one of the wildest of mountain hamlets, I hoped to indulge in the luxury of my tent, and it was actually unrolled, when all the village men came to me and with gestures of appeal besought me not to pitch it, as it would not be safe for one hour and would " bring trouble upon them." The hamlet is suffering terribly from the Kurds, who are not only robbing it of its sheep and most else, but are attempting to deprive the peasants of their lands in spite of the fact that they possess title-deeds. This Berwar-Lata valley has been reduced from a condition of pastoral wealth to one of extreme poverty. Kotranis, and Bilar a little lower down, from which the best hones are exported, are ruined by Kurdish exactions. The Christians sow and the Kurds reap : they breed cattle and sheep and the Kurds drive them off when they are well grown. One man at —— a few miles off, had 1000 sheep. He has been robbed of all but sixty. This is but a specimen of the wrongs to which these unhappy people are exposed. The Kurds now scarcely give them any respite in which " *to let the sheep's wool grow*," as their phrase is.

Kotranis is my last Syrian halting-place, and its miseries are well fitted to leave a lasting impression. It is included in the *vilayet* of Van, in which, according to the latest estimates, there are 80,000 Syrian Christians.

The *rayahs* either own the village lands or are the dependants or serfs of a Kurdish Agha or master. In either case their condition is deplorable, for they have practically no rights which a Kurd or Turk is bound to respect. In some of their villages they have been robbed till they are absolutely without the means of paying taxes, and are beaten, till the fact is established beyond dispute. They are but scantily supplied with the necessaries of life, though their industry produces abundance. Squeezed between the rapacity and violence of the Kurds and the exactions of the Turkish officials, who *undoubtedly connive at outrages so long as the victims are Christians*, the condition of these Syrians is one of the most pitiable on earth. They have no representatives in the cities of Europe and Asia, and no commercial instincts and habits like the Armenians. They have the Oriental failings of untruthfulness and avarice, and the cunning begotten by centuries of oppression, but otherwise they are simple, grossly ignorant, helpless shepherds and cultivators; aliens by race and creed, without a rich or capable man among them, hemmed in by some of the most inaccessible of mountain ranges, and by their oppressors the Kurds; without a leader, adviser, or friend, rarely visited by travellers, with no voice which can reach Europe, with a present of intolerable bondage and a future without light, and yet through all clinging passionately to the faith received by tradition from their fathers.

As I have no lodging but a dark stable, I am utilising the late afternoon, sitting by the village threshing-floor, on which a mixed rabble of animals is treading corn. Some buffaloes are lying in moist places looking amiable and foolish. *Boy* is tied to my chair. The village women knit and stare. Two of the men, armed with matchlock guns, keep a look-out for the Kurds. A crystal stream tumbles through the village, over ledges of white quartz. Below, the valley opens and discloses ranges bathed in ineffable blue. The mountain sides are aflame with autumn tints, and down their steep paths oxen are bringing the tawny gold of the late harvest on rude sledges. But the shadow of the Kurd is over it all. I left English-speaking people so lately that I scarcely realise that I am now alone in Central Kurdistan, in one of the wildest parts of the world, among fierce predatory tribes, and a ravaged and imperilled people.

I bade the Patriarch farewell at six this morning, and even at that early hour men were seated all round his room. After shaking hands with about thirty people, I walked the first mile accompanied by Mr. Browne, who then left me on his way to seek to enlighten the wild tribesmen of the Tyari valley. From the top of the Kamerlan Pass, above Kochanes, the view was inconceivably beautiful. On the lovely alp on which the village stands a red patch of autumnal colouring flamed against the deep indigo and purple mountains of Diz and Shaw-utha, which block up the east end of the lofty valley; while above these rose the Jelu ranges, said to be from 12,000 to 15,000 feet in altitude, bathed in rich pure blue, snow-fields on their platforms, new-fallen snow on their crests, indigo shadows in their clefts and ravines,— a glorious group of spires, peaks, crags, chasms, precipices, rifts, parapets, and ridges perfect in their beauty as seen in the calm coloured atmosphere in which autumn loves to die. Higher up we were in vast solitudes, among splintered peaks and pasturages where clear streams crashed over rock ledges or murmured under ice, and then a descent of 1800 feet by steep zigzags, and a seven hours' march in keen pure air, brought us through rounded hills to this village.

Van, November 1.—There was a night alarm at Kot-ranis. A number of Kurds came down upon the threshing-floor, and the *zaptiehs* were most unwilling to drive off the marauders, saying that their only orders were to protect me. The Kurds, who were at least ten to one, retired when they saw the Government uniforms, but the big dogs barked for the rest of the night.

The next day's march occupied eleven hours. It was very cold, "light without heat," superb travelling weather. One *zaptieh* was a Moslem, the other an Armenian, and there were strong differences of opinion between them, especially when we halted to rest at a Christian village, and the Kurdish *katirgi* took several sheaves of corn from a threshing-floor without paying for them. The Moslem insisted that he should not pay, and the Christian that he should, and it ended by my paying and deducting the sum from his *bakhsheesh*. The *zaptiehs* are usually men who have served five years with the colours. In Eastern Asia Minor they are well clothed in dark blue braided uniforms, and have ulsters in addition for cold weather. They provide their own horses. Their pay is eighty piastres a month, with rations of bread for themselves and of barley for their animals, but the pay is often nine months in arrear, or they receive it in depreciated paper. They are accused of being directly or indirectly concerned in many robberies, and of preying on the peasantry. They are armed with Snider rifles, swords, and revolvers. From the top of a high pass above Kotranis there was a final view of the Jelu mountains, and the remainder of the day was spent among hills, streams, and valleys, with rich fertile soil and abundant water, but very thinly peopled.

A very ingenious plough has taken the place of the primitive implement hitherto used. The share is big and heavy, well shod with iron, and turns up the soil to a great depth. The draught is from an axle with two wheels, one of them two feet in diameter and the other only ten inches. The big wheel runs in the last furrow, and the little one on 'the soil not yet upturned, the axle being level. Some of these ploughs were drawn by eight buffaloes, with a boy, singing an inharmonious tune, seated facing backwards on each yoke. After the ploughing, water is turned on to soften the clods, which are then broken up by the husbandmen with spades.

There is a great charm about the scenery as seen at this season, the glorious colouring towards sunset, the fantastic forms and brilliant tints of the rocks, and the purity of the new-fallen snow upon the heights; but between Kotranis and Van, except for a little planting in the " Valley of the Armenians," there is scarcely a bush. If I had warm clothing I should regard the temperature as perfect, nearly 50° at noon, and falling to about 25° at night. After a severe march, a descent and a sudden turn in the road brought us in the purple twilight to Merwanen, the chief village of Norduz, streamily situated on a slope—a wretched village, semi-subterranean; a partly finished house, occupied by a newly arrived *Kaimakam* and a number of *zaptiehs*, rising above the miserable hovels, which, bad as they are, were all occupied by the *Kaimakam's* attendants. *Zaptiehs*, soldiers, Kurds, and villagers assured me that there was no room anywhere, and an officer, in a much-frogged uniform, drove my men from pillar to post, not allowing us standing room on the little dry ground that there was. I humbly asked if I could pitch my tent, but a rough negative was returned. A subterranean buffalo stable, where there was just room among the buffaloes for me to lie down in a cramped position, was the only available shelter, and there was none for the servants. I do not much mind sharing a stable with *Boy*, but I " draw the line " at buffaloes, and came out again into the frosty air, into an inhospitable and altogether unprepossessing crowd.

Then there was a commotion, with much bowing and falling to the right and left, and the *Kaimakam* himself appeared, with my powerful letter in his hand, took me into the unfinished house, at which he had only arrived an hour before, and into a small room almost altogether occupied by two beds on the floor, on one of which a man very ill of fever was lying, and on the other an unveiled Kurdish beauty was sitting. The *Kaimakam*, though exceedingly " the worse of drink," was not without a certain dignity and courtesy. He apologised profoundly for the incivility and discomfort which I had met with, and for his inability to entertain me " with distinction " in " so rough a place," but said that he would give up his own room to so " exalted a personage," or if I preferred a room outside it should be made ready. Of course I chose the latter, with profuse expressions of the gratitude I sincerely felt, and after a cup of coffee bade him good-night.

The room was the justice or injustice room over the *zaptieh* barracks, and without either door or glazed windows, but cold and stiff as I was after an eleven hours' march, I was thankful for any rest and shelter. Shortly my young Kurdish *katirgi*, a splendid fellow, but not the least " tame," announced that he must leave me in order to get the escort of some *zaptiehs* back to Julamerik. He said that " they all " told him that the road to Van was full of danger, and that if he went on he would be robbed of his mules and money on the way back. No transport however, was to be got, and he came on with me very pluckily, and has got an escort back, at least to Merwanen. In the morning the *Kaimakam* rose early to do me honour, but was so tipsy that he could scarcely sit upright on his chair on a stone dais amidst a rabble of soldiers and scribes. We were all benumbed with cold, and glad that the crossing of an expanse of frozen streams rendered walking a necessity. A nine hours' march through mountains remarkable for rocky spires and needles marvellously coloured, and for the absence of inhabitants, took us to the Armenian village of Khanjarak, finely situated in a corrie upon a torrent bank ; but it is so subterranean, and so built into the hillside, that a small square church and conical piles of *kiziks* are the only obvious objects, and I rode over the roofs without knowing what was underneath.

All the women and children, rabbit-like, came out of their holes, clothed in red rags, and some wore strings of coins round their heads. The men were dressed like Kurds, and were nearly as wild-looking. They protested against my tent being pitched. They said the Kurds were always on the watch, and would hack it with their swords in half an hour to get at its contents, that they had only three matchlock guns, and that the Kurds were armed with rifles. I felt that I could scarcely touch a lower depth in the matter of accommodation than when they lodged me in a dark subterranean stable, running very far back into the hill, with a fire of animal fuel in the middle giving off dense and acrid fumes. A recess in this, with a mud bench, was curtained off for me, and the rest of the space was occupied by my own horses and baggage mules, and most of the village asses, goats, cows, calves, and sheep. Several horses belonging to travellers and to my own escort were also there, and all the *zaptiehs*, servants, travellers, and *katirgis* were lodged there. There were legions of fleas revelling in a temperature which rose to 80° at midnight, though there were 5° of frost outside. In the part of the roof which projected from the hill there were two holes for light, but at night these were carefully closed with corks of plaited straw.

The wretched poverty of the people of this place made a very painful impression on me. They *may* have exaggerated when they told me how terribly they are oppressed by the Kurds, who, they say, last year robbed them of 900 sheep and this year of 300, twenty-five and some cattle having been driven off a few days before, but it is a simple fact that the night of my visit the twenty-four sheep for which there was no room in the stable were carried away by a party of well-armed Kurds in the bright moonlight, the helpless shepherds not daring to resist. It is of no use, they say, to petition the Government; it will not interfere. The Kurds come into their houses, they say, and terrify and insult their women, and by demands with violence take away all they have. They say that the money for which they have sold their grain, and which they were keeping to pay their taxes with, was taken by the Kurds last week, and that they will be cruelly beaten by the *zaptiehs* because they cannot pay. Their words and air expressed abject terror.[1]

Their little church is poorer than poverty itself, a building of undressed stone without mortar, and its length of thirteen feet includes the rude mud dais occupied by the yet ruder altar. Its furniture consists of an iron censer, an iron saucer containing oil and a wick, and an

---

[1] I must ask my readers to believe that I crossed the Turkish frontier without any knowledge of or interest in the "Armenian Question;" that so far from having any special liking for the Armenians I had rather a prejudice against them; that I was in ignorance of the "Erzerum troubles" of June 1890, and of yet more recent complications, and that the sole object of my journey by a route seldom traversed by Europeans from Urmi to Van was to visit the Patriarch of the Nestorians and the Kochanes station of the Archbishop of Canterbury's Assyrian Church Mission, and that afterwards I travelled to Erzerum *viâ* Bitlis only to visit the American missionaries there. So far as I know, I entered Turkey as a perfectly neutral and impartial observer, and without any special interest in its Christian populations, and it is only the "inexorable logic of facts" which has convinced me of their wrongs and claims.

earthen flagon. There are no windows, and the rough walls are black with candle smoke. The young man who showed the church took a Gospel from the dais, kissing the cross upon it before handing it to me, and then on seeing that I was interested went home and brought a MS. of St. Matthew's Gospel, with several rudely-illuminated scenes from our Lord's life. "Christos," he said with a smile, as he pointed to the central figure in the first illustration, and so on as he showed me the others, for in each there was a figure of the Christ, not crowned and risen, but suffering and humiliated. Next morning, in the bitter cold of the hour before sunrise, the clang of the mallet on the sounding-board assembled the villagers for matins, and to the Christ crowned and risen and "sitting on the right hand of power" they rendered honour as Divine, though in the midst of the grossest superstition and darkness, and for Him whom they "ignorantly worship" they are at this moment suffering the loss of all things. Their empty sheepfold might have been full to-day if they had acknowledged Him as a Prophet and no more.[1]

Leaving this wretched hamlet, where the unfortunate peasants are as avaricious as they are poor and dirty, and passing a Kurdish village with a stone fort picturesquely situated, we crossed a pass into a solitary valley, on which high rounded hills descend in harmonised buffs and browns, both hills and valleys covered with uncut hay. The *zaptiehs* said that this was a specially dangerous place, and urged the caravan to its utmost speed. We met three Armenian *katirgis* in their shirts. They complained most bitterly that they had been robbed an hour before of five mules with their equipments, as well

---

[1] In another village, a young man in speaking of their circumstances said : " We don't know much, but we love the Lord Jesus well enough to die for Him."

as of their clothing and money. The ascent and the very tedious descent of the Kasrik Kala Pass brought us into the large and fertile plain of Haizdar, the "plain of the Armenians," sprinkled with Armenian villages, and much cultivated.

Mirza and one *zaptieh* had gone back for a blanket which had been dropped, and after halting in an orchard till I was half-frozen I decided to proceed without them, having understood that we could reach Van in three hours. I started my party by signs, and after an hour's riding reached a village where Johannes spoke fluently in an unknown tongue, and the *zaptieh* held up five fingers, which I learned too late meant that Van was five hours off. I thought that they were asking for instructions, and at every pause I repeated *Van*.

After a brief consultation we went up among the hills, the young Kurdish *katirgi* jumping, yelling, singing, and howling, to keep his mules at a trot, the *zaptieh* urging them with his whip, and pointing ominously at the fast sinking sun. On we clattered with much noise, nor did we slacken speed till we gained a high altitude among desert solitudes, from which we looked down upon the Dead Sea of Van, a sheet of water extending in one direction beyond the limits of vision, lying red and weird, with high mountains jutting into it in lofty headlands hovered over by flame-coloured clouds. High up along the mountain side in a wavy line lay the path to Van in the deepening shadows, and the *zaptieh*, this time holding up three fingers, still urged on the caravan, and the Kurd responded by yells and howls, dancing and jumping like a madman.

Just as it was becoming dark, four mounted men, each armed with two guns, rode violently among the mules, which were in front of me, and attempted to drive them off. In the *mêlée* the *katirgi* was knocked down. The *zaptieh* jumped off his horse, threw the bridle to me, and shouldered his rifle. When they saw the Government uniform these Ḳurds drew back, let the mules go, and passed on. The whole affair took but a few seconds, but it was significant of the unwillingness of the Kurds to come into collision with the Turks, and of the power the Government could exercise in the disturbed districts if it were once understood that the marauders were not to be allowed a free hand.

After this attack not a word was spoken, the bells were taken off the mules, the *zaptieh*, as fine and soldierly a man as one could wish to see, marched in front, quiet and vigilant, and so in a darkness in which I could not see my horse's ears we proceeded till, three hours later, the moon rose as we entered Van. It was one of the *eeriest* rides I ever made, and I had many painful reflections on having risked through ignorance the property of my faithful Kurdish *katirgi*. The first light of Van was a welcome sight, though after that there was a long ride to "the gardens," a large wooded suburb chiefly inhabited by Armenians, in which the American missionaries live. Dr. Reynolds, the medical missionary, has given me a most hospitable welcome, though his small house is more than full with new arrivals from America. I wanted to re-engage my jolly *katirgi* for Bitlis, but he went back at once with the *zaptieh*, and after the obvious perils of the road it would not have been fair to detain him. Visitors are scarce here. Van does not see more than one non-official European in three years. The Vice-Consul says that he should have doubted the sanity of any one who had proposed to travel from Urmi to Van by the route I took, but now that the journey is safely over I am glad that no one at Urmi knew enough to dissuade me from it. The Vice-Consul and all the mission party are as kind as they can be, and Van is for me another oasis.   I. L. B.

LETTER XXXI

VAN,[1] ARMENIA, *Nov. 4.*

VAN and its surroundings are at once so interesting and picturesque that it is remarkable that they are comparatively seldom visited by travellers. Probably

[1] Van may be considered the capital of that part of Kurdistan which we know as Armenia, but it must be remembered that under the present Government of Turkey Armenia is a prohibited name, and has ceased to be "a geographical expression." Cyclopædias containing articles on Armenia, and school books with any allusions to Armenian history, or to the geography of any district referred to as Armenia, are not allowed to enter Asia Minor, and no foreign maps which contain the province of Armenia are allowed to be used in the foreign schools, or even to be retained in the country. Of the four millions of the Armenian race 2,500,000 are subjects of the Sultan, and with few exceptions are distinguished for their loyalty and their devotion to peaceful pursuits.

The portion of Armenia which lies within the Turkish frontier consists for the most part of table-lands from 5000 to 6000 feet in elevation, intersected by mountain ranges and watered by several rivers, the principal of which are the Euphrates, the Tigris, and the Aras. Of its many lakes the Dead Sea of Van is the principal, its dimensions being estimated at twice the area of the Lake of Geneva, and at eighty miles in length by twenty-five in breadth. From its exquisitely beautiful shores rise the two magnificent extinct volcanoes, the Sipan Dagh, with an altitude of over 12,000 feet, and the Nimrud Dagh, with a crater five miles in diameter and 1600 feet in depth, the top of its wall being over 9000 feet in height.

The Armenians claim an antiquity exceeding that of any other nation, and profess to trace their descent from Haik, the son of Togarmah, the grandson of Japhet, who fled from the tyranny of Belus, King of Assyria, into the country which in the Armenian tongue is known by his name, as *Haikh* or *Haizdani*. It may be said of the Armenians that the splendour and misery of their national history exceed those of any other race.

the insecurity of the roads, the villainous accommodation *en route*, and its isolated position account for the
neglect.[1]   Here as elsewhere I am much impressed
with the excellence of the work done by the American
missionaries, who are really the lights of these dark
places, and by their exemplary and honourable lives
furnish that *moral model* and standard of living which
is more efficacious than preaching in lifting up the lives
of a people sunk in the depths of a grossly corrupted
Christianity.   The boys' and girls' schools in Van are on
an excellent basis, and are not only turning out capable
men and women, but are stimulating the Armenians to

Their national church claims an older than an apostolic foundation, and
historically dates from the third century, its actual founder, S. Gregory
the Illuminator, having been consecrated at Cæsarea as Bishop of Armenia
in the second year of the fourth century. In the fifteenth century a schism
brought about by Jesuit missionaries resulted in a number of Armenians
joining the Church of Rome, and becoming later a separate community
known as the "Catholic Armenian Church." Within the last half-century,
under the teaching of the American missionaries, a Reformed Church has
arisen, known as the Protestant Armenian Church, but with these exceptions
the race and the national church may be regarded as one. The Armenians
have had no political existence since the year 1604, but form an element
of stability and wealth in Turkey, Russia, and Persia, where they are
principally found.

Their language is regarded by scholars as an off-shoot of the Iranian
branch of the Indo-Germanic group of languages. Their existing literature
dates from the fourth century, and all that is not exclusively Christian has
perished. Translations of the Old and New Testaments dating from the
fifth century are among its oldest monuments, and the dialect in which
they are written, and in which they are still read in the churches, known
as Old Armenian, is not now understood by the people. During the last
century there has been a great revival of letters among the Armenians,
chiefly due to the *Mekhitarists* of Venice, and a literature in modern
Armenian is rapidly developing alongside of the study and publication of
the works of the ancient writers.

[1] It has, however, received due attention both from scholars and anti-
quaries, and among the popularly-written accounts of it are very interesting chapters in Sir A. H. Layard's *Nineveh and Babylon*, and in a charming volume by the Rev. H. F. Tozer, *Turkish Armenia and Eastern Asia
Minor*.

raise the teaching and tone of their own schools in the
city, with one of which I was very greatly pleased. The
creation of churches, strict in their discipline, and pro-
testing against the mass of superstitions which smother
all spiritual life in the National Armenian Church, is undoubtedly having a very salutary effect far beyond the
limited membership, and is tending to *force reform* upon
an ancient church which contains within herself the
elements of resurrection. Great honour is due to Dr.
Reynolds for the way in which, almost single-handed, he
has kept the valuable work of this Mission going for
years, and now that colleagues have arrived a considerable development may be hoped for.

I have confessed already to a prejudice against the
Armenians, but it is not possible to deny that they are
the most capable, energetic, enterprising, and pushing race
in Western Asia, physically superior, and intellectually
acute, and above all they are a race which can be raised
in all respects to our own level, neither religion, colour,
customs, nor inferiority in intellect or force constituting
any barrier between us. Their shrewdness and aptitude
for business are remarkable, and whatever exists of commercial enterprise in Eastern Asia Minor is almost altogether in their hands. They have singular elasticity, as
their survival as a church and nation shows, and I cannot
but think it likely that they may have some share in
determining the course of events in the East, both
politically and religiously. As Orientals they understand
Oriental character and modes of thought as we never can,
and if a new Pentecostal *afflatus* were to fall upon the educated and intelligent young men who are being trained in
the colleges which the American churches have scattered
liberally through Asia Minor, the effect upon Turkey
would be marvellous. I think most decidedly that
reform in Turkey must come through Christianity, and

in this view the reform and enlightenment of the religion which has such a task before it are of momentous importance.

Islam is "cabined, cribbed, confined." Its forms of belief and thought and its social and political ideas remain in the moulds into which they were run at its rise. Expansion is impossible. The arrogance which the Koran inculcates and fosters is a dead weight on progress. If the Turk had any disposition to initiate and carry out reforms his creed and its traditions would fetter him. Islam, with its fanaticism, narrowness, obstructiveness, and *grooviness* is really at' this moment the greatest obstacle to every species of advance both in Turkey and Persia, and its present activity and renewed proselytising spirit are omens of evil as much for political and social progress as for the higher life of men.

The mission houses and schools are on fairly high ground more than two miles from Van, in what are known as "the Gardens," where most of the well-to-do Armenians and Turkish officials reside. These gardens, filled with vineyards and all manner of fruit trees, extend for a distance of five miles, and being from two to three miles wide their mass of greenery has a really beautiful effect. Among them are many very good houses, and the roads and alleys by which they are intersected are well planted with poplars and willows, shading pleasant streams which supply the water for irrigation.

The view from the roof is a glorious one. Looking west over the gardens, which are now burning with autumn tints, the lofty crests of the huge crater of Nimrud Dagh are always visible across the lake of Van, intensely blue in the morning, and reddening in the sunsets of flame and gold. In the evenings too, the isolated rock on which the castle of Van is built bulks as a violet mass against the sinking sun, with a foreground of darkening greenery. The great truncated cone of the Sipan Dagh looms grandly over the lake to the north ; to the east the rocky mass of the Varak Dagh, with white villages and monasteries in great numbers lying in its clefts and folds, rises precipitously to a height of 10,500 feet; and to the south the imposing peaks of Ardost, now crested with snow, and Mount Pelu, projecting into the lake, occupy prominent positions above the lower groups and ridges.

The town of Van is nearly a mile from the lake, and is built on an open level space, in the midst of which stands a most picturesque and extraordinary rock which rises perpendicularly to a height of about 300 feet. It falls abruptly at both extremities, and its outline, which Colonel Severs Bell estimates at 1900 yards in length, is emphasised by battlemented walls, several towers, and a solitary minaret rising above the picturesque irregularity of the ancient fortifications. Admission to the interior of the castle is refused, consequently I have not seen the chambers in the rock, supposed to have been the tombs of kings. The most celebrated of the cuneiform inscriptions cut on tablets smoothed in the rock is on the south side in an inaccessible position, and was with difficulty copied by the murdered traveller Schulz with the aid of a telescope. It is well seen from below, looking, as has been remarked, like an open copy of a newspaper. Like the tablets of Persepolis and Mount Elwend, it relates in august language the titles and deeds of Xerxes.

The founding of Van is ascribed to Semiramis, who, according to Armenian history, named it Shemiramagerd, and was accustomed to resort to its gardens, which she had herself planted and watered, to escape from the fierce heat of the summer at Nineveh. The well of Semiramis and other works attributed to her bring her

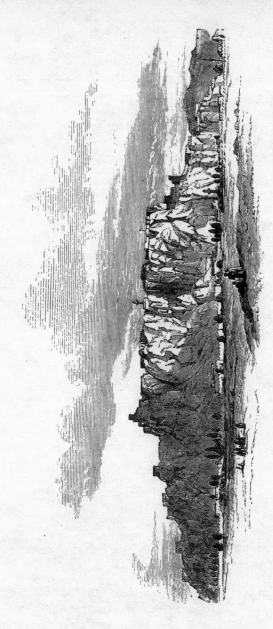

ROCK AND CITADEL OF VAN.

To face p. 338, vol. II.

name frequently into conversation—indeed she is mentioned as familiarly as Queen Elizabeth is among us !

The town, which is walled, is not particularly attractive, but there is one very handsome mosque, and a very interesting Armenian church, eleven centuries old, dedicated to St. Peter and St. Paul. The houses are mean-looking, but their otherwise shabby uniformity is broken up by lattice windows. The bazars are poorly built, but are clean, well supplied, and busy, though the trade of Van is suffering from the general insecurity of the country and the impoverishment of the peasantry. It is very pleasant that in the Van bazars ladies can walk about freely, encountering neither the hoots of boys nor the petrifying Islamic scowl.

Fifty years ago Venetian beads were the only articles imported from Europe. Now, owing to the increasing enterprise of the Armenians, every European necessary of life can be obtained, as well as many luxuries. Peek and Frean's biscuits, Moir's and Crosse and Blackwell's tinned meats and jams, English patent medicines, Coats' sewing cotton, Belfast linens, Berlin wools, Jæger's vests,

KURDS OF VAN.

and all sorts of materials, both cotton and woollen, abound. I did not see such a choice and abundance of European goods in any bazar in Persia, and in the city of Semiramis, and beneath the tablet of Xerxes, there is a bazar devoted to Armenian tailors, and to the clatter of American sewing machines stitching Yorkshire cloth! One of these tailors has made a heavy cloth ulster for me, which the American ladies pronounce perfect in fit and "style!"

The Armenians, with their usual industry and thrift, are always enlarging their commerce and introducing new imports. Better than this, they are paying great attention to education, and several of their merchants seem to be actuated by a liberal and enlightened spirit. It is, however, to usury not less than to trade that they owe their prosperity. The presence of Europeans in Van, in the persons of the missionaries and vice-consuls, in addition to the admirable influence exerted by the former, has undoubtedly a growing tendency towards ameliorating the condition of the Christian population.

In the *vilayet* of Van it is estimated by Colonel Severs Bell that the Christians outnumber the Moslems by 80,000, the entire population being estimated at 340,000. In the city of Van, with a population estimated by him at 32,000, the Christians are believed to be as 3 to 1.[1]

The formalities required for Turkish travelling are many and increasing, and from ignorance of one of them Johannes has been arrested, and Mirza marched to the Consulate by the police. I have been obliged to part with the former and send him back to Hamadan, as it would not be safe to take the risky journey to Erzerum with such an inexperienced and untrustworthy servant. Through Mr. Devey's kindness I have obtained an interpreter and servant in Murphy O'Rourke, a British subject, but a native of Turkey, and equally at home in English, Turkish, and Armenian, though totally illiterate.

I. L. B.

---

[1] An estimate by Mr. Devey, Her Britannic Majesty's Vice-Consul at Van, gives a population of only 250,000 for the whole *vilayet*.

LETTER XXXII

BITLIS, Nov. 10.

I ARRIVED here two days ago, having ridden the ninety miles from Van in three and a half days. Dr. Reynolds accompanied me, and as we had a couple of *zaptiehs* on good horses we deserted the caravan, and came along at as good a pace as the mountainous nature of the road would allow. The early winter weather is absolutely perfect for travelling. All along I am quite impressed with the resemblance which the southern shores of Lake Van bear to some of the most beautiful parts of the Italian Riviera—Italian beauty seen under an Italian sky. Travellers lose a great deal by taking the easier route round the north shore of the lake.

The first day's half march ended at Angugh, an Armenian village on the river Hashal, on the plain of Haizdar or Haigatsor, where the people complained of some Armenian women having been despoiled of their jewels by some Kurds during the afternoon. The views are magnificent *en route*, especially of the Christian village of Artemid, on a spur on a height, with a Moslem village in gardens below, with green natural lawns sloping to the lake. At Angugh I was well accommodated in a granary on a roof, and as there was no room for my bed, found a comfortable substitute in a blanket spread upon the wheat. The next day's march was through exquisitely beautiful scenery, partly skirting deep bays on paths cut in the rock above them, among oaks and ferns,

and partly crossing high steep promontories which jut
out into the lake. A few villages, where strips of level
ground and water for irrigation can be obtained, are
passed, and among them the village of Vastan, the " Seat
of Government " for the district, and a Turkish telegraph
station, but in the eleventh century the residence of the
Armenian royal family of Ardzrauni.

Art aids nature, and there are grand old monasteries
on promontories, and Kurdish castles on heights, and
flashing streams and booming torrents are bridged by
picturesque pointed arches. There are 150 monasteries
in this region, and the towers of St. George at the
mountain village of Narek, high on a rocky spur above
one of the most beautiful of the many wooded valleys
which descend upon the lake of Van, lend an air of
medieval romance to a scene as fair as nature can make
it. Nearly all the romantic valleys opening on the lake
are adorned with one or more villages, with houses tier
above tier in their rocky clefts, and terrace below terrace
of exquisite cultivation below, of the vivid velvety green
of winter wheat. These terraces often " hang " above
green sward and noble walnut trees. Occasionally the
villages are built at the feet of the mountains, on small
plateaux above steep-sided bays, and are embosomed in
trees glowing with colour, from canary-yellow to crimson
and madder-red, and mountains, snow-crested and forest-
skirted tower over all. Lake Van, bluer than the blue
heavens, with its huge volcanic heights—Sipan Dagh,
Nimrud Dagh, and Varak Dagh, and their outlying
ranges—its deep green bays and quiet wooded inlets ;
its islets, some like the Bass Rock, others monastery-
covered ; its pure green shadows and violet depths ; its
heavy boats with their V-shaped sails ; and its auburn
oak-covered slopes, adds its own enchantment, and all is
as fair as fair can be.

Though the state of things among the Christians is not nearly so bad as in some of the Syrian valleys, the shadow of the Kurd is over this paradise. The Armenians complain of robbery with violence as being of constant occurrence, and that they have been plundered till they are unable to pay the taxes, and it is obvious that travellers, unless in large companies, are not safe without a Government escort. In each village the common sheepfold is guarded from sunset to sunrise by a number of men—a heavy burden on villagers whose taxation should ensure them sufficient protection from marauders.

In one of the fairest bays on this south side of the lake is the island rock of Akhtamar, crowned with a church and monastery built of red sandstone. The convent boat, which plies daily to the mainland for supplies, is available for travellers. Eleven monks with their pupils inhabit the rock. It is a very ancient foundation, dating from A.D. 633, and the church is attributed to the Armenian King Kakhik, who reigned in the tenth century. It is a cruciform building, with a hexagonal tower and a conical terminal at the intersection of the cross. The simple interior is decorated with some very rude pictures, and a gilded throne for the Patriarch stands at the east end. This Patriarchate of Akhtamar, the occupant of which has at times claimed the title of *Catholicos*, was founded in 1113 by an archbishop of Akhtamar who declared himself independent of the *Catholicos* of the Armenian Church who resides in Echmiadzin, but at the present time he has only a few adherents in the immediate neighbourhood of Van, and has the reputation of extreme ignorance, and of being more of a farmer than an ecclesiastic. He was at Haikavank, at the fine farm on the mainland possessed by the convent, but we had not time to call.

Plain as is the interior of the Church of Akhtamar,

the exterior is most elaborately ornamented with bas-reliefs, very much undercut. Three of the roofs rest on friezes on which birds and beasts in singularly vigorous action are portrayed, and there are besides two rows of heads in high relief, and a number of scripture subjects very boldly treated, in addition to some elaborate scroll-work, and bands of rich foliage. On this remarkable rock Dr. Reynolds and his family took refuge a few years ago, when it was apprehended that Van would be sacked by the Kurds.

The vivid colouring of the lake is emphasised by a line of pure white deposit which runs round its margin, and vivacity is given to its waters by innumerable wild fowl, flamingoes, geese, ducks, pelicans, cormorants, etc. From a reedy swamp near it ducks rose in such numbers as literally to darken the air. Carbonate of soda and chloride of sodium are obtained from the lake water by evaporation, but it is not nearly so salt as that of the Sea of Urmi. Not very far from the south shore a powerful fresh-water spring bubbles up in the midst of the salt water. The only fish known of is a species said to be like a small herring. These are captured in enormous quantities in the spring as they come up into the streams which feed the lake.

On the last two nights at Undzag and Ghazit I had my first experiences of the Turkish *odah* or village guest-house or *khan*, of which, as similar abodes will be my lodgings throughout my journey to Erzerum, I will try to give you an idea. Usually partially excavated in the hillside and partly imbedded in the earth, the *odah* is a large rambling room with an irregular roof supported on rough tree-stems. In the centre, or some other convenient place, is a mud platform slightly raised; in the better class of *odahs* this has a fireplace in the wall at one end. Round this on three sides is a deep manger, and similar mangers run along the side walls and into the irregular recesses, which are lost in the darkness. The platform is for human beings, and the rest of the building for horses, mules, oxen, asses, and buffaloes, with a few sheep and goats probably in addition. The *katirgis* and the humbler class of travellers sleep among the beasts, the remainder, without distinction of race, creed, or sex, on the enclosed space. Light enters from the door and from a few small holes in the roof, which are carefully corked up at night, and then a few iron cups of oil with wicks, the primitive lamp in general use, hanging upon the posts, give forth a smoky light.

In such an *odah* there may be any number of human beings cooking, eating, and sleeping, and from twenty to a hundred animals, or more, as well as the loads of the pack-horses and the arms of the travellers. As the eye becomes accustomed to the smoke and dimness, it sees rows of sweet ox faces, with mild eyes and moist nostrils, and wild horse faces surrounding the enclosure, and any number more receding into the darkness. Ceaseless munching goes on, and a neigh or a squeal from some unexpected corner startles one, or there is a horse fight, which takes a number of men to quell it. Each animal is a " living stove," and the heat and closeness are so insupportable that one awakes quite unrefreshed in the morning in a temperature of 80°. The *odah* is one of the great features of travelling in Eastern Asia Minor. I dined and spent the evenings in its warmth and cheeriness, enjoying its wild picturesqueness, but at Undzag I pitched my small tent at the stable door, and at Ghazit on the roof, and braved the cold in it.

Boy is usually close to me, eating scraps from my dinner, and gently biting the back of my neck when he thinks that I am forgetting his presence. He amuses all the men everywhere by his affectionateness, and eating out of my hand, and following me like a dog. I never saw so gentle and trustworthy a creature. His hair has grown very long, thick, and woolly, and curls in parts like that of a retriever. His sweet ways have provided him with a home after his powerful legs and big feet have trudged with me to Trebizond, for my hosts here, who are old and somewhat frail, have taken such a fancy to his gentleness and winsomeness that he is to return to them when the roads open in the spring.

It was a grand ride from Undzag over lofty mountain passes to the exquisitely-situated village of Ghazit, built in a deep *cul de sac* above the lake. Terraces, one above another, rise from the lake shore, so beautifully cultivated as to realise Emerson's description of the appearance of English soil, "Tilled with a pencil instead of a plough." A church stands on a height, and the village, almost hidden among magnificent walnuts, is crowded upon a terrace of green sward at the foot of a semicircle of mountains which wall it in from the world. The narrow village road, with its low, deep-eaved stone houses, was prettily brightened by colour, for all the women were dressed more or less in red, and wore high red coronets with dependent strings of coins, and broad aprons, reaching from the throat to the feet, of coarse dark blue cotton, completely covered with handsome patterns worked in cross-stitch in silk.

Fine walnut trees are one of the specialities of this part of Turkey. They provide much of the oil which is used during the long fasts which both Armenians and Syrians observe, and they develop very large woody excrescences or knots, the grain and mottling of which are peculiarly beautiful. These are sought for by buyers for Paris houses even in the remote valleys of Kurdistan for use in the making and veneering of furniture, especially of pianos. Fortunately the removal of this growth does not

kill the tree, and after a time the bark grows over much
of the uncovered portion of the trunk, only a scar being
left.

At sunset that evening 800 sheep were driven into
the village sheepfold just below the roof on which my
tent was pitched, and it was a very picturesque scene,
men pushing their way through them to find their own
sheep by ear-mark, women with difficulty milking ewes
here and there, big dogs barking furiously from the roofs
above, and all the sheep bleating at once. In winter they
are all housed and hand fed. The snow lies six feet
deep, and Ghazit can communicate neither with Bitlis
nor Van. It is the " milk of the flocks " which is prized.
Cows' milk is thought but little of. I made my supper
of one of the great articles of diet in Turkey, boiled
cracked wheat, sugar, and *yohoort*, artificially soured milk,
looking like whipped cream.

I was glad to escape to my tent from the heat and
odours of the *odah*, even though I had to walk over sheep's
backs to get up to the roof. I had a guard of two men,
and eight more armed with useless matchlock guns
watched the sheepfold. I was awakened by a tremendous
noise, the barking of infuriated dogs close to me, the
clashing of arms and the shouts of men, mixed up with
the rapid firing of guns not far off on the mountain side,
so near, indeed, that I could see the flashes. It was a
Kurdish alarm, but nothing came of it. A village which
we passed a few hours later was robbed of 600 sheep,
however.

Leaving beautiful Ghazit before the sun rose upon it
the next morning, we spent some hours in skirting the
lake, and in crossing elevated passes and following paths
along hillsides covered with oaks, the russet leaves of
which are being cut for winter "keep." The dwarf
juniper is also abundant. After crossing a pass on the

top of which are graves covered with heavy stone slabs
with inscriptions on their sides, and head-stones eight
feet high inscribed with epitaphs in Kufic or early Arabic,
we descended upon the great plain of Rahwan, separated
from the plain of Mush only by a very low ridge, which,
however, is a remarkable water-parting, dividing the
drainage systems of the Tigris and the Euphrates. On
this solitary plain there are the ruins of a magnificent
building, known as " the Persian Khan," built of large
blocks of hewn stone.   Parts of it are still available
for shelter during snowstorms.   It has courtyards with
stately entrances, domes, arches, and vaulted chambers,
and is a very striking object.   Two other *khans* are
placed as refuges in the valley nearer Bitlis.

Shortly afterwards we reached the meeting-place of
three valleys and three roads, leading respectively to the
plain of Mush, the lake of Van, and Bitlis.   It is in
this neighbourhood that the eastern source of the Tigris
is situated, and here there is also the great interest of
coming upon one of the landmarks on the retreat of the
Ten Thousand.   Scholars appear to agree in general that
this gallant band must have come up by these eastern
sources of the Tigris, for then, as now, the only practicable
entrance into Armenia from the Karduchi territory, the
modern Kurdistan, was by this route.[1]

The march was very long and fatiguing, and as we

---

[1] It does not present any difficulty to me that Xenophon omits all
mention of the lake of Van, for a range of hills lies between it and the
road.   I have travelled over the track twice, and failed to see anything
in the configuration of the country which would have led me to suppose
that the region to the eastward was anything but a continuity of ranges of
hills and mountains, and if the Ten Thousand took the route from the
eastern head-waters of the Tigris to the Murad-chai at the farther end of
the plain of Mush, directing all their investigations and inquiries in a
westerly direction, there are very many chances against their having been
informed, even by their prisoners, of the existence of the sea of Van.

were compelled to rest for two hours at the beautifully-situated village of Toogh, evening was coming on with a gray sky and a lurid sunset before we left the Rahwan plain, after which we had a ride of more than three hours down the wild and stony Bitlis valley before we reached our destination. If I had made this march in spring, when herbage and flowers drape the nakedness of the rocky and gravelly mountains and precipices, it would not have made such an impression upon me as it did, but seeing the apparently endless valley for ever winding and falling to the south, with two bars of lurid light for ever lying across what never proved to be its opening, and the higher peaks rising snow-crested into a dark and ominous-looking sky, I think it one of the weirdest and wildest rides I ever took.

The infant Tigris is rapidly augmented by a number of streams and torrents. The descent was like taking leave of the bright upper world to go down into some nether region, from which there would be no exit. The valley, at times narrowing into a ravine, is hemmed in by sterile mountains, so steep as not to afford sites for villages. There are parapetless ancient arches of stone, flung across torrents which have carved hideous pathways for themselves through hideous rocks, scoriæ, and other signs of volcanic action, rough gulches, with narrow paths hanging on their sides, and in spite of many climbs upwards the course is on the whole downwards.

Darkness settled upon the valley long before lights, in what looked like infinite depths, and straggling up remarkable heights, trees, stone walls, and such steep ups and downs that it felt as if the horses were going to topple over precipices, denoted that we had entered Bitlis. Then came a narrow gateway, a flagged courtyard choked with mules and men, a high house with heavily-barred windows, a steep outside stair, and at the top sweet faces and sweet voices of European women, and lights and warm welcomes.

Bitlis, November 12.—This is the most romantically-situated city that I have seen in Western Asia. The dreamy impressions of height and depth received on the night of my arrival were more than realised the following morning. Even to the traveller arriving by daylight Bitlis must come as a great surprise, for it is situated in a hole upon which the upper valley descends with a sudden dip. The Bitlis-chai or Eastern Tigris passes through it in a series of raging cataracts, and is joined in the middle of the town by another torrent tumbling down another wild valley, and from this meeting of the waters massive stone houses rise one above another, singly, and in groups and terraces, producing a singularly striking effect. Five valleys appear to unite in Bitlis and to radiate from a lofty platform of rock supported on precipices, the irregular outlines of which are emphasised by walls and massive square and circular towers, the gigantic ruins of Bitlis Castle.

The massiveness of the houses is remarkable, and their courtyards and gardens are enclosed by strong walls. Every gate is strengthened and studded with iron, every window is heavily barred, all are at a considerable height, and every house looks as if it could stand a siege. There is no room to spare ; the dwellings are piled tier above tier, and the flagged footways in front of them hang on the edges of precipices. Twenty picturesque stone bridges, each one of a single arch, span the Tigris and the torrents which unite with it. There are ancient ruins scattered through the town. It claims immense antiquity, and its inhabitants ascribe its castle and some of its bridges to Alexander the Great, but antiquarians attribute the former either to the Saracens or to the days when an ancient Armenian city

called Paghesh occupied the site of the present Bitlis.
It seems like the end of the world, though through the
deep chasms below it, through which the Tigris descends
with great rapidity to the plains, lies the highway to
Diabekir.   Suggestions of the ancient world abound.
The lofty summits towering above the basin in which
this extraordinary city lies are the termination of the
Taurus chain, the Niphates of the ancients, on the highest
peak of which Milton localised the descent of Satan.[1]

Remote as Bitlis seems and is, its markets are among
the busiest in Turkey, and its caravan traffic is enormous
for seven or eight months of the year.   Its altitude is
only 4700 feet, and the mercury in winter rarely falls to
zero, but the snowfall is tremendous, and on the Rahwan
Plain snow frequently lies up to the top of the telegraph
poles, isolating the town and shutting up animals in their
stables and human beings in their houses for weeks, and
occasionally months, at a time.   Bitlis produces a very
coarse, heavy cotton cloth which, after being dyed madder
red or dark blue, is largely exported, and is used for the
embroidered aprons which the Armenian women wear.
It also exports *loupes*, the walnut whorls or knots of
which I have written before, oak galls, wax, wool, and
manna, chiefly collected from the oak.   The Bitlis
people, and even some Europeans, regard this as a
deposit left by the aromatic exhalations which the wind
brings in this direction from Arabia, and they say that it
lies on any plant without regard to its nature, and even
on the garments of men.   The deposit is always greatest
in dry years.   In addition to the white manna, obtained
by drying the leaves and allowing the saccharine matter to
fall off—and the green, the result of steeping the leaves in
water, which is afterwards strained, there is a product much
like golden syrup, which is used for the same purposes.

[1] *Paradise Lost*, iii. 741, "Nor stayed, till on Niphates' top he lights."

Bitlis is one of the roughest and most fanatical and turbulent of Turkish cities, but the present Governor, Raouf Pasha, is a man of energy, and has reduced the town and neighbourhood to some degree of order. Considerable bodies of troops have been brought in, and the garrison consists of 2500 men. These soldiers are thoroughly well clothed and equipped, and look remarkably clean in dress and person. They are cheery, soldierly-looking men, and their presence gives a little confidence to the Christians.

The population of Bitlis is estimated at 30,000, of which number over 20,000 are Kurds. Both men and women are very handsome, and the striking Kurdish costume gives a great brilliancy and picturesqueness to this remarkable city. The short sleeveless jackets of sheepskin with the black wool outside which the men are now wearing over their striped satin vests, and the silver rings in the noses of the girls give them something of a " barbarian " look, and indeed their habits appear to be much the same as those of their Karduchi ancestors in the days of Xenophon, except that in the interval they have become Moslems and teetotallers ! Here they are Sunnis, and consequently do not clash with their neighbours the Turks, who abhor the Kurds of the mountains as Kizil-bashes. The Kurdish *physique* is very fine. In fact I have never seen so handsome a people, and their manly and highly picturesque costume heightens the favourable effect produced by their well-made, lithe, active figures.

The cast of their features is delicate and somewhat sharp ; the mouth is small and well formed ; the teeth are always fine and white ; the face is oval ; the eyebrows curved and heavy ; the eyelashes long ; the eyes deep set, intelligent, and roving ; the nose either straight or decidedly aquiline, giving a hawk-like expression ; the chin slightly receding; the brow broad and clear; the hands and feet remarkably small and slender.

The women when young are beautiful, but hard work and early maternity lead to a premature loss of form, and to a withered angularity of feature which is far from pleasing, and which, as they do not veil, is always *en évidence*.

The poorer Kurds wear woollen socks of gay and elaborate patterns; cotton shoes like the *gheva* of the Persians; camlet trousers, wide at the bottom like those of sailors; woollen girdles of a Kashmir shawl pattern; short jackets and felt jerkins without sleeves. The turban usually worn is peculiar. Its foundation is a peaked felt cap, white or black, with a loosely-twisted rope of tightly-twisted silk, wool, or cotton wound round it. In the girdle the *khanjar* is always seen. Over it the cartridge belt is usually worn, or two cartridge belts are crossed over the chest and back. The girdle also carries the pipe and tobacco pouch, a long knife, a flint and steel, and in some cases a shot pouch and a highly-ornamented powder horn.

The richer Kurds dress like the Syrians. The undergarment, which shows considerably at the chest and at the long and hanging sleeves, is of striped satin, either crimson and white or in a combination of brilliant colours, over which is worn a short jacket of cloth or silk, also with long sleeves, the whole richly embroidered in gold. Trousers of striped silk or satin, wide at the bottom; loose medieval boots of carnation-red leather; a girdle fastened with knobbed clasps of silver as large as a breakfast cup, frequently incrusted with turquoises; red felt skull-caps, round which they wind large striped silk shawls, red, blue, orange, on a white or black ground, with long fringed ends hanging over the shoulders, and floating in the wind as they gallop; and in their girdles they carry richly-jewelled *khanjars* and pistols decorated with silver knobs, besides a number of other glittering appointments. The accoutrements of the horses are in keeping, and at marriages and other festivities the head-stalls, bridles, and breast-plates are completely covered with pendent silver coins.

The dress of the women is a foil to that of their lords. It consists of a blue cotton shirt; very wide trousers, drawn in at the ankles; a silver saucer on the head, from which chains depend with a coin at the end of each; a square mantle hanging down the back, clasped by two of its corners round the neck, and many strings of coins round the throat; a small handkerchief is knotted round the hair, and in presence of a strange man they hold one end of this over the mouth. The Turks in Bitlis are in a small minority, and the number of Armenian Christians is stated at from 2000 to 5000. The Old Church has a large monastery outside the town and several churches and schools. The Protestant Armenians have a substantial church edifice, with a congregation of about 400, and large boarding-schools for boys and girls.

The population is by far the wildest that I have seen in any Asiatic city, and is evidently only restrained from violence by the large garrison. It is not safe for the ladies of this mission to descend into the Moslem part of the city, and in a residence of more than twenty years they have never even passed through the bazars. The missionaries occupy a restricted and uncertain position, and the Armenian Christians are subject to great deprivations and restraints, and are distrusted by the Government. Of late they have been much harassed by the search for arms, and Christian gunsmiths have been arrested. Even their funeral ceremonies are not exempt from the presence of the police, who profess to believe that firearms are either carried in the place of a corpse or are concealed along with it.   Placed in the midst of a preponderating and fully-armed Kurdish population, capable at any moment of being excited to frenzy against their faith, they live in expectation of a massacre, should certain events take place which are regarded as probable within two or three years.

It was not to see the grandeur and picturesqueness of Bitlis that I came here so late in the season, but to visit the American missionaries, especially two ladies.   My hosts, Mr. and Mrs. Knapp, have returned from a visit to America to spend their last days in a country which has been their home for thirty years, and have lately been joined by their son, who spent his boyhood in Bitlis, and after graduating in an American university has come back, like so many sons of missionaries, to cast in his lot with a people to whom he is bound by many links of sympathy, bringing his wife with him.   The two Misses ———, who are more than half English, and are highly educated and accomplished, met Mr. and Mrs. Knapp long ago in a steamer on the Mediterranean, and decided to return with them to this dangerous and outlandish place, where they have worked among the women and girls for twenty-three years, and are still full of love and hope.   The school for girls, in which fifty boarders are received in addition to fifty day pupils, has a *kinder-garten* department attached to it.   The parents of all are expected to contribute in money or in kind, but their increasing poverty is telling on their ability to do so, and this winter the supply of food contributed by them is far short of the mark.

The tastefulness and generosity of these ladies have produced as bright and beautiful a schoolroom as could be found anywhere, and ivy trained round the windows, growing plants, and pictures which are not daubs give a look of home. With them "Love is the fulfilling of the law"—love in every tone, look, and touch, and they have that true maternity of spirit which turns a school into a family, and trains as well as educates. They are now educating the children, and even grandchildren, of their earliest pupils, and have the satisfaction of seeing how very much their school has effected in permeating the household and social relationships of the Armenian women with the tone of Christian discipleship, so that one would scarcely hear from the lips of any of their married pupils the provoking question, "We are only women, what can we do?" Many of them have gone to homes in the roughest and wildest of mountain villages, where they sweeten village life by the gentle and kindly ways acquired in the Bitlis school. These ladies conduct a mothers' meeting, and I thought that the women were much developed in intelligence and improved in manner as compared with the usual run of Armenian women. On being asked to address them, I took their own words for my text, "We are only women," etc., and found them intelligent and sympathetic.

These ladies have endured great hardships, and their present position is one of continual deprivation and frequent risk. One of them was so severely stoned in Bitlis that she fell unconscious from her horse. In the winter Miss —— itinerates among the Armenian villages of the Mush and Rahwan Plains and the lake shore, travelling over the crust of the enormously deep snow in a hand-sled drawn by a man, braving storms which have nearly cost her her life, sleeping and living for a month or more at a time chiefly in *odahs*, and fearlessly encountering the very roughest of Kurds and others in these dim and crowded stables. The danger of village expeditions, and the difficulty of obtaining *zaptiehs* without considerable expense, have increased of late, and the Mush Plain especially has been ravaged all the summer and autumn by the Kurds, with many barbarities and much loss of life, so that travelling for Christians even in companies has been dangerous. Caravans have lately been attacked and robbed, and in the case of one large mixed caravan the Christians were robbed but the Moslems were unmolested. A traveller was recently treacherously murdered by his *katirgis*, and Miss ——, having occasion to employ the same men a few days ago, saw and heard them rehearse his dying agonies more than once for the amusement of Kurds on the road.

Luxury is unknown in this mission house. It is so small that in order to receive me the ladies are sleeping in a curtained recess in the kitchen, and the reception-room for the natives is the eating and living room of the family. Among them all there is a rare devotion, and lives spent in cheerful obedience to God and in loving service for man have left on their faces the impress of "the love which looks kindly and the wisdom which looks soberly on all things." The mission has had a severe struggle. The life on this mountain slope above the fanatical city is a very restricted one,—there is nothing of what we are accustomed to regard as "necessary recreation," and a traveller is not seen here above once in two or three years. All honour to those who have courage and faith to live such a life so lovingly and cheerfully !   I. L. B.

LETTER XXXIII

PIKHRUZ, *Nov. 14.*

I WAS indeed sorry to leave the charming circle at the Mission House and the wild grandeur of Bitlis, but a certain wan look in the sky and peculiar colouring on the mountains warned my friends that winter might set in any day, and Dr. Reynolds arranged for *katirgis* and an escort, and obtained a letter from the Governor by means of which I can procure additional *zaptiehs* in case of need. My Turkish *katirgi*, Moussa, is rich, and full of fun and jollity. He sings and jokes and mimics Mirza, rides a fine horse, or sprawls singing on its back, and keeps every one alive by his energy and vitality. My loads are very light, and his horses are strong, and by a peculiar screech he starts them off at a canter with no other object than the discomfiture of Mirza, who with all his good qualities will never make a horseman. Unluckily he has a caravan of forty horses laden with ammunition for the Government on the road, so things may not be always so smooth as they are now. Descending by a track more like a stair than a road, and crossing the Tigris, my friends and I performed the feat of riding through some of the bazars, even though Mr. Knapp and I had been pelted with stones on an open road the day before. There was no molestation, for the people are afraid of the *zaptiehs'* swords. Bitlis is busy, and it is difficult to get through its crowded markets, low, narrow,

and dark as they are, the sunbeams rarely entering
through their woven roofs.   The stalls were piled with
fruits, roots, strange vegetables, red home-dyed cottons,
gay gear for horses, daggers and silver chains such as
Kurds love, gay Kurdish clothing, red boots with toes
turned up for tying to the knees, pack-saddles, English
cottons (" *Mankester* "), mostly red, and pipes of all kinds.
There was pottery in red and green, huge earthen jars
for the storage of water, brooms, horse-shoes, meat, curds,
cheeses, and everything suited to the needs of a large
and mixed population, and men seated in the shops plied
their curious trades.

Emerging into the full sunlight on the waggon road
to Erzerum, we met strings of girls carrying water-jars
on their backs from the wells, and long trains of asses
and pack-bullocks bringing in produce, mixed up with
foot passengers and Kurds on showy horses.   Bitlis
rejoices in abundant streams, wells, fountains, and mineral
springs, some strongly chalybeate, others resembling the
Vichy waters.   The grandly picturesque city with its
piled-up houses, its barred windows suggestive of peril,
its colossal ruins, its abounding waters, its bridges, each
one more remarkable than the other, its terraced and
wooded heights and the snow-crested summits which
tower above them, with their cool blue and purple shadows,
disappeared at a turn of the road, and there too my
friends left me to pursue my perilous journey alone.

The day was superb, and full of fine atmospheric
effects.   As we crossed the Rahwan Plain the great
mountains to the west were enshrouded in wild drifting
mists, through which now and then peaks and ledges,
white with recent snow, revealed themselves, to be
hidden in blackness the next moment.   Over the plain
the blue sky was vaulted, and the sun shone bright and
warm, while above the mountains to the south of Lake

Van white clouds were piled in sunlit masses. After halting at Tadvan, a pleasant village among streams, fountains, gardens, and fruit trees, we skirted the lake along pleasant cultivated slopes and promontories with deep bays and inlets to Gudzag, where I spent the evening in an *odah*, retiring to sleep in my small tent, pitched in the village, where a big man with a gun, and wearing a cloak of goatskin reaching to his feet, kept up a big fire and guarded me till morning. The water froze in my basin during the night. The *odah* was full of Armenians, and Murphy interpreted their innumerable tales of wrong and robbery. " Since the Erzerum troubles," so the tales ran, " the Kurds kill men as if they were partridges." On asking them why they do not refuse to be robbed by "demand," they replied, " Because the Kurds bring big sticks and beat us, and say they will cut our throats." They complained of the exactions of the *zaptiehs* and of being tied to the posts of their houses and beaten when they have not money wherewith to pay the taxes.

Starting at sunrise on the following morning I had a very pleasant walk along the sweet shore of the lake, while water, sky, and mountains were blended in a flood of rose and gold, after which, skirting a wooded inlet, on the margin of which the brown roofs of the large village of Zarak were scarcely seen amidst the crimson foliage, and crossing a low range, we descended upon a plain at the head of a broad bay, on the farther side of which, upon a level breezy height, rose the countless monoliths and lofty mausoleums of Akhlat, which I had made a long detour to see. The plain is abundantly watered, and its springs were surrounded with green sward, poplars, and willows, while it was enlivened by numerous bullock-carts, lumbering and creaking on their slow way with the latest sheaves of the harvest.

After winding up a deep ravine we came upon a great

table of rock scarped so as to be nearly perpendicular, at the base of which is a stone village. On the other side is a fine stream. I had purposed to spend the night at Akhlat, but on riding up the village street, which has several shops, there was a manifest unfriendliness about its Turkish inhabitants, and they went so far as to refuse both lodgings and supplies, so I only halted for a few hours. Few things have pleased me more than Akhlat, and the dreamy loveliness of the day was altogether propitious.

I first visited the Kharaba-shahr or "ruined city." The table rock is honeycombed with a number of artificial chambers, some of which are inhabited. Several of these are carefully arched. A very fine one consists of a chamber with an arched recess like a small chancel, and a niche so resembling a piscina at one side that one involuntarily looks for the altar. These dwellings are carefully excavated, and chisel marks are visible in many places. Outlining this remarkable rock, and above these chambers, are the remains of what must have been a very fine fortress, with two towers like those of the castle of Bitlis springing from below the rock. The whole of it has been built of hewn red sandstone. The walls have been double, with the centre filled up with rough stones and mortar, but not much of the stone facing remains, the villages above and below having been built of it. Detached pieces of masonry, such as great masses of walls, solitary arches, and partially-embedded carved fragments extend over a very large area, and it is evident that investigators with time and money might yet reap a rich reward. Excavators have been recently at work— who or what they were I could not make out, and have unearthed, among other objects of interest, a temple with the remains of a dome having a cornice and frieze, and two small circular chambers, much decorated, the whole about twenty-five feet long.

Akhlat Kalessi, or the castle of Akhlat, stands on the sea-shore, on which side it has no defences. It is a fortress with massive walls, with round and square towers at intervals, and measures about 700 paces from the water to the crest of the slope, and about 330 across. The enclosure, which is entered by two gates, contains two ancient mosques solidly built, and a few houses among fruit trees, as well as some ruins of buildings. The view of the Sipan Dagh from this very striking ruin is magnificent.

There are many Circassian villages on the skirts of the Sipan Dagh, and their inhabitants bear nearly as bad a reputation as that of the Kurds. They are well armed, and defy the local government. They are robbers and pilferers, and though they receive, or did receive, an allowance raised by a tax on the general community, they wring what they please out of the people among whom they live.

A mile from Akhlat, on a table-land of smooth green sward high above the silver sea, facing southwards, with a glorious view of the mountains of Central Kurdistan whitened with the first snows of winter, lies in an indescribable loneliness—the city of the dead. The sward is covered though not crowded with red sandstone monoliths, from six to fourteen feet in height, generally in excellent preservation. Each has a projecting cornice on the east side with carved niches, and the western face is covered with exquisite tracery in arabesques and knot-work, and inscriptions in early Arabic. On the graves are either three carved stones arranged on edge, or a single heavy hewn stone with a rounded top, and sides decorated with arabesques. Few of these beautiful monoliths have fallen, but some are much time-worn, and have a growth of vivid red or green lichen upon them.

Besides these there are some lofty *turbehs* or mausoleums, admirably preserved and of extreme beauty. The form is circular. The sepulchre is a closed chamber, with another above it open half-way round on the lake side, and a colonnade of very beautiful pillars supports round arches, above which are five exquisitely-carved friezes. The whole is covered with a conical roof of carved slabs of red stone, under which runs an Arabic inscription. Each of these buildings is decorated with ornament in the Saracenic style, of a richness and beauty of which only photography could give any adequate representation. Close to the finest of these *turbehs* is an old mosque with a deeply-arched entrance, over which is a recess, panelled and carved like one in the finest of the rock chambers. The lintels of the door are decorated with stone cables. Mirza counted more than 900 monoliths.

As I sketched the finest of these beautiful mausoleums some *mollahs* came up and objected to the proceeding, and Moussa urged me to desist, as the remainder of the march was "very dangerous," he said, and must be "got over" in full daylight. This phrase "very dangerous," as used in Armenia, means that there is a serious risk of having the baggage and horses driven off, and the men stripped to a single garment. Such things are happening constantly, and even Moussa ceases his joking when he speaks of them.[1] The remaining march was over great solitary sweeps of breezy upland to Pikhruz, an Armenian village of 100 houses, which has an intelligent Protestant teacher with sixty boys in his school.

[1] Akhlat was a place of immense importance in ancient days, and its history epitomises the vicissitudes of Armenia ; Abulfeda, Bakani, Deguignes, Ritter, and Finlay in his *History of Greece* are among the best-known authorities on its history, and Mr. Tozer in his work on *Turkish Armenia*, p. 318, etc., gives an interesting popular sketch of the way in which it was conquered and reconquered by Saracens, Greeks, Kurds, Turks, Khoarasmians and Georgians, till eventually the Turks reconquered it from the Kurds. Its ancient Armenian name of Khelat is altogether unknown to its present inhabitants.

The villagers possess 4000 sheep, and have not been much harassed by the Kurds. They employ Kurdish shepherds and four night watchmen, two of whom are Kurds. The head-dresses of the women are heavy with coins, and they wear stomachers and aprons so richly embroidered that no part of the original material is visible.

The *khan* is an exceptionally bad *odah*, and is absolutely crowded with horses, oxen, and men, and dim with the fumes of animal fuel and tobacco. It is indeed comically wretched. The small space round the fire is so crowded with *zaptiehs*, *katirgis*, and villagers that I have scarcely room for my chair and the ragamuffin remains of my baggage. Murphy is crouching over a fire which he is trying to fan into a state in which it will cook my un-varying dinner—a fowl and potatoes. Moussa is as usual convulsing the company with his stories and jokes, and is cracking walnuts for me ; the schoolmaster is enlarging to me on that fruitful topic—" the state of things," the sabres and rifles of my escort gleam on the blackened posts, the delectable ox and horse faces wear a look of content, as they munch and crunch their food, the risk of sleeping in a tent is discussed, and meanwhile I write spasmodically with the candle and ink on a board on my lap. I am fast coming to like these cheery evenings in the *odahs*, where one hears the news of the country and villages. The *khanji,* the man who keeps the guest-house, provides fire, light, horse-food, and the usual country diet at so much per head, and obtains the daily fowl, which costs about 6d., and is cooked while warm. Milk can be got from one of the cows in the stable. My expenses for food and lodging are from 4s. to 6s. a night.

Matchetloo, November 19.—One of the most un-pleasant parts of the routine of the journey is the return to the *odah* at 5 A.M. after a night in the fresh air, for the atmosphere is so heated and foul as almost to knock one down. The night frosts are sharp, and as we start before sunrise we are all glad to walk for the first hour. The night in my tent at Pikhruz was much disturbed, and I realised that it is somewhat risky for me to have my servants out of hearing in the depths of a semi-subterranean dwelling. The village dogs raged at times as though the Kurds were upon them, and every half-hour the village guards signalled to each other with a long mournful yell. I was awakened once by a confusion of diabolical sounds, shots, shrieks, roars, and yells, which continued for some time and then died away. In the morning the guards said that the Kurds had attacked a large caravan on the plain below, but had been repulsed, and that men on both sides had been wounded.

The following day's march by the silver sheet of the Kuzik Lake, alive with ducks, divers, and other water fowl, was very charming. Snow had fallen heavily, and the Sipan Dagh and the Nimrud Dagh were white more than half-way down their sides. From the summit of a very wild pass we bade adieu to the beautiful Sea of Van, crossed a plain in which is a pretty fresh-water lake with several villages and much cultivation on its margin, and, after some hours of solitary mountain travelling, came down upon the great plain of Norullak, sprinkled with large villages, very fertile, and watered by the Murad-chai, the eastern branch of the Euphrates.

I was to have had an easy march of five hours, and to have spent Sunday at Shaoub in the comfortable house of a Protestant pastor with an English-speaking wife, but the *zaptiehs* took the wrong road, and as twilight came on it was found that Shaoub had been left hours behind. I have been suffering very much from the fatigue of the very long marches, and only got through this one by repeatedly lying down by the roadside while the *zaptiehs* went in search of information. After it was quite dark and we were still astray, news came that Shaoub was occupied by 400 Turkish soldiers, and that there were neither supplies nor accommodation, and after two more hours of marching and counter-marching over ploughed lands and among irrigation ditches, we emerged on the Erzerum road, six inches deep in dust, forded a river in thick darkness, got very wet, and came out upon the large village of Yangaloo, a remarkable collection of 170 ant-hills rather than houses, with their floors considerably below the ground. The prospects in this hummocky place were most unpromising, and I was greeted by Moussa, who, on finding that Shaoub was full of troops, had had the wits to go on to Yangaloo, with the information that there was " no accommodation."

A womanly, Christian grip of my arm reassured me, and I was lodged for Sunday in the Protestant church, the villagers having arranged to worship elsewhere. A building forty feet long with small paper-covered windows under the eaves was truly luxurious, but the repose of Sunday morning was broken by loud and wearisome noises, lasting for several hours, which received a distressing explanation. I was informed by the priests and several of the leading men of the village that Yangaloo for some time past had suffered severely from the Kurds, and that just before a heavy demand for taxes had been made by the Government, the three days' grace usually granted having been refused. The local official had seized the flax seed, their most profitable crop, at half-price, and had sold it for full price, his perquisite amounting to a large sum. Fifteen *arabas*, each one loaded with seven large sacks of " linseed," were removed in the morning.

The people were very friendly. All the " brethren " and " sisters " came to kiss hands, and to wish that my departure " might be in great peace," and on Sunday evening I was present at a gathering of men in a room

with the door carefully bolted and guarded, who desired
me to convey to "the Consul" at Erzerum, with the
attestation of the names of the priests of the Old and
Reformed Churches, certain complaints and narratives of
wrong, which represented a condition of living not to be
thought of without grief and indignation, and not to be
ignored because it is partially chronic.

Yangaloo is a typical Armenian village, its ant-hill
dwellings are half-sunk, and the earth which has been
excavated is piled up over their roofs and sides.   The
interior of each dwelling covers a considerable area, and
is full of compartments with divisions formed by low
clay walls or by the posts which support the roof, the
compartments ramifying from a widening at the inner
end of a long dark passage.   In Yangaloo, as in other
villages on the plains, the earth is so piled over the houses
as to render them hardly distinguishable from the surrounding ground, but where a village burrows into a
hill-side only a small projection needs an artificial roof.
The people live among their live stock; one entrance
serves for both, and in winter time the animals never
leave the stables.   The fireplace or *tandūr* is in the floor,
but is only required for cooking purposes, as the heat
and steam of the beasts keep the human beings comfort-
ably warm.   From two to five families live in every
house, and the people are fairly healthy.[1]

[1] Xenophon in his *Anabasis* describes the Armenian dwellings of his
day thus :—

"Their houses were underground, the entrance like the mouth of a well,
but spacious below ; there were passages dug into them for the cattle, but
the people descended by ladders.   In the houses were goats, sheep, cows,
and fowls, with their young.   All the cattle were kept in fodder within
the walls."   I have not seen the entrance by a well, but have understood
that it still exists in certain exposed situations.   Xenophon mentions
buried wine, and it is not unlikely that the deep clay-lined holes in which
grain is stored in some of the villages are ancient cellars, anterior to the
date when the Karduchi became Moslems and teetotallers.

All the male members of a family bring their brides to live under the parental roof, and one " burrow " may contain as many as three generations of married couples with their families.   On becoming an inmate of her father-in-law's house, each Armenian bride, as in the country districts of Persia, has to learn the necessity of silence.   Up to the day of the birth of the first child she is the family drudge, and may not speak to any one but her husband, and not to him in the presence of his parents.   Maternity liberates her tongue; she may talk to her child, and then to the females of the household; but she may not speak freely till some years of this singular novitiate have passed by.   She then takes a high place in the house, and eventually rules it if she is left a widow.   The Armenian women are veiled out of doors, but only in deference to the Moslems, who regard an uncovered head as the sign of a bad woman.   The girls are handsome, but sheepish-looking; their complexions and eyes are magnificent.

Sunday was windy, with a gray sky, and the necessity of getting over the Ghazloo Pass before the weather absolutely broke was urged upon me by all.   On the plain of Norullak, not far from Yangaloo, I forded the Euphrates,—that is, the Murad-chai, a broad, still, and deep river, only fordable at certain seasons.   The fine mountain Bijilan is a landmark in this part of the country.   Leaving the Euphrates we ascended for some hours through bleak uninteresting regions to Kara Kapru, and on the road passed thirty well-armed Kurds, driving a number of asses, which the *zaptiehs* said had been driven off from two Christian villages, which they pointed out.   I was interested in the movements of some mounted men, who hovered suspiciously about my caravan, and at one time galloped close up to it, but retired on seeing the Government uniforms, and were apparently "loafing about" among the valleys. The *zaptiehs* said that they were notorious robbers, and would not go home without booty. Towards evening they re-appeared with several bullocks and asses which they had driven off from the village of ——, the headman of which came to me in the evening and asked me to report the robbery to "the Consul," adding that this was the third time within a week that his village had been robbed of domestic animals, and that he dared not complain.

At Kara Kapru, the best-looking Armenian village I have seen, while I was looking for an *odah*, Moussa, in spite of Murphy and the *zaptiehs*, dashed off with his horses at full speed, and never stopped till he reached Ghazloo, three hours farther on. This barbarous conduct was occasioned by his having heard that two of his forty horses ahead had broken down, and he hurried on to replace them with two of mine! I was so tired and in so much pain that I was obliged to lie down on the road-side for a considerable time before I could proceed, and got a chill, and was so wretched that I had to be tied on my horse. It was pitch dark, the *zaptiehs* continually lost the way, heavy rain came on, and it was 9 P.M. when we reached Ghazloo, a village high up on a hill-slope, where Mirza and Murphy carried me into a small and crowded stable, and later into my tent, which was pitched in the slime at the stable door. Moussa was repentant, borrowed a *kajaveh*, and said he would give me his strong horse for nothing!

Torrents of rain fell, changing into sleet, and sleet into snow, and when the following day dawned dismally my tent was soaked, and standing in slush and snow. My bed was carried into the stable, and I rested while the loading was going on. Suleiman, my special *zaptieh*, said that the *khanji* was quadrupling the charges, and wanted me not to pay him anything. The *khanji* retorted that I gave the *zaptieh* money to pay, and that he gave only a few coppers to the people—a glaring untruth, for Murphy pays everything in my presence. Thereupon Suleiman beat the *khanji* with his scabbarded sword, on which the man struck him, and there was a severe fight, in the course of which the combatants fell over the end of my bed. So habituated does one become to scenes of violence in this country that I scarcely troubled myself to say to Murphy, "Tell them to fight outside."

It was a severe day's march over the Bingol Dagh, and I know little about the country we passed through. We skirted a bleak snowy hillside, first in rain and then in a heavy snowstorm, made a long ascent among drifting snow clouds, saw an ass abandoned by a caravan shivering in the bitter wind, with three magpies on its back picking its bleeding wounds, and near the summit of the Ghazloo Pass encountered a very severe "blizzard," so severe that no caravan but my own attempted to face it, and sixty conscripts *en route* for Bitlis in charge of two officers and some cavalry turned back in spite of words and blows, saying, "We may be shot; better that than to die on the hillside"! Poor fellows, they are wretchedly dressed, and many of them have no socks. The "blizzard" was very awful—"a horror of great darkness," a bewildering whirl of pin-like snow coming from all quarters at once, a hurricane of icy wind so fearful that I had to hold on by the crupper and mane to avoid being blown out of the saddle; utter confusion, a deadly grip at my heart, everything blotted out, and a sense of utter helplessness. Indeed I know of no peril in which human resources count for so little. After reaching the summit of the pass the risk was over, but we were seriously delayed in forcing a passage through the drift, which was fully seven feet deep. The men were much exhausted, and they say that "half an hour

of it would have finished them." All landmarks were
lost in the storm, and after some hours of struggling
through snow, and repeatedly losing the way, the early
darkness compelled us to take refuge in a Kurdish
village of bad repute on a bleak mountain side.

The *odah* was not only the worst I have yet seen, but
it was crammed with handsome, wild-looking Kurds, and
with the conscripts who had turned back at the pass,
some of whom were suffering from fever, and with
cavalrymen and their horses, every man trying to get
near the fire. I cannot say that any of them were rude,
indeed the Kurds did their best for what they supposed
to be my comfort. I spent the evening among them,
but slept in my tent outside, in two feet of snow, 100
yards from the stable, in spite of the protestations of the
zaptiehs. In fact I trusted to Kurdish watchmen, who
turned out faithful, and when an attempt was made to
rob my tent in the night they sprang on the robbers,
and after a struggle got two of them down and beat them
with their guns, both sides yelling like savages. When I
left the *odah* for the tent two Kurds gripped my arms
and led me to it through the deep snow. It was better
to run some risk than to be suffocated by the heat and
overpowering odours of the stable, but it was an eerie place.

November 21.—The weather considerably delayed my
farther progress. The days were severe, and the nights
were spent in a soaked tent, pitched in slush or snow.
Mist and snow concealed the country, and few travellers
were stirring. We marched with the powder caravan
for the sake of the escort and for its services in beating
the track, and Moussa and his men watched at night.
The going was very bad, and both Moussa and I fell
down hill slopes with our horses, but the animals luckily
alighted on their feet. Moussa's jollity was very useful.
He is a capital mimic, and used to " take off" Mirza in

the *odahs* at night, and as Murphy lost no opportunity
of showing up the poor fellow's want of travelling *savoir-
faire*, he would have had a bad time but for his philo-
sophical temperament and imperturbable good-nature.   I
suffered very much from my spine, but the men were
all kind, and tried to make things easy for me, and the
zaptiehs were attentive and obliging.

Kurdistan is scarcely a "geographical expression," and
colloquially the word is used to cover the country inhabited by the Kurds.   They are a mysterious people,
having maintained themselves in their original seats and
in a condition of semi-independence through all the
changes which have passed over Western Asia, though
they do not exceed numerically two and a quarter
millions of souls.   Such as they were when they opposed
the retreat of the Ten Thousand they seem to be still.
War and robbery are the business of Kurdish life.

One great interest of this journey is that it lies

through a country in
which Kurds, Turks,
and Armenians live
alongside each other—
the Kurds being of two
classes, the tribal, who
are chiefly nomads,
owning no law but the
right of the strongest;
and the non-tribal or
settled, who, having
been conquered by
Turkey, are fairly or-
derly, and are peace-
able except in their
relations with the

A HAKKIARI KURD.

Christians.   The strongholds of the tribal Kurds are in

the wild mountains of Kurdistan, and especially in the Hakkiari country, which is sprinkled with their rude castles and forts.   An incurable love of plunder, a singular aptitude for religious fanaticism, a recklessness as to the spilling of blood, a universal rapacity, and a cruel brutality when their passions are roused, are among their chief vices.   The men are bold, sober, and devoted to their kinsmen and tribe ; and the women are chaste, industrious, and maternal.   Under a firm and equitable Government, asserting vigorously and persistently the supremacy of law and the equal rights of race and creed, they would probably develop into excellent material.

The village Turk, as he is described by Europeans well acquainted with him and speaking his language, and as I have seen him on a long journey, is a manly, hospitable, hard-working, kindly, fairly honest fellow, domestic, cheerful, patriotic, kind to animals, usually a monogamist, and usually also attentive to his religious duties.

The Christians, who, in this part of Kurdistan, are all Armenians by race, live chiefly on the plains and in the lower folds of the hills, and are engaged in pastoral and agricultural pursuits.   My letters have given a faithful representation of them as dwelling with their animals in dark semi-subterranean hovels.   The men are industrious, thrifty, clannish, domestic, and not given to vices, except that of intoxication, when they have the means and opportunity, and the women are hardworking and chaste.   Both sexes are dirty, hardy, avaricious, and superstitious, and ages of wrong have developed in them some of the usual faults of oppressed Oriental peoples. They cling desperately to their historic church, which is represented among the peasants by priests scarcely less ignorant than themselves.   Their bishops constitute their only aristocracy.

They are grossly ignorant, and of the world which lies outside the *sandjak* in which they live they know nothing. The Sultan is to them a splendid myth, to whom they owe and are ready to pay a loyal allegiance. Government is represented to them by the tax-gatherer and his brutalities. Of justice, the most priceless product of good government, they know nothing but that it is a marketable commodity. With the Armenian trading communities of the cities they have slender communication, and little except nationality and religion in common.

As a rule, they live in villages by themselves, which cluster round churches, more or less distinguishable from the surrounding hovels, but there are also mixed villages in which Turks and Armenians live side by side, and in these cases they get on fairly well together, though they instinctively dislike each other, and the Turk despises his neighbour both for his race and creed. The Armenians have not complained of being maltreated by the Turkish peasants, and had there been any cause for complaint it would certainly have reached my ears.

On this journey hundreds of stories have been told to me by priests of both the Old and Protestant Churches, headmen, and others, of robbery by demand, outrages on women, digging into houses, killing, collectively and individually, driving off sheep and cattle, etc., etc.[1]

On the whole, the same condition of alarm prevails among the Armenians as I witnessed previously among the Syrian *rayahs*. It is more than alarm, it is *abject terror*, and not without good reason. In plain English,

---

[1] It was not possible to ascertain the accuracy of these narratives, and though many of them appeared to be established by a mass of concurrent and respectable testimony, I forbear presenting any of them to my readers, especially as the report presented to Parliament in January 1891 (*Turkey*, No. 1) not only gives, on British official authority, a mass of investigated facts, but states the case of the Armenian peasantry in language far stronger than any that I should have ventured to use.

general lawlessness prevails over much of this region. Caravans are stopped and robbed, travelling is, for Armenians, absolutely unsafe, sheep and cattle are being driven off, and outrages, which it would be inexpedient to narrate, are being perpetrated. Nearly all the villages have been reduced to extreme poverty by the carrying off of their domestic animals, the pillage, and in some cases the burning, of their crops, and the demands made upon them at the sword's point for every article of value which they possess, while at the same time they are squeezed for the taxes which the Kurds have left them without the means of paying.

The repressive measures which have everywhere followed " the Erzerum troubles " of last June,—the seizure of arms, the unchecked ravages of the Kurds, the threats of the Kurdish Beys, who are boldly claiming the sanction of the Government for their outrages, the insecurity of the women, and a dread of yet worse to come,—have reduced these peasants to a pitiable state.

The invariable and reasonable complaint made by the Christians is, that though they are heavily taxed they have no protection from the Kurds, or any advantage from the law as administered in Kurdistan, and that taxes are demanded from them which the Kurds have left them without the means of paying. They complain that they are brutally beaten when they fail to produce money for the payment of the Government imposts, and they allege with great unanimity that it is common for the *zaptiehs* to tie their hands behind them, to plaster their faces with fresh cow-dung, and throw pails of cold water at their eyes, tie them to the posts of their houses and flog them severely. In the village of ———, which has been swept bare by the Kurds, the people asserted that the *zaptiehs* had tied twenty defaulters together, and had driven them round and round barefooted over the thistles of the threshing-floor, flogging them with their heavy whips. My *zaptiehs* complain of the necessity they are under of beating the people. They say (and I think correctly) that they can never know whether a man has a hoard of buried money or not without beating him. They tell me also that they know that half the peasants have nothing to pay their taxes with, but that unless they beat them to "get what they can out of them" they would be punished themselves for neglect of duty.

On the plains to the west and north-west of the lake of Van, where the deep, almost subsoil, ploughing and carefully-constructed irrigation channels testify to the industry of a thrifty population, great depredations are even now being committed, and though later the intense cold and tremendous depths of snow of the Armenian highlands will proclaim the "Truce of God," the Kurds are still on the alert. Nor are their outrages confined to small localities, neither are they the result of "peculiar local circumstances," but from the Persian frontier near Urmi, along a more or less travelled road of several hundred miles, there is, generally speaking, no security for life, traffic, or property, and I hear on good authority that on the other side of Erzerum, even up to the Russian frontier, things are if possible worse.

I have myself seen enough to convince me that in the main the statements of the people represent accurately enough the present reign of terror in Armenia, and that a state of matters nearly approaching anarchy is now existing in the *vilayet* of Erzerum. There is no security at all for the lives and property of Christians, law is being violated daily, and almost with perfect impunity, and peaceable and industrious subjects of the Porte, taxed to an extent which should secure them complete protection, are plundered without redress. Their feeble complaints are ignored, or are treated as evidence of

" insurrectionary tendencies," and even their lives are
at the mercy of the increased audacity and aroused
fanaticism of the Kurds, and this not in nearly inaccessible and far-off mountain valleys, but on the broad
plains of Armenia, with telegraph wires above and
passable roads below, and with a Governor-General and
the Fourth Army Corps, numbering 20,000 seasoned
troops, within easy distance !

I have every reason to believe that in the long winter
evenings which I have spent in these sociable *odahs*, the
peasants have talked to me freely and frankly.   There
are no reasons why it should be otherwise, for my
zaptiehs are seldom present, Moussa is looking after his
horses in distant recesses, quite out of hearing, and my
servants are Christians.   If the people speak frankly,
I am compelled to believe that the Armenian peasant
is as destitute of political aspirations as he is ignorant
of political grievances ; that if he were secured from the
ravages of Moslem marauders he would be as contented
as he is loyal and industrious ; and that his one desire
is " protection from the Kurds " and from the rapacity
of minor officials, with security for his life and property.
Not on a single occasion have I heard a wish expressed
for political or administrative reform, or for autonomy.
The Armenian peasants are " of the earth, earthy," and
the unmolested enjoyment of material good is their idea
of an earthly Paradise.

With regard to the Kurds, they have been remorse-
less robbers for ages, and as their creed scarcely hesi-
tates to give the appropriation of the goods of a *Kafir* a
place among the virtues, they prey upon the Syrian and
Armenian peasants with clear consciences.   To rob them
by violence and " demand," month after month and year
after year, till they have stripped them nearly bare, to
cut their throats if they resist, to leave them for a while

to retrieve their fortunes,—" *to let the sheep's wool grow*," as their phrase is,—and then to rob them again, is the simple story of the relations between Kurd and Christian. They are well armed with modern rifles and revolvers. I have rarely seen a Kurd with an old-fashioned weapon, and I have *never* seen a Christian with a rifle, and their nearly useless long guns have lately been seized by the Government. The Kurds hate and despise the Turks, their nominal rulers; but the Islamic bond of brother-hood is stronger than the repulsion either of hatred or contempt, and the latent or undisguised sympathy of their co-religionists in official positions ensures them, for the most part, immunity for their crimes, for the new Code, under which the evidence of a Christian has become nominally admissible in a court of law, being in direct opposition to the teaching of the Koran, to the practice of centuries, to Kurdish fanaticism, and to the strong religious feelings and prejudices of those who administer justice, is practically, so far as the Christians are concerned, a dead letter.[1]

I am writing in an *odah* in the village of Harta, after a wild mountain ride in wind, sleet, and snow. The very long marches on this journey have been too much for me, and I made a first and last attempt to travel in a *maffir* or covered wooden pannier, but the suffering was so great that I was glad to remount my faithful woolly *Boy*. We had a regular snowstorm, in which nothing could be seen

---

[1] In a Minute by the late Mr. Clifford Lloyd (*Turkey*, No. 1, 1890-91, p. 80) the condition of the Christian peasant population of Kurdistan is summarised thus :—

"Their sufferings at present proceed from three distinct causes—

"1. The insecurity of their lives and properties, owing to the habitual ravages of the Kurds.

"2. The insecurity of their persons and the absence of all liberty of thought and action (except the exercise of public worship).

"3. The unequal status held by the Christian as compared with the Mussulman in the eyes of the Government."

but the baggage horses struggling and falling, and occasional glimpses of caverned limestone cliffs and precipitous slopes, with a foamy torrent at a tremendous depth below. On emerging from the pass, Moussa, Suleiman, and I came at a good pace through the slush to this *odah*, and I arrived so cold that I was glad to have to rub my horse dry, and attend to him. Murphy describes him thus: "That's a strange horse of yours, ma'am; if one were to lie down among his legs he'd take no notice to hurt one. When he comes in he just fills hisself, then he lies down in the wettest place he can find, and goes to sleep. Then he wakes and shakes hisself, and hollers, he does, till he gets his grub"—an inelegant but forcible description of the excellences of a travelling horse. *Boy* is truly a gentle pet; it afflicts me sorely to part with him. A few nights ago as I took some raisins to him in a dark recess of the stable, my light went out, and I slipped and fell among the legs of some animal. Not knowing whether it was a buffalo or a strange horse I did not dare to move, and said, "Is this you, my sweet *Boy*?" A low pleasant snuffle answered "yes," and I pulled myself up by the strong woolly legs, which have carried me so sturdily and bravely for several hundred miles.

The Christians appear not to have anything analogous to our "family worship," but are careful in their attendance at the daily prayers in church, to which they are summoned before dawn, either by loud rappings on their doors or the striking of a wooden gong or sounding-board. The churches differ very little. They usually have an attempt at an outer courtyard, the interior of the edifice is generally square, the roof is supported by two rows of poplar pillars, and the rough walls are concealed by coarse pictures and dirty torn strips of printed cotton. Dirty mats or bits of carpets cover the floor, racks are provided for the shoes of the worshippers, and if there is not a gallery a space is railed off for the women. The prayers are mumbled by priests in dirty vestments, while the women knit and chatter. Candle-grease, dust, and dirt abound. There is such an air of indifference about priests and people that one asks what motive it is which impels them to leave their warm stable dwellings on these winter mornings to shiver in a dark and chilly church. They say, "We will tread the paths our fathers trod; they are quite good enough for us." Two nights ago, in an *odah* full of men, the Kurdish *khanji*, at the canonical hour, fell down on his forehead at prayer in the midst of us, all daggers, pistols, and finery as he was. In which case is the worship most ignorant, I wonder?

I. L. B.

LETTER XXXIV

ERZERUM, *Dec. 1.*

I LEFT Harta in a snowstorm without the caravan, and wherever the snow was well beaten got along at a good pace, passing on the right the fortress of Hassan-Kaleh, with several lines of fortifications and a town at its base, which, with the surrounding district, consumes, it is said, an amount of strong drink equal in value to its taxation. The adjacent Pasin Plain, watered by the Araxes, has suffered severely from the Kurds. A short time ago all its Christian villages were plundered, and *at least* 20 horses, 31 asses, 2282 sheep, and 750 head of cattle, nearly the whole pastoral wealth of the people, were carried off by these marauders, while the Moslem villages were exempt from their attacks. After winding among uninteresting hills crowned with forts, along valleys in which military posts occur at frequent intervals, and making a long ascent, the minarets and grim fortifications of the unhappy town of Erzerum loomed through the snow-mist; the city itself lying on a hill slope above a very extensive plain at a height of over 6000 feet. It was a solemn scene. The snow was deep and was still falling, the heavens were black, and swirls of mist driven by a strong wind blotted out at times the surrounding mountains. A dead calm followed, and snow clouds hung suspended over the city.

My first impression of Erzerum was of earthworks of

immense size extending for miles, with dismounted guns upon them looking very black in the snow; of a deep ditch, and a lofty rampart pierced by a fine granite tunnel; of more earthworks, and of forts crowning all the heights directly above the city, and of many flags drooping on their staffs. Between the fortifications and the town there is a great deal of open ground sprinkled with rifle pits, powder magazines, and artillery, cavalry, and infantry barracks, very solidly built and neatly kept up. After passing through cemeteries containing thousands of gravestones, we abruptly entered the principal street, wide and somewhat European-looking, in which are some of the Consulates and the Protestant Armenian church and schools. The houses in this street are very irregular, and most of them have projecting upper fronts.

I was received with the utmost kindness at the American Mission House, where it has seemed likely that I might be detained for the winter! I understood that when I reached Erzerum I should be able to drive to Trebizond in a *fourgon*, so I sent Murphy to Van on *Boy*, and thought with much satisfaction of the ease of the coming journey. Then I was ill, and afterwards found that the *fourgons* were long rough waggons without springs, in which one must lie or sit on the top of the baggage, and that I should never be able to bear the jolting. There was another heavy snowstorm, and winter set in so rigorously that it was decided that driving was out of the question, and that I must hire a horse. After the matter had been settled thus, Murphy and *Boy*, both in very bad case, were found in a low part of the town, and though Murphy asserts that he encountered Kurds near Hassan-Kaleh who robbed him of everything, it is not believed that he ever passed through the city gate. He looks a pitiable object, and his much-frogged uniform, and the blanket, revolver, and other things that I had given him are all gone. In spite of his fatal failing, I have re-engaged him, and shall again ride my trusty pet. The Vali, ignoring my official letter, has insisted on a number of formalities being complied with, and though the acting-Consul has undertaken all the formal arrangements, the delays have been many and tiresome. There are two bugbears on the Trebizond road,—the Kop and Zigana mountains, which are liable to be blocked by snow.

As compared with Persian towns, Erzerum looks solid and handsome, and its uncovered bazars seem fairly busy. The through traffic between Trebizond and Tabriz, chiefly in British goods, is very heavy. The Custom House is in sight from my windows, and in one day I have counted as many as 700 laden camels passing through it, besides horse and mule caravans. There are about 2000 Persians in the city, and the carrying trade is mainly in their hands. The present population is estimated at from 20,000 to 24,000. The Armenians are not very numerous, but their enterprise as traders gives them an importance out of proportion to their numbers. The Armenian cathedral, the "Pair of Minarets," the "Single Minaret," and the castle,. which stands on a height in the middle of the city, and contains a small Saracenic chapel, are the chief "sights."

Nothing is talked about but "the troubles,"[1] and the European Consuls, who possess trustworthy information, confirm my impressions of the seriousness of the present latitude allowed to the Kurds. The Turkish Govern-

[1] The reader will recollect that the "Erzerum troubles" so frequently referred to consisted of riot and bloodshed following upon a search for arms which was made under the floors of the Armenian Cathedral and the Sanassarian College, on the strength (it is said) of an anonymous telegram in June 1890. The lucid account given of this deplorable affair and of the subsequent inaction of the local Government by Her Britannic Majesty's Consul-General for Kurdistan, in the "White Book," to which allusion has been made, should be studied by all who are interested in the so-called "Armenian Question."

ment has just taken a step which is regarded as full
of hazard.   Certain Kurdish Beys were summoned to
Erzerum, nominally for the purpose of being reprimanded
for their misdeeds ; but they were allowed to enter the
gates with a number of armed followers, and afterwards
went to Erzingian, where, from the hands of Zeki Pacha,
the Commander of the Fourth Army Corps, they received
commissions as officers of irregulars.   The Christians (but
I hope erroneously) regard this step as a menace, and the
Kurds appear to think that it gives them license to maraud.

These Beys, after receiving their commissions, went
through the Christian quarter of the Erzingian bazars,
making gestures as of cutting throats, and saying to the
Christian merchants, " Your time has come now; hitherto
we have not had the co-operation of the Government,
but we have it now."   It remains to be seen whether
the Porte will succeed in bringing these men and their
wild followers under the conditions of military discipline.

The excitement following upon the "troubles" last
June has only partially subsided, and I learn from the
Europeans that the state of suspicion, fear, distrust, and
repression within the city has undergone little diminu-
tion.   Every day brings fresh reports of robbery and
outrage, and for murders of well-known Christians no
arrests are being made.[1]   Trade among the Armenians
is suffering, for those merchants whose transactions are
with Kurdish districts dare not collect their debts for
fear of losing their lives.   Arrests of Christians on
frivolous and worthless pretexts are being made daily,
Armenian houses are being searched continually, and indi-
viduals are being imprisoned for long terms of years for

---

[1] In a despatch in the "White Book" (*Turkey*, No. 1, 1890-91) Mr.
Clifford Lloyd sums up the condition of things in Kurdistan thus : "In
a country such as this is, lawlessness is to be expected ; *but unfortunately
in nearly every instance armed and ungoverned Kurds are the aggressors,
and unarmed and unprotected Armenian Christians the victims.*"

having books in their possession containing references to the past history of Armenia, and the Government is, or affects to be, in constant dread of an insurrectionary rising among the Christians. The accounts from the country districts are so very bad that one of the ablest and best-informed of the European Consuls, a very old resident in Asia Minor, remarked indignantly, " It's no longer a question of politics but of humanity."

One of the most interesting sights in Erzerum is the Sanassarian College, founded and handsomely endowed by the liberality of an Armenian merchant. The fine buildings are of the best construction, and are admirably suited for educational purposes, and the equipments are of the latest and most complete description. The education and the moral and intellectual training are of a very high type, and the personal influence of the three directors, who were educated in Germany and England, altogether " makes for righteousness." The graduation course is nine years. The students, numbering 120, wear a uniform, and there is no distinction of class among them. They are, almost without exception, manly, earnest, and studious, and are full of enthusiasm and *esprit de corps*. Much may be hoped for in the future from the admirable moral training and thorough education given in this college, which is one of the few bright spots in Armenia.

I have seen Erzerum under very favourable circumstances, for, since the last snowstorm, the weather has been magnificent, and everything that is untidy or unsightly has an unsullied covering. The winter sunsets reddening the white summits of the Deveh Boyun and other lofty ranges, and the absolute purity of the whiteness of the plain, between thirty and forty miles long and from ten to twenty broad, which lies below the city, exercise a witchery which the scorching heats of summer must utterly destroy.   I. L. B.

LETTER XXXV

TREBIZOND, *Dec. 13, 1890.*

THE journey from Erzerum to Trebizond in the winter season occupies from ten to twelve days, and involves a transition from an altitude of 6000 feet to the sea-level, and from treelessness, aridity, and severities of cold to forests and moisture, a temperate climate, and the exquisite greenness of the slopes which descend upon the Black Sea.   There is a well-made waggon road, carefully engineered, for the whole distance, with stone bridges in excellent repair ; many of the *khans* are tolerable, supplies can be procured, and the country is passably safe.

I left Erzerum on the 2d of December, escorted by my kindly hosts as far as Elijeh, having an Armenian *katirgi*, who in every respect gave me the greatest satisfaction, and the same servants as before.   The mercury fell rapidly the following night, was 2° below zero when I left Elijeh for Ashkala the next morning, and never rose above 15° during the whole day.   The road follows the western branch of the Euphrates, the Frat, a reedy and winding stream.   The horsemen and foot passengers were mostly muffled up in heavy cloaks with peaked hoods, and the white comforters which wrapped up their faces revealed only one eye, peering curiously out of a cavern of icicles.   Icicles hung from the noses and bodies of the horses, it was not possible to ride more than half an hour at a time without being benumbed, and the snow was very deep for walking. After crossing the Euphrates twice by substantial stone bridges, I halted at Ashkala, a village of *khans*, at a clean but unfinished *khan* on the bank of the river, and in a room with unglazed windows and no possibility of making a fire experienced a temperature of 5° below zero. My dinner froze before I could finish it, the stock of potatoes for the journey, though wrapped in a fur cloak inside my *yekdan*, was totally spoilt, and my ink froze. The following day was cloudy and inclined to snow rather than frost, and the crossing of the much-dreaded Kop Dagh was managed without difficulty in five hours, in snow three feet deep. There is a refuge near the summit, but there are no habitations on the ascent or descent. It is a most dangerous pass, owing to the suddenness and fury of the storms, and only last winter sixty fine camels and ten drivers perished there in a blizzard. My *zaptieh* was left behind ill at the refuge, and I made the remainder of the journey without an escort. The Kop Dagh, 7500 feet in altitude, forms the watershed between the Euphrates valley and the Black Sea, and on such an afternoon as that on which I crossed it, when wild storms swept over successive mountain ranges, and yet wilder gleams lighted up the sinuous depression which marks the course of the Frat, the view from its lofty summit is a very striking one.

It was dark when I reached the very miserable hamlet on the western side of the Kop, and as earlier caravans had taken up the better accommodation, I had to content myself with a recess opening out of a camel stable. The camels sat in circles of ten, and pleasant family parties they looked, gossiping over their chopped straw, which, with a ball of barley-meal dough in the morning, constitutes their slender but sufficient diet. Nothing gives a grander idea of the magnitude and ramifications of commerce than the traffic on the road from Erzerum to

Trebizond.   During eleven days there has scarcely been
a time when there has not been a caravan in sight, and
indeed they succeed each other in a nearly endless procession, the majority being composed of stately mountain
camels, gaily caparisoned, carrying large musical bells,
their head-stalls of crimson leather being profusely tasselled and elaborately decorated with cowries and blue
beads.   The leader of each caravan wears a magnificent
head-dress covering his head and neck, on which embroidery is lavishly used in combination with tinsel and
coloured glass, the whole being surmounted by a crown
with a plume set between the ears.   There is one driver
to every six animals; and these men, fine, robust, sturdy
fellows, are all dressed alike, in strong warm clothing,
the chief feature of which is a great brown sheepskin
cap of mushroom shape, which projects at least nine
inches from the head.   The road is a highway for
British goods.   The bales and packing cases are almost
invariably marked with British names and trade marks.
The exception is Russian kerosene, carried by asses and
horses, of which an enormous quantity was on the road.

I was glad to leave Kop Khané at daybreak, for
caravan bells jingled, chimed, tolled, and pealed all night,
and my neighbours the camels were under weigh at 3 A.M.
The road descends gently down the wide valley of the
Tchoruk, the ancient Acampsis, and then ascends to Baiburt, a town with a population of about 12,000 souls, 1800
being Christians.   It is very picturesquely situated at the
junction of two or three valleys, the houses rise irregularly
as at Bitlis tier above tier, and the resemblance is
heightened by a great reddish-yellow rock which rises
in the centre, the long and varied contour of which is
followed by the walls of a fortress imposing even in its
ruins, round and square towers cresting the remarkable eminence.   A handsome military college on a height,

wide streets lined by well-built houses with projecting upper stories, and well-supplied and busy markets, in which an enormous quantity of mutton is exposed for sale, are among the chief features of this very striking town. A domiciliary visit from a courteous chief of police, who assured me that an escort was not needed, and re-sealed my passports, was my only contact with Turkish officialism between Erzerum and Trebizond.

After leaving Baiburt I diverged a little, in spite of very deep snow, to visit the ruined Armenian ecclesiastical edifices at Varzahan, a village from which a mountain road to Trebizond passing near the Greek monastery of Sumelas branches from the main road. The most interesting and best-preserved of these buildings is an octagonal chapel of a very elaborate design, with remains of a circle of slender shafts, a very fine west window, round arches, and some curious designs in fresco. In another a pointed arch, and a fragment of a blind arcade with niches on its outer face, remain, along with some very carefully-executed cable and twisted moulding. It was truly refreshing to come upon such very beautiful relics of Christian art in so wild a country. These edifices are attributed to the eleventh or twelfth century. In an ancient and adjacent cemetery there are several monumental stone rams, very much like the stone lions of the Bakhtiari country.

I quite broke down on that march, and was obliged to bribe the Turkish occupants of a most miserable hovel to vacate it for me, and on the following day was only able to ride three hours to Getchid. The sky was grim and threatening, and the snow deep, and when after a long ascent we descended into a really magnificent defile, so narrow that for a long distance the whole roadway is blasted out of the rock, a violent snowstorm came on, with heavy gusts of wind. There were high mountains with a few trees upon them dimly seen, walling in the wildest and most rugged part of the defile, where some stables offered a shelter, and I was glad to be allowed to occupy the wood house, a damp excavation in the mountain side! No words can convey an impression of the roughness of Asia Minor travelling in winter!

It was lonely, for the stable where the servants were was a short distance off, and the *khanji* came several times to adjure me to keep the bolt of the door fastened, for his barley was in my keeping, and there was a gang of robbers on the road! I fell asleep, however, but was awakened at midnight by yells, shouts, tramplings, and a most violent shaking of my very insecure door. It was the Turkish post, who, being unable to get into the stable, was trying to bring his tired horses into my den for a little rest! Fine fellows these Turkish mail riders are, who carry the weekly mail from Trebizond into the interior. The post drives two horses loaded with the mail bags in front of him at a gallop, urging them with yells and his heavy whip, the *zaptieh* escort galloping behind, and at this pace they dash up and down mountains and over plains by day and night, changing at short intervals, and are only behind time in the very worst of weather.

Snow fell heavily all night, and until late in the afternoon of the following day, but we started soon after seven, and plodded steadily along in an atmosphere of mystery, through intricate defiles, among lofty mountains half-seen, strange sounds half-heard, vanishing ravines and momentary glimpses of villages on heights, fortress-crowned precipices, suggestive of the days of Genoese supremacy, as in the magnificent gorge of Kala, and long strings of camels magnified in the snow-mist, to the Kala village, with its dashing torrent, its fine walnut trees, and its immense camel stables, in and outside of

which 700 camels were taking shelter from the storm
We pushed on, however, during that day and the next,
through the beautiful and populous Gumushkhané valley
to Kupru Bridge, having descended almost steadily for
five days.

The narrow valley of the Kharshut is magnificent,
and on the second day the snow was only lying on the
heights.   The traveller is seldom out of sight of houses,
which are built on every possible projection above the
river, and on narrow spurs in wild lateral ravines, and
wherever there are houses there are walnut, pear, apple
and apricot trees, with smooth green sward below, and
the walnut branches often meet over the road.   The
houses are mostly large, often whitewashed, always brown-
roofed, and much like Swiss *châlets*, but without the
long slopes of verdure which make Switzerland so fair.
Instead of verdure there is the wildest rock and mountain scenery, a congeries of rock-walls, precipices, and
pinnacles, and the semblance of minarets and fortresses,
flaming red, or burnt sienna, or yellow ochre, intermingled
with bold fronts of crimson and pale blue rock, the
crimson cliffs looking in the rain as if torrents of blood
were pouring over them   The roadway has been both
blasted out of the rock and built up from the river.   Far
up picturesque ravines oxen were ploughing the red
friable soil on heights which looked inaccessible ; there
was the velvety greenness of winter wheat ; scrub oak
and barberry find root-hold in rocky rifts, and among
crags high up among the glittering snows contorted
junipers struggle for a precarious existence.

The road was enlivened by local as well as through
traffic, and brightened by the varied costumes of Turks,
Greeks, Armenians, and Lazes.   The latter do not
resemble the Turks in physiognomy or costume.   All of
them carry rifles and sabres, and two daggers in their

girdles, one of which always has a cloven hilt. They are on their way to their native province of Lazistan with droves of horses, and are much dreaded by both the *katirgis* and *khanjis* on the road for their marauding habits. The Turkish Government has a very difficult task in ruling and pacifying the number of races which it has subjugated even in Asiatic Turkey. Between the Arabs of the Chaldæan Plains and the Lazes of the shores of the Black Sea I have met even in my limited travels with Sabeans, Jews, Armenians, Syrians, Yezidis, Kurds, Osmanlis, Circassians, and Greeks, alien and antagonistic in creed and race, but somehow held together and to some extent governed by a power which is, I think, by no means so feeble as she is sometimes supposed to be.

The Kharshut is crossed at Kupru Bridge by a very fine stone arch. This village, at the foot of the Zigana Mountain, is entirely composed of inferior *khans*, food shops, and smiths' shops. The clang of hammers lasted late into the night, for the road was reported as " icy," and more than 400 horses and mules were having their shoes roughed for the passage of the Zigana Mountain. I arrived late in the evening, when all the *khans* were full, and had to put up in a hovel, the door of which was twice attempted during the night by a band of Lazes, about whose proceedings Stephan, my *katirgi*, had been very suspicious. After the servants and *katirgis*, roused by my whistle, had rushed out of an opposite stable upon the marauders, I lay awake for some time trying to realise that my ride of 2500 miles was nearly at an end, and that European civilisation was only five days off; but it was in vain. I felt as if I should *always* be sleeping in stables or dark dens, *always* uttering the call to " boot and saddle " two hours before daylight, *always* crawling along mountain roads on a woolly horse, *always* planning marches, *always* studying Asiatic character, and *always* sinking deeper into barbarism !

From the summit of the Zigana Mountain to Trebizond is a steady descent of twelve hours. The ascent from Kupru Bridge occupied five hours and a half. It was a much more serious affair than crossing the Kop Dagh, for the snowstorm had lasted for three days, the snow was from four to nine feet deep on the summit, and the thawing of its surface at the lower altitudes, succeeded by keen frost, had resulted in the production of slopes of ice, over which I had to walk for two hours, as *Boy* could scarcely keep on his feet.

The early snow has a witchery of its own, and it may be that the Zigana Mountain and the views from it are not so beautiful as I think them, but under the circumstances in which I saw them, I was astonished with the magnificence of the scenery, and with the vast pine forests which clothe the mountain sides. Villages of *châlets*, with irregular balconies, and steep roofs projecting from two to six feet, are perched on rocky heights, or nestle among walnuts with a blue background of pines, above which tower spires and peaks of unsullied snow; ridges rise into fantastic forms and mimicries of minarets and castles ; pines, filling gigantic ravines with their blue gloom, stand sentinels over torrents silenced for the winter; and colossal heights and colossal depths, an uplifted snow world of ceaseless surprises under a blue sky full of light, make one fancy oneself in Switzerland, till a long train of decorated camels or a turbaned party of armed travellers dissipates the dream.

The last hour of the ascent was very severe. The wind was strong and keen, and the drifting snow buffeted us unmercifully. The mercury fell to 3° below zero, and the cold was intense. Murphy complained of " trembles " in his knees and severe pain in his legs, and when we reached the summit was really ill. The drift was not only blinding and stinging but suffocating. I was quite breathless, and felt a chill round my heart. I could not even see *Boy's* neck, and he cowered from the blast; but just as all things were obliterated I found myself being helped to dismount in the shelter of a camel stable full of Lazes, but was so benumbed that I could not stand. Some *zaptiehs* had the humanity to offer me the shelter of a hovel nearly buried in the snow, and made a fire and some coffee, and I waited there till the wind moderated. It came in such fierce gusts as actually to blow two of the baggage horses over on their sides. Murphy was really ill of fever for two days from the cold and exposure. The altitude of the pass is about 6627 feet.

The first part of the descent was made on foot, for the snow had drifted on the road to a height of fully twenty feet, leaving only a path of shelving ice on the brink of a precipitous slope. Earlier in the day twenty laden camels had gone over, and were heaped in the ravine below, not all dead. The road dips with some suddenness into a deep glen, dark with pine and beech forests; large rhododendrons and the *Azalea pontica* forming a dense undergrowth. Long gray lichen hung from the branches, Christmas roses and premature primroses bloomed in sheltered places, the familiar polypody and the *Asplenium adiantum nigrum* filled every crevice, soft green moss draped the rocks, there was a delicious smell of damp autumn leaves, and when we reached the Greek village of Hamzikeuy clouds were rolling heavily up the valley from the not far distant ocean.

The two days which followed were easy and pleasant, through a prosperous and peopled valley brightened by the rushing waters of the Surmel, the ancient Pyxites. Orchards and tillage beautify the lower slopes of the mountains, the road is excellent, the homesteads are in good repair, the people are bright and cheery-looking, and Greek villages with prominent churches on elevated spurs add an element of Christian civilisation to the landscape. The exceeding beauty of natural forests, of soft green sward starred with the straw-coloured blossoms of the greater hellebore, of abounding ferns and trailers, of " the earth bringing forth grass, the herb yielding seed, and the tree yielding fruit after his kind," of prosperous villages with cheerful many-windowed houses and red-tiled deep-eaved roofs, can only be fully appreciated by the traveller who has toiled over the burning wastes of Persia with their mud villages and mud ruins, and across the bleak mountains and monotonous plateaux of the Armenian highlands, with their ant-hill dwellings, and their poverty-stricken population for ever ravaged by the Kurd.

" Tilled with a pencil," carefully weeded, and abundantly manured, the country looks like a garden. The industrious Greek population thrives under the rule of the Osmanlis. Travellers on foot and on horseback abound, and *khans* and *cafés* succeed each other rapidly. When the long descent alongside of the Surmel was accomplished, the scenery gradually became tamer, and the look of civilisation more emphasised. The grass was if possible greener, the blossoming hellebore more abundant, detached balconied houses with their barns and outhouses evidenced the security of the country, the heat-loving fig began to find a place in the orchards, the funereal cypress appeared in its fitting position among graves, and there was a briny odour in the air, but, unfortunately for the traveller, the admirable engineering of the modern waggon road deprives him of that magnificent view of the ocean from a height which has wrung from many a wanderer since the days of the Ten Thousand the joyful exclamation, " *Thalatta* ! *Thalatta* ! "

The valley opened, there was a low grassy hill, beyond it, broad yellow sands on which the "stormy Euxine" thundered in long creamy surges, and creeping up the sides of a wooded headland, among luxuriant vegetation, the well-built, brightly-coloured, red-roofed houses of the eastern suburb of Trebizond, the ancient Trapezus.[1] It was the journey's end, yet such is the magic charm of Asia that I would willingly have turned back at that moment to the snowy plateaux of Armenia and the savage mountains of Kurdistan.   I. L. B.

[1] The itineraries will be found in Appendix B.

APPENDIX A

AMONG the prayers recited by the Hadjis are those with which the pilgrims circle the Kaaba at Mecca, a translation of which was given by Canon Tristram in a delightful paper on Mecca contributed to the *Sunday at Home* volume for 1883. The following is a specimen :—

"O God, I extend my hands to Thee : great is my longing towards Thee. Accept Thou my supplication, remove my hindrances, pity my humiliation, and mercifully grant me Thy pardon.

"O God, I beg of Thee that faith which shall not fall away, and that certainty which shall not perish, and the good aid of Thy prophet Mohammed — may God bless and preserve him ! O God, shade me with Thy shadow in that day when there is no shade but Thy shadow, and cause me to drink from the cup of Thy prophet Mohammed—may God bless him and preserve him !—that pleasant draught after which is no thirst to all eternity."

APPENDIX B

APPENDIX B

ITINERARIES WITH APPROXIMATE DISTANCES

1
From BAGHDAD to KIRMANSHAH.

	MILES
Orta Khan	16
Yakobieh	14
Wiyjahea	16
Sheraban	11
Kizil Robat	18
Khanikin	17
Kasr-i-Shirin	16
Sir-i-pul-i-Zohab	18
Myan Tak	15
Kirrind	14
Harunabad	20
Mahidasht	22
Kirmanshah	14
	———
	211

2
From KIRMANSHAH to TIHRAN.[1]

Besitun	22
Sannah	16
Kangawar	21
Phaizalpah	24
Hamilabad	12
Nanej	18
Dizabad	24
Saruk	22
Ahang Garang	12
Siashan	20
Jairud	18
Taj Khatan	14
Kûm	25
Shashgird	16
Aliabad	24
Husseinabad	28
Tihran	28
	———
	344

3
From TIHRAN to ISFAHAN.

	MILES
Husseinabad	28
Aliabad	28
Shashgird	24
Kûm	16
Passangham	16
Sinsin	24
Kashan	24
Kuhrūd	28
Soh	24
Murchehkhurt	28
Gez	24
Isfahan	16
	———
	280

4
From ISFAHAN to BURUJIRD.

The actual distance travelled, about 700 miles.

5
From BURUJIRD to HAMADAN.

Deswali	16
Sahmine	13
Daulatabad	12
Jamilabad	22
Mongawi	6
Yalpand	9
Hamadan	8
	———
	86

[1] Probably the distance by this route is over-estimated, as it is the computation of the *charvadars*.

6
From Hamadan to Urmi.

	MILES
Bahar	8
Kooltapa.	24
Gaukhaud	20
Babarashan	20
Bijar	20
Karabulak	16
Jafirabad	16
Takautapa	15½
Geokahaz	16
Sanjud	14
Sain Kala	14½
Kashawar	15
Miandab	21
Amirabad	12
Sujbulāk	16
Mehemetabad	14
Dissa	25
Turkman	12
Urmi	10
	309

8
From Van to Bitlis.

	HOURS
Angugh	4.45
Undzak	8.30
Ghazit	7
Bitlis	8

90 Miles.

From Bitlis to Erzerum.

Gudzag	8
Pikhruz	8
Yangaloo	9
Ghazloo	10
Ama	6.30
Matchetloo	6
Herta	7
Erzerum	5

177 Miles (?)

7
From Urmi to Van.

	HOURS
Anhar	2
Merwana	3½
Marbishu	9
Pirzala	10
Gahgoran	2
Shawutha	8
Kochanes	6
Kotranis	7
Merwanen	10
Khanjarak	9
Van	9

188 Miles.

10
From Erzerum to Trebizond.

Elijeh	3½
Ashkala	7½
Kop Khané	8½
Baiburt.	7
—— Bridge	6½
Getchid	4
Gumush Khané	8
Kupru Bridge	7
Hemizkeuy	8¾
Atli Killessi	8
Trebizond	6

199 Miles by Measurement.